Distinguished Flying Cross by Ruth Mayer

On Heroic Wings:

STORIES OF THE
DISTINGUISHED FLYING CROSS

Dr. Barry A. Lanman
and
Dr. Laura M. Wendling

Dedication:

On Heroic Wings: Stories of the Distinguished Flying Cross is dedicated to the past, the present and the future recipients of the Distinguished Flying Cross.

The Distinguished Flying Cross Society gratefully acknowledges and publicly thanks the following individuals/organizations for their financial support of this publication.

Elizabeth B. Cope

The Rodney and Guille Tuttle Charitable Remainder Trust

Copyright © 2012 by the Distinguished Flying Cross Society

On Heroic Wings: Stories of the Distinguished Flying Cross
By: Barry A. Lanman and Laura M. Wendling

Published by: The Distinguished Flying Cross Society
P.O. Box 530250
San Diego, California, 92153

Edited by: Jennifer Braithwait Darrow

Design, Layout & Graphics by: Linda A. Schisler

Printed by: United Book Press, Inc.
1807 Whitehead Road
Baltimore, Maryland 21207

Library of Congress Cataloging-in-Publication Data

Lanman, Barry A. and Wendling, Laura M.
On Heroic Wings: Stories of the Distinguished Flying Cross - Barry A. Lanman and Laura M. Wendling

ISBN: 978-0-615-52024-7 (hard cover)

Library of Congress Control Number: 2011933548

The authors wish to extend their appreciation to the following individials
for their valuable contribution to the publication.

Design, Layout and Graphics

Linda A. Schisler

Edited by

Jennifer Braithwait Darrow

Coordinator of Research and Visual Images

Chuck Sweeney

Research Consultants

**Dr. Charles P. McDowell, Bailey Ball, Jennifer Braithwait Darrow,
Barry M. Lanman, Mary-Anne Mulcahy, Johanna Seymour,
Brennan Willard, John D. Willard V and Paul Weisko**

Oral History Committee

Reed Phillips, Chair, Jim Baker and Dick Tyhurst

Oral History Interviewers

**Chuck Sweeney, Dick Tyhurst,
John D. Willard V and Brennan Willard**

Development Committee and Supporting Personnel

**Greg Mac Neil, Bill Bradfield, Michael O'Neil, Richard Deihl, Richard Stricker,
Chuck Sweeney, Tom Equels and David Bentler**

Contents

From the first engagements in the air, military aviators have captured a special place in the hearts and minds of Americans. The vast majority of these aviators performed their duties in an admirable manner; however, the most courageous and valiant have been awarded the Distinguished Flying Cross.

The Distinguished Flying Cross was created by an Act of Congress in 1926 and except for a brief period when a select group of civilians received the Distinguished Flying Cross, the medal has been conferred for military actions involving heroism or extraordinary achievement while participating in aerial flight. As a recipient of the Distinguished Flying Cross during World War II, I hold this honor in high regard. I also take great pride in being a member of the Distinguished Flying Cross Society and a part of this outstanding cadre of individuals.

Coming from a wide range of backgrounds, cultures and races, the recipients of the Distinguished Flying Cross represent a microcosm of America. Accordingly, the justification for which the DFC has been awarded is as varied as its recipients. Nonetheless, there are common threads that bond the aircrew, aviators and astronauts who have been awarded this high honor. Each individual performed beyond the call of duty during high risk endeavors in rapidly changing environments. Each individual made a commitment to the achievement of the assigned mission beyond all other considerations. And, each individual developed an unwavering loyalty to his or her brethren.

For decades, most of these stories have never been told, even to loved ones. *On Heroic Wings: Stories of the Distinguished Flying Cross*, is the first comprehensive publication dedicated to the history of the Distinguished Flying Cross, and to the men and women whose extraordinary contributions merited this recognition.

The stories contained in this publication, based primarily on oral history interviews, are compelling accounts of those awarded the Distinguished Flying Cross. They are unique in the depth and richness of the experience. They also characterize the personal exploits of individuals who put their country above their own lives and changed the course of history. *On Heroic Wings: Stories of the Distinguished Flying Cross*, recounts the glory of these true American heroes who quietly yet proudly wear the Distinguished Flying Cross.

George Bush
Forty-first President of the United States

Introduction

Since the infancy of aviation, awards, medals and trophies have been a way to recognize individual accomplishments contributing to the advancement of flight. Among the honors have been the Robert J. Collier Trophy, the Wright Brothers Medal, the Gordon Bennett Trophy and the Katherine Wright Memorial Award. For military aviators and aircrews, however, the Distinguished Flying Cross is one of the most prestigious honors which can be bestowed.

The DFC is awarded for heroism and/or extraordinary achievement during aerial flight. It is the only medal conferred by the Air Force, Army, Navy, Marines and Coast Guard, in all wars and campaigns from World War I to the present.

While it is hard to fathom, records on the presentation of DFCs were not collectively preserved by a central governmental repository. The data resided at the lower echelons of the various military services, usually at the unit level. Thus, no comprehensive database exists which allows America to revere all of its heroes from aloft. Only as an estimate is it safe to say that after more than eight decades, thousands of Distinguished Flying Crosses have been conferred on individuals for their humanitarian acts, for setting records and for combat missions which protected American lives.

To obtain, preserve and disseminate this significant part of American history, the Distinguished Flying Cross Society was established in 1994. As conservators, the DFCS commissioned an oral history program and a publication so that this heritage would not be lost.

On Heroic Wings: Stories of the Distinguished Flying Cross skillfully traces the Distinguished Flying Cross from its origin through the major eras of military aviation involving the five services. As I read the accounts, I became immersed in the stories that represent a wide range of time periods, missions, aircraft and theaters of operation. In addition to the stories told from the recipients' perspectives, the Memorable Moments captured my interest as they demonstrated the depth and breath of the situations for which Distinguished Flying Crosses were awarded. I was also amazed by the number of notable individuals who received the DFC, and those who did not share the spotlight of fame but made contributions which often defied classification under the traditional headings of wars, conflicts or military actions.

While this publication is highly researched and contains stunning photographic documentation, the volume has a dual purpose. Beyond the content, the stories from our American heroes and role models provide a source of motivation…they serve to teach and inspire. They bring out the best in our collective character and instill a sense of pride in being a United States citizen.

In 1965, I piloted the Gemini 7 mission and received a DFC. A year later, I was awarded a second DFC for the Gemini 12 space flight I commanded. As a member of the Distinguished Flying Cross Society, I am proud to be associated with this tribute to my fellow compatriots who received this legendary honor.

Captain James A. Lovell
United States Navy, Retired

Authors' Note

Research leading to a publication entails the willingness to take on a challenging journey. Some aspects of the journey may be anticipated while others yield to unexpected paths of exploration. In the case of *On Heroic Wings: Stories of the Distinguished Flying Cross*, our travels involved a decade of research, the creation of over 130 formal oral history interviews, countless investigations in museums and archives and the crafting of a manuscript reflective of such an extensive heritage. While the rewards were many, it was the human interaction with true American heroes and patriots that proved to be our experience of a lifetime.

As oral historians, we were trained in the acquisition of biographical and thematic historical accounts. We were not aviation aficionados by formal education; thus, our learning curve was steep. But rather than prove a liability, our detachment from the field provided an objectivity which brought a balanced and fresh approach to this specialized area of military aviation history.

Given our professional backgrounds, we embarked on a quest to uncover those exceptional stories that would take your breath away. As the process unfolded and the oral interviews were conducted, time after time we were mesmerized by narratives that gave new meaning to the concepts of bravery, courage and heroism.

In telling the stories of the Distinguished Flying Cross, we were intent on capturing the factual content of the events that merited this prestigious medal. It was important to document the accounts in terms of cause and effect, chronology and historical context. Our most critical responsibility though, was to separate lore and legend from reality. To determine the veracity of the oral accounts, we corroborated the stories with a variety of documents including the Distinguished Flying Cross citation, which officially identified the circumstances for the award.

In addition to the facts and figures, we were resolute in capturing the subjective elements of the story that allowed these heroes' voices to resonate. By doing so, the men and women revealed their motivations, training, bonds of comradeship and the trials and tribulations thrust upon them. The respondents' words reflect private thoughts as they engaged history with incredible skill tempered by human emotion. The aviators and aircrew acted, often in a blink of an eye, with valor and selflessness; their deeds frozen in time for all to witness.

On the completion of this amazing journey, an unexpected happenstance transpired beyond the resulting archival collection of aviation history and the production of this book. The experience galvanized our own beliefs about the American spirit and the power of patriotism. As the stories are read, there is a sense of inspiration reflecting honor, duty and commitment. It is a reaffirmation of what is so impressive about the human character when it intersects with American values. We share these stories collected through our journey with respect, admiration and an immense debt of gratitude to the men and women who received the Distinguished Flying Cross and secured the American way of life.

Dr. Barry A. Lanman and Dr. Laura M. Wendling

Annotations for the Reader and Researcher

Based on the range of criteria for the Distinguished Flying Cross and the five military services that were authorized to confer the medal, a balanced representation of awards is included in this brief historical discourse. The absence of collective statistics relating to the Distinguished Flying Cross is not an oversight. Because Congress and the branches of the military did not keep comprehensive records, there is no way to accurately gauge how many medals were conferred. Suffice it to say that no matter how many DFCs have been awarded since its inception, every Distinguished Flying Cross citation is unique and the stories reflect the collective character of the United States.

Two principal sources of documentation were used in preparing this publication along with supporting data and photographs: Oral history interviews with the recipients of the Distinguished Flying Cross and the Distinguished Flying Cross citations. For the awards included in this volume, a copy of the original Distinguished Flying Cross citation or a copy of the General Orders authorizing a DFC was obtained and resides in the Distinguished Flying Cross Society Archives located in San Diego, California. In most cases, the Distinguished Flying Cross citation was obtained from the recipient. But, in some situations, the documentation had to be researched and obtained from family members, experts in military history, military museums, the National Personnel Records Center, Military Personnel Records in St. Louis, Missouri or other repositories. Thus, considerable effort was made to verify the accuracy of the personal reflections and associated sources used to tell the stories of the Distinguished Flying Cross.

For the aviators and aircrew mentioned, their name, highest rank and military service is included in the title of their account. In the case of individuals who served in multiple branches of the military, each service is listed. To address the subordinate role of the United States Army Air Corps when the United States Army Air Forces was established in June 1941, the World War II era recipients were listed according to the issuance of the citation for the medal. In addition, the service history was explained in the individual's account where appropriate.

With the establishment of the United States Air Force, the DFC recipients who served in the United States Army Air Forces during the 1940s and transitioned to the United States Air Force were listed as "USAFF / USAF" in the title with an explanation of the aviator's history summarized in the text. Because the data is frequently inaccurate, the designation of "retired" was not used in the title of an account but the recent status of a recipient was mentioned in the narrative.

Unless otherwise stated, photographic documentation and authority to use visual images is attributed to the Distinguished Flying Cross recipient and/or the recipient's family. A comprehensive listing of research sources for the photographic and narrative documentation is included in the back of this publication.

While the accuracy of the factual content was of paramount importance, capturing the personal feelings, perceptions and perspectives of American aviation heroes was of equal significance. Therefore, the stories of the Distinguished Flying Cross provide both objective and subjective insights into the history of this revered medal.

To access the Distinguished Flying Cross citations, transcripts of oral history
interviews and associated documentation used in this publication, contact
the Distinguished Flying Cross Society.

Chapter 1

Establishing the Legacy

From Idea to Reality – One Man's Dream

Inspired ideas often come to fruition as a result of one dedicated individual. The establishment of the Distinguished Flying Cross for the United States was no exception. Hiram Bingham, III, originally from Connecticut and a graduate of both Harvard and Yale, was content traveling the world as a noted professor and archeologist. However, when World War I (WWI) erupted, Bingham's sense of adventure compelled him to become a pilot. He organized the United States School of Military Aeronautics in May 1917, and just a month later was commissioned as a major in the Aviation Section of the Signal Corps. Showing promise, Bingham quickly attained the rank of lieutenant colonel and spent the duration of the war in France commanding a flight school in Issoudun; though he never had the opportunity to fly actual combat missions.[1]

When the Armistice of 1919 was signed, ending the devastating war, Bingham entered politics. By 1922 he was in the midst of serving as governor-elect from his home state of Connecticut when he was also elected to the United States Senate to complete the balance of a vacant term. He ultimately chose the national office and the press quickly dubbed Bingham "The Flying Senator."

Capitalizing on the public's fascination with flight and his knowledge of British aviation decorations, Senator Bingham proposed a similar medal for aviators in the United States. Beyond personal sentiment, there was justification for the bill. During WWI, by Royal Warrant dated 3 June 1918, the British Crown created several aviation awards. According to British hierarchical tradition, the medals differed for officers and enlisted men. Thus, the Distinguished Flying Cross was awarded to British officers engaged with an enemy, while the Distinguished Flying Medal was conferred on British enlisted ranks for acts of valor.

The Air Force Cross was also created for non-combat heroism and given to officers, while enlisted personnel received the Air Force Medal.[2]

As well intentioned and researched as it was, Bingham was unsuccessful at gathering enough support for his Distinguished Flying Cross bill. Undaunted, the air power advocate used his political power to obtain a post on the Aircraft Board through a presidential appointment from Calvin Coolidge. From this position of influence, Bingham once again proposed that Congress create an aviation award to recognize the contribution of aviators.

Working diligently, he made a strong case that aircraft proved invaluable for military reconnaissance and as a weapons platform during WWI. Bingham also garnered support for recognizing pilots who demonstrated both courage and endurance in combat and non-combat situations. This time, Bingham's colleagues agreed and established the Distinguished Flying Cross on 2 July 1926. The legislation was incorporated into the Air Corps Act, Section 12, Public Law No. 446, 69th Congress.[3]

The law stated that the Distinguished Flying Cross could be presented, "to any person who, while serving in any capacity with the Air Corps of the Army of the United States, including National Guard and the Organized Reserves, or with the United States Navy,

Hiram Bingham, III (top) was a noted professor and archeologist. Some speculate that he was the real-life inspiration for the movie character, Indiana Jones.

Senator Hiram Bingham, III was responsible for the establishment of the Distinguished Flying Cross in the United States.

since [6 April] 1917, had distinguished, or who after this act, distinguishes himself by heroism or extraordinary achievement while participating in an aerial flight."[4]

Therefore, the legislation permitted WWI aviators to be recognized, retroactively for their valor along with other individuals who met the award's criteria. A joint board of officers from the Army and Navy assisted with the establishment of additional regulations that helped each service refine their specific selection process.

The language of the law permitted awards for combat actions, emergency rescues and awards based on aerial achievement which involved such categories as altitude, distance, endurance and speed. As compared to some other military medals, the Distinguished Flying Cross was standardized for all service branches and included an identical medal, ribbon and award criteria.

Section 12 of the Air Corps Act also permitted members of the armed forces of friendly foreign nations, who served with the United States, to receive the Distinguished Flying Cross for meritorious actions. There was also a section that allowed the DFC to be presented to military instructors and students who displayed heroism while participating in flight training.

While mosr of the criteria for the Distinguished Flying Cross was the same as that of its British counterpart, the United States award was intentionally designed in a more egalitarian fashion. The highest aviation medal in the United States could be awarded to enlisted ranks as well as officers.

Designing the Medal and the Ribbon

After passage of the legislation authorizing the Distinguished Flying Cross, the creation of the actual medal was of paramount importance. Due to a lack of records from the Department of the Treasury concerning this matter, as well as conflicting sources, the exact evolution of the planning process has remained uncertain. It appears that the joint military board charged with the development of the award regulations was also given the responsibility of designing the medal. However, not wishing to undertake that task, the board dispatched a letter to the Chairman of the Commission of Fine Arts on 20 September 1926, which asked if the commission would, "be good enough to have prepared and submit...an appropriate design for this cross." The letter also stated that, "Unfortunately, there is no money available for the purchase of designs or for compensating you for this work."[5]

Given the lack of funding, a competition was not formally initiated. Instead, the creation of the medal was entrusted to the Army's Heraldic Section (now known as the Institute of Heraldry). Even so, it seems that additional designs may have been submitted from private commercial artists and from the Office of the Quartermaster General.

Once the basic concept was completed by the Heraldic Section, several other variations were made based on the original theme. The proposals were then sent to the Commission of Fine Arts with a request that they accept one of them because, "there was an immediate necessity for approval of a design in order to present a cross to Captain Lindbergh."[6]

Responding to the urgency, the commission tentatively made its selection even though they were not completely satisfied with any of the proposed medals. The commission made it known that they felt

The Distinguished Flying Cross medal, designed by Arthur E. Dubois and Elizabeth Will, incorporated a bronze cross pattee on which is superimposed a four-bladed propeller, 1 11/16 inches in width. Five rays extend from the re-entrant angles, forming a one-inch square. The medal is suspended from a rectangular-shaped bar. The cross symbolizes sacrifice, and the propeller symbolizes flight. The combination of those symbols made it clear that the Distinguished Flying Cross was meant as an award for heroism and/or achievement for individuals involved in aviation. Subsequent awards of the Distinguished Flying Cross are indicated by oak-leaf clusters for Army and Air Force personnel and by additional award stars for members of the Naval services.

the design was "commonplace and insignificant." Despite some revisions by the Heraldic Section, the Commission remained unsatisfied, believing that the changes actually detracted from the original design. Ultimately, it was the original concept that the Commission recommended.[7]

The Distinguished Flying Cross Comes to Life

Following passage of the law which established the Distinguished Flying Cross, the initial awards were conferred and occurred in a relatively short period of time; the Pan American Good Will Flight and Charles A. Lindbergh's trans-Atlantic flight.

The Pan American Good Will Flight of 1926-1927 was planned by the United States to encourage friendship with the governments and people of Central and South America. In addition, the US hoped to promote commercial aviation and develop aerial routes throughout the Americas. The plan required the first aerial circumnavigation of South America at the risk of flying more than 21,000 miles of uncharted territory.

The Air Corps selected ten men for their flying prowess and their mechanical expertise. Major Herbert Dargue was chosen to command the mission involving five Loening OA-1A amphibian aircraft, which included components of both land-based and sea planes. The aircraft were named after American cities chosen by their crew.

Crew of the *New York*:   Major Herbert Dargue and Lieutenant Ennis Whitehead
Crew of the *San Antonio*:   Captain Arthur McDaniel and Lieutenant Charles Robinson
Crew of the *San Francisco*:   Captain Ira Eaker and Lieutenant Muir Fairchild
Crew of the *Detroit*:   Captain Clinton Woolsey and Lieutenant John Benton
Crew of the *St. Louis:*   Lieutenant Bernard Thompson and Lieutenant Leonard Weddington

To plan for the flight and provide the necessary logistics, a cadre of Air Corps officers traveled ahead to pre-position 50,000 gallons of aviation fuel and 5,000 gallons of oil along the route. They also orchestrated ceremonies and events in advance of the expedition.

On 21 December 1926, the five Pan American aircraft took off from Kelly Field in San Antonio, Texas, to begin their extended journey. At each stop, the flying ambassadors stayed for a few days to attend the planned festivities in their honor. After a ceremony in Buenos Aires, Argentina, the flyers left for an overnight stay in the nearby town of Palomar. As the planes prepared to land, Lieutenant Benton went out on the wing of the *Detroit* to lower the landing gear by hand, since it had been damaged and could not be lowered by the pilot. To increase his freedom of movement, Lieutenant Benton elected not to wear a bulky parachute.

President Calvin Coolidge presented the eight surviving Pan American aviators with Distinguished Flying Cross citations on 2 May 1927.

At an altitude of about 1,500 feet, the *Detroit* accidentally drifted into the *New York*. The aircraft locked together and spun out of control. Major Dargue and Lieutenant Whitehead parachuted to safety, however, Captain Woolsley elected to stay in the doomed plane with Lieutenant Benton, and they both perished when the *Detroit* crashed. Despite the horrific accident, the balance of the Pan American flyers continued their mission.

After their arduous journey of more than four months, the Pan American Flyers landed at Bolling Field in Washington, DC, arriving 2 May 1927. Their homecoming coincided with the opening of the Pan American Air Commission Conference. President Calvin Coolidge, Cabinet members, diplomats from various countries and a cheering crowd greeted the aviators upon their return. For their achievement, President Coolidge awarded each flyer with a Distinguished Flying Cross citation.[8] The aviators did not receive their actual medals at the ceremony because they were still in the process of being struck.[9]

Just three weeks after the Pan American Good Will Flight, Charles A. Lindbergh, the daring "Lone

Distinguished Flying Cross citations were posthumously presented to Lieutenant John Benton and Captain Clinton Woolsey. Both were killed in an accident during the Pan American Good Will Flight.

Eagle," gained immediate international prominence for his solo flight across the Atlantic. Lindbergh was hailed as a hero and was presented the first actual DFC medal along with his citation which included the following description of the historic accomplishment, "The President of the United States of America… takes pleasure in presenting the Distinguished Flying Cross to Captain…Charles Augustus Lindbergh…

THE UNITED STATES OF AMERICA

TO ALL WHO SHALL SEE THESE PRESENTS, GREETING:

THIS IS TO CERTIFY THAT
THE PRESIDENT OF THE UNITED STATES OF AMERICA
PURSUANT TO ACT OF CONGRESS APPROVED JULY 2, 1926.
HAS AWARDED TO
Charles A. Lindbergh
Captain, National Guard and Air Corps Reserve, United States Army

THE DISTINGUISHED FLYING CROSS
FOR
EXTRAORDINARY ACHIEVEMENT
WHILE PARTICIPATING IN AN AERIAL FLIGHT

and in recognition of his courage, his skill and his resourcefulness in piloting unaccompanied
"The Spirit of St. Louis" from New York City across the Atlantic Ocean to Paris, France, a distance
of 3600 miles, the longest nonstop flight ever made by man.
GIVEN UNDER MY HAND AT THE CITY OF WASHINGTON
THIS first DAY OF June 1927.

RECORDED IN THE OFFICE OF
THE ADJUTANT GENERAL
Robert C. Davis
MAJOR GENERAL
THE ADJUTANT GENERAL

Dwight F. Davis
SECRETARY OF WAR

for extraordinary achievement while participating in an aerial flight and in recognition of his courage, his skill and his resourcefulness in piloting unaccompanied the *Spirit of St. Louis* from New York City across the Atlantic Ocean to Paris, France, on 20 - 21 May 1927, a distance of 3,600 miles, the longest non-stop flight ever made by man."[10]

Lindbergh was presented the Distinguished Flying Cross medal on 11 June 1927 by President Calvin Coolidge. As far as the public was concerned at the time, and even to this day, Lindbergh was the first person to receive the Distinguished Flying Cross. While that is technically true for the presentation of the actual medal, he received his award after the ten Pan American aviators. However, the prominent attention Charles Lindbergh brought to the Distinguished Flying Cross, and to aviation in general, was profound.

After Charles Lindbergh and the Pan American flyers received their medals, every effort was made to account for, number and register the Distinguished Flying Cross medals authorized and presented. Despite the intentions of military and civilian authorities, at some point the process became convoluted. While Bailey, Banks and Biddle was contracted to produce the first fifty medals, number forty-three was actually created by August Frank who made many of the medals after the Bailey, Banks and Biddle contract came to an end.

Making it even more complicated to accurately document the award of DFCs before World War II (WWII), was that some medals were stamped with the manufacturer's hallmark while some did not have any markings on the reverse or sides of the medal. There also appears to have been some duplication of registered numbers before 1941. Once the United States became engaged in war, it was no longer a priority to keep detailed records of medals by number throughout the military services.[11]

Research by United States medal expert and past President of the Orders and Medals Society of America, Dr. Charles P. McDowell and author James W. Patrick, indicated that from 1927 through most of 1941, more than one-hundred and sixty Distinguished Flying Cross

Charles A. Lindbergh was the first person to receive a Distinguished Flying Cross medal.

medals were awarded. The few mentioned in this chapter are representative of the awards made before the war turned the focus of the Distinguished Flying Cross from peacetime aerial achievement and rescues to heroism under fire.[12]

Aviation Pioneers are Recognized for Their Accomplishments

Once the aviators of the Pan American Good Will Flight and Charles Lindbergh were awarded the Distinguished Flying Cross, retroactive awards were considered for the pioneers who, through their daring and ingenuity, contributed to the advancement of flight. The earliest event for which the new award was presented went to Orville and Wilbur Wright for the first heavier-than-air flight at Big Kill Devil Hill in Kitty Hawk, North Carolina which occurred 17 December 1903. The 605 pound *Wright Flyer* traveled 120 feet in twelve seconds under the controls of Orville Wright and paved the way for all others to follow. Since the law permitted only awards for aerial events after 1917, Congress passed special legislation to present the Distinguished Flying Cross to Orville Wright and Wilbur Wright.

Building on the work of the Wright Brothers and other early aviators, Eugene Ely pioneered a new military application of the airplane. Ely worked with Captain Washington Chambers, USN, who had been appointed by the Secretary of the Navy to study the ways in which the airplane could be used within

Orville and Wilbur Wright were awarded DFCs on 23 February 1929 for the first flight of a powered aircraft. Wilbur Wright received his medal posthumously.

After his death, Eugene Ely was awarded a DFC for pioneering the concept of the aircraft carrier and the first tailhook system.

the Navy.

On 14 November 1910, Ely took off in a Curtiss pusher from a temporary wooden platform erected over the bow of the USS *Birmingham*, a light cruiser located in Norfolk, Virginia. As Ely came to the end of the eighty-three foot temporary runway, the airplane immediately dipped and headed for the water. With the wheels touching the water and spray on his goggles, Ely was able to obtain enough speed to gain altitude and avert a catastrophe. Erring on the side of caution, he decided to land on the nearby beach rather than completing circles in the harbor and landing at the Norfolk Navy Yard as planned.

Two months later, on 18 January 1911, Eugene Ely landed his Curtiss pusher on a wooden "runway" aboard the armored cruiser USS *Pennsylvania* which was anchored in the San Francisco Bay. This unique experimental landing employed the first tailhook system to "capture" planes safely. Ely was famous for his newspaper quote about the adventure, "It was easy enough. I think the trick could be successfully turned nine times out of ten." From these initial experiments, the concept of the aircraft carrier was born. Ely was awarded a Distinguished Flying Cross for the improvement of naval aviation and for demonstrating the feasibility of operating aircraft from ships. He was the only civilian to receive a DFC awarded directly from the Navy. Unfortunately, the award by President Hoover dated 16 February 1933 was made posthumously.[13]

Glenn Hammond Curtiss had an interest in all things mechanical. He developed engines for balloons and became fascinated with flight. After winning the St. Louis International Exposition in a balloon powered by a Curtiss engine, he was instrumental in manufacturing the first dirigible adopted by the US Army.

A year later Curtiss won the Scientific American trophy for flying his famous plane called the *June Bug*. During the next several years, he won many air races in the United States and abroad, barnstormed across the country and established a number of flying schools, which benefited from the publicity of his racing victories. In 1919, he produced the NC4 for the US Navy which became the first airplane to cross the Atlantic Ocean.

After the outbreak of WWI, Curtiss moved his manufacturing facilities to Buffalo, NY and built more than 5,000 Jennies. Although he had become wealthy, those years were marred by a court fight with the Wright brothers over the invention of the aileron, a wing device to maintain

Glenn Curtiss received a DFC as a civilian for his overall advancement of aviation.

vertical stability.

Unlike the Wright Brothers, Eugene Ely and other pioneers, Curtiss was not awarded a Distinguished Flying Cross for a specific experiment, flight or mission; instead he was awarded a Distinguished Flying Cross for his overall contributions to aviation as a US civilian. The award was given posthumously as directed by general orders from the War Department in 1933.

Honoring Military Aviation During World War I

The dogfights above the trenches and battlefields of Europe provided classic tales of wartime adventures. Accordingly, the first aviators in combat were revered as heroes, and the law that had established the Distinguished Flying Cross permitted awards for meritorious actions in the Great War; finding documented proof of such recognition has, however, proven challenging.

An initial investigation of the archives of the Distinguished Flying Cross Society has not produced a single DFC citation for WWI. This revelation nevertheless set in motion a wider search for WWI pilots who received the medal under the retroactive provision of the law.

The current president of the Distinguished Flying Cross Society, Chuck Sweeney, was joined by various board members on a quest to uncover the records of these early aviators and their decorations. Army, Navy and Air Force museums across the United States were consulted along with other repositories such as the National World War I Museum in Kansas City, Missouri. To the surprise of all parties, no Distinguished Flying Cross citations were found and no written documentation of such awards was forthcoming. At best, the results were inconclusive after the exhaustive efforts to obtain the anticipated data.

Several American WW I aces and top-rated pilots received foreign decorations. Some were given the British Distinguished Flying Cross in the absence of an American Distinguished Flying Cross. Existing US decorations for heroism and achievement were also awarded to military aviators during and after WWI. The Medal of Honor, Distinguished Service Cross and the Navy Distinguished Service Medal were among the decorations bestowed on US pilots for their aerial exploits. For example, American top ace Eddie Rickenbacker was awarded the Distinguished Service Cross multiple times and the Medal of Honor but he was not awarded a Distinguished Flying Cross after the law was enacted.[14]

Another possibility for the lack of retroactive approval of WWI awards during the 1920s and 30s may have been America's focus on aviation pioneering rather than wartime combat.[15] For that matter, Congress, the military services and the public seemed to be content with the recognition already dispensed for WWI flyers. The vision of the Distinguished Flying Cross appeared to be on the future of aviation rather than on its past.

While no Distinguished Flying Cross was discovered for a pilot involving WWI combat, a unique award was

Sergeant Ralph W. Bottriell made the first military parachute jump in 1919 and received a DFC fourteen years later.

found for one of the more daring aviation exploits of its era. Army Air Corps, Master Sergeant Ralph W. Bottriell, attached to the 68th Service Squadron, was the first to perform a jump by Army personnel with a manually operated free-type parachute at McCook Field in Dayton, Ohio. The date was 19 May 1919.

Sergeant Bottriell's citation, which was authorized by General Orders No. 6 in 1933, indicated that, "At the time, parachute jumping was considered extremely hazardous. In spite of this, Sergeant Bottriell repeatedly jeopardized his life making parachute test jumps from airplanes…Sergeant Bottriell aided materially in proving the free-type parachute not only possible but practical for airplane use."[16] Bottriell's Distinguished Flying Cross may have been the first award for actions which did not involve the actual operation of an aircraft.

Advancing Aviation by Establishing Records

During the relative era of peace between WWI and World War II (WWII), a multitude of adventurous and daring pilots sought to establish aviation records and advance the development of airplanes through experimentation. Those who "pushed the envelope" and accomplished major records of time, distance and/or speed were rewarded with the Distinguished Flying Cross.

Jimmy Doolittle, who became a military icon during WW II, joined the Army Signal Corps in 1917 but did not have the experience of combat during WWI because he remained in the US as a flight instructor. Doolittle received his initial DFC as a first lieutenant for a one-stop flight from Pablo Beach, Florida to San Diego, California between 4-5 September 1922. The flight took only twenty-two hours and thirty minutes. Awarded retroactively, the citation stated that, "the flight was an extraordinary achievement with the equipment available at the time." He was also cited for his skill, endurance and resourcefulness. The most significant aspect of the flight, however, demonstrated the possibility of moving

Jimmy Doolittle was awarded two Distinguished Flying Crosses before he became famous for his raid on Tokyo during the beginning of World War II.

Air Corps units to any portion of the United States in less then twenty-four hours.

Lieutenant Doolittle received a second Distinguished Flying Cross for a series of acceleration tests in a Fokker PW 7 pursuit airplane in 1924 at McCook Field in Dayton, Ohio. A recording accelerometer was mounted in the airplane and the accelerations were taken for the following maneuvers according to the Distinguished Flying Cross citation. The citation also commended Doolittle for putting, "...the airplane through the most extreme maneuvers possible in order that the flight loads imposed upon the wings of the airplane under extreme conditions of air combat might be ascertained."

In 1925, Doolittle received one of the first US doctorates in aeronautical engineering from the Massachusetts Institute of Technology, and on 24 September 1929 he made the first blind flight and landing. However it was his attack on Tokyo, the Doolittle Raid, that was his most prestigious accomplishment because it raised American morale and changed the psychological balance of power with Japan in the Pacific during WWII. For this historic mission, he received the Medal of Honor and each of his men received the Distinguished Flying Cross. Among other commands, General Doolittle headed the 8th Air Force in Britain until the end of WWII.[17]

The first person to make a non-stop flight across the United States was Army Air Service First Lieutenant Oakley G. Kelley. Kelley and his copilot, Lieutenant John A. MacCready departed Mitchel Field, Long Island, New York at 12:36 the afternoon of 2 May 1923 in the Army transport Airplane T-2, on a non-stop transcontinental flight. They arrived at Rockwell Field, Coronado, California at 12:26 on the afternoon of 3 May 1923. By doing so, they obtained a record and each received a Distinguished Flying Cross in 1928. The citation stated that, "they encountered practically every hazard of flying and displayed remarkable ingenuity, skill, and perseverance."[18]

Eighteen years before the United States entered into WWII, a daring experiment took place which had significant implications for military aviation and proved of great value for future combat situations. Over two days, 28 and 29 June 1923, the first successful experiment in refueling an airplane in the air took place. Army Air Service Lieutenant Virgil Hine flew the refueling airplane and was honored for making, "repeated contacts with another airplane in flight, and by supplying gasoline, oil, and water to the latter, enabl[ing] it to break the then existing endurance, speed and distance records."

First Lieutenant Lowell H. Smith and Lieutenant John P. Richter were the pilots of the plane that was refueled. With the transfer of the vital supplies mid-air, Smith and Richter were able to stay aloft for more than thirty-seven hours.

First Lieutenant Oakley G. Kelley (left) was the first pilot to make a non-stop flight across the United States in 1923.

The three aviators were awarded the Distinguished Flying Cross having served as pioneers in establishing the practicality of refueling and expanding the horizons of military aircraft. The awards, though, were not authorized until 30 April 1940.[19]

Richard E. Byrd learned to fly during WWI after his graduation from the United States Naval

Academy where he developed a passion for aviation exploration. He subsequently pioneered many navigational techniques for airplane travel over the oceans. Included in these developments were drift indicators and bubble sextants. It was 9 May 1926, when then Lieutenant Commander Byrd claimed to have flown over the North Pole and was awarded the Medal of Honor by President Coolidge. His exploit, however, remains disputed.

Following Lindbergh's success across the Atlantic, Byrd commanded a four man crew in the aircraft *America*. The expedition was a planned

First Lieutenant Lowell H. Smith (left) along with Lieutenant John P. Richter (right) were the first pilots of a plane to be refueled in mid-air.

flight from New York to Paris which took off on 29 June 1927. Due to extremely poor weather, when the plane reached Paris two days later the expedition was forced to land in the breakers on the shore at Ver-sur-Mer. For this accomplishment, Byrd and his copilot, Lieutenant George O. Noville, were presented the first two Naval Distinguished Flying Crosses. These awards occurred shortly after the Army presented its initial set of Distinguished Flying Cross medals.

Commander Richard E. Byrd and Lieutenant George O. Noville (not shown) were awarded the first two Distinguished Flying Crosses by the Navy for a flight across the Atlantic Ocean in June 1927.

In 1928 and 1930, Byrd explored the South Pole. Instead of a military medal, he received a gold medal from the American Geographical Society. Richard E. Byrd was ultimately promoted to rear admiral.

In the spring of 1928, another trans-Atlantic flight took place setting a record. It was the first successful non-stop east to west crossing. Baron Ehrenfried Gunther von Huenefeld, Captain Hermann Koehl, a former WWI pilot and Major James C. Fitzmaurice of the Irish Free State Air Force took off from

Baron Ehrenfried Gunther von Huenefeld (left), Captain Hermann Koehl (center) and Major James C. Fitzmaurice (right) were the first foreigners to receive DFCs for a non-stop east to west flight across the Atlantic Ocean.

Baldonnel, Ireland on 12 April 1928, in a Junkers monoplane named the *Bremen,* they crash-landed the next day on Greenly Island in Labrador. When rescued, Friday the 13th turned out to be very lucky for the German-Irish crew that came to be known as the "Three Musketeers."

Authorized by an Act of Congress, and approved 2 May 1928, President Coolidge presented each of the three aviators with a Distinguished Flying Cross. The men were the first foreigners to receive this honor for aerial achievement. When Huenefeld, Koehl and Fitzmaurice toured the United States, they were met with immense adulation.[20]

Henry H. "Hap" Arnold became a general during WWII and he had a significant impact on the creation of the United States Air Force. Not surprisingly, his roots extended back to the early days of flight experimentation with his fellow military aviation pioneers.

In 1911, he became a pilot and was detailed to the Signal Corps. Arnold was also one of the first flyers taught by the Wright Brothers. In June, 1912, Arnold, established a new altitude record when he piloted a Brugree-Wright airplane to a height of 6,540 feet.

After establishing several aeronautical records, Lieutenant Colonel Hap Arnold received a Distinguished Flying Cross for participating in an aerial flight as pilot and commanding officer of a bombardment squadron of ten airplanes that traveled from Washington, DC to Fairbanks, Alaska and returned between 19 July and 20 August 1934. His citation was awarded for "untiring energy, fearless leadership and extraordinary professional skill" and for having "completed over 18,000 miles of exceptionally dangerous flying…over water under extremely adverse weather conditions, without the loss of personnel or equipment, to demonstrate successfully the mobility of the Air Force…"

He progressed rapidly through the ranks and by 11 February 1935 he had received the temporary rank of brigadier general. Then on 29 September 1938 he was named Chief of Staff

Lieutenant Colonel "Hap" Arnold was awarded a DFC for the demonstration of aviation mobility in 1934. He eventually became the commanding general of the USAF.

of the Air Corps. By 1941 Hap Arnold was promoted to major general and then became Chief of the Army Air Forces. He was also instrumental in the creation of the Women Airforce Service Pilots (WASP) and appointed Jacqueline Cochran as its director. An ardent supporter of the United States Air Force, he became the first five-star general of the newest service on 7 May 1949.[21]

Wiley Hardeman Post, a distinctive flyer with an eye patch, first gained national prominence in 1930 when he won the Men's Non-stop Cross Country Derby, from Los Angeles to Chicago. His plane, actually owned by a wealthy oilman named C.H. Hall, was a Lockheed Vega called the *Winnie Mae* after the owner's daughter.

With support from Hall, Post attempted a new speed record for around-the-world travel the next year. To navigate, the pilot chose Harold Gatty. It was 23 June 1931, when the two aviators took off from Roosevelt Field, Long Island, the same field Charles Lindbergh had started from four years earlier.

Eight days, fifteen hours and fifty-one minutes later, they landed back on Long Island on 1 July and broke the previous record which had been twenty days. Post and Gatty became heroes overnight. Wiley Post was awarded the Distinguished Flying Cross.

In 1933, Post flew solo around the world with the assistance of two new pieces of equipment: a Sperry gyroscope and a radio direction finder. This time, he made the journey in seven days, eighteen hours

Wiley Post was an adventurer who focused his talents on setting records for long distance and high-altitude flights.

and forty-nine minutes. Post had broken his own record by twenty-one hours.

Always fascinated by the scientific challenges of flight, in 1934 he focused on high-altitude, long distance flight. Since the *Winnie Mae's* cabin could not be pressurized, he developed an early pressure suit with the assistance of the B.F. Goodrich Company. In his first flight using the pressure suit on 5 September 1934 above Chicago, he reached 40,000 feet. In the super-charged equipped *Winnie Mae*, Post set unofficial altitude records, as high as 50,000 feet, discovering the jet stream in the process.

Wiley Post's most notable friend was Will Rodgers, the famous humorist. Rodgers loved to fly and enjoyed various adventures while in the company of Post. Unfortunately, while flying together in an airplane Post had designed, and built from the parts of two other planes, the duo crashed during take-off near Point Barrow, Alaska on 15 August 1935. Both prominent men were killed on impact. Post's widow was able to have the record-breaking *Winnie Mae* donated to the Smithsonian as a lasting tribute to her husband.[22]

Some people are born to fly and possess innate skills to pilot an aircraft. Amelia Earhart was not one of those individuals. However, her first ride in an airplane sealed her destiny – she knew that she must fly. Taught by the pioneer aviatrix Anita "Neta" Snook, Amelia worked hard to gain skills as an aviator. Despite several mishaps and accidents along the way, she gained valuable confidence and experience.

It was 22 October 1922 when Earhart set a women's altitude record of 14,000 feet. She continued to set records for the next few years. By June 1928, she became the first woman to fly across the Atlantic, but as a passenger, not the pilot. Nevertheless, she gained national celebrity status and realized the power she

By a joint resolution of Congress in 1932, Amelia Earhart Putnam was presented a Distinguished Flying Cross for being the first female to solo across the Atlantic Ocean. She was an inspiration to female pilots.

possessed to advance the role of women both in and out of the cockpit.

Four years later, she soloed across the Atlantic on the fifth anniversary of Lindbergh's Atlantic flight and received the National Geographic Society's Gold Medal from President Herbert Hoover. Amelia Earhart Putnam was also awarded the Distinguished Flying Cross in a joint resolution of Congress. The citation read, "…That the President of the United States is authorized to present the Distinguished Flying Cross to Amelia Earhart Putnam for displaying heroic courage and skill as a navigator, at risk of her life, by her [non-stop] flight in her plane, unnamed, from Harbor Grace, Newfoundland, to Londonderry, Ireland, on 20 May 1932, by which she became the first and only woman, and the second person, to cross the Atlantic Ocean in a plane in solo flight, and also establish new records for speed and elapsed time between the two continents."

Although the law authorizing a Distinguished Flying Cross officially required a recipient to serve in the military, a number of awards were made to early civilian aviation pioneers. Due to gender bias of the era, as a result of Earhart's Distinguished Flying Cross, the president signed an executive order prohibiting such civilian awards.

Not willing to rest on her laurels, the world's most famous female aviator went on to set other aviation records. Earhart was attempting to fly around the world in 1937 with her navigator, Fred Noonan, in their Lockheed Electra when she disappeared sometime during her flight 2 July 1937. President Roosevelt authorized an immediate search but she was never found.

While her legacy was cut short by this tragedy, the legend of Amelia Earhart grew and she served as an inspiration to countless women. The fact that an increasing number of women now serve as combat pilots and have received the Distinguished Flying Cross is a testament to Earhart's vision concerning the role of women in aviation.[23]

Many pilots of the golden era of aviation were colorful, Roscoe Turner was the quintessential barnstorming daredevil. Combining showmanship with serious aviation, Turner demonstrated that he was one of the era's most significant pilots, he won multiple air races, set aviation records and received other prestigious awards.

Having only completed the tenth grade, Roscoe was rejected when he tried to enlist as a pilot in 1917.

Roscoe Turner (left) a colorful aviator, received a Distinguished Flying Cross through a special act of Congress in 1952.

However, he served as an ambulance driver, and was eventually transferred into the Army Signal Corps' Aviation Section where he became a trainee as a balloon pilot and observer. He learned to fly airplanes from military pilots who taught him on the side.

After the war was over, Turner became a barnstormer and did his own mechanics, wing-walking and parachute jumping. His most colorful endeavor was the "Roscoe Turner Flying Circus." As interest declined in barnstorming, Turner went to Hollywood and worked as a stunt pilot for movies. His most impressive work was in *Hell's Angels*, produced by Howard Hughes.

In 1929, Turner was hired to organize Nevada Airlines. The airline purchased four Lockheed aircraft, one of which Turner converted into a racy showpiece. He took four passengers and flew them to New York, proving the practicality of transcontinental air service. Upon his return to Nevada, the governor bestowed upon him the honorary title of "Colonel." Roscoe then acquired a military uniform and began donning a beautifully waxed mustache.

He also started to compete in the Bendix Air Race and the Thompson Trophy Contest. When he obtained sponsorship from Gilmore Oil Company, he capitalized on the company's logo--a lion--by flying with a lion cub named Gilmore. The publicity stunt was quite popular until the cub became too large to fly. During that time, though, Turner continued to set air records. After his racing career, Turner established a flight school in Indianapolis, Indiana and assisted the training of more than 3,300 pilots during WWII.

A variety of sources, both military and civilian, were interested in recognizing Turner for his life-long achievements. Since he had not actually been a member of the military, legislation was required to enact official acknowledgement of his services. After three years of work by his supporters, Roscoe Turner received a Distinguished Flying Cross, authorized by a Special Act of Congress on 14 August 1952, putting him in a select group of people who received a Distinguished Flying Cross in that manner.[24]

THE UNITED STATES OF AMERICA

TO ALL WHO SHALL SEE THESE PRESENTS, GREETING:
THIS IS TO CERTIFY THAT
THE PRESIDENT OF THE UNITED STATES OF AMERICA
AUTHORIZED BY SPECIAL ACT OF CONGRESS
HAS AWARDED

THE DISTINGUISHED FLYING CROSS

TO

Roscoe Turner

FOR
EXTRAORDINARY ACHIEVEMENT
WHILE PARTICIPATING IN AERIAL FLIGHT

GIVEN IN THE CITY OF WASHINGTON
THIS 14TH DAY OF AUGUST 1952

ACTING CHIEF OF STAFF

SECRETARY OF THE AIR FORCE

Roscoe Turner received a Distinguished Flying Cross for his long-term aviation achievements.

Military and Peacetime Heroism

Record setting and aviation improvements were categories for which a large portion of the Distinguished Flying Cross medals were awarded prior to WWII. Between 1919 and 1941 the United States was officially at peace. However, various engagements overseas dictated the use of aviation in situations which elicited bravery beyond the call of duty, particularly for the Marine Corps who played a dominant role in these military actions.

During an insurrection in Nicaragua, US Marine Corps Major Ross E. Rowell was awarded a Distinguished Flying Cross for a situation that occurred on 16 July 1927. The citation recounted that, "during an insurrection in Nicaragua having been notified by his patrol that the garrison at Ocotal, one hundred miles away was in danger, he at once took to the air, and leading a flight of five planes in the face of a tropical storm, conducted the attack with the highest tactical skill, destroying a greater part of the enemy, thereby saving the little garrison from almost certain destruction."[25] While these types of attacks had originally been conducted during WWI and in Haiti, the Navy considered this the first organized dive-bombing attack in its history.

Major Rowell received what was considered to have been the first Marine Corps Distinguished Flying Cross, presented 22 November 1927, followed by First Lieutenant Hayne D. Boyden for rescue actions in Nicaragua on the same day. In fact, of the twenty-five Distinguished Flying Cross medals awarded to Marines before WWI, fifteen were presented for military engagements and/or rescues in Nicaragua.[26]

Second Lieutenant William W. Caldwell and Lieutenant Irvin A. Woodring, of the Army Air Corps were selected to carry out secret orders given by the War Department. It was 15 October 1930, when they were dispatched in two planes to receive a document of "international importance"

In 1927, Major Ross E. Rowell, was the first Marine aviator to receive a Distinguished Flying Cross.

in Vancouver, Canada and deliver it to representatives of the State Department in Newark, New Jersey. The deadline given for this mission was 18 October 1930.

The Distinguished Flying Cross citation provided an account of the situation. "The orders given to the pilots stressed the necessity of disregarding the ordinary peacetime precautions in order to get the document to its destination on scheduled time. Extremely hazardous flying conditions were encountered in Wyoming, snow and sleet destroying all visibility…[T]he airplanes being used in the flight were of pursuit type, selected for speed and not suitable for extensive blind flying…Lieutenant Caldwell remained

Major Rowell, USMC and his fellow aviators contributed to the success of military operations in Nicaragua during the summer of 1927.

with his flight leader until the total lack of visibility caused a separation between them, and he crashed to Earth at 2:15 p.m. 15 October 1930."

Through extremely hazardous flying conditions, Lieutenant Woodring continued on the secret mission. By doing so, he was successful in the delivery of the secret document in the evening 16 October 1930, and completed the mission as ordered.

Lieutenant Irvin A. Woodring, USAAC, received a DFC for risking his own life in order to deliver secret documents to State Department officials.

In 1931, Second Lieutenant Caldwell was posthumously presented the Distinguished Flying Cross. Lieutenant Woodring also received a Distinguished Flying Cross for completing the vital mission.[27]

Dirigibles were a major part of aviation before WWII. Being equally risky to fly, these pilots were also noted for their heroism and were awarded the Distinguished Flying Cross. Two examples demonstrated the gallant actions taken by dirigible pilots during emergency situations.

Lieutenant Commander Robert Rudolph Paunack was an early Navy pilot. He was Aviator Number 27. While serving as the commander of the dirigible C-8 on 3 June 1919, the craft caught fire as a result of a backfiring engine. As the flames threatened the ship and crew of six, which flew at 8,500 feet, Paunack quickly moved into action and grabbed the nearest fire extinguisher. Climbing out to the nacelle (a cover housing the engine) with no handholds or lifeline, he put himself in peril and extinguished the fire. The courageous officer was eventually awarded a Distinguished Flying Cross dated 13 December 1927; however, he did not receive his medal until 1928. Paunack was later made the commanding officer of the Naval Air Station at San Diego and retired in 1935. However, he was recalled in WWII and retired a second time as a captain.[28]

Another award of the Distinguished Flying Cross for heroism during a dirigible disaster was made to Rear Admiral Charles E. Rosendahl and presented 30 June 1947 for heroic actions displayed more than two decades earlier. Rosendahl, the commander of the Navy dirigible *Shenandoah* encountered bad weather over Ohio on 3 September 1925. Unfortunately, the storm became so violent that the *Shenandoah* was being torn apart by forces beyond the commander's control. The naval report, NAVWEPS 00-80-P (B), stated that the rigid airship then lost the control car and rear section which fell to the ground killing fifteen individuals. Even so, Rosendahl was able to use his skills as an airman to free-balloon the forward section for over an hour and eventually land twelve miles from the site of the disaster. The Distinguished Flying Cross citation commended Rosendahl for the, "successful navigation of the airborne remnant of the airship without injury to the survivors of the catastrophe." Twenty-nine people

As a result of his heroism in 1919, Lieutenant Commander Robert Paunack, USN, saved dirigible C-8 from being destroyed by fire while aloft. He was an early naval aviator.

survived as a result of Rosendahl's heroic actions.[29]

Sea rescues have long been a Coast Guard tradition. With the addition of aviation, the Coast Guard became even more efficient and successful in their life-saving endeavors.

In accordance with an Act of Congress dated 30 July 1937, the Coast Guard was granted the authority to award the Distinguished Flying Cross along with the other branches of the military.[30] Ten months later, Lieutenant Carl B. Olsen was selected as the first Coast Guard recipient. Receiving his award on 12 May 1938, the citation stated that it was conferred for, "outstanding heroic action in flying an airplane of the Coast Guard approximately 300 miles to sea under the difficulties of darkness, storms and rough seas for the purpose of removing and transporting to a hospital on shore an officer of the Army, on board the United States Army Transport *Republic*, who was critically ill, saving his life."[31] Once this precedent was

The Navy dirigible *Shenandoah* was a massive airship which was torn apart by a violent storm in 1925. Charles E. Rosendahl, the commander, was able to save many lives as a result of his skill as an aviator.

set, a judicious number of awards were considered and made to deserving Coast Guard aviators.

Two months before the bombing of Pearl Harbor, heroic actions prevented the loss of a high ranking official in the United States Government. It was 3 October 1941, when the Secretary of the Treasury, Henry Morgenthau, Jr., was on board a Coast Guard flight to New Hackensack, New Jersey. Lieutenant William E. Sinton, pilot and Chief Aviation Pilot, Edmund T. Preston, copilot, were responsible for the Secretary's safety and well-being.

With weather a factor, the official documentation explained the tense situation. "While executing an instrument let down procedure to break through an overcast preparatory to landing at New Hackensack, New Jersey, the aircraft struck the treetops and was severely damaged. An imminent crash landing seemed certain, but the pilot and crew kept the damaged airplane in the air. After a flight of almost two hours in low visibility and darkness, the airplane arrived over Philadelphia where clear weather prevailed.

Because of the condition of the airplane, a dangerous landing at high speed was necessary and it was accomplished without injury to the persons on board or further damage to the airplane. The courage, quick thinking, skill, resourcefulness and efficient teamwork of the pilot and crew transformed almost certain disaster into a safe

In Washington, DC, USCG Lieutenant Carl B. Olsen (right) received the Coast Guard's first Distinguished Flying Cross on 12 May 1938 for an action which took place in June 1935. Rear Admiral R.R. Waesche, Commandant of the Coast Guard (left) and Secretary of the Treasury, Mongenthau (center) presented the citation and medal.

In an emergency situation, USCG Academy graduate, Lieutenant William E. Sinton made a difficult landing in a highly damaged aircraft on 3 October 1941. Secretary of the Treasury, Henry Morgenthau, Jr., was a passenger on board the aircraft.

landing which was incredible in light of the damage to the airplane."

Secretary Henry Morgenthau, Jr. arrived safely at his destination. The entire Coast Guard crew: Lieutenant Sinton, Chief Aviation Pilot Preston, Aviation Radioman First Class Stephen J. Brodnan and Chief Aviation Machinist Mate Lonnie Bridges each received a Distinguished Flying Cross personally written and presented by Morgenthau with deep appreciation. As time unfolded, the Secretary went on to fulfill his destiny as the financial architect for the United States during WWII.[32]

Henry Morgenthau, Jr. continued his service to humanity until his death in 1976.

The Way had Been Shown…

When the United States entered WWII, the Distinguished Flying Cross had been authorized for fifteen years. During that time, the Distinguished Flying Cross went from a theoretical concept to a well respected honor. The aviation award had been conferred on our aerial pioneers, individuals who advanced the science of flight, pilots who established records and those who performed beyond the call of duty in a variety of military situations.

The tradition of aviators and aircrews displaying courage, duty and honor was well established by this initial cadre of individuals who wore the red, white and blue stripped ribbon of the Distinguished Flying Cross. The way had been shown and the legacy has grown through war and peace to the present day.

"A Nation that does not Honor its Heroes will not endure."

Abraham Lincoln

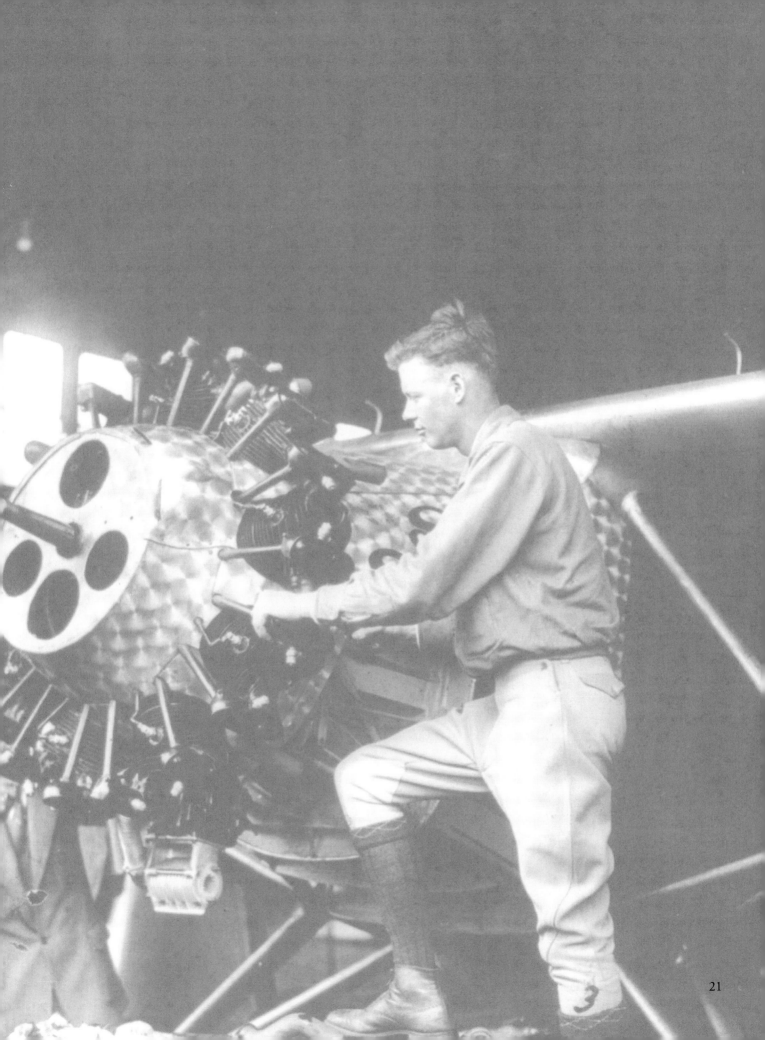

Photographs courtesy of:

Page   2: Yale University Manuscripts & Archives Digital Images Database
Page   3: Library of Congress
Page   4: Distinguished Flying Cross Society
Page   5: Top, The National Museum of the United States Air Force
Page   5: Bottom, The National Museum of the United States Air Force
Page   6: Top, Missouri History Museum
Page   6: Bottom, San Diego Air & Space Museum
Page   7: San Diego Air & Space Museum
Page   8: Top, Naval Historical Foundation
Page   8: Bottom, United States Air Force
Page   9: National Museum of the United States Air Force
Page 10: San Diego Air & Space Museum
Page 11: Library of Congress
Page 12: Top, United States Air Force
Page 12: Bottom, Coronado Library
Page 13: Top, San Diego Air & Space Museum
Page 13: Bottom, National Museum of the United States Air Force
Page 14: San Diego Air & Space Museum
Page 15: San Diego Air & Space Museum
Page 16: Top, Library of Congress
Page 16: Bottom, University of Wyoming, American Heritage Center
Page 17: Top, Coronado Library
Page 17: Bottom, Tailhook Association
Page 18: Top, San Diego Air & Space Museum
Page 18: Bottom, National Naval Aviation Museum
Page 19: Top, National Naval Aviation Museum
Page 19: Bottom, Library of Congress
Page 20: Top, United States Coast Guard
Page 20: Bottom, United States Coast Guard

Notes

[1] Yale Peabody Museum History and Archives, Hiram Bingham, III, http://www.peabody.yale.edu/archives/ypmbios/bingham.html. Accessed on 23 May 2011.

[2] "The Medal," The Distinguished Flying Cross Society website, available from http://www.dfcsociety.org. Accessed 27 October 2011.

[3] Charles P. McDowell, Ph.D., *The Distinguished Flying Cross*, unpublished paper, Archives, the Distinguished Flying Cross Society, San Diego, CA, 5-6.

[4] James W. Patrick, *Wood & Canvas Heroes: Awards of the Distinguished Flying Cross and Other Airmen Stories, 1927 to December 1941* (Fullerton, CA: James W. Patrick Publishing, 2002), xvii.

[5] Letter, Major S. W. Fitzgerald (Recorder) to the Commission of Fine Arts, 20 September 1926, Record Group 66, Entry 17, National Archives, Washington, DC.

[6] McDowell, 5-6.

[7] Letter from Charles Moore, Chairman of the Commission on Fine Arts to the Assistant Secretary of War and Assistant Secretary of the Navy, 24 January 1929, Group 66, Entry 17, National Archives, Washington, DC.

[8] Pan American Good Will Flight, Distinguished Flying Cross citations, US Army Air Corps, presentation date: 2 May 1927, Archives, the Distinguished Flying Cross Society, San Diego, CA.

[9] Patrick, 3-8, Appendix V.

[10] Charles A. Lindbergh, Distinguished Flying Cross citation, Civilian, Act of Congress, action date: 20-21 May 1927, Archives, the Distinguished Flying Cross Society, San Diego, CA.

[11] Ibid.

[12] Ibid.

[13] Ibid., 106-107, Appendix VI.

[14] McDowell, 3.

[15] Ibid.

[16] Master Sergeant Ralph W. Bottriell, Distinguished Flying Cross citation, action date 19 May 1919 in Office of the Adjutant General, *American Decorations,* Supplement I, 1937, (1 January 1927 - 30 June 1937), (Washington, D.C.: The Secretary of War, 1937). 18.

[17] Ibid., 66.

[18] First Lieutenant Oakley G. Kelly, Distinguished Flying Cross citation, action date: 2-3 May 1923 in Office of the Adjutant General *American Decorations,* Supplement I, 1937, (1 January 1927 – 30 June 1937), (Washington, D.C.: The Secretary of War, 1937), 69.

[19] Lieutenant Virgil Hine, Lt. Lowell Smith and Lt. John Richter, Distinguished Flying Cross citation, action date: 28-29 June 1923, Archives, the Distinguished Flying Cross Society, San Diego, CA.

[20] Public Law No. 341, 70th Congress (H.R. 13331), approved 2 May 1928.

[21] Patrick, 120, 122, 133.

[22] Office of the Adjutant General, *American Decorations,* 72.

[23] Amelia Earhart Putnam, Distinguished Flying Cross citation, Civilian, Act of Congress: 2 July 1932, in Office of the Adjutant General, *American Decorations,* Supplement I, 1937, (1 January 1927 – 30 June 1937), (Washington, D.C.: The Secretary of War, 1937), 66.

[24] Roscoe Turner, Distinguished Flying Cross citation, Civilian, Special Act of Congress, 14 August 1952, the Distinguished Flying Cross Society, San Diego, CA.

[25] Patrick, xviii, 28.

[26] Ibid., Appendix V.

[27] Office of the Adjutant General, *American Decorations,* 65, 75.

[28] Patrick, xviii, 26-27.

[29] Ibid., 152.

[30] Stephen B. Gibbons, Coast Guard Memorandum for Secretary Morgenthau, Jr., 4 May 1937, Franklin Roosevelt Library, Hyde Park, NY.

[31] Lieutenant Carl B. Olsen, Distinguished Flying Cross citation, presentation date: 12 May 1938, Archives, the Distinguished Flying Cross Society, San Diego, CA.

[32] Lieutenant William E. Sinton and Chief Aviation Pilot Edmund T. Preston, Aviation Radioman First Class Stephen J. Brodnan and Chief Aviation Machinist Mate Lonnie Bridges, Distinguished Flying Cross citations, action date: 3 October 1941, Archives, the Distinguished Flying Cross Society, San Diego, CA.

Chapter 2

Stories of the Distinguished Flying Cross:

World War II

*A*s Pearl Harbor smoldered, young men lined-up in unprecedented numbers to defend America and secure their future in military aviation. World War II became the quintessential opportunity for pilots and aircrews to demonstrate their combat heroism. It would be the first significant military confrontation since the establishment of the Distinguished Flying Cross in 1926, but it would not be the last.

Along with prodigious human resources, the American industrial complex was unleashed, pulling the United States out of the Depression through the production of the materials of war, especially airplanes. In the process, the country was transformed from a sleeping giant to an aviation colossus.

As the war progressed, the Army and Navy gained experience in orchestrating their assets. At sea, aircraft carriers loaded with a dynamic mix of aircraft demonstrated a formidable presence in the Pacific. The Navy, which oversaw Marine and Coast Guard aviation during the war, coordinated their combined assets for both defensive and offensive objectives.

Meanwhile, Army aviation expanded at a phenomenal rate as did the overall organization. The Army Air Corps, established in 1926, was transitioned into the Army Air Forces, led by General Henry "Hap" Arnold, in June of 1941; six months before World War II began. Despite their inclusion in the Army Air Forces, however, many aviators continued to refer to themselves as members of the Army Air Corps out of loyalty.

Navy and Marine aviation predominately operated within the Pacific while the Army generally took on the air war in Europe, thus allowing for a two front war to be effectively managed. Together, they provided air coverage, bombarded Axis strongholds and destroyed enemy targets while effectively protecting friendly forces.

By 1945, the United States procured the largest, most technologically advanced aviation force ever assembled which included a vast array of formidable bombers, fighters, transports and other aircraft that were revered along with the men who flew them. Without question, it was air superiority on both fronts that turned the tide of World War II and led the way to victory in Europe and then Japan.

In addition to the economic and political repercussions of World War II, there were also social developments. Women and African American men benefited from opportunities in military aviation during the war. Female pilots were recruited to transport airplanes to strategic locations throughout the US, freeing up male pilots for combat overseas. These pioneers were known as the Women Airforce Service Pilots (WASP). African Americans, previously restricted from flying, were given the opportunity to participate in combat as an experiment. Though they were segregated, the Tuskegee Airmen proved themselves in all regards with an impressive war record. Their stellar performance gave impetus to President Truman's Executive Order to desegregate the military by 1948.

World War II was a defining moment in aviation history for pilots and crews who flew aircraft in search of the enemy. They were the ones who performed aerial deeds in heroic proportions, fulfilling their destinies and assuring victory. Then, most went home and remained silent for decades until the media later honored them as "The Greatest Generation." The stories of Distinguished Flying Cross recipients chronicle these amazing sagas of World War II.

Personal Accounts of the Distinguished Flying Cross:

World War II

"The ones who truly deserve the Distinguished Flying Cross are the ones who didn't make it back..."

Sergeant Sidney "Sid" Zimman, USMC

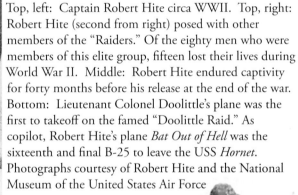

Top, left: Captain Robert Hite circa WWII. Top, right: Robert Hite (second from right) posed with other members of the "Raiders." Of the eighty men who were members of this elite group, fifteen lost their lives during World War II. Middle: Robert Hite endured captivity for forty months before his release at the end of the war. Bottom: Lieutenant Colonel Doolittle's plane was the first to takeoff on the famed "Doolittle Raid." As copilot, Robert Hite's plane *Bat Out of Hell* was the sixteenth and final B-25 to leave the USS *Hornet*. Photographs courtesy of Robert Hite and the National Museum of the United States Air Force

Thirty Seconds Over Tokyo: A Mission That Lasted Forty Months

Lieutenant Colonel Robert L. Hite, USAAF / USAF

"I was willing to go anywhere with Jimmy Doolittle."_____

Thousands of missions were flown in the European and Pacific Theaters during World War II. However, few rival the significant impact of the Doolittle Raid on Tokyo. In the dark days after Pearl Harbor, Americans were stunned by their vulnerability to attack. Decisive military and psychological retaliation was mandatory. Boosting morale at home was also of paramount importance.

Just four months after the smoke had cleared from Pearl Harbor, Lieutenant Colonel James H. Doolittle led an air attack on Japan. It was, without question, the most daring operation undertaken to that point in the war. The plan was conceived in January of 1942, after the realization that it was theoretically possible to launch Army twin-engine bombers from an aircraft carrier. Admiral Ernest J. King, US Fleet Commander, and General Henry "Hap" Arnold, Air Forces Commander, strongly supported the aggressive plan.

General Arnold assigned Lieutenant Colonel James H. Doolittle to organize and lead the air group. Doolittle was the obvious selection because of his impressive aviation accomplishments during the 1920s and 30s.

The attack on Japan, which came to be known as the Doolittle Raid, was orchestrated to accomplish several goals. On the surface, it was a traditional bombing mission aimed at military targets. Perhaps more important, however, was the profound psychological significance the bombing inflicted on the enemy's homeland. Its success boosted American and Allied morale and shook the confidence of the Japanese, proving that they were not invincible. The Raid also signaled a change in basic US tactics from a defensive to an offensive strategy.

After extensive evaluations, the B-25B "Mitchell" medium bomber was selected as the plane that could accomplish the mission. Tests showed it could take-off from a carrier with the necessary bomb load and carry enough fuel to attack Japan and fly onward to airfields in China. Gathering volunteers for a secret but admittedly dangerous undertaking was no problem, and Doolittle embarked on selecting the best men to carry out the mission.

Robert L. Hite was one of the men chosen. He stated, "Everybody knew General Doolittle as being one of the top airmen in the whole country and everybody wanted to volunteer to go with him, so it wasn't any problem to establish the B-25 outfit. We were the 17th Bomb Group, and we were the only ones that had the B-25s. I was willing to go anywhere with Jimmy Doolittle."

Hite also remembered the extensive training and testing required for the secret mission. "We tried everything, including full throttle takeoffs…After we practiced several times, we found out that we could get the aircraft up in about three hundred to four hundred feet…so the ones of us that did the best were selected."

While the training commenced, the new carrier *Hornet* was sent to the Pacific to carry out the Navy's part of the mission. The Raid was so secret that the captain of the aircraft carrier, Marc A. Mitscher, was not apprised of the mission until sixteen B-25s were loaded on the flight deck. With non-folding wings and no room to move the planes, the B-25s were arranged on the flight deck in the order of take-off.

Bob Hite's plane was not on board because it had needed spark plugs in California and sixteen planes had already been loaded on the carrier. That relegated Hite and his crew to surplus status. However, two days before the mission Bill Farrow came to Hite after an argument with his copilot and made a proposition. Farrow said "Hey, would you go with me as my copilot?" Hite responded "Heck yeah, I'll go with you as your copilot. I'll go as your gunner. I'll go as anything to go on this mission. I just want to go!" Thus, Hite became part of the crew for the sixteenth and final plane nicknamed *Bat Out of Hell*.

Each B-25 had been stripped of some of their defensive guns and given extra rubber fuel bladders to extend their range. Two wooden dowels were cleverly placed in each plane's plastic tail cone, simulating extra machine guns that were designed to persuade enemy fighters to keep their distance. Four, 500 pound bombs were their major weapons.

Joined in mid-ocean on 13 April 1942 by Vice Admiral William F. Halsey's flagship *Enterprise*, which would provide air cover during the approach, the *Hornet* headed toward a planned afternoon launch, on 18 April, approximately 400 miles from Japan. However, before dawn on the 18th, Japanese ships were encountered much further east than expected. These vessels were either evaded or sunk. However, concerned that the ships had sent warnings of an attack, the launch was moved up to 8:00 a.m. The largest concern was that they were still more than 600 miles from the Japanese coast. Despite the rushed takeoff and extended distance, the trust in Doolittle was incredible.

"We had the best person to lead us off the aircraft carrier." The last instructions given by Doolittle still reverberate in Hite's head: "You are to bomb military targets only and, whatever you do, stay away from the Imperial Palace…Bombing military targets is an act of strategic warfare, but hitting the 'Temple of Heaven' or other non-military targets such as hospitals or schools would be interpreted as an inexcusable barbarian act. It could mean your life if captured…besides, it isn't worth a plane factory, a shipyard or an oil refinery, so leave it alone!"

Doolittle's aircraft was the first off of the carrier. Everybody followed right behind him and did the same thing. The planes were helped off by a Navy launching officer, who timed the start of each B-25's take-off roll to ensure that it reached the forward end of the flight deck as the ship pitched up in the heavy seas and gave extra lift at a critical time.

Once off the deck of the *Hornet*, the B-25s flew at a very low altitude over the ocean. The trip to Japan was relatively uneventful. As they approached land, the planes separated and headed for their specific targets. "The horizon was speckled with flak and anti-aircraft fire exploded around us as we approached Nagoya. Within a short time our first target, a battery of oil storage tanks, came into view. Bill Farrow pulled up over the target and Jake DeShazer let the first bomb fly. A successful hit! We then flew on to our primary target. With three direct hits on the aircraft factory, we headed across the bay.

I think we saw one enemy aircraft…It was quite a surprise for them and we thought it was a pretty good attack." As they made their egress from their target and headed to China, Hite recalled flying over a school and seeing the children playing and waving to their plane. "I don't think they understood we had just dropped bombs on their homeland."

As the *Bat* headed for the China Sea, they saw one B-25 head north and one head south. Farrow decided to split the difference. "The hours dragged on and we shivered with the constant cold." To make matters more difficult, the weather worsened and they were compelled to fly through a vicious storm, forcing Farrow and Hite to make a decision on a final heading. They ultimately chose and continued in a southwesterly direction, maintaining a speed that would use less fuel but put them over land as darkness fell. "Because we did a really great job of fuel consumption, we flew the furthest of anyone before our engines quit and we were forced to bail out. But we bailed out in the wrong spot." They had to jump out of *Bat* into territory occupied by the Japanese.

Once on the ground, Hite tried to evade the Japanese, however he was eventually captured. Hite and four other Raiders were flown to Shanghai and put in solitary confinement. "By the time I was put in front of the Japanese interrogators, all hope of concealing my participation in the raid on Tokyo evaporated. The officer in charge held a complete list of the airmen from the sixteen crews. They asked about Jimmy Doolittle. They asked about the *Hornet*… I told them that the planes came from the Aleutians."

After this ordeal, the POWs were taken to Tokyo. "Even though conversation was forbidden, I found solace in the company of my crewmates…We faced the unknown but we faced it together…I peeked under my blindfold and realized that I was returning to Tokyo as a prisoner of war."

Starved, blindfolded, handcuffed, stripped, beaten and deprived of sleep, interrogations took place around the clock, every two to three hours. One such technique was a form of water-boarding. "They placed a towel over my face and formed a cup-like pocket over my mouth and nose. I tried to hold my breath when the bucket of water hit my face and pooled in the towel cup. Sputtering, I held out as long as possible…Drowning in the onslaught of water, I fell unconscious…only to be revived by the guard applying pressure to my lungs and abdomen. As soon as my breathing returned to normal, the process started over again and again.

Food for the day often consisted of six slices of bread and hot tea. This created malnutrition and dysentery…I spent endless hours between interrogations in my solitary cell worrying about my mother and sister, and wondering about the welfare of my crewmates and the whereabouts of Doolittle and the other Raiders."

Eventually, the men were returned to Shanghai and imprisoned in the Bridge House, a former British hotel. Seven Raiders were interred with Bob Hite: George Barr, Jake DeShazer, Bill Farrow, Dean Hallmark, Bob Meder, Chase Nielson and Harold Spatz. It often went through Hite's mind if any would survive; if they would see their families again. Emaciated, their clothes hung loose. Unfortunately, the worst was yet to come.

A "trial" was convened on 28 August 1942 and the Raiders stood before five Japanese officers. Since there was no provision that allowed the Japanese to charge the airmen as war criminals, one was enacted and applied ex post facto to the Raiders. During the proceedings, Hite remembered giving his story but he carefully avoided any mention of the Raid – no one took notes. On 14 October 1942, five of the men, including Hite, were marched into a small room and were informed, through an interpreter, that they were convicted of war crimes punishable by death. However, their sentences were commuted to life imprisonment but with "special treatment." Special treatment meant solitary confinement and if the United States won the war, they would be shot. The fate of the other three men was not known. Sadly, it turned out that Farrow, Hallmark and Spatz had already been executed by firing squad.

"The hours of solitary confinement wore away at each man differently. My health declined and my spirit suffered…Robert Meder died of beriberi and malnutrition on 1 December 1943 and his death was a personal blow. Shortly after that, I wrote a letter to the prison governor requesting a Bible…The words in the Bible saved my life…Faith probably attributed to our being able to hang in to the last."

Three years and two months after he had been taken prisoner the Japanese moved the remaining Raiders to Peking on 15 June 1945. Four of the original eight captured Raiders remained in solitary confinement. Hite and DeShazer found a way to communicate with each other through knocks on the wall and by talking through the connecting benjos (the open toilets in the floor of the cells). "One day, Jake told me that he had prayed for peace and that the Lord told him that he didn't need to pray anymore because the war had been won." The date was 9 August 1945; the day that the second atomic bomb was dropped on Nagasaki…American paratroopers found us eleven days later and we were released from prison on 20 August 1945 – forty months after we were captured."

Getting word home to the Raiders' families was critical. "I was in solitary confinement thirty-six months out of forty and none of our families knew for sure whether we were dead or alive. In fact, the film Thirty Seconds Over Tokyo, was dedicated to those who did not return…and I am listed in that dedication…but I made it back! Well, the first thing I wanted was to go back home and have some biscuits and gravy that I had as a young fellow. And when I got home, that is the first thing I asked for…"

After family reunions, the returning Raiders were taken to the Pentagon for a ceremony. "A General at the ceremony said 'You know you guys have been awarded the Distinguished Flying Cross'… and that was a very special moment." He also learned that the actual damage on Tokyo and Nagoya was modest and that none of the planes had reached the Chinese airfields as planned. Three of the eight American airmen the Japanese had captured were executed. Hite also learned that because of the raid on Japan, the Japanese military resolved to eliminate the risk of future attacks and decided to destroy America's aircraft carriers; a decision that led the Japanese to a disastrous defeat at the Battle of Midway.

"Sixteen Raiders lost their lives during the war. Some died on the Doolittle Raid, some died flying the Hump and others were killed in Europe…If I hadn't flown with Bill, I might have been on one of those planes that went down…I'll never know."

The surviving airmen eventually returned to duty. Their leader, Lieutenant Colonel, Jimmy Doolittle was promoted to Brigadier General and awarded the Medal of Honor while the balance of the Raiders received the Distinguished Flying Cross and other military awards and honors.

After regaining his health, Bob Hite became a B-25 flight instructor, remained in the military and retired as a Lieutenant Colonel in the Air Force. "Jake DeShazer, the bombardier on my aircraft went back to Japan and became a missionary for about thirty years."

The 1944 best-selling book *Thirty Seconds Over Tokyo*, authored by Raider Second Lieutenant Ted W. Lawson made the event well-known and along with the film of the same name elevated the Raid to the status of lore and legend. To honor the Raiders, the citizens of Tucson, Arizona presented a set of eighty sterling goblets to the Raiders following World War II. In turn, they were presented to the Air Force Academy in Colorado Springs by General Doolittle on behalf of the surviving members of the Raiders for safekeeping and display between reunions. Thus, a tradition was born. A bottle of brandy was included to be used by the remaining two Raiders at a final reunion to toast their departed comrades.

As in past years, Bob Hite attended the Doolittle Raider Reunion in 2009. With only a few Raiders remaining, the reunion was much more sedate than the reunions just after the war. One tradition yet remains to be enacted which will close the chapter on this remarkable saga in American aviation; the final toast. Asked if he was determined to taste the brandy and drink a toast to his fellow Raiders, Lieutenant Colonel Hite responded, "It doesn't really matter who it will be…it will be one of us."

Few individuals have endured as much pain and suffering at the hands of their captors as Doolittle Raider, Robert Hite. Yet with courage, grace and a faith that endured, he survived the ordeal.

Hite's son, Wallace, best described the importance of his father's role in history. "The Raiders had an integral role in changing the course of the war…There was a great sense of duty to our country. My Dad never really spoke of this historic event at home. There was just a great sense of patriotism. I hope his legacy is that people understand the cost of freedom, and that he was willing to pay the price. Dad has a grandson who is a doctor in the Army. He's served four tours of duty, two in Iraq and two in Afghanistan. Honor and service is a family tradition."

Notes

Jonna Doolittle Hoppes, Calculated Risk: (Santa Monica, CA: Santa Monica Press, 2005, 336.

Lieutenant Colonel Robert L. Hite, Distinguished Flying Cross citation, action date: 18 April 1942, Archives, the Distinguished Flying Cross Society, San Diego, CA.

Lieutenant Colonel Robert L. Hite and Wallace Hite, oral history interview, interviewed by Dr. Barry A. Lanman, 8 May 2009, transcribed, the Distinguished Flying Cross Society Oral History Collection, the Distinguished Flying Cross Society, San Diego, CA.

Top: Ensign Rudy Matz participated
in the Battle of the Philippine Sea,
nicknamed "The Marianas Turkey
Shoot." He progressed through the
ranks to become an enlisted pilot and
was eventually promoted to Lieutenant
Commander. Middle: Ensign Matz
shot down four enemy planes during
the Battle of the Philippine Sea.
Bottom: During his combat tour,
he flew forty-four missions and was
never hit by enemy fire. Photographs
courtesy of Rudy Matz

Dog Fighting in the Pacific: A Carrier Pilot Remembers

Lieutenant Commander Rudolph "Rudy" W. Matz, USN

"We were only in actual combat for twenty-nine days. But we lost thirty-three percent of our squadron in that time and they sent us home."_____

On 7 December 1941, a "day that will live in infamy," the United States was propelled into war following the attack on Pearl Harbor. With the retaliatory Doolittle Raid on Japan, the sleeping giant signaled that it had every intention of regaining the Pacific and winning World War II.

Among the names of revered naval and air confrontations in the Pacific are the Battle of the Coral Sea, the Battle of Midway and the Battle of the Philippine Sea. For Lieutenant Commander Rudy Matz, these are not just names in a history textbook. They are personal bitter-sweet combat experiences seared into his memory.

During the Depression, life on a small farm in Newark, Ohio was austere to say the least. The house in which Matz lived had no electricity or running water. Like the pioneers of the region before him, he attended a one-room grade school. However, he did have the opportunity to complete a high school education. Due to the fact that there were no employment options available, Matz's father took him to the Navy recruiting office two days after his graduation and he joined the Navy on 19 July 1939. While there was no previous military tradition in his family his siblings all entered the service; his brother Otto followed his lead and joined the Navy in 1942, his sister Elfrieda joined the WAVES in 1942 and his brother, Robert enlisted in the Army in 1943.

Matz was originally scheduled for aviation mechanics school as an enlisted man after boot camp, which coincided with his early interest in aviation. However, when Germany invaded Poland the school was cancelled and he found himself at sea, on board the USS *Hughes*. He saw action for the first time in May and June of 1942. Matz recounted his two memorable battles while on board the destroyer. "During May, I was in the Battle of the Coral Sea…before the battle, we were escorting the *Neosho*, which was an oil tanker for refueling the ships, and our gun director jammed, so we swapped places with the USS *Sims* because they had an empty tanker and they sent us back. But before we left we transferred twelve men and one officer to the *Sims*…The following week, the Battle of Coral Sea started and the first two ships that were sunk were the *Sims* and the *Neosho*. So, you just don't know…It was one of those lucky things.

During the Battle of Midway [4-7 June 1942], I was a fire controlman on the destroyer, so I had a ring-side seat…During the battle, I served as the pointer/tracker operating next to the gunnery officer and we were the plane guard for the *Yorktown*…we got credit for two planes shot down…When the *Yorktown* was hit, we started picking up survivors…and we were assigned to stay with her that night. The *Hammann* was tied up alongside the *Yorktown* and the *Hughes* was ordered to go alongside the *Hammann* (we thought to transfer the survivors we had picked up) but the order was cancelled. We just pulled away and I'd say within five minutes a Japanese submarine fired four torpedoes. One hit the *Hammann*; two hit the *Yorktown* and one missed. The *Hammann* sank in four minutes. And the *Yorktown* finally sank the following day."

Narrowly escaping tragedy on two separate occasions, Matz felt extremely lucky. He also realized that the combination of the Battle of the Coral Sea and the Battle of Midway had successfully reduced Japan's naval strength. However, even with a diminished capacity, Japan still represented a formidable naval force well into 1944. Matz, like most men in the Navy, realized that if they were going to be successful in executing a major assault east across the Pacific to advance into the Marianas, they would have to engage the Japanese Navy. The Japanese had come to the same conclusion from a different vantage point. During this interlude, Second Class Fire Controlman Matz decided to make a more significant contribution and went through flight training. He received his wings on 10 July 1943 as an enlisted pilot, aviation pilot first class. After that, he was commissioned an ensign and became a carrier fighter pilot.

By late May of 1944, both sides had amassed an enormous number of ships and aircraft. The Japanese believed that only a major sea and air battle would restore their superiority so more than 563 Japanese planes were put in place for a grand confrontation by June that year. The Americans countered with Task Force 58, a massive carrier component of the 5th Fleet comprised of 896 aircraft, most of which were the venerable F6F Hellcats. By 19 June, the enemies were now poised for an epoch confrontation. As a fighter pilot in VF-1, Lieutenant Matz explained his role in the Battle of the Philippine Sea as he took off from the *Yorktown* [the new *Yorktown*] as part of Air Group 1.

"The squadron took off. We knew that the Japanese were coming because they picked it up on the radar by the ship and I think there were about twenty-four planes in our squadron, but there were several squadrons from all the other carriers…When we got up to twenty-thousand feet, we saw all these planes coming. Our skipper said it looked like a hundred…I think there were twenty enemy planes in about a mile radius…

So, first thing you know, you're into a dogfight and, in my particular case, I was the fourth man in the division and when all hell broke loose everybody got separated or moved, between the different divisions. My division leader had just shot down a Japanese Zero and we were starting to descend into a steep starboard turn. Since I was on the outside, I was sliding underneath. And just as I slid underneath this plane was coming head-on at me and all I did was squeeze the trigger and went through a big ball of fire. I started to open my cockpit because I thought I was going to have to bail out, but when I got through the fireball and I was by myself. I looked down and here's another plane below me, a Japanese Zero, and I shot it down.

I'm just kind of recovering and here's three planes coming at me, but there were two F6Fs chasing them and they chased them off. Then, this one Tony, which was an inline Zero, rolled over and the first thing I did was squeeze my trigger again and I went underneath him, and he was smoking. And again, I'm all by myself, and that's the worst thing you can do – is be by yourself. I looked below me again and here's another one. I started out at twenty-thousand feet and I'm now down to about six. And he was below me and I made a pass at him and had him smoking…but I never saw him hit the water… you're not looking to see them hit the water anyway. Hell, you're too busy. It happens so fast – the entire dogfight was most likely about five minutes.

When you're in a dogfight, everything is so instantaneous and you see planes all over, either coming at you or they're fighting somebody else, and you're basically up there trying to find somebody else to shoot at. And you hope it's the right guy.

It's not as easy as they say or as the textbook describes it. Just like the Thatch Weave, [a complex aerial combat maneuver] which on paper looks very good, but do you ever get to use it? Dogfights don't really happen like the textbook tells you…The interesting thing is that you aren't scared during combat. You're more scared on a pre-dawn take off when it is dark, the ship is rolling and you don't have a horizon."

As the air battle subsided, Matz explained how he got back. "I joined up on another airplane, which happened to be from the *Hornet*. I found out later, it was the skipper of the Fighter Squadron 2 (VF-2). We came back and landed at 14:40.

Throughout the entire battle, Japan lost an estimated 375 planes as compared to 14 American planes. Due to the tremendous victory, the Battle of the Philippine Sea was nicknamed 'The Marianas Turkey Shoot.' VF-1 downed 37 Japanese aircraft." Lieutenant Matz shot down four of them himself and was awarded a Distinguished Flying Cross when he returned to the United States.

With additional providence, Lieutenant Matz was again in the right place at the right time. The next day, 20 June 1944, the Americans aggressively pursued the retreating Japanese forces. The first wave of 216 planes from all the carriers in the task force took off at 4:30 p.m. The second flight was scheduled to depart at 5:30 and Matz was on the port catapult ready to launch when the flight was cancelled. While the first flight was successful, because of the length of the mission, the planes did not get back to their respective carriers until well after dark. Since most pilots had not been trained to land in the dark, this situation presented a major problem. To avoid a disaster after a huge success, the commanders illuminated their ships with flood lights despite the risk of being spotted by Japanese submarines. Even with the bold move, only 116 landed safely on any carrier they could find…there were six crashes on the flight decks of the various carriers with two on the *Yorktown*. A pilot from the *Hornet* took a cut on a waveoff with no tailhook down and landed on top of VF-1s highest scoring pilot, killing him. A total of ninety-four planes ditched in the sea and most of those pilots and crew were picked up the next day by destroyers. A total of fifty-four pilots and aircrew were lost that day. This part of the battle became know as the "Mission Beyond Darkness."

His second DFC came shortly after the Turkey Shoot (25 June – 9 July 1944) when Lieutenant Matz successfully strafed and bombed Japanese shipping and greatly contributed to the success of Fighter Squadron 1's mission from the *Yorktown*. Before the end of his combat tour, Matz received his final DFC for combat actions in the vicinity of the Mariana Islands. The award was given for his engagement of a large enemy force en route to attack his task force. The citation indicated that, "his coolness, bravery and resourcefulness were at all times inspiring…" As with the first DFC, he would actually receive his second and third Distinguished Flying Cross when he returned from combat.

Matz stated "I had forty-four combat missions and I never got hit. However, the squadron I was in… we lost thirteen pilots out of forty…so they sent us back early. We were only out in actual combat for roughly twenty-nine days but we lost thirty-three percent of our squadron in that time. I just happened to be very fortunate…I was in the right place at the right time…It was a true adventure and I enjoyed flying. Looking back on it, the Distinguished Flying Cross means a great deal…It puts me in a group with Charles Lindbergh, Amelia Earhart and other great pilots. In reality, I was just doing what I was assigned to do."

In retrospect, Rudy Matz, with his intimate knowledge of various planes that had played a critical role in the Pacific war, noted he clearly had a favorite fighter plane. "I flew all the Grumman propeller fighter planes, the Wildcat, the Hellcat, the Tigercat and the Bobcat. The fastest of them, of course, was the Bobcat which is much faster than the Hellcat, but the Hellcat was very, very stable and almost forgiving of any mechanical problems. We had planes that would come back with holes in it. We had one guy come back with part of a palm tree in the engine - it was buried into the engine because he went too low and he still made it back. We also had a lot of planes that would come back all shot up…once the pilot landed on the carrier, they would just push the plane overboard because it was so damaged, but the Hellcat got the pilot back.

I went from the Wildcat to the Hellcat, and the Hellcat was such an improvement over the Wildcat because to get the landing gear up on a Wildcat, you had to crank it up by hand and there were thirty-two turns on a ratchet, and if you missed the ratchet and let go, you'd get snapped with the handle and break your wrist.

The Hellcat was much more refined. Picking up the landing gear was so easy … Landing it on a carrier was much easier than the Wildcat, and also much safer than the Corsair.

The Hellcat could carry a 150 gallon belly tank or it could carry two 500 pound bombs or a 1000 pound bomb. But when they had the bomb on, then they would leave the belly tank off. So it could be used as a fighter which was used in the fighter sweeps, without a belly tank, then after the fighter sweep they would put a belly tank on and possibly one 500 or two, 250 pound bombs. With a belly tank, you could stay up around four hours, but over Iwo Jima we stayed up about five hours and four minutes.

It was just an amazing aircraft and if they had the Hellcat much sooner I think the war would've been a lot different. The ratio of kills with the Hellcat was nineteen to one - nineteen Zeros shot down to one Hellcat."

After World War II, Rudy Matz stayed in the Navy as a career and retired as a Lieutenant Commander after twenty-one years of military service. However, for six decades, Matz did not really discuss his combat experiences outside of his squadron reunions. For him and many of his comrades of the "Greatest Generation," it was a past event that had been buried deep in their memories. Only when national interest was awakened by several books and movies were these stories unlocked.

For Matz's children, they finally heard the stories of their father's heroic actions as a fighter pilot when he participated in an oral history interview conducted by the Distinguished Flying Cross Society in 2006. From the interview transcripts and subsequent published sources about the Battle of the Philippine Sea, Matz's children gained a new appreciation for their father.

Lindsey Matz, Matz's youngest daughter, remembered "When I was growing up, he was a pilot and we lived everywhere across the United States for about fifteen minutes…We didn't have much of an opportunity to know him when we were growing up because he was gone so frequently. It is nice, now that I am an adult, to have an opportunity to really get to know him; not only as a father but as a recognized person of the military. He was an employer. He had a business locally. He has worked hard on behalf of a number of non-profit organizations, missionaries, the blind, veterans organizations and so on... He gives back in a million different ways, so I am very proud of what he's accomplished in his lifetime."

Matz's oldest daughter, Carolyn Matz Robertson, concurred with her sibling. "What an amazing job he did in World War II…He never really talked about it and we just found out about his exploits in recent years…It means a lot to me and I can pass along his values of service and commitment to my children… We are so proud of him."

Rudy Jr. reflected on his relationship with his father. "I am highly honored that he was able to fight for our country and come back alive…I know it was difficult for my mom. I am honored that he did what he did for the United States…and that he received the Distinguished Flying Cross."

Matz's children now realize the stories about their dad are an important part of their heritage. Matz Jr. added that, "It's going to be a living legacy and the grandchildren and future generations will be able to understand what Grandpa did in World War II."

Eric, the youngest son, summed up their perspective by saying, "To learn about his life before mine gives me a new appreciation of what he'd been through and what he'd done…"He doesn't consider himself a hero, but I think at the same time, most heroes usually don't. Yeah, he's a hero!

Notes

Lieutenant Commander Rudolph (Rudy) Walter Matz, Distinguished Flying Cross citations, action dates: 19 June 1944, 25 June – 9 July 1944 and July 1944 Archives, the Distinguished Flying Cross Society, San Diego, CA.

Lieutenant Commander Rudolph (Rudy) Walter Matz, oral history interview, interviewed by Dr. Barry A. Lanman, 16 August 2006 and 18 April 2007, transcribed, the Distinguished Flying Cross Society Oral History Collection, the Distinguished Flying Cross Society, San Diego, CA.

Top: Lieutenant George Walsh flew the Curtis Helldiver during WWII. Middle: At the age of twenty-three, Lieutenant Walsh took this photograph of six pilots posed on and around a SB2C. Bottom: George Walsh received a DFC for his role in the attack on Manila Harbor on 13 November 1944. Photographs courtesy of George Walsh

The Attack on Manila: Reflections of a Dive Bomber Pilot

Lieutenant Commander George L. Walsh, USN

"I always felt confident in my ability to survive." _____

As a young child growing up in Brooklyn, New York during the 1920s, George Walsh was enthralled by the exploits of the pioneer aviators of World War I over the fields of France and Germany. In grammar school, he passed the time at his desk drawing stick figures of the German and Allied airplanes dog-fighting in the skies with little dots that represented bullets aimed at the enemy. As a teenager, he examined illustrated books about World War I written by relatives who had fought in the trenches on the Western Front. The scenes were horrible and left an enduring impression on the young man. For Walsh, a quick death in a crashing aircraft seemed preferable to the suffering, maiming and amputations that resulted from warfare on land.

In 1939, Walsh was enrolled in Brooklyn College when World War II broke out in Europe. He had a premonition that the United States would be drawn into the war and he would be part of the action. Walsh realized, however, that the infantry was not the place for a 128 pound, skinny kid. Therefore, he decided to enlist early in an elite service. Naval Aviation seemed his best option and he was eventually accepted in the Naval Aviation Cadet Program after several rejections. Since he enlisted before the draft, Walsh was even offered a five-hundred dollar enlistment bonus and required to finish college. On 7 December 1941, with the attack on Pearl Harbor, the trajectory of Walsh's life abruptly changed as he was immediately called to active duty.

With accelerated cadet training, Walsh completed his pre-flight training in New Orleans within ninety days. He was then sent to Pensacola Naval Air Station for six months of advanced training where he completed all of the flights without a "down check," graduating first in his class.

Ensign Walsh was initially assigned to VS 34 flying inshore patrols from Floyd Bennett Field. He flew convoy ships in and out of New York Harbor due to the activity of German submarines along the Atlantic shipping lanes early in the war. However, Walsh wanted to be part of the "real war" and asked to be reassigned to carrier duty in the Pacific. His wish was granted and he got his chance to fly the Curtis SB2C Helldiver, often referred to as "The Beast."

At twenty-three years of age, the aviator found himself joining the VB 80 dive bombing squadron for the commissioning and the shakedown of the new Essex class carrier USS *Ticonderoga*. The *Ticonderoga* was part of the Fast Carrier Task Force 38 of the Third Fleet. In addition to being a bomber pilot, Walsh also served as the squadron photographer.

After qualification for night carrier landings on the *Saratoga*, he joined Task Force 38 just after the Battle of Leyte Gulf. While heading toward the island of Luzon in the Philippines with twenty-three other dive bombers, Walsh spotted the Japanese cruiser *Kiso* in the harbor of Manila. He recounted the events of the day: "After a briefing in the ready room the night before the attack on Manila of 13 November 1944, we knocked off for some sleep, lying restlessly in the bunk as we raced to get into launching position. At any moment we expected to be aroused by a submarine contact, but this time the night was uneventful. Before dawn, before the ship was aroused, the pilots arose and had breakfast. After breakfast, we reported to the ready room for the last minute briefings and crammed the last of a thousand vital details into our sleepy heads. All were excited but not quite so cheerful this early in the morning. When the word to 'man the planes' was given, the pilots not going helped the others into their parachute harness[es] and we filed out of the room cursing as we stumbled in the dark passages heading for the flight deck.

Above on the darkened deck, all was quiet but the hiss of the ocean that rushed past. An occasional order barked a discordant note and broke the silence. The sun was below the horizon, but already flaming red streaks in the eastern clouds could be observed. Our eyes became accustomed to the darkness, the weird but familiar shapes of the planes, roosting with folded wings, loomed up and we picked our way among them to the one which shared our fate. We were helped into the cockpit and I fastened the safety belt and shoulder harness. My fingers seemed unusually clumsy.

With a few words over the bull horn, the day burst alive as the engines were turned up. Smoke and fumes dissipated as the big ship heeled over into the wind. The red disk of the sun seemed to suddenly rise, resting on the horizon like an orange on a window sill. One by one, the heavily loaded planes staggered off the deck, picked up speed and disappeared... into the rising sun. How symbolic!

Once in the air, all nervousness seemed to vanish. The squadron circled as they joined...from independent units into a few patterns of power headed for the target. The climbing journey to the target was uneventful, but as reports were received over the radio and land came into sight, you could see a wave of unsteadiness – a ripple through the formation. Perhaps, the pilots were rechecking all the cockpit controls. Perhaps, they are taking their eyes off their lead plane to check their geographical position. This was happening as we passed over the mountains of eastern Luzon and the inland plains.

As we arrived, a heavy layer of clouds covered the city of Manila and the harbor. The skipper, Anderson, turned toward the southern end of the city and sent our division, headed by Paul Kalat, toward the northern end. As we began a high speed run in at about 12,000 feet, nothing was visible but a pall of overcast smoke. Kalat signaled for a let down through the overcast for a glide bombing run from lower altitude and began his descent.

Just as I was about to follow with my two wingmen, I spotted a doughnut-sized hole - an opening in the clouds to the west and headed toward the clearing. Puffs of anti-aircraft fire studded the opening as the Japanese sighted in their guns at that point. Suddenly, I had an open view to the sea below. Two miles below me, a Japanese warship steamed at high speed toward the open sea. It was centered in the clearing as if sighted on a target range. Without a second thought, I signaled to my wingmen, peeled off, dropped my dive brakes, adjusted the throttle, blower and propeller pitch, opened the bomb bay doors, armed the bomb and pointed the nose of the plane straight down at the target; lined up stern to bow.

At 300 knots, the vertical two-mile dive only took about thirty seconds, but it seemed like a long time with anti-aircraft shells bursting around you. The dive brakes held the speed of the plane from approaching terminal velocity as it would in a free fall or a power dive. I was pressed forward against my shoulder straps because the aircraft was held back as if suspended from a rope...There was time to adjust the aiming point by using the elevators and ailerons as the ship grew bigger and bigger in the windscreen. With luck, there was no wind factor to be compensated.

A cruiser is a narrow target. Thus, I stayed in my dive until I was confident of scoring a hit, and then I released the bombs. At that speed, another two seconds would have made me a Kamikaze suicide pilot... and at the precise moment, I pulled out hard. I would imagine I probably pulled thirteen G's and blacked out momentarily but quickly regained my senses. At that point, I was low over the water and took evasive action while I retracted the dive brakes, adjusted the throttle, blower and pitch, closed the bomb bay, and raced south toward the rendezvous point.

Virgil Gordon, my gunner, reported a direct hit but I did not look back. My instinct was to get the hell out of there and get back to the protection of the group. We were also so low over the water that all of my attention was on flying the plane, looking where I was headed and watching out for other planes in the area, including enemy fighters...I flew southeast toward Manila and Virgil took a photo of the city waterfront in flames as we passed to rejoin our squadron south of Cavite and Corregidor.

Throughout November, we repeatedly struck targets in and around the Philippines and Formosa. In December, we endured the famous typhoon that did so much damage to the Task Force. Then, Admiral Halsey took the fleet into the China Sea to provide support for McArthur's landings on northwest Luzon at Lingayen Gulf. We attacked Canton, Saigon, Swatow, Hong Kong, Hainan and other targets along the coast of China.

After coming out of the China Sea, the *Ticonderoga* was hit by two Kamikaze causing much damage and severe casualties. Our Air Group was transferred to the carrier *Hancock* and we went on to participate in the Iwo Jima invasion, Okinawa, and the first naval air attacks on mainland Japan."

Of the fifty-seven original pilots of VB 80, Walsh was one of only seventeen who served the entire tour of duty aboard the carriers *Ticonderoga* and *Hancock*. By the war's end, Air Group 80 had completed forty bombing missions and destroyed thirty-one ships and dozens of aircraft.

Given his combat record for the attack on Manila, Walsh was awarded the Distinguished Flying Cross. Walsh stated, "I always felt confident in my ability to survive, but at the same time I went out of my way to study all the survival training…I was a studious pilot, rather than a reckless pilot." Upon completion of his second fleet tour, Walsh was assigned to the Carrier Air Acceptance Test Center at Mustin Field in Philadelphia and remained there until the end of the war.

As a civilian, George Walsh opened an advertising agency and also worked as an SEC registered money manager until 2001. In retirement, Walsh has been actively involved in service activities for his home town of Darien, Connecticut and prolifically writes about World War II dive bombing and the Battle of Midway. When asked what the Distinguished Flying Cross means to him, Lieutenant Commander Walsh said, "I always wear my DFC lapel pin as a personal reminder of my days in combat."

Notes

Lieutenant Commander George L. Walsh, Distinguished Flying Cross citation, action date: 13 November 1944, Archives, the Distinguished Flying Cross Society, San Diego, CA.

Lieutenant Commander George L. Walsh, personal written account, 8 April 2007, the Distinguished Flying Cross Society Oral History Collection, the Distinguished Flying Cross Society, San Diego, CA.

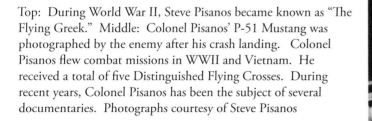

Top: During World War II, Steve Pisanos became known as "The Flying Greek." Middle: Colonel Pisanos' P-51 Mustang was photographed by the enemy after his crash landing. Colonel Pisanos flew combat missions in WWII and Vietnam. He received a total of five Distinguished Flying Crosses. During recent years, Colonel Pisanos has been the subject of several documentaries. Photographs courtesy of Steve Pisanos

"The Flying Greek"
Colonel Steve N. Pisanos, USAAF / USAF

"I had a dream when I came to this country and I was able to accomplish that dream - I flew for Uncle Sam."

The Flying Greek is a book that captures your heart, imagination and sense of patriotism while telling the story of Colonel Steve N. Pisanos. The biography is filled with incredible adventures and romance. It is a work that only the best novelist could dare to dream of writing – but the story is actually true.

It is not the author's name or the wonderful graphic on the book's cover depicting Pisanos' death-defying crash landing that is first noticed; it is the words "Foreword by Walter Cronkite." The revered journalist, in his own unique style, told how he and Pisanos met in Europe during World War II and remained life-long friends. In placing Pisanos, an ace with five DFCs, in context with the thousands of interviews accomplished over the course of his entire career, Cronkite stated that, "Of all the people I've interviewed in a lifetime of journalism, Steve Pisanos ranks right among the most interesting." Anyone would consider this the recommendation of a lifetime.

Born in 1919 with the given name Spiro N. Pisanos, the young boy grew up in Athens, Greece. He was thirteen when he saw his first airplane in flight and Pisanos was forever changed as a result of the experience. Combining his love for flying and all things American, Spiro decided to come to the United States. Even though his father vehemently opposed his plans, Pisanos pursued his dream and made his way to Baltimore and then to New York as a Merchant Marine in 1938.

Following the traditional pattern of immigrants, Pisanos worked hard to make a living, learned English and even adopted a new first name: Steve. By 1941, Steve Pisanos saved enough money to obtain a private pilot's license, and in doing so realized the second part of his dream. However, the next set of events had not been planned. After Germany invaded Greece, Steve felt compelled to fight. He joined the British Royal Air Force and served in the 268th and 71st Eagle Squadrons. The 71st was one of three squadrons comprised of American volunteers and was absorbed into the US Army Air Force in 1942. While in London during early 1943, at the Debden Airdrome, Pisanos was interviewed by a UPI reporter. The reporter's name was Walter Cronkite and their paths would cross again in a few months resulting in a lifelong friendship.

By the spring of 1943, officials of the Greek Air Force (exiled in London) were aware of Pisanos' prowess in the air and they tried to obtain him from the RAF to go to Egypt and join a Greek Spitfire Squadron; something he did not want to do. With the political backing of the British and American governments, he was quickly made a citizen of the United States in May of 1943. With this he became the first person in American history to be naturalized outside the continental limits. To add to the aura of the occasion, Walter Cronkite and Edward R. Morrow were in attendance and recorded the event for posterity. Now a member of the United States Army Air Forces, he was officially flying for his adopted country.

Lieutenant Pisanos' first aerial victory occurred on 21 May 1943. "I shot down a FW-190 with my P-47 and that was my first ever mission with the P-47. We were flying Spitfires before that and I had finished my training in the P-47. The incident occurred over Belgium somewhere after we took care of the bombers. I got mixed up with the Luftwaffe and I chased this guy…and got on the tail of this FW-190. I was very excited…You tremble a little bit. Your feet are shaking. Your heart is pumping fast and your mouth becomes dry all of a sudden…I felt it in my gut… 'I'm going to kill a man - and I felt kind of guilty. But then on the other hand, my adopted country was at war and as far as things were concerned the Luftwaffe was the enemy and I went ahead and fired... He just got in my way and I shot him down.

When I came back to the base, my roommate, Don Gentile [top 8th Air Force Ace] said 'They want you on the parade ground.' I said, 'What for?' And he said, 'You're getting the Distinguished Flying Cross today.' I said, 'I wish my friends in the place of my birth, Athens, Greece, were here to see this - what I had been able to accomplish for my adopted country.' I was very excited when the brigadier general, pinned this American decoration on me. I felt tremendously happy."

Just seven months after his first victory and his first DFC, Pisanos had become an Ace and received two additional Distinguished Flying Cross medals. By March of 1944, he had shot down ten enemy planes. When asked about his most memorable mission, Pisanos did not have to ponder the response. "It was my 110th mission on the 5th of March, 1944 for which I would receive my fourth and final DFC of World War II...We had a big fight down at Bordeaux and I lost my engine on the way back...after I shot down two enemy planes and damaged two more which were later confirmed as destroyed.

My engine quit at about twenty-two thousand feet as I was approaching Le Havre and the Germans lost no time to 'greet' me with the heaviest flack I had ever encountered anywhere over Germany. It was so heavy that I knew that one of those puffs would hit my engineless aircraft. After I had given 'Mayday' to the fighter controller, my idea was to see if I could glide the crippled aircraft over the English Channel and bail out at low altitude. I didn't want to bail out at high altitude because, at that time, the Germans were shooting anybody coming down in a parachute. I soon realized that I couldn't glide far enough to bail out over the Channel, so I decided to turn right back and proceed south and bail out at a low altitude.

When I was well south of Le Havre and my altitude was about 2000 feet, I prepared to leave the aircraft. I trimmed the crippled Mustang so it would fly on its own for awhile. Then I released my harness, tossed my gloves and helmet on the floor and released the Mustang's canopy. With the wind pushing my body backward, I tried desperately to hold myself steady as I stood up. As I struggled to step on the wing, I could feel something holding me to the cockpit. I looked down and saw the dingy [inflatable rubber raft] cord, which I had failed to connect to the 'Mae West' [life jacket]. The plug at the end of the nylon cord appeared to be jammed somewhere underneath the seat. I pulled the cord to free it, but it wouldn't come loose. I had to sit down. I tried again to free the trapped plug by pulling at it from a seated position, but I was unsuccessful. I began to panic and sweat with fear...I tried again to dislodge the cord pulling it to the left and right. Finally, a miracle: the plug came loose!

Losing no time, I jammed it into the plug of my 'Mae West', stood up and braved the wind again. This time I was able to step onto the wing and prepare to jump. But the time I had lost trying to free myself from the cockpit had brought the plane too close to the ground to bail out...I knew that my time was almost up, as I held tight to the cockpit.

I looked ahead and saw my engineless plane gliding straight for the roof of a barn, which was adjacent to the only farmhouse in the area. I held on the longeron, bracing myself for the inevitable. For a moment I considered getting back in the cockpit and trying to glide the Mustang away from the barn to a belly landing. But I didn't have time. I looked ahead and estimated that the aircraft was about 100 to 150 feet in the air – headed straight for the barn...I reached inside the cockpit and pulled the stick back gently, causing the Mustang to pass just over the barn. This action, of course, killed some of the Mustang's gliding speed and I was about to crash.

I prayed and held onto the longeron with all my strength, my knees against the surface of the wing. The Mustang's right wingtip scraped the ground and its belly skidded along the soft farmland. Despite my grip, I was thrown forward and to the left, barely missing the stopped propeller. My eyes were closed as I tumbled through the air and I never saw the ground rushing to meet me...."

Miraculously, Lieutenant Pisanos was not killed but from the impact he was rendered unconscious for an undetermined amount of time. As he regained his senses, he felt intense pain. His first thought was that he had been seriously injured from the impact. However, with as much luck as his crash landing, he only sustained a superficial cut and a dislocated shoulder. Summoning all of his strength, he retrieved his escape kit from the 'Mae West' and started to set the plane on fire so it could not be of use to the enemy.

However, he was interrupted before he could do so. He recalled, "All of a sudden, I heard machine gun fire and spotted two German soldiers at a distance walking rather briskly towards my crashed Mustang while firing their automatic weapons intermittently. For a moment, I thought they were trying to scare me until the bullets flew over my head and hit the vertical stabilizer of my crashed aircraft. And that did it! I dropped everything and I ran into a nearby forest. The two soldiers kept firing their weapons at me while I was on the run and up to the moment I entered the wooded area.

I got into the forest and they followed me inside the forest as well. Then, they began to talk in German and I could hear them but I didn't understand German. They were probably saying, 'You better give up. We're going to kill you if we find you.' But somehow I got away from them and quickly came out of the forest. I walked by the farm house and my Mustang on its belly and jumped a fence and found myself on a paved road.

I then started walking down the road and ran into a parked motorcycle. No doubt, it must have been the one the two soldiers used to come to the site of the crash. At that point, I decided to jump another fence and get away from the area. I wandered around for about five days; drinking water from running creeks, eating dandelions and whatever I could find. And then, I walked into a small farm and saw some cabbage, so I did a little stealing. I grabbed a cabbage and ate the whole thing. On my fifth day of wandering, I made contact with the underground.

Because D-Day was being planned, the Resistance couldn't help me to get to the Spanish frontier as they used to help downed aviators in the past. So after spending some two weeks in a village well south of Le Havre, I was taken to Paris in a truck loaded with firewood. I stayed there until the city was liberated in August 1944. Because I spoke a little French, I got involved with some resistance 'characters' in one of the safe houses I was staying. Their aim was to sabotage the German machinery and kill Germans; an escapade in which I took part several times… The Liberation of Paris was an experience I will never forget. Several hundred aviators, British and Americans, came out from hiding."

For this combat situation, Pisanos received his fourth Distinguished Flying Cross but he was prohibited from flying in combat again. He was sent to Wright Field as a test pilot where he attended the Air Force's Test Pilot School along with his close friend Don Gentile. There, he also met Chuck Yeager and eventually realized that Yeager had been shot down on the same mission as Pisanos' crash landing in France. A kindred friendship ensued.

When the Korean War started, Pisanos had anticipated a combat assignment; however, he did not see action in Korea because he was assigned to the Pentagon working on aircraft allocations, specifically taking P-51s from the Air National Guard and sending them to Korea. Feeling on the sidelines, Pisanos said, "I asked my general if I could be released and go to Korea. The general said 'Sit down at your desk, and do what you're doing.' And I guess I missed Korea…"

Vietnam was a different story. Lieutenant Colonel Pisanos was determined to get back in the air. "I was in Germany when I volunteered to go to Vietnam. I was a senior officer then and I knew that if I came back to the States I would probably end up at a desk shuffling papers. I felt all my life that Uncle Sam had helped me tremendously to achieve my dream and I had an obligation, to really do something worthwhile. My adopted country was at war in Vietnam. I didn't care what type of war, but the country was really in a bind.

So I went to USAFE Personnel and I said 'What do I have to do to go to Vietnam?' The personnel officer said only one word; 'Volunteer'…He gave me a form and I completed it. I went home and I told my wife and, boy, I thought I was going to have the biggest divorce ever. But, thank God, she began to see my way of thinking. I told her I'm obligated to the country and as a soldier I needed to go there, and 'Please, please, don't worry about me.'

I went to Vietnam and I had volunteered for fighters. I had orders when I left Wiesbaden, Germany to go to Williams Air Force Base to get checked out on the F-4. But somewhere along the line they discovered that I was a senior Lieutenant Colonel, had an airline transport license, flown for the airlines and what on earth are we doing with a guy like this signed up in Fighters? They had so many lieutenants from the academy who needed combat experience. So they changed my assignment and I went to a Caribou C-7 (twin-engine) Unit in Sewart Air Force Base in Tennessee. I got checked out on the aircraft and I was sent to Cam Ranh Bay, Vietnam; first as operations officer and then commander of 457 TAS.

I flew three hundred and seventy-five missions supporting the Special Forces in the jungles of Vietnam. There was no enemy air force in South Vietnam but we had an enemy on the ground; the Vietcong. They would hide in the foliage and when they saw a helicopter or a low-flying Caribou, they would fire. And on one of the missions, I came back and my crew chief said 'Hey Colonel, we've got many bullet holes in the tail of the aircraft.'"

While this was a memorable event for Pisanos, an incident concerning ice cream was just as important to the veteran aviator. "My wing commander came into my office and said, 'We have some ice cream here and we don't know how on earth to deliver it to the Special Forces.' I said, 'I'll deliver it.' The wing commander said 'How are you going to do it? By the time you get there it's going to be milk.' So, I just connected the oxygen system and took the Caribou to about eighteen thousand feet when I got close to the Special Forces Camp. Then, I told the camp commander I had special cargo – ice cream! I said, 'Get your guys and come out with cups and spoons because it is going to melt within minutes due to the extreme heat'…I landed immediately and you should have seen the GIs in that Special Forces camp waiting with pots, pans, spoons and what-have-you. That was the greatest enjoyment they ever had, to have real ice cream delivered to them…and it meant a great deal to me as well.

I got my fifth Distinguished Flying Cross for doing an airdrop of ammunition and other supplies into a lost Army Special Forces Patrol that was surrounded by the enemy for a few days." The DFC citation commended Lieutenant Colonel Steve N. Pisanos, "for heroism while participating in aerial flight in connection with military operations against an opposing armed force near Cung Son, Republic of Vietnam, on 6 December 1967. On that date, Colonel Pisanos made a tactical emergency airdrop to a besieged patrol of Special Forces personnel in danger of being overrun by a superior hostile force.

After overcoming extremely adverse weather conditions and mountainous terrain to locate the patrol, and overruling the patrol commander's warning not to attempt the drop due to hostile activity, Colonel Pisanos, in complete disregard for his personal safety, airdropped the needed supplies to the patrol. His unusual skill and determination was directly responsible for the preservation of the Special Forces unit, which was subsequently rescued. The outstanding heroism and selfless devotion to duty displayed by Colonel Pisanos reflect great credit upon himself and the United States Air Force."

When Pisanos had completed his assignment in Vietnam, he was given a well-deserved leave that he spent in Kansas City, Missouri with his family. During that time, the Pentagon informed him that he had been promoted to a "Full-Bird" Colonel and that his new assignment was Deputy Commander of the 308th Ballistics Missile Wing at Little Rock AFB, Arkansas. When trained, Pisanos spent three years working with Titan II ICBM Missiles and explained what transpired next.

"I received another call from the Pentagon informing me that I had been reassigned to Athens, Greece as Chief of the Air Force Section, under the military mission for aid to Greece, JUSMAAG. Yes, the place of my birth and the place where it all began. I cannot express how wonderful this assignment turned out to be, helping the Greek Air Force, meeting ambassadors and all kinds of diplomats. I even had the opportunity to meet the Prime Minister of Greece and conversed with him in Greek as he didn't speak English. But the most interesting part of this assignment was when I, along with the people who worked for me in the section, managed to sell two squadrons of F-4Es to the Greek Air Force, beating two competitors; the British and the French.

As a decorated Ace and recipient of five Distinguished Flying Crosses, Colonel Pisanos commanded immense respect. However, it was his father's respect that he most prized. "When I was on my last assignment with the Air Force and I had completed some thirty years of active duty, my father saw me in the Colonel's uniform, with all my decorations on my left breast; he began to cry. He couldn't believe that

48

his son was able to accomplish the dream he had when he was just a youngster. My father was the happiest man."

When he retired, Colonel Pisanos and his wife made San Diego their home. Pisanos appeared in a Discovery Channel series hosted by Walter Cronkite in January 1997 and was later included in Oliver North's series, *War Stories,* shown on the Fox Channel during January 2007. An episode featured Colonel Pisanos called "Yanks in the RAF."

By 2008, Colonel Pisanos completed his biography called, *The Flying Greek* with the foreword written by his famous journalist friend, Walter Cronkite. Bringing the words to life from his book, when asked he expressed to people; "I am proud to be an American…I am proud because I accomplished the impossible. I had a dream when I came to this great country and I was able to accomplish that dream - I flew for Uncle Sam and the American Flag… The United States of America is a country worth loving, serving, defending, fighting for and dying for…I have decorations from four other countries but to me, being decorated with the Distinguished Flying Cross was one of the greatest achievements in my life."

Notes

Colonel Steve N. Pisanos, Distinguished Flying Cross citations, action dates: 21 May 1943, March 1944, 6 December 1967, Archives, the Distinguished Flying Cross Society, San Diego, CA.

Colonel Steve N. Pisanos, oral history interview, interviewed by Dr. Barry A. Lanman, 19 July 2009, transcribed, the Distinguished Flying Cross Society Oral History Collection, the Distinguished Flying Cross Society, San Diego, CA.

Colonel Steve N. Pisanos, *The Flying Greek* (Dulles, VA: Potomac Books, Inc., 2008), 349.

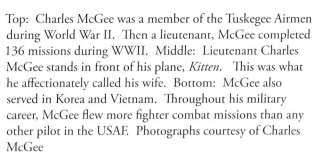

Top: Charles McGee was a member of the Tuskegee Airmen during World War II. Then a lieutenant, McGee completed 136 missions during WWII. Middle: Lieutenant Charles McGee stands in front of his plane, *Kitten*. This was what he affectionately called his wife. Bottom: McGee also served in Korea and Vietnam. Throughout his military career, McGee flew more fighter combat missions than any other pilot in the USAF. Photographs courtesy of Charles McGee

NO STEP

The Tuskegee Experience

Colonel Charles E. McGee, USAAF / USAF

"Talent doesn't come in color or happenstance of birth…It comes from education and confidence in yourself."

During the "Summer of 42," when Charles E. McGee first became a member of the Tuskegee Airmen, he never imagined that one day he would be a highly decorated Air Force colonel with three Distinguished Flying Crosses and a record that included the most fighter combat missions of any pilot in the United States Air Force. He also never dreamt of standing in the Capitol being honored by Congress and President George Bush as he was conferred the Congressional Gold Medal in 2007. For Colonel McGee, the Tuskegee experience has been a profound one, lasting a lifetime.

Born in Cleveland Ohio on 7 December 1919, Charles McGee spent most of his youth in Keokuk, Iowa and a small town near Chicago, Illinois. After graduation from high school in 1938 he wanted to go to college, but the Depression deferred that dream, even though his father was a prominent social worker and African Methodist Episcopal minister. He joined the Civilian Conservation Corps in northern Illinois and worked for a year with the CCC where he learned engineering, contour farming, and saved enough money to attend the University of Illinois in 1940. He studied engineering, joined the Reserve Officer Training Corps (ROTC) program, and became a member of the Pershing Rifles. McGee described his early goals in succinct terms: "I just knew that education was important to be able to open doors and so that was my focus." That intense focus would continue as a lifelong quest for achievement and self improvement.

Once World War II began, McGee, who became known as "Mac," received a draft card and had to make a decision that would significantly impact his life. He did not have any love for the infantry and trudging through the mud, so he had considered applying to a new program for aviation technicians open to African Americans at Chanute Field. However, before that transpired, his ROTC instructor said, "You ought to sign up to be a pilot, not a mechanic." McGee's response: "That sounds good to me! So I took the exams in the spring of '42 and passed them, and then it was a waiting game to be called up, which came in October of 1942. By the time I got to Tuskegee in the fall of 1942, the airfield had been completed, although they had been training on it even while it was under construction. The 99th had completed its 33-pilot cadre by the time I arrived…I started out in [class] 43G and, I assume, it was due to my ROTC training I skipped upper pre-flight, so I graduated with 43F in June of 1943. And, of course, that was dual training; I was commissioned a Second Lieutenant and received my silver wings."

From the summer of 1943 to the end of the war, Lieutenant McGee flew one hundred and thirty-six missions: eighty-two tactical missions and fifty-four strategic missions. "We started out with the 12th Air Force in Italy doing harbor and coast patrol, flying the P-39 Belair Cobra…Our mission was patrol at the time and I had eighty-two such missions flying out of the Naples area of Italy. But in the spring of 1944, our bombers flying from Southern Italy penetrated deep into German protected territory and the losses were extremely high…Thus, they formed the 15th Strategic Air Force, and four fighter groups were initially picked to begin escorting our B-17s and B-24s. Of course, the P-39 wasn't the aircraft for that so we gave them to the Russians and they used it in ground support. We then started the escort work with the P-47 Thunderbolt and then got the pilots' favorite; the P-51 Mustang. The P-51 was just a wonderful little aircraft because of its range, speed and maneuverability at altitude. My P-51 was named *Kitten*; the nickname for my wife, and because my crew chief kept the plane purring like a kitten."

While bomber escorts were the bulk of his missions with the Mustang, he did participate in a type of mission called a "fighter's sweep." These activities involved striking targets on the ground such as aircraft, oil fields and manufacturing facilities. He clearly stated that "if we caught them on the ground, that's better than having to fight them in the air. And we had a couple missions like that that were very successful, so it's kind of a combination of all of the things that went about into giving us air superiority."

With so many different missions seemingly alike, a few stick out as unique in McGee's memory, and for good reason. "I was very fortunate to have a wonderful crew chief. In fact, in all of my missions I only had one abort, early return, where about twenty minutes out I started having an engine problem that made me return the aircraft. Another memorable mission was the flight I ended up with a victory - I certainly won't forget that because the enemy pilot made a mistake in turning the wrong way. It put him right in my gun site and range, and I shot him down."

During his hundred and thirty-six missions in World War II, Lieutenant McGee did not receive a DFC. However, for one mission, he had anticipated such recognition. "I flew a mission during the Normandy landings; we struck German facilities in Southern France, attacked radar stations and kept enemy troops from moving to the northern part of France. So we were quite active at that time…From the intelligence and the nature of the targets, you get an idea, and the talk, but I guess our intelligence folks didn't get around to writing that up, so I came home without a Distinguished Flying Cross in Europe; but I received twelve air medals."

In analyzing the rationale for the lack of a DFC for this mission and a general under-awarding of DFCs for the Tuskegee Airmen as a group (approximately 110), two factors have been considered by McGee. "I've had the feeling since our unit was segregated even overseas, we didn't have the privilege of experienced intelligence officers who made the recommendations for medals." The second conjecture was simply that of racism.

Colonel McGee also has an interesting perspective concerning the overall performance record of the Tuskegee Airmen. While some individuals will state that the Airmen didn't lose a bomber under their protection during the 200 plus escort missions they flew, McGee is careful to consider all the circumstances. "It's just so many factors, and when you look at some reports, the details are skimpy…Was the rendezvous on time? How many? Who? Where? Was a loss a straggler out of the formation? We just have to be careful of how we look at it and how we use the data. So, if you say the Tuskegee Airmen never lost a plane, you certainly better qualify it… However, if you look at the record in terms of percentage; the percentage was formidable."

At the conclusion of World War II, Captain McGee had every desire to stay in the military because of his love of flying; however, the "Johnson Purges" by the Secretary of Defense Louis A. Johnson grounded a large number of pilots in a cost-cutting measure. McGee was unfortunately one of those placed on Non-Flying Duty and sent to the Philippines with an assignment in operations. However, as the Korean War came to pass, the need for P-51 pilots was significant considering all the surplus Mustangs housed in Japan.

McGee stated "I was assigned to one of two squadrons of pilots leaving the Philippines, who went to Japan, picked up P-51s and started flying against the North Koreans. In fact, we flew out of Japan while they built the first airstrip within the Pusan perimeter…So the P-51s were in place and immediately put to work. I was with the 67th Squadron of the 18th Group…And so, with my background, I started out in the squadron as a squadron maintenance officer as well as a pilot.

Of course, to me, that was another phase of the aviation experience, because this was all ground support and interdiction. I never saw a MiG during my tour there, but they weren't down in the trees where we were. They were up a little higher…Looking back at my log, it reminds me of the way we flew. We would fly from our base, conduct a mission and land somewhere farther north, rearm, fly another mission and then go back home.

I received a Distinguished Flying Cross for a mission on the 20th of August 1950. We carried frag bombs and rockets and, of course, our internal guns and worked with our men on the ground to destroy forces and equipment that had been moved in place against our ground forces. But that was the nature of the fighting…All pretty much low level…and, as I recall, on that mission we flew through bad weather from our base, fortunately, were able to get into the target area and do our job and then get back. Receiving a DFC depended on the intelligence reports and the ground report on the effectiveness of our work…A few weeks after that mission, I was notified that I had received a Distinguished Flying Cross." In his normal understated manner, McGee didn't mention the heroic actions taken to accomplish the strategically importance mission.

Major McGee received a second DFC on 17 December 1950, shortly before he completed his hundred mission tour. "That mission was a little longer than the one that I had earlier, but also a little different because we carried napalm and rockets." According to the DFC citation, Major McGee and his flight leader penetrated deep into enemy occupied territory near Hwasan-dong. They located and destroyed a large quantity of enemy and well camouflaged war material even though McGee's engine was not performing properly.

After his Korean combat tour along with the transition to P-80 jets and a variety of assignments, McGee found himself headed for Vietnam in 1967 as a Lieutenant Colonel assigned to reconnaissance, flying the RF-4C and took the 16th Tactical Reconnaissance Squadron (TRS) at Tan Son Nhut ARB near Saigon. There, he flew a hundred and seventy-three missions along with commanding the squadron.

McGee recounted one rather difficult mission. "Late in 1967, I was flying a day recon mission over one of the roads in Laos. It was a suspected infiltration route, but I'd received no intelligence of heavy defenses. As I was letting down, however, I took a high-caliber hit in my left wing, which left a big hole. I was losing fluids, though I couldn't tell which ones. I had to divert to the nearest base on the coast, Da Nang, and it was the only time I had to make a front-end engagement landing, using my tail hook to make sure we wouldn't run off the runway. It turned out we needed major repairs. I took the film out of the plane and hitched a ride with a general who happened to be going to Saigon in a twin-engine North American Rockwell T-39. When I got back, I turned in the film and resumed flying the next day."

When the Tet Offensive broke out on 31 January 1968, most of the squadron pilots were at their walled compound off base. There were only six pilots on base including Mac and for three days they flew all of the squadron's missions, since there was no movement allowed off base. "We didn't lose a mission. Soon hutches were built for us to live in on the base. At one point, the VC started mortaring the place. We had foxholes, but I'd just put my helmet over my head and stayed in bed. Who knew where a round would land?"

While he did not receive a DFC for flying in the Tet Offensive, less than a month later on 25 January 1968, Lieutenant Colonel McGee was chosen for a specific mission. He flew a top priority day reconnaissance over classified targets in a high threat target area. Because of the success of his reconnaissance and the strategic success of the overall mission, Mac was awarded his third DFC.

"My tour was up in May of 1968, and after being given the choice, I went on a wonderful year's tour in Heidelberg, Germany, as air liaison officer to the Seventh Army Headquarters. I was promoted to Colonel and became chief of maintenance for the 50th Tactical Fighter Wing. I got to fly the F-4C Wild Weasels, F-4E air defense fighters and the F-4D, which I flew at Mach 2. Eventually, back in the States, Major General Paul Stoney, commander of Air Force Communications Service, asked me if I'd like to take command of Richards-Gebaur AFB. I'd always wanted this administrative task, so on 24 June 1972 I got my opportunity, and with it came getting a 'key to the city of Belton.' It ended too soon, though, due to a mandatory retirement policy based on 30 years unless you were made a general officer. Thus, I retired on 31 January 1973."

Looking back at his entire career and comparing three wars McGee recounted that, "I enjoyed going through the different phases of the aviation experience. In Europe, predominantly the nature of assignment and work was providing for air superiority so that we could move freely. That experience in Korea was interdiction and ground support…Then, Vietnam was tactical intelligence - no weapons. Our defense was speed and yet you're being fired at. As I say, I got through Europe unscathed. Had an aircraft hit in Korea and was able to get back to my home base...Had the aircraft hit in Vietnam...Couldn't get back home and had to leave it at a friendly base. The nature of each war was different." And, as for the Distinguished Flying Cross, he modestly replies, "The recognition is wonderful...it inspires...and is most appreciated but it is the accomplishment of a job well done that is most important."

Charles E. McGee never saw himself as a pioneer in breaking down the barriers of segregation and racism. "My feeling is that I look at it that way in retrospect."

"As Tuskegee Airmen, we came from all different parts of the country; different backgrounds and different levels. Some already had college degrees; some didn't as they changed the requirements. And, the attitudes and experiences were quite different, so we were each individuals. But number one, we were patriotic...There were opportunities to serve in the military and opportunities for jobs as the war build up. So, our coming together was individual. But only over time and looking back do you suddenly realize that it had a profound impact on change. So it took all of that coming together and time to make us what we are now."

Following his retirement from the military, Col. McGee spent the next decade in business, received a degree in business administration and served as manager of the Kansas City Downtown Airport. After a second retirement, he was selected as a member of the Aviation Advisory Commission.

Colonel McGee was a charter board member when the Tuskegee Airmen, Inc., was established in Washington, DC, in 1972 and served as President of the association from 1983 to 1985 and 1998 to 2002. In these roles, Mac pondered the significance of his Tuskegee experience and the important lessons learned. For more than two decades after his official role with the group, the mantra remains the same. "Talent doesn't come in color or happenstance of birth...It comes from education and confidence in yourself." He inspires young people to make the most of their educational opportunities and to give their best effort in what ever they do. He also emphatically points out that "the lessons out of our past shouldn't be forgotten." By embracing these values, Colonel Charles McGee comments that, "It brings out the very best in every person and as a result, it means a better community; a better country."

Notes

Colonel Charles E. McGee, Distinguished Flying Cross citations, action dates: 20 August 1950, 17 December 1950 and 25 January 1968, Archives, the Distinguished Flying Cross Society, San Diego, CA.

Colonel Charles E. McGee, oral history interview, interviewed by Dr. Barry A. Lanman, 2 December 2008, transcribed, the Distinguished Flying Cross Society Oral History Collection, the Distinguished Flying Cross Society, San Diego, CA.

Top: The unmistakable shape of the B-17 was a common site over the skies of Europe during World War II. Middle: Staff Sergeant Donald Smith was a ball turret gunner on B-17s during WWII. Bottom: Donald Smith spent many hours in a B-17 ball turret like this one. He loved his job. Photographs courtesy of Donald L. Smith and the National Museum of the United States Air Force

The Best Seat in the House: Perspectives of a B-17 Ball Turret Gunner

Staff Sergeant Donald L. Smith, USAAF

"The flak was so thick you could walk on it."_____

On 14 August 1942, Donald L. Smith turned eighteen and enlisted in the United States Army Air Corps with a passion to become a pilot. After basic training, Smith went to Santa Anna, California for pre-flight training in December of that year, and then on to primary flight training. As Smith put it, "somewhere in that period of time they decided I was not pilot material but I still wanted to fly so I volunteered to enter gunnery school."

After completing gunnery school in Las Vegas, he was assigned to a B-17 crew and was "volunteered" as a ball turret gunner. By April 1944, Smith was assigned to the 447th bombardment group, USAAF, based at Rattlesden Airbase, England, part of the 4th Combat Wing. "We flew seven missions and we had an outstanding crew so after those missions we were taken off operations and put into training as a lead crew…We finished training in early July 1943 and immediately began flying as a lead crew…We flew missions all over Germany, but in July of '44 we led two missions to bomb the St. Lo area of France. That was to facilitate Patton's breakout.

We also flew on D-Day. When we went to the briefing on June 6th and they announced it was D-Day, there was a loud cheer…we were overjoyed because that was our entire purpose in life at the moment. Our purpose was to invade France and eliminate the Germans. I mean, that's why I enlisted. We were gung-ho…We flew three missions in just over a thirty-six hour period. So we were in and out like a bus driver…We'd just go over, drop, come back, load up, get some food, sleep while they were servicing the planes and then back out again.

Our first mission on D-Day, we did not drop our bombs. We were scheduled to drop on Sword beach right under the British troops, but we had solid undercast and we were in a timeframe where there was a possibility of dropping on the friendlies. So, we went inland looking for targets of opportunity but didn't find any. So, the first mission we brought our bombs home. The second and third missions we went further inland and we were doing 'intervention' bombing - preventing the Germans from bringing in reinforcements."

When asked if he realized the significance, Sergeant Smith put the events into perspective. "We all knew what it was because we'd had the invasion of North Africa. We had the invasion of Sicily. We had the invasion of Italy. All those preceded Normandy so we knew exactly what it was. And we all knew that it was a momentous occasion. The only thing we really didn't know was the lack of air opposition. We were told there wasn't going to be any…but we didn't believe that. But there was none…and there was no flak either, because the Germans were not prepared for what happened…and they were not prepared for the masses of aircraft. So we totally overwhelmed them and the same thing happened at St. Lo.

As the war progressed we bombed all the standard targets, like Bremen, Bremerhoffen, Regensburg, Berlin and Kassel. The scariest one was a place called Merseburg. That's where they had the synthetic oil plants. It's near the town of Leipzig and they had more anti-aircraft guns in that area than any other area outside of Berlin, but they were more concentrated there. I think it was a more confined area than Berlin. That was one of the places where the expression, 'the flak was so thick you could walk on it,' fit. It was pretty spooky there."

As time went on, Sergeant Smith's love affair with his airplane continued to grow. "The B-17 looked like a fighter. The B-24, although it was faster and could carry more bombs, was not as agile at high altitude. It wasn't as rugged and it wasn't as romantic. And I think the romantic part was more to it than anything else. One of my five brothers had served as radio operator in a B-24. So we had a lot of inter-family rivalry over that…The B-17 was a very wonderful aircraft and it got the job done."

While he was totally committed to the B-17, Smith also loved his job as ball turret gunner. "I had the best view in the house because I could rotate the turret three-hundred and sixty degrees and I could point it straight down or horizontal. So I had a complete panoramic view of everything going on in front and behind, and to the sides. I just couldn't see what was above." In response to the issue of flak, Sergeant Smith recounted, "One fellow told me that he used to hide from the flak…You have to understand what the inside of a ball turret looks like. When you pointed it straight down [the gun sight], which is the size of a medium box, it was right in front of your face and then the glass that you looked through pointed straight down…if I put my head up over the gun sight I had that to deflect any flak that would come up through.

It really scared me when I put my head up and couldn't see anything, but I could hear the flak bursting…when you could hear the flak burst, that meant it was very, very close because a B-17 made an awful lot of noise. So when we heard the explosion of the flak you were going to get hit. That scared me because I couldn't see. As soon as I took my head out from under there and rotated the ball up to where I could see the flak, then I calmed down. In situations like that everybody's afraid. But I think its more apprehension than fear because fear is something different…We were afraid, but I don't think fear took over…"

Reflecting on the people who served as ball turret gunners, Sergeant Smith was very emphatic, "Many movies and documentaries talk about the 'suicide people' who flew in the ball turret…and people believe that anybody who flew in a ball turret was semi-nuts to begin with. I'd like to debunk that. Number one, the ball turret was the safest place to be and had the fewest injuries statistically…the ball turret, being a sphere, when the flak hit the ball turret; it was more apt to bounce off. This happened to me on more than one occasion. However, if you're up in the cockpit or any other part of the plane, the aluminum skin was very thin and the flak would go right through it like melted butter.

Number two, many people seem to think that I was in the ball turret when we took off and when we landed - Not true! When the guns were pointed straight down the hatch was up inside the plane. Open the hatch and step up in the plane. So we did not get into the ball turret until we were above five thousand feet, and when we got down to five thousand feet I got out of the ball turret. When we landed I was sitting in the radio room.

The reason that we did not get in it until five thousand feet, is above five thousand feet there was German radar, so they could direct fighter planes at us. Therefore, we had to be in at our station. And as I said before, I had the best view and I could watch the bombs as they came out of the bomb bay, and one of my jobs was to inform the pilot of the moment of impact. Thus, the ball turret really was a nice place.

Number three, many people will say to me, 'How could anybody be in there?' I was in the ball turret for about seven hours of a mission that usually lasted ten hours… It was comfortable! When the guns were horizontal I was laying on my back and in the fetal position. And what is the most comfortable position to be in? The fetal position. A couple times, yes, I did fall asleep. So, I wanted to de-bunk these myths."

With objectivity, Smith also pointed out some of the unpleasant parts of flying in the B-17. "We were on oxygen six or seven hours at a time…Once we got above ten thousand feet we're supposed to be on oxygen, but we never went on oxygen until roughly fifteen because we wanted to conserve it. Besides, our oxygen masks were awfully uncomfortable…Our standard bombing level was at about twenty-five thousand feet. You've got to have oxygen then…and we were penetrating, by the time we got to the enemy coast, we were at our bombing altitude. So all the way in and all the way out we wore the masks, and we cruised at a hundred and fifty-five miles an hour if we were lucky. So it took a long time to get there and back." The temperature was also a factor that was not pleasant. "It's mighty cold up there over

Northern Europe…Sixty-five degrees below zero at twenty-five thousand feet was standard. I had an electrically heated suit on and I wasn't really cold."

Without a doubt, Donald Smith's recollections of his experiences flying in the B-17 are vividly remembered with exceptional detail, however, the exact reason for which he was awarded the Distinguished Flying Cross is somewhat a mystery. Smith was awarded the DFC after he had completed his missions. "I was sent to the 94th Bomb Group, which was our headquarters group. I remember receiving the medal and the citation from a colonel as he pinned the DFC on me…but the thirty combat missions flown, had a tendency to blur together." Thus, Sergeant Smith did not remember the specific circumstances for which he was awarded the medal, and like most men completing their combat experience, that information wasn't important at the time; getting home was! As the decades went by, Smith misplaced the citation. However, with a resurgence of public interest in World War II since the dawn of the twenty-first century, Smith became curious and decided to obtain a new copy of the Distinguished Flying Cross citation. To his horror, he learned that his records, along with thousands of others, had been destroyed in a fire which occurred at the National Personnel Records Center in St. Louis, Missouri in 1973. Smith lamented, "Now there is no way I will ever know exactly why I received the DFC."

From his perspective, Sergeant Smith theorized that he received the medal for one of his flak suppression missions. One memorable mission was an assault on Market Garden. "That was when Monty [General Montgomery] wanted to make an end-run up through Holland into Germany…We went in and bombed the flak guns before the paratroopers got in, right ahead of them. We were going out as they were coming in. Unfortunately, the paratroopers really got nailed…It was a compete fiasco [on the ground]."

Another theory suggested by Smith, for his DFC, was one of the missions where he was part of the lead crew. "Being the lead crew was a little different than being in the middle or back of the pack. The other planes bombed, but when our bombardier dropped his bombs, others dropped their bombs. The bombardier and the navigator we had were very, very good. I can brag about them and it's not crew loyalty that I'm talking about. They were that good." Thus, Smith theorized that the DFC was for one of those intensive experiences. He dispels the notion that the Distinguished Flying Cross was awarded for a set number of missions as some of his contemporaries in the 8th Air Force contend. He makes his case by saying, "I flew thirty missions and I met many who flew thirty-five missions who did not receive the DFC.

Even with the specific circumstances not known by Sergeant Smith, he remembered the feeling of pride as he was honored for his exploits in the ball turret. In fact, each member of his entire crew received a Distinguished Flying Cross.

More than six decades later, Donald Smith still loves to talk about his World War II experiences. His purpose is specific, though, to educate people about the ball turret gunner's life aboard a B-17. His eyes sparkle and he becomes animated as he relives this unique episode of his life. It is evident that Sergeant Smith holds a special place in his heart for the B-17, the ball turret and his Distinguished Flying Cross. Concerning this military honor, he states with reverence, "It's something special – a mark of distinction." What makes his story unique is that he does not extol his own legacy but the legacy of the ball turret gunner. To Smith, this is the real story to be remembered.

Notes

Staff Sergeant Donald L. Smith, DD-214 documentation, action date: circa 1944, Archives, the Distinguished Flying Cross Society, San Diego, CA.

Staff Sergeant Donald L. Smith, oral history interview, interviewed by Dr. Barry A. Lanman, 28 July 2007, transcribed, the Distinguished Flying Cross Society Oral History Collection, the Distinguished Flying Cross Society, San Diego, CA.

Top, left: Lieutenant Richard Tyhurst was a B-17 navigator in Europe. Top, right: Tyhurst (top row, fifth from left) posed with his crew during World War II. Bottom: Tyhurst spent many combat hours flying in B-17s through flak-filled skies. Photographs courtesy of Richard Tyhurst and the National Museum of the United States Air Force

European Bombing Runs, Milk Runs and Shuttle Raids

Lieutenant Colonel Richard W. Tyhurst, USAAF / USAF

"A micro-second's difference is all that saved us from a direct hit because they were right on us…"

When the United States entered World War II, Richard William Tyhurst was twenty-one years old and knew his destiny. He wanted to be in the air fighting the enemy. By the fall of 1942, Tyhurst enlisted in the Army Air Corps as an aviation cadet, however, his dream was deferred because he wasn't called to active service until February of 1943.

Finally inducted in New York, he was sent to Hondo, Texas for navigation school and graduated the following April. As a second lieutenant, USAAF, he was then sent to Lincoln, Nebraska for redeployment to Rapid City, South Dakota for overseas training where he was assigned to a B-17 crew. After two and a half years, the young aviator was about to realize his dream and experience the events of a lifetime.

"We finished our overseas training and were on a train heading to Kearney, Nebraska to pick-up our new B-17 to fly it over to England. The date was 6 June 1944. We were in a train station in some little town in Nebraska when the newsboys came and hollered 'D-Day, US Invades the Continent.' So I always remember being on that troop train when I found out about D-Day."

After flying from Nebraska to Newfoundland and on to Prestwick, Scotland, the officers in command took the new B-17 away and put Lieutenant Tyhurst and his crewmates on another train to Horam, East Sussex in the United Kingdom which was the field where the 95th Bomb Group, a B-17 outfit, was stationed.

"My first mission was a flight from Horam to Munich. We were a brand new crew, hadn't any idea what it was going to be like, and it was reasonably easy enough going in there until we got close to Munich. Then the sky suddenly became black with puffs of anti-aircraft fire (flak)…When we were doing overseas training back in the United States, everything was practice runs on railroad marshalling yards. They were assuming that those would be our principal targets. There was no opposition and it was not a problem. Of course, when you get to a heavily flak-defended target the whole experience was different…They tell me that I was calm counting down time for my bombardier, time to target and so on. But personally I was scared silly because it was obvious if they hit us we were going to get killed.

Our second mission turned out to be what they called a 'milk run.' It was an easy flight. Actually, we were carrying supplies to the Marquis, French underground. They had captured the top of a mountain and were able to hold it just west of Mount Blanc in the French Alps. The top of this mountain was a plateau about five or six thousand feet high, so we could fly down to within a couple of hundred feet of the ground, drop our parachute supplies right there in the field directly to them. The Germans were down in the lower valley and couldn't do anything about it.

The missions after that seemed either rough or easy, but no in-between…In our bomber group, if we could get a maximum effort up, three of our four squadrons would get twelve ships per squadron in two six-ship boxes. We always flew in a three-ship element. Three - a lead plane and two wingmen, and then another set of planes right behind in a six-ship formation. Then there would be a high squadron and a low squadron and one in-between.

By the summer of '44 we had actually established air superiority. The Germans were able to bring up fighters to some extent, but they had to concentrate their fighters and look for formations that were stragglers and that sort of thing. A well flown formation of B-17s was rarely attacked and the 95th flew good formations. We flew with our wingtip between the wingtip of our lead man and the tail, so that no fighter would've gotten through there, and our guns would reach all over. We were never attacked by

German fighters during any of my combat flying.

The three roughest missions I ever flew were three days in succession when we were trying to wipe out a synthetic oil refinery at a field in a city called Zeitz. It's in the Leipzig area. The second day we lost eight planes out of our twelve ship squadron, including a wingman. We had been quite friendly with the crew and we never knew what happened to them.

To me, all the synthetic oil refinery missions that we flew were the rough ones. I can remember a synthetic oil refinery mission in a place called Politz. It's up along the Baltic Coast, just up at the northeast corner of Germany, before you get to the Polish border. And there—you have to fly 'straight and steady' on a bomb run and just tool along. I could see a flak burst and another and another. I had it calculated. The next one was going to be right at us. With luck, it turned out to be right behind our plane. You know, a micro-second's difference is all that saved us from a direct hit because they were right on us…That's the kind of thing that scared you to death. It was really terrifying. At that point in time, it seemed like if you got through your first five missions and got enough experience, you could get through.

We also flew interesting missions called shuttle raids. We couldn't fly deep into Eastern Europe and get back against the prevailing westerly winds. Thus, the Air Force made arrangements with the Russians so that we could hit a target which was deep in Eastern Europe, and then we could land in the Ukraine, (some distance behind the German/Russian front lines). We would then refuel and fly south from there to Italy, and then from Italy back up to England.

My first shuttle raid was the bombardment of a Messerschmitt factory in Gdinya. Gdinya is a small coastal town just north of the big port city of Gdansk. Apparently, the Germans were completely unprepared with any kind of anti-aircraft defenses because they didn't think we could go that far eastward. In fact, I later met a German soldier who was stationed at that field, or at the Messerschmitt factory, and he told me when that raid occurred they were so unprepared. They didn't have any kind of defenses, no slip trenches to jump into or anything, and he said they were hopping around like a bunch of scared rabbits in the field.

Sometimes weather would prevent our missions. The longest period I can remember when we weren't able to fly was during the Battle of the Bulge. In December there was a heavy fog and it was so bad we couldn't get off the ground to provide aerial support against that invasion…I had never seen fog that heavy. On Christmas Day of 1944, we finally got up but had difficulty getting back down. We made a pass and the fog just covered the runway so they diverted us to one of the emergency fields just north of the Thames. It was for 'cripples' coming back from Europe. They had a trench along the sides of this runway and they poured aviation gas in there, lit it and it burned a hole in the fog up to about a thousand feet. So we could get down and into this hole and find the runway. We landed around ten o'clock at night. I remember at the time thinking, 'Damn, we're going to miss Christmas dinner.' They sent a truck from our base and we got back around midnight and got Spam for Christmas dinner. But c'est la vie!

The mission for which we received the Distinguished Flying Cross was a bombing raid to Berlin. We had just dropped our bombs and were at about twenty-five thousand feet when we got hit which severely damaged our wings. The two port engines were lost and we had trouble with the third engine on the starboard wing. The pilot lost about five-thousand feet of altitude but got things under control and nobody was hurt; all the damage was on the outside.

We didn't realize it, but we had actually lost control of the third engine; it went to automatic control. The pilot was unaware that he didn't have control of it and tried feathering. Of course, you have to feather engines when you lose them. Otherwise, the props will windmill and drag. We got two of the engines feathered…and had twenty-thousand feet of altitude which we could trade for a long careful glide supported by the one engine. The problem was we couldn't stay with our formation…I remember saying to myself 'oh no, I'm nearly done with a combat tour and now we're going to get shot down and be either a prisoner of war in Germany or we aren't going to even survive it.' But then, right away, reality takes over and you say, 'hey, you've got problems - get with it!'

One saving grace was that we had been up in the front of the bomber stream. It was one of these big multi-hundred plane raids, and most of the bomber stream was coming in, so we were able to stay under them. We weren't crippled, and never saw a German fighter trying to catch us nor did we stray into flak-defended areas along the Dutch coast because by that time we were down to about eight or nine-thousand feet. Our last challenge was to get across the North Sea, that hundred and forty miles.

With fortune on our side, the damaged B-17 made it back to the base but as we landed, the pilot realized that we still didn't have control of the one engine and couldn't shut it off. It pulled us off the runway and the tires shot up. Fortunately, before we hit the tower, the damaged wheels stopped us in the grass…Everybody jumped up and I said 'get me out of this thing!' That was kind of harrowing to say the least.

The pilot got put in for a DFC and I got put in for a DFC as the navigator for avoiding the flak areas… It was midway through my second tour when I found out I had received the Distinguished Flying Cross. On a Sunday, we had a big formal parade and ceremony. General Doolittle, who was at that point in charge of the 8th Air Force, was there and our wing commander was Elliot Roosevelt. He's the one who actually presented the DFC to me at that ceremony. So I made the *New York Times* and that made it quite memorable."

Lieutenant Tyhurst's thirty-fourth and last combat flight in a B-17 was 6 January 1945. He then volunteered to serve in the 25th Bomb Group flying reconnaissance in the British Mosquito rather than chance being sent to the Pacific to fly B-29s. While the tour would have normally been fifty missions, he had flown twenty-two missions when the war in Europe ended on 8 May 1945.

In 2005, Lieutenant Colonel Richard Tyhurst who had long been retired from the Air Force, put his B-17 experiences in perspective after climbing into the nose of a restored B-17 six decades after his last combat flight. He stated that, "I had almost three-hundred hours of flight time and maybe two hundred of those hours were in combat…It was a big team effort and our crew was one big family. We really stayed together a lot, even during off duty hours, and we acted instinctively to do the right things. Except when you were worried about getting killed—it was thrilling and I always enjoyed it. Those were marvelous experiences."

Notes

Lieutenant Colonel Richard William Tyhurst, DD-214 documentation, Archives. The Distinguished Flying Cross Society, San Diego, CA.

Lieutenant Colonel Richard William Tyhurst, oral history interview, interviewed by Dr. Barry A. Lanman, 22 April 2007, transcribed, the Distinguished Flying Cross Society Oral History Collection, the Distinguished Flying Cross Society, San Diego, CA.

Top: Lieutenant Rosenberg was a navigator on a B-24 Liberator. Middle: This well-worn photograph is the only known image of Larry Rosenberg from WWII. Bottom: By chance, Larry Rosenberg (left) met Paul Hartal (right) in 2006. Hartal and his family were saved from being transported to a work camp in Germany as a result of Rosenberg's bombing of their train near Vienna, Austria. Photographs courtesy of National Museum of the United States Air Force

Surviving the Skies over Europe and the Russians on the Ground

Lieutenant Larry Rosenberg, USAAF

"The chances of surviving what I went through... were more than a thousand-to-one against me."

Like so many young men in 1942, Larry Rosenberg enlisted in the United States Army Air Corps after Pearl Harbor. In fact, about half of his class at the University of Pennsylvania had registered for the Officer Reserves program, and by February of 1943 had traveled en mass by train to Florida for induction. After his flight training, he became a B-24 navigator and was sent to the European Theater.

Up to that point in his life, Larry Rosenberg never really considered himself a particularly lucky individual; that is until his brush with death on multiple occasions. The story of how fate seemed to be on his side, how he survived in the skies over Europe and with the Russians on the ground, is best expressed by Rosenberg himself:

"I got to Italy to join the 15th Air Force [USAAF]. We flew from Gander to the Azores, Azores to Casablanca, Casablanca to Tunis and Tunis to Italy. My first mission was 30 August 1944 and as a supply mission it was uneventful. On another early mission…it wasn't a bombing mission…we were ferrying military equipment to the 7th Army. The 7th Army landed in the South of France shortly after the D-Day invasion. As luck would have it, I got very ill from something I ate – horrible pains in my stomach, vomiting and nausea…The reason it was good luck was that I was sent to a hospital and then to the Island of Capri for a week of rest camp…As I got back, I walked across the tarmac to return to the squadron and everybody came over to me saying, 'Rosenberg, you're dead.' I said, 'What are you talking about?' They said 'Well, you're plane blew up on takeoff. Everyone was killed.' That started my lucky streak.

As a navigator, I flew several supply missions and a few bombing raids until the day I got my Distinguished Flying Cross which took place on 3 November 1944. On that raid we were bombing the Blechhammer synthetic oil refineries at Auschwitz. The Germans were in trouble because they didn't have enough oil. Yasi was just about taken over by the Russians, which was a big oil supply base for the Germans. Thus, Blechhammer was extremely important. And from my perspective, that is why I believe the Americans and the British were losing the air war until such time as they realized the targets they had to bomb were the enemy's oil refineries.

During the raid, all the planes were up…and we were 'throwing everything.' We didn't realize what Auschwitz meant. We just knew that bombing the two synthetic oil refineries was very important. There was Blechhammer South and Blechhammer North, both on Auschwitz territory. For the record, Auschwitz must have been almost as big as the state of Rhode Island because I spoke to someone who was an inmate, way after the war, and he remembered bombs exploding but didn't see the planes. That means the factory was pretty far away from where the inmates were kept.

Once we started to reach our target, the Germans threw everything up they had and by the time I was supposed to bomb the target I saw planes blowing up all around me. After the bombs were dropped, I said, "Bombs away." Just then the pilot screamed, 'Larry, get up here!' So, I put on my oxygen mask and went to the area right near where the pilot could see me, and he said, 'A bomb hung up. You gotta get rid of that bomb.' I said, 'Yes, sir!' I asked the flight engineer to close the other bomb bay door so I could crawl out and get rid of the bomb. The engineer said, 'I can't close the bomb bay door…It's frozen.' As this was normally the engineer's job, I expected him to do it. However, he told me, 'Rosenberg, you're the officer. You do it!' So, I had to take off my parachute, take off my oxygen mask, and crawl out to get rid of that bomb, holding on for dear life, with planes exploding all around us. Luckily I got rid of that bomb.

I then backed up very carefully and the engineer helped me up into the plane itself, and just at that point of safety, I fell unconscious from the lack of oxygen.

When we got back to the squadron we checked in and the CO was waiting for us. He said to us, 'You all can have two dinners tonight because you're the only plane that came back.' Out of the seven planes in my squadron, six were lost. We were the only plane that made it. Twenty-five out of the thirty-one planes in the group were shot down that day, which was the worst day in the history of the 15th Air Force. And that is the day my CO, Bob Baker, recommended me for the Distinguished Flying Cross.

My reactions, once we got back on the ground were varied…I was sort of in shock…Then I realized this was about my seventh mission and I had twenty-eight to go so I figured how am I going to survive twenty-eight more missions? We always had fear going to bed but when we woke up we were okay. I continued on to my thirtieth mission.

During my "lucky thirteenth mission," we were bombing the Strausa Railroad Station, which was about ten miles east of Vienna, and we successfully caused tremendous explosions on the ground. However, we got hit and decided to try and make it to Russian territory. The Russians were fighting the Germans in Hungary at the time and, with luck, maybe we could get to the Russian lines. We had to crash land on the side of a hill. My copilot told me that if we hadn't made that landing, we would've exploded…but we made it.

After the crash landing, we got picked up by some Bulgarian troops wearing SS uniforms. They were in the 1st SS Bulgarian Division, now fighting for the Russians. We were afraid because they had pulled their guns on us and we thought they were going to shoot us. However, before we all got slaughtered, some Russians came up and intervened, and we thought we were totally safe. But thirty days went by between that time and the time I left Russia on a British vessel carrying two hundred British, thirteen Americans, and about two thousand French back to Naples and then on to England.

In any case, the thirty days in Russia were extremely interesting. We went into a cauldron where Americans were being killed. We weren't aware of the dangers…and I was having a ball. We went through Hungary by truck and then by train and we saw things I've always been interested in. As a stamp collector I knew what countries and what cities I was going through, and finally we got to Bucharest and into the hands of the Americans. The Americans put us in a nunnery and the nuns were wonderful to us. However, I got bored and didn't want to stay in the nunnery so I walked around Bucharest because I figured we were allies with the Russians. It turned out at that time the king was locked in his stamp safe in his palace in Bucharest and the Russian embassy was surrounded by Russian tanks, and there I am wandering around looking for, as any other red-blooded American, women. There were plenty of them, especially at a hotel…across the street from the palace.

As I was having a drink, because officers got forty-eight dollars escape money and I wasn't able to use it before, I ordered a scotch. All of a sudden a beautiful redhead came up to me at the bar, and sat down right next to me. I offered her a drink and within five minutes she invited me upstairs to her room…so what could I do? I went upstairs and was confronted by two Americans (of Russian descent) in civilian clothes who talked to me in perfect Bronx English. They started to 'grill' me and ask all kinds of questions about Allied plans. I quickly realized I was in really big trouble and then, all of a sudden, they said, 'Okay Rosenberg, get lost' – just like that. So I ran down six flights of steps and back to the nunnery. I never set foot outside again until an American drove us by truck to Yasi, which was the oil capital of Europe. During that trip, I couldn't believe all the holes in the ground. It was one pock-marked area of bombings after another because the Americans bombed it, the Russians bombed it, and the British bombed it.

As we started to get on a train, the Russians demanded my pistol, which I refused to give them. They didn't argue with me and let me get on the train. After about a week, we got to Odessa where we marched to this bombed out area of town, to a destroyed hospital. For the most part, Odessa was totally wiped out. They put me together with the twelve other Americans into this hospital. The only other people were about seventy-five to a hundred British enlisted men. There was an armed guard at the hospital but we just gave them a couple of cigarettes and we were allowed to leave and explore Odessa…We went to the opera and had some good Russian food. We also marched in an unusual parade. It was a victory parade, the first anniversary of the recapture of Odessa by the Russians. The lady in charge of greeting us was Mrs. Winston Churchill, who flew to Odessa in honor of the occasion. She waved at the Americans and British, who were put in one unit marching together, while the Russians were screaming at us, 'Go to hell, Americans. Go to hell.' That was a very interesting day in the life of Larry Rosenberg.

Finally, we were put on a British ship, the HMS *Lancashire*, and I got back about a week before the war was over. I had been declared Missing in Action, so I wrote my parents to let them know I was alive. Because my brother had been killed in 1943, they were relieved to know I had survived – and that was the end of my war.

In retrospect, we didn't realize that fifty-five hundred Americans had been captured by the Russians and that Stalin had given orders to kill all the prisoners. Of the fifty-five hundred American MIA's, only thirteen of us would survive…Even after decades, this atrocity has been kept quiet and most US citizens are not aware of this piece of history. When I think about my experiences, the chances of surviving what I went through...were more than a thousand to one against me. But I made it – I was really lucky."

After World War II, Larry Rosenberg became a highly successful attorney and practiced law in New York City before retiring in San Diego, California. One day Rosenberg serendipitously came upon a story by Paul Hartal that appeared in *The 461st Liberator*, a publication for veterans. While reading Hartal's account of being transported from a Jewish Labor camp with his mother and little sister in a locked boxcar, and the detailed saga of how they survived a bombing by the Americans, Rosenberg realized he had been responsible for the attack. But in a peculiar twist of fate, the bombs had actually allowed Hartal and his family to escape, which ultimately saved their lives. Before Rosenberg passed away in 2008, he and Hartal had the chance to meet. It was a joyous epilogue to an amazing story.

Notes

Lieutenant Larry Rosenberg, Distinguished Flying Cross citation, action date: 3 November 1944, Archives, the Distinguished Flying Cross Society, San Diego, CA.

Lieutenant Larry Rosenberg, oral history interview, interviewed by Dr. Barry A. Lanman, 28 July 2007, transcribed, the Distinguished Flying Cross Society Oral History Collection, the Distinguished Flying Cross Society, San Diego, CA.

Memorable Moments of the Distinguished Flying Cross

World War II

Naturally you are scared, but you are also excited when flying in combat. We were all in the same boat so we just concentrated on the job we were asked to do...It was the best thing that ever happened to me."

Lieutenant Colonel Noble Newsom, Jr.

Captain Alexander "Al" Ciurczak, USAAF
Gunner/Photographer in the Pacific

A photographer in WWII, Ciurczak was twice awarded the Distinguished Flying Cross for "extraordinary achievement and heroism in aerial flight." On the morning of 11 September 1943, Ciurczak was aboard a B-24 on a bombing mission from the Aleutian Islands to Paramushiru in Japan's northern islands. Every available B-24 and B-25 of the 11th Air Force (about two dozen) was involved.

After dropping the bombs, Ciurczak's B-24 was attacked by Japanese fighter planes and he watched as the bomber on his right wing, carrying friend and fellow photographer Walter Feuer, was shot down and crashed into the ocean. Ciurczak's bomber was also severely hit. A shell blasted through the front windshield striking the copilot in the face and the pilot in the arm. Ciurczak pulled the copilot out of his seat and used everything he could find to stop the bleeding.

Another shell hit the cockpit, setting the bomber's felt lining on fire but Ciurczak was able to extinguish the fire. When the Japanese fighters retreated, the one-armed pilot, with help from the engineer, was able to return the plane to safety.

Ciurczak's second DFC was awarded for the numerous missions he flew in the Aleutian Islands during his duty from May 1943 to April 1944.[1] Al Ciurczak was the founder of the Distinguished Flying Cross Society.

John R. Rossi, The American Volunteer Group
A Member of the Flying Tigers

For most Americans, the 1st American Volunteer Group (AVG) was actually known as the Flying Tigers. As part of the Chinese Air Force between 1941 and 1942, most of the pilots and aircrew were former US military aviators who had been recruited under presidential sanction and led by Claire Lee Chennault. There were three squadrons of about twenty planes each and the overall mission was to defend China from a Japanese invasion. The "shark" face painted on the front of each fighter was one of the most recognizable symbols of WWII.

John R. Rossi, a member of the Flying Tigers received a Distinguished Flying Cross for his participation as a volunteer. The citation indicated that Rossi, "participat[ed] in aerial flight in the South China and Southeast Asia theater, from 7 December 1941 to 18 July 1942. The American Volunteer Group, the Flying Tigers, compiled an unparalleled combat record under extremely hazardous conditions. This volunteer unit conducted aggressive counter-air, air defense, and close air support operations against a numerically superior enemy force occasionally twenty times larger. Members of the All Volunteer Group destroyed some 650 enemy aircraft while suffering minimal losses. Their extraordinary performance in the face of seemingly overwhelming odds was a major factor in defeating the enemy's invasion of South China. The professional competence, aerial skill, and devotion to duty displayed by John R. Rossi reflect great credit upon himself and the Armed Forces of the United States."[2] Rossi was also an ace, credited with six aircraft.

Sergeant Sidney "Sid" Zimman, USMC
SBD Dauntless Rear Gunner

Sid Zimman joined the Marine Corps in 1942 after training when he was just eighteen years old. He became a rear gunner on the SBD Dauntless dive-bomber. The plane was often nicknamed the "Slow but Deadly Douglas" which described the bomber and its prominent role in the Pacific.

Sergeant Zimman was stationed in the Pacific and he explained that his missions were primarily to dive and destroy targets specifically involving gun emplacements. The runs began at 12,000 feet and they would roll over and dive at a controlled speed of about 270 miles per hour. He called the SBD "the guided missile of its day" because it could travel two miles in about 26 seconds during a dive.

Zimman had always been proud of his wartime experiences and the knowledge that he helped save the lives of fellow Marines. However, it was not until 6 June 1998 that he found out he had been awarded two Distinguished Flying Cross medals for his missions with Marine Scout Bomber Squadron 341 from 7 - 26 April 1944 and 30 July -30 August 1944.[3] He is currently on another mission to educate people about the SBD and its importance during WWII. Zimman also enjoys wearing his dress uniform alongside his granddaughter who was also a Marine.

Lieutenant Colonel Noble Newsom, Jr., USMC
Received Two DFCs Fifty Years after his Missions

Noble Newsom Jr. received two Distinguished Flying Crosses almost a half-century after World War II. The time delay for the awards was caused by a bureaucratic oversight and was rectified when he was finally presented the medals and citations by Brigadier General E. C. Kelly, Jr. at a ceremony on the Marine Corps Recruit Depot in San Diego on 16 June 1994.[4] He also received nine Air Medals on the same day.

Newsom was one of the first pilots assigned to the Marine Corps Air Station in Santa Barbara, California where he started flying SBC-4 dive-bombers, a fabric-covered bi-wing plane built by Curtis. Shortly thereafter, the squadron began flying the SBD-3 Douglas Dauntless; the dive-bomber used during the five Solomon Island battles. In 1943, Newsom's squadron spent five months at Midway Island where he completed 89 submarine combat patrols. After the Battle of Midway he was sent to Henderson Field on Guadalcanal.

His tent was next to Charles A. Lindbergh's for awhile when the "Lone Eagle" toured the Pacific. Newsom also spent three combat tours as the Division Leader of dive-bombers in all five of the Solomon Island battles. He stated, "Naturally you are scared, but you are also excited when flying in combat. We were all in the same boat."

Staff Sergeant James R. Richardson, USMC
Volunteered at Age 17 to be a Radio - Gunner

James R. Richardson joined the United States Marine Corps at the age of seventeen on 28 April 1942 and became a radio – gunner in the Pacific with VMSB-245 and 231. Flying in SBDs, Richardson received a Distinguished Flying Cross, "for extraordinary achievement while participating in aerial flight with Marine Scout Bombing Squadron 231 from 22 to 29 August 1944.[5] In the successful completion of these missions, Sergeant Richardson contributed materially to the success of United States efforts. By his undaunted courage, superb airmanship and unyielding devotion to duty in the face of hazardous flying conditions, Sergeant Richardson reflected great credit upon himself and upheld the highest traditions of the Marine Corps and the United States Naval Service."

Major Charles T. Goldsmith, Jr., USAAF
Radio Operator/Gunner flew Over the Hump

Charles T. Goldsmith, Jr. flew "over the hump" on 198 missions as a radio operator and gunner from July 1943 to December 1944. Due to circumstances involving the enemy and the hazardous flying conditions, all of the Staff Sergeant's flights were logged as combat missions.

Named by Allied pilots, "the hump" referred to the eastern end of the Himalayan mountains over which the aircrews flew military transport aircraft from India to China in order to provide supplies for the Chinese and the Flying Tigers.

As Goldsmith explained, "flying over the Himalayas was extremely dangerous because of a lack of reliable navigational charts, an absence of radio navigation aids, and the extremely bad weather conditions that would change in an instant."

Flying in C-46s and C-47s, the planes would usually carry 55 gallon drums of fuel for the Flying Tigers, although on one unique mission, Goldsmith's plane carried a load of donkeys which kicked the sides of the plane during the entire flight.

Two Distinguished Flying Cross medals were awarded to Goldsmith for successfully completing his missions which helped prevent the Japanese from taking over China.[6]

Aviation Ordinance Chief Herman J. Herdt, USN
Bombardier of a PB4Y-1 Participated in Daring Pacific Rescue_____

As a bombardier of a PB4Y-1, Aviation Ordinance Chief Herman J. Herdt had a rare opportunity to participate in a daring rescue near Bougaville Island in the Pacific. For his part in this heroic rescue, Herdt would receive a Distinguished Flying Cross.

A Navy radioman, was the only survivor of a plane shot down during the Battle of the Eastern Solomon's on 24 August 1942, he spent fifteen days in a rubber raft and eventually landed on the Carteret Islands. He endured the next five months with natives until he was joined by the five surviving members of a B-17 who were shot down on 9 February 1943. Given their location in enemy territory, their chances of survival looked bleak.

However, as the story of the men spread, an ingenious plan was devised between Herdt's PB4Y Squadron VB-101 and VP-44, a PBY seaplane Squadron. The resources needed for the mission involved two PB4Ys, a PBY and thirty-two men. Three requests in top secret code were sent before permission was granted. With the men ready, after a message drop by a B-17, the three planes took off on 15 April 1943 and flew just fifteen feet off the water to avoid the Japanese radar and arrived at sunset. Once at the pick-up location, the PBY was able to rescue all of the men and the return flight occurred without incident.[7]

Captain Alfred L. Cope, USN
Received Distinguished Flying Crosses for Lighter-than-Air Missions_____

Very few pilots have received a Distinguished Flying Cross for missions involving a blimp. Captain Alfred "Al" Cope was such a pilot who received two DFCs during World War II for lighter-than-air missions.

After graduating from the Naval Academy in 1932, Cope became a submariner but in 1937 attended a lighter-than-air class at Lakehurst, New Jersey and qualified as an airship pilot. Thus, he was in a very unique category. He could wear both the submariner's dolphins and the aviator's gold wings on his uniform.

As blimps became an important part of the anti-submarine patrols in the Atlantic, he was sent back to Lakehurst, New Jersey in the role of instructor and by 1943, he took command of Airship Patrol Squadron 21 flying ASW patrols from Florida. On 30 October 1943, a blimp under his command took direct fire from a German submarine while on patrol. The disabled blimp tried to make it back to shore, while it continued to deflate. It finally settled on the water and the crew abandoned the craft.

When Cope reached the scene of the floating wreck, he estimated the extent of the damage and the chance of salvaging the blimp. Aware of the dangers involved in flying a ship with one propeller and a completely wrecked power plant, Cope re-inflated the blimp with the assistance of a volunteer crew and "free-ballooned" the craft off the water, returning it safely to base. For this action, he received a Distinguished Flying Cross. The DFC citation, which accompanied the medal, commended Cope for "his courageous determination [which] enabled him to save a valuable airship for further service."[8] Cope would receive a second DFC for the same type of courageous action before the end of World War II. Later in his career, he obtained the rank of Captain and qualified to fly jets and helicopters. Before his death at the age of ninety-four in 2004, he was the most senior blimp pilot in the world.

Commander Sam L. Silber, USN
Strafed Shipping and Downed Two Planes All in the Same Day

During his tour of duty in the Pacific, Commander Sam Silber received four Distinguished Flying Cross medals in 1943 when he served as part of Fighting Squadron Eighteen, attached to the USS *Bunker Hill*. While each was significant, Silber's DFC for his actions on 11 November 1943 was most noteworthy. The citation accompanying his medal tells the account of Silber, leader of a squadron of fighter planes, who was assigned to escort a bomber group in an attack on enemy shipping at Rabaul, New Britain. "Despite intense anti-aircraft fire and enemy fighter planes, [Silber] provided excellent cover for the attacking bombers at all times. By skillful airmanship, he strafed two enemy surface vessels and still maintained his proper escort position with the bomber formation and in so doing, enabled it to complete its mission without damage.

On the afternoon of the same day, Silber's squadron intercepted and thwarted many Japanese dive-bombing attacks on a carrier task force, he himself destroying two enemy aircraft in the engagements. His outstanding leadership and courageous spirit were in keeping with the highest traditions of the United States Naval Service."[9] The citation was personally signed by W. F. Halsey, Admiral, US Navy.

First Lieutenant Robert W. Sternfels, USAAF
Bombed the Ploesti Oil Refineries

First Lieutenant Robert W. Sternfels received a Distinguished Flying Cross for participating in operations against the Ploesti Oil Refineries of Romania on 1 August 1943. As part of the 345th Bombardment Squadron, 98th Bombardment Group, their heavy bombardment aircraft assaulted the major fuel supply of the Axis. The Distinguished Flying Cross Citation stated, "In a mission which involved extraordinary difficulty of execution and very great danger, they performed their tasks assigned to them with such efficiency, application to duty and fearlessness that in the face of almost overwhelming odds, the operation was successfully accomplished. Flying through enemy flak, bursting bombs, smoking oil tanks and a balloon barrage, they bombed and strafed their objective with such satisfactory effect as to destroy the source of more than one third of the enemy's refined fuel. Their achievement adds a new and brilliant chapter to the record of the Army Air Forces."[10] Sternfels was the pilot of the B-24 "The Sandman" which is the aircraft in the iconic picture of the historic raid.

First Lieutenant Lester H. Ronsberg, USAAF
Helped to Destroy Axis Fuel Supply in Romania

First Lieutenant Lester H. Ronsberg, USAAF, was part of a raid on the Ploesti Oil Refineries of Romania on 1 August 1943. Flying as a pilot of a B-24, with the 512th Bombardment Squadron, 376th Bombardment Group, the Distinguished Flying Cross Citation commended Ronsberg for his part, "in one of the most spectacular, daring and destructive raids ever attempted in aviation history. Skimming in at a level barely above the installations to be attacked, they encountered withering gunfire from some of the world's heaviest concentrations of anti-aircraft batteries. Yet he continued in the  performance of his duty, and in the face of seemingly insurmountable obstacles, bombed and strafed, with enormously destructive effect, the heart of the enemy's fuel supply. His success in this most daring and hazardous enterprise not only brought great honor to himself, but contributed definitively to the final defeat of the enemy and the shortening of the war."[11]

First Lieutenant Charles Bloom, USAAF
Served as a Bombardier in the Mediterranean and North African Theaters

As a B-17 bombardier, First Lieutenant Charles H. Bloom, USAAF, served in the Mediterranean and North African theaters as part of the 817th Bomb Squadron, 483rd Bomb Group. Lieutenant Bloom received a Distinguished Flying Cross, along with several of his compatriots, on 18 July 1944 for participating in, "many long and hazardous combat missions against the enemy despite severe and adverse weather conditions and enemy opposition by large numbers of fighter aircraft and intense, accurate and heavy anti-aircraft fire. Displaying great combat spirit and aggressiveness, these men have met, engaged and defeated the enemy regardless of the odds and in spite of the fact that at times their aircraft were so severely damaged that only by extraordinary skill and fortitude were they able to fight their way through to the objective and aid in the grave damage inflicted upon the enemy…during this period of intense combat operations against the enemy."[12]

First Lieutenant Jack K. Mates, USAAF
Sixty-One Missions over Europe in a B-17

Jack Mates initially joined the United States Army Air Corps in 1942 and then became part of the 97th Bombardment Group, 341st Bombardment Squadron of the 15th Air Force, USAAF, based in Naples, Italy. He completed sixty-one missions flying B-17s and received a Distinguished Flying Cross for a flight on 3 December 1944 heading to Vienna, Austria.

The DFC Citation states that, "Second Lieutenant Jack M. Mates is awarded the Distinguished Flying Cross for extraordinary achievement while participating in aerial flight against the enemy in the Mediterranean Theater of Operations. Throughout many long and hazardous combat missions against vital strategic targets deep in enemy occupied territory, though confronted by heavy enemy opposition from highly aggressive enemy fighters and intense and accurate anti-aircraft fire, Lieutenant Mates consistently displayed outstanding courage, aggressiveness and intense devotion to duty throughout all engagements.

With his aircraft frequently severely damaged by heavy enemy fire, Lieutenant Mates courageously remained at his station, battling his way through to his targets to aid materially in the utter destruction of vitally important enemy installations and supplies. Heedless of severe and adverse weather conditions encountered over rugged mountainous terrain, and surmounting many other major obstacles that faced him during these hazardous combat missions, Lieutenant Mates gallantly engaged, fought and defeated the enemy with complete disregard for his personal safety and against overwhelming odds."[13]

Despite heavy flak damage, the plane was able to make it back to base with only a few gallons of fuel in the tanks remaining as it landed. Mates was promoted to First Lieutenant and discharged from the USAAF in November of 1945. He became a founding member of the Distinguished Flying Cross Society.

Commander Dean "Diz" Laird, USN
Ace who Shot Down German and Japanese Planes

Commander Dean "Diz" Laird was a Navy ace during World War II. An example of his skill as a fighter pilot is lauded in his DFC citation for, "participating in aerial flight as pilot of a Fighter Plane in Fighting Squadron Four, attached to the USS *Essex* in action against enemy Japanese forces in the Tokyo area, 17 February 1945. While protecting friendly bomber planes attacking heavily defended aircraft engine factories, Lieutenant Laird engaged and destroyed two hostile fighter aircraft, thereby assisting materially in the accomplishment of the assigned mission."[14] As an ace, flying the F4F and the F6F, Diz shot down two German airplanes and three Japanese airplanes. This feat put him in a very unique category of being the only Navy ace to achieve victories in both theaters of war. In addition to his military exploits, Laird accumulated 150 hours flying simulated Japanese aircraft in the movie *Tora, Tora, Tora*.

First Lieutenant Herbert S. Leopold, USAAF
Pin-point Bombing Accuracy

First Lieutenant Herbert S. Leopold, USAAF, flew on B-24s in Europe and specialized in bombing, gunnery and navigation. He was awarded the Distinguished Flying Cross for, "extraordinary achievement while participating in aerial flight as a bombardier, 466th Bombardment Group, European Theater of Operation, on 22 February 1945. On that date, Lieutenant Leopold demonstrated excellent bombing capabilities which resulted in sixty-five percent of the bombs landing within the 500 foot circle and 100 percent of the bombs landing within the 1000 foot circle over the target. The

professional competence, aerial skill and devotion to duty displayed by Lieutenant Leopold reflect great credit upon himself and the United States Air Force."[15] (Leopold – top row, far left)

Master Sergeant Edward F. Gouveia, USAAF
Sixty-Nine Round Trips Over the Hump

On 6 May 1941, Edward Gouveia enlisted in the United States Army Air Corps which later became part of the United States Army Air Forces. He was one of four boys and two girls from the Gouveia family who served in the military during World War II. Gouveia became a crew chief and engineer on the B-17, B-24, C-47 and C-109.

Sergeant Gouveia made a total of sixty-nine round trips "over the hump" flying from India, over the Himalayan Mountains, to China and back. During those trips over a fourteen month period, he logged 702 hours of flight time hauling fuel, bombs and Chinese troops. Gouveia's DFC citation, issued from the USAAF, stressed his contributions to the war effort between 3 November 1944 and 15 March 1945.[16]

Overall, the airlift delivered approximately 650,000 tons of war material to China during its forty-two month history. By early 1945, there were 722 aircraft involved in the transport of 44,000 tons of supplies to China each month and the loss of life was cut in half. This event served as a model for the Berlin Airlift.

Lieutenant Commander Philip S. Ball, USN
Strafed Hostile Warships at Rabaul with Famed Squadron Nine

Philip Ball, Jr. received a Distinguished Flying Cross serving as, "a pilot of a Fighter Plane and Wingman in Fighter Squadron NINE, attached to the USS Essex, during operations against enemy Japanese forces at Rabaul Harbor, New Britain, 11 November 1943. Flying wing in the first division of fighters assigned to cover a striking group during an attack on Japanese shipping, Lieutenant [then Lieutenant, Junior Grade] Ball proceeded to the target area in advance of the bombers and, maneuvering skillfully in the face of intense enemy anti-aircraft fire, relentlessly strafed hostile warships in the harbor…He continued to provide unusually effective protection for both the Division Leader and the attack group, personally destroying two Japanese fighter planes."

In addition, Lieutenant Ball received a second DFC for, "action against enemy forces in the vicinity of Tokyo, Iwo Jima, Kyushu and Nansei Shoto from 10 February to 9 May 1945."[17] Ball participated in twenty missions during this time period as part of Fighter Squadron NINE. Through his actions, he inflicted extensive damage on enemy shipping, airfields and installations. Ball ultimately achieved the rank of Lieutenant Commander as a result of his heroic efforts.

Colonel Ward Macauley, USAAF
Bombardier – Navigator in Europe

When he was a first lieutenant, Ward Macauley, 47th Bombardment Group (L), USAAF, was awarded the Distinguished Flying Cross for participating in aerial flight as a bombardier in A-20 and A-26 type aircraft. On the night of 19 April 1945, Lieutenant Macauley flew in an attack upon heavily fortified military buildings at Sassuolo, Italy. The DFC Citation explained that the Lieutenant displayed, "superior professional skill and resourcefulness…

Lieutenant Macauley guided his pilot through adverse weather to the briefed initial point; then setting course for a perfect run over the objective. Lieutenant Macauley released his bombs with devastating effect

on these vital military positions. On more than fifty combat missions, he demonstrated outstanding proficiency and steadfast devotion to duty.[18]

After WWII, Ward Macauley became part of the USAF and attained the rank of colonel before his retirement in 1974. In the 1990s, he became an early member of the Distinguished Flying Cross Society. The DFCS Scholarship program was named in his honor.

Aviation Radioman Second Class Wayne Turner, USN
Twenty Anti-shipping and Patrol Missions in the Pacific_____

Wayne Turner graduated from high school in Vevay, Indiana in the spring of 1943 and later that year joined the Navy. After extensive training in Tennessee, Florida and San Diego, Turner was assigned to VPB 109 as an Aviation Radioman. Their first combat area was on Palawan in the Philippine Islands followed by patrols of the east coast of China, the South China Sea and finally a multitude of islands in the Philippine Sea.

Aviation Radioman Second Class Turner received a Distinguished Flying Cross for his combat expertise during the period between 19 April and 15 August 1945 against Japanese forces in the western Pacific Area. The citation stated that he participated in "twenty anti-shipping and patrol missions during this period…" and that, "Turner contributed materially to the success of his squadron. His gallant devotion to duty was in keeping with the highest traditions of the United States Naval Service."[19] When the war ended, Wayne Turner was discharged and pursued a civilian career. He was on the first Board of Directors of the Distinguished Flying Cross Society. (Turner – top row, far right)

Photographs courtesy of the DFC recipients and/or their families
except for the following:

Page 68: Robert W. Sternfels over Astra Romana Refinery on 1 August 1943
Page 73: Top, Tailhook Association
Page 73: Bottom, United States Navy
Page 75: National Museum of the United States Air Force
Page 78: Library of Congress

Photograph – following page:

On 2 September 1945, the formal surrender of Japan took place on the USS *Missouri* which was anchored in Tokyo Bay. After the conclusion of the ceremony, a massive flyover took place involving several hundred Army and Navy aircraft. Lieutenant Commander Robert Page Ross, USN, was chosen to fly the lead plane. This honor was bestowed on Ross because he had been awarded two Distinguished Flying Crosses and achieved the status of an ace. (Photograph courtesy of the Naval Historical Foundation)

Notes

[1] Captain Alexander "Al" Ciurczak, Distinguished Flying Cross citation, action date: 11 September 1943, Archives, the Distinguished Flying Cross Society, San Diego, CA.

[2] John R. Rossi, Distinguished Flying Cross citation, action date: 7 December 1941-18 July 1942, Archives, the Distinguished Flying Cross Society, San Diego, CA.

[3] Sergeant Sidney "Sid" Zimman, Distinguished Flying Cross citation, action date: 1-26 April 1944, Archives, the Distinguished Flying Cross Society, San Diego, CA.

[4] Lieutenant Colonel Noble Newsom, Distinguished Flying Cross citation, presentation date: 16 June 1994, Archives, the Distinguished Flying Cross Society, San Diego, CA.

[5] Staff Sergeant James R. Richardson, Distinguished Flying Cross citation, action date: 22-29 August 1944, Archives, the Distinguished Flying Cross Society, San Diego, CA.

[6] Major Charles T. Goldsmith, Jr., Distinguished Flying Cross citation, action date: July 1943-December 1944, Archives, the Distinguished Flying Cross Society, San Diego, CA.

[7] Aviation Ordinance Chief Herman J. Herdt, Distinguished Flying Cross citation, action date: April 1943, Archives, the Distinguished Flying Cross Society, San Diego, CA.

[8] Captain Alfred L. Cope, Distinguished Flying Cross citation, action date: 30 October 1943, Archives, the Distinguished Flying Cross Society, San Diego, CA.

[9] Commander Sam Leonard Silber, Distinguished Flying Cross citation, action date: 11 November 1943, Archives, the Distinguished Flying Cross Society, San Diego, CA.

[10] First Lieutenant Robert W. Sternfels, Distinguished Flying Cross citation, action date: 1 August 1943, Archives, the Distinguished Flying Cross Society, San Diego, CA.

[11] First Lieutenant Lester H. Ronsberg, Distinguished Flying Cross citation, action date: 1 August 1943, Archives, the Distinguished Flying Cross Society, San Diego, CA.

[12] First Lieutenant Charles Bloom, Distinguished Flying Cross citation, action date: 18 July 1944, Archives, the Distinguished Flying Cross Society, San Diego, CA.

[13] First Lieutenant Jack K. Mates, Distinguished Flying Cross citation, action date: 3 December 1944, Archives, the Distinguished Flying Cross Society, San Diego, CA.

[14] Commander Dean "Diz" Laird, Distinguished Flying Cross citation, action date: 17 February 1945, Archives, the Distinguished Flying Cross Society, San Diego, CA.

[15] First Lieutenant Herbert S. Leopold, Distinguished Flying Cross citation, action date: 22 February 1945, Archives, the Distinguished Flying Cross Society, San Diego, CA.

[16] Sergeant Master Edward Gouveia, Distinguished Flying Cross citation, action date: 3 November 1944-15 March 1945, Archives, the Distinguished Flying Cross Society, San Diego, CA.

[17] Lieutenant Commander Philip Ball, Jr., Distinguished Flying Cross citations, action dates: 11 November 1943 and 10 February-9 May 1945, Archives, the Distinguished Flying Cross Society, San Diego, CA.

[18] Colonel Ward Macauley, Distinguished Flying Cross citation, action date: 19 April 1945, Archives, the Distinguished Flying Cross Society, San Diego, CA.

[19] Aviation Radioman Second Class Wayne Turner, Distinguished Flying Cross citation, action date: 19 April-15 August 1945, Archives, the Distinguished Flying Cross Society, San Diego, CA

Chapter 3

Stories of the Distinguished Flying Cross:

Korea

*W*hen the instrument of surrender was signed by the representatives of Japan ending World War II, it seemed surreal to imagine that the United States would be involved in another significant military engagement in fewer than five years. However, that was precisely what transpired when that which began as a civil war in Korea played out as part of the Cold War between the United States and the Soviet Union, who supported China's participation on behalf of the North. In the summer of 1950, North Korea, under the communist regime of Kim Il Sung, invaded South Korea, led by Syngman Rhee and backed by the United States.

Unlike the early days of World War II, the United States entered this military commitment with a surplus of the commodities for war. This was especially true of airplanes, pilots and aircrew including a cadre of battle-hardened flight leaders.

The most significant aviation challenge at the onset of this conflict was re-configuring equipment and strategies for combat in Korea. The mountainous terrain, poor weather conditions and night operations all posed unique challenges during most missions. In accordance with these tasks, the United States Air Force, newly created in 1947, rose to the occasion along with its aviation counterparts from the other military branches, to oppose communist forces that ultimately included both the North Koreans and the Chinese.

Initially, the backbone of aviation in Korea was the time-tested propeller driven aircraft which were once again utilized. With the introduction of jet fighters, increased speed added an element of surprise which proved to be a tactical advantage when used in conjunction with the propeller driven "slow movers." Interdiction missions on strategic objectives along with targets of opportunity comprised a major component of the air war. Close air support was also of the highest priority as it provided protection for American and UN troops in contact with the enemy. Both missions used guns, rockets, bombs and napalm to obliterate the targets.

Along with jet fighters, the helicopter made its introduction into combat; not as a platform for weapons but as a vehicle of mercy. With the ability to make vertical take-offs and landings, helicopters became instrumental in evacuating wounded soldiers. Coupled with the Mobile Army Surgical Hospital (MASH), a new concept in military medicine was created and credited with saving countless lives.

Both aircraft and weapons had significantly advanced from World War II, but bravery, commitment and skill were consistent, making air engagements successful. Some aviators sent to Korea were already well seasoned and shared their experience with novice pilots who quickly learned the art of combat.

After the loss of more than 36,000 American soldiers and at an estimated cost of fifty billion dollars, a cease fire was established on 27 July 1953. Korea remained divided along the 38th parallel. Soon after, the vast majority of aviators and aircrew returned home with a lifetime of memories and wisdom. Some were praised for their actions in posthumous ceremonies. The Distinguished Flying Cross recipients may not have received the same adulation for serving in the "Forgotten War" as did their predecessors from WWII, but they shared their stories with pride and their documented heroism has been preserved for posterity.

Personal Accounts of the Distinguished Flying Cross:

Korea

"It was never just about the Distinguished Flying Cross, it was the total military experience... Yes, you're proud of the DFC, but it is how the total military experience impacts your life... It makes you a better citizen."

Major Rex W. Warden, USAAF / USAF

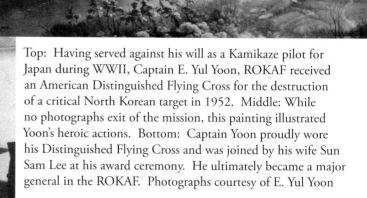

Top: Having served against his will as a Kamikaze pilot for Japan during WWII, Captain E. Yul Yoon, ROKAF received an American Distinguished Flying Cross for the destruction of a critical North Korean target in 1952. Middle: While no photographs exit of the mission, this painting illustrated Yoon's heroic actions. Bottom: Captain Yoon proudly wore his Distinguished Flying Cross and was joined by his wife Sun Sam Lee at his award ceremony. He ultimately became a major general in the ROKAF. Photographs courtesy of E. Yul Yoon

Kamikaze Pilot and Distinguished Flying Cross Recipient
General E. Yul Yoon, ROKAF

"I fought for freedom at every turn. You have to choose it!"_____

Upon first hearing General E. Yul Yoon's life story, most people listen in disbelief to a saga filled with anguish, survival, intrigue, love and most of all, uncommon valor. To them, it seems almost incomprehensible that a kamikaze pilot could receive an American Distinguished Flying Cross. However, the biography of E. Yul Yoon is the fulfillment of a legacy that reads more like an epic drama.

Born in Korea in 1927, E. Yul Yoon grew up in the town of Pyongyang in northern Korea and had a rather normal, uneventful childhood. However, as the world plummeted into war and Yoon reached young adulthood, he was forcefully conscripted into service for the Japanese military. Since Korea was a colony of Japan at that time, he was a human resource considered expendable by the Japanese. To avoid the draft, Yoon entered the Japanese Aviation School in 1944. To his surprise, Yoon learned that he would be trained in combat as a kamikaze pilot. Given only forty hours of basic flight training and seventy hours of combat pilot training in Indonesia, seventeen-year old Yoon flew for the Japanese. One week before his final kamikaze mission in Indonesia (Cambodia) fate intervened as World War II came to an end. The young pilot was elated that he had not been forced to make the ultimate sacrifice.

Once free from the Japanese, Yoon made his way back to Pyongyang but all was not well. The city was under communist control and the Soviet forces had gathered in the north preparing for war. For a second time, Yoon was forced to join the military. This time, he was conscripted into Kim Il Sung's air force. Ater a year, he was arrested in 1948 for making negative comments about the new leader's power. He stated, "My Soviet interrogator could have sent me to a labor camp but he didn't. He revoked my flying privileges… I don't know why he had mercy on me but he saved my life…if he sent me to a Siberian labor camp, I would have died. If he kept me as a fighter pilot up there, I would never have escaped." Realizing he could not live under oppression again, and knowing his family had already made their way to the south, he developed his own daring plan to make it to freedom and reunite with his family.

The young aviator made his way to the Haeju coast near the 38th parallel, the dividing line between North and South Korea, waited for the tide to go out and for the cover of darkness. When he thought the conditions were ideal, he made a dash for the water, far away from the military patrols. He didn't hesitate and started to swim. "I placed all my bets on that run…I was gambling with my life." Yoon knew that if he stopped he would drown and if he turned back it meant he would surely be executed. Thus, with every bit of adrenaline, he managed to swim under a hail of gunfire to the shoreline of a South Korean village. The experience was so traumatic that he still dreams about the escape.

Greeted by an American soldier, he was extensively questioned but also given a Coke. "That was the first time I had a Coke and that's my favorite drink to this day." After proving his convictions, Yoon voluntarily joined the newly formed Republic of Korea Air Force and within two years fought along side the United States and United Nations Forces once the Korean War began. Initially, the Republic of Korea Air Force only had antiquated L-4, L-5 and T-6 aircraft, so Yoon carried small bombs on them to drop on enemy targets. Ultimately, given training in the propeller driven P-51 Mustang, Yoon realized he was still flying an outdated airplane when compared with the American F-86 jet or the MiG-15 jet produced by the Russians; statistics proved his assessment. One in seven South Korean pilots was killed flying the Mustang. Yoon, therefore, realized he had to be well trained and use every tactical advantage to compete in the air. Of course, meeting the love of his life gave him every motivation to survive. Within two weeks of his marriage to Sun Sam Lee his combat abilities would be tested.

During the early part of the Korean War, the Seunghori Railroad Bridge was a major North Korean target because it was the central supply route used in transporting war materials from Communist China to central and eastern North Korea. While the United Nations Forces had tried to destroy the bridge on several occasions, they failed in every attempt. "It was a very complicated mission and they assigned me to destroy the bridge because I was familiar with the bridge and the location. You see, the bridge was close to my hometown and I had made several trips across the bridge each year as a child." Yoon was as familiar with the strategic target as anyone and was the perfect aviator to lead the mission.

The attack required intensive planning and a departure from normal combat tactics. "In a Mustang you generally needed an altitude of 8,000 feet to start your dive so you could drop your bombs and pull up at 3,000 feet. But because of its location, it was not so easy to attack the bridge from that altitude. We decided to start diving at 4,000 feet and pull up at around 1000 feet. It was a very aggressive and dangerous plan but we knew that is what it would take to be successful for the interdiction mission."

Captain Yoon as first fighter lead pilot was assigned to the 10th Fighter Group at Kanguung Air Base. Six Republic of Korea P-51 fighters took off with Yoon and headed to Pyongyang on 17 January 1952. As the planes approached the target, they executed the plan without regard to personal safety, descended to the pre-arranged altitude of 4,000 feet and commenced the precision attack. In all, the six planes dispensed twelve bombs, twenty-four rockets and 47,000 rounds of machine gun ammunition which resulted in the destruction of two spans of the supply bridge. Six anti-aircraft firing positions, one supply point, three bunkers and other structures were also destroyed. Thus, the P-51 pilot from the Republic of Korea Air Force was ultimately successful in destroying the Seunghori Railroad Bridge in Pyongyang, the capital of North Korea. He executed his plan to perfection and returned safely with all of his wingmen. Happily, Yoon also returned to his new bride.

For this act of military achievement and heroism, Yoon and the other five pilots on the mission received citations in person from the Chief of Staff of the South Korean Air Force and Yoon's entire 10th Fighter Group received a citation from the President of the United States. "We were honored and proud to be able to accomplish a mission along side the United States Air Force and together, fight for freedom." In addition, E. Yul Yoon was personally awarded a Distinguished Flying Cross from the United States His reaction was as follows: "It was very glorious. We never expected to get a US medal ourselves... It was honorable for me and also my family. The Distinguished Flying Cross is very special!"

After the Korean War, Yoon became a fighter wing commander, the superintendent of the Korean Air Force Academy and the commander of the combat air command, 2nd highest command in the ROK Air Force. Ultimately Yoon rose to the rank of major general in the South Korean Air Force. He also became a military attaché to France and Mexico, and a vice minister for defense development, Seoul Korea. Throughout his career, along with the Distinguished Flying Cross, he was awarded the Korean Distinguished Service Medal, the Republic of China Distinguished Service Medal and eight individual ROK medals, five of which were combat related.

For General Yoon, retirement from military and government service in 1973 did not mean retirement in the traditional sense. With his vast military and political experience, he became the CEO of the Korea Tacoma Shipbuilding Ind. and continued in that capacity until 1976 when he became president and CEO of Buyeon Company. Yoon provided leadership to the company until 1985 when he decided he wanted to enjoy beautiful weather and his avocation - golf. General Yoon bought a home in Rancho Santa Fe, California and has remained there pursuing leisure activities, directing his business interests and enjoying his extended family. General Yoon has also shared his historical and political perspectives with the international community and is resolute in his current politics about his homeland and surrounding region. When opportunities arise, he makes it his mission to educate the public about many of the false stereotypes surrounding kamikaze pilots. He is quick to relate that not all kamikaze were Japanese and that most were not fanatical; instead they were forced to comply.

General Yoon's life is an amazing story of a brave pilot who refused to acquiesce in the face of danger and who ultimately became one of South Korea's most decorated and revered aviation heroes. Yet the end of this military saga did not come to fruition until a concluding chapter took place on 27 April 2005. Fifty-three years earlier, Yoon was awarded the Distinguished Flying Cross medal by Lieutenant General Glenn Barcus, commander of the US 5th Air Force, in Sachun (K-4 Air Base), South Korea. However, he was not given the actual citation which made the medal official. Through the efforts of the Distinguished Flying Cross Society, an official citation was obtained which described the mission in detail.

A ceremony was held at the San Diego Air & Space Museum in honor of General Yoon's vast accomplishments. General Cardinas, multiple DFC recipient and the aviator who released Chuck Yeager from the B-29 for his sound barrier flight, presented the citation and a new medal in front of a large gathering which included several generations of General Yoon's family. In his remarks, he stated that "I'm nearing the end of my life...I will be leaving a legacy for my children and I wanted them to have that citation." Kyung-im, Yoon's daughter commented, "He's gone through things we can't even imagine... that's probably why he's so passionate and stubborn about every little detail he believes in."

General Yoon's final reaction on that beautiful San Diego day was short but profound. "I fought for freedom at every turn. You have to choose it!"

Notes

General E. Yul Yoon, Distinguished Flying Cross citation, action date: 17 January 1952, Archives, the Distinguished Flying Cross Society, San Diego, CA.

General E. Yul Yoon, oral history interview, interviewed by Dr. Barry A. Lanman, 26 April 2005, transcribed, the Distinguished Flying Cross Society Oral History Collection, the Distinguished Flying Cross Society, San Diego, CA.

Lee Booyeon, "He's Earned His Wings," San Diego Union-Tribune, April, 28, 2005, B1, B4.

Top: Lieutenant Paul Butler posed with a Douglass B-26. Although he was a private pilot before the war, Butler was a navigator-bombardier during Korea. Bottom: Butler flew forty-five missions in Korea and received a Distinguished Flying Cross along with a Bronze Star. Photographs courtesy of Paul Butler and the National Museum of the United States Air Force

Interdicting the Enemy in Korea

Colonel Paul Butler, USAF

"We would interdict a railroad and fly right down until we saw the steam coming out of the locomotive...we were flying at a hundred feet, then pop up...and drop a bomb."_____

As a child, Paul Butler became fascinated with airplanes as he watched C-47s conduct low-level practice over the family farm, located near Syracuse, New York. Butler fondly recalled his youth and how these planes motivated him to take to the air. "My original flight training occurred when I was fourteen and fifteen years old, in Syracuse, at Amboy Airport. A good friend went with me...we decided to fly. And we did. I had eight hours of instructions and then I soloed having just turned fifteen years old. We flew occasionally for the next couple of years. It was '43 and I went to college in '45."

In college, he pursued this passion for flight and his fascination for science by obtaining a Bachelor's Degree in aeronautical engineering in 1948. The next challenge was to find an exciting job that would let him use his newly acquired skills. "After I had graduated from college I applied for several jobs in my field. One of these was for an engineer at Wright Patterson Air Force Base, and I took the examination for a position. I found out I had the third highest score - they were hiring five. However, it turned out I was actually tenth in the overall ranking. That was because all the ex-GI's got ten or fifteen extra points... Rightly so! Therefore, I didn't get the job.

After that...the Army said you're "1A" [Top category to be drafted] and I said, 'No, I'm not'...In other words, I avoided the draft by enlisting in the United States Air Force, in October 1948...They sent me to Lackland Air Force Base in San Antonio, Texas. When I was there, I applied for flying school and was accepted. But nothing happened. I was just held in what's called a "Casual Squadron" for almost a year before they sent me off to Aviation Cadets...where I played baseball. Well, officially, I was a clerk typist..."

When he finally got his slot as an aviation cadet at Ellington Air Force Base, Paul Butler used his previous experience as a private pilot to complete his training in nine-and-a-half months and become a navigator-bombardier. The reason he chose this route was clear. "I actually went into this area, even though I had a pilot's license, because it consisted of navigation, radar, electronics and mathematics. It was really good training and I was already an Aeronautical Engineer, so it made sense to combine all my skills.

After graduating from school, I stayed there as an instructor - in radar. I was also an engineer...and after the Korean War had started, the commanding officer, General Lee, who had been [General] Mac-Arthur's pilot at one time, asked for volunteers to go over to replace the first group of combat troops... They needed forty navigator-bombardiers and they got thirty-eight volunteers. I was not one of them and they took everybody else who was there as instructors, who had no overseas experience, and put their names in a hat and went to Officer's Call at the Officer's Club and he drew out names. I wasn't the first out, I was the second..."

While this might have seemed to be bad luck, Butler looked at it a different way by the end of his tour. "Yes, in a way it was bad luck, the remaining instructors who didn't get picked made fun of me, giving me the 'ha, ha, ha'...but nine months later, I met them in Hawaii and they were all going to Korea while I was coming home...

I went to combat crew training first, at Langley Air Force Base in Virginia. It was a really nice experience in August of '51. We got a lot of combat training and experience in a B-26. We did low level missions, long range missions. We did it all... One of the missions was that we took off from Langley, went to St. Louis, flew north to Chicago, and practiced a reconnaissance route, just like we would in combat. We flew the length of Lake Erie, and counted the trains along the railroad track from Buffalo to Cleveland. We had a lot of [practice] missions, and a lot of flying in a short period of time. It should have been a four to six month program but we did it all in two months because of the Korean War.

I got to Korea in 1951 on Thanksgiving Day and was a first lieutenant. We got a little bit of training there. They gave you what's called a 'Dollar Ride.' Your first ride, your first combat mission, was with an experienced man in the crew with the same position that you were flying. You did the work and he'd just observe. You were checked out. After that, I was actually assigned missions because a lot of navigator-bombardiers went home because they got their allotted number of missions…The squadron commander made me the scheduling officer for all the navigator bombardiers. So, I worked in operations as well as doing the flying."

The young aviator felt comfortable with his range of skills in the Douglas B-26. "It was a wonderful airplane, easy to handle, easy to fly. It was crew friendly. But in ice it flew like a rock…I could navigate, be the bombardier. And since I already had a pilot license, I could actually fly the airplane if I had to. There were experiences with a lot of people who were navigators, without training in flying, who had to bring the airplane home…"

Butler explained what it was like flying combat missions in a Douglass B-26 during the Korean War. "Each squadron was assigned a given route, which is a segment of roads and railroads in the Northern Korea area that we patrolled. We attacked targets of opportunity most of the time. Sometimes we went after specific targets. Our primary job was low-level night interdiction missions on supplies. You interdict, interfere, with ground transportation in any form: locomotives, trains, trucks, marching troops, whatever. We only got chased by a MiG-15 a couple of times but our F-86 jets protected us…The MiGs didn't really want us…they wanted to go after the B-29s. We could see the MiGs' search lights and see them track a B-29. That was not pleasant to watch…

We would normally do one mission a night…The only day missions I ever flew were two close air support missions for the Army. That was when they were being severely attacked. But there were occasions when I did fly two missions a night…

Between flights, we had other jobs…I did all the scheduling for the navigators and the bombardiers in my squadron. So, I had to be at Operations during the day, and then we always had to go to the pre-mission briefings held late in the afternoon. After that we did our night missions. When you came back, you were free to go to sleep.

We brought back pieces of our own bombs a few times. It was winter and there was snow on the ground, and you get a clear night with the big moon out there. We had a route that was over fairly level terrain. We would interdict a railroad and fly right down until we saw the steam coming out of the locomotive…we were flying at a hundred feet, then we'd pop up to four hundred and drop a bomb. It was a 500 pound bomb with a parachute on it. The idea…you drop the bomb and it should open just before it hits. Lots of times it didn't open quick enough. It would explode and we'd end up bringing back pieces in the tail.

On one mission, in February 1952, we flew several close air support missions for the ground troops…pretty close to the front lines for two hours…did a lot of strafing and maneuvers like that. We had to keep track of where we were, because the Chinese were coming over the hill, and we did what we could to protect our guys. The airplane got shot up pretty badly, but fortunately no one got hurt and we were able to bring it home". For this mission, Lieutenant Butler received the Bronze Star.

"We were allocated specific routes, and they were numbered P, our number was P4. They were always numbered, purple four, purple seven and so forth. P4 was on the west part of Korea and a very, very level plain, north from Pyongyang which is the capital of North Korea now. That was a very good route for trains. It was a dual railroad track that ran from Sinanju to Sunan…and, at Pyongyang [there] was a big marshalling (train) yard. So, on 11 March 1952, we used the same technique, interdict the rail system, find the railroad and then fly right up or down it…until we found a train. Usually you found a train by the steam coming out of the engine. I was able to successfully drop a bomb in front of one and back of one. We wrecked the rails, they couldn't move and they were stuck, two trains side by side. One of them was an ammunition train. Colonel Morgan did the strafing, and I did the bombing. That's how we received the Distinguished Flying Cross. We blew up two locomotives, fully loaded trains with ammunition."

On his forty-fifth and final mission, Butler sustained personal injury and the nose of his B-26 was severely damaged. Thus, he was unable to complete fifty missions, which was customary for Korean era pilots. Colonel Butler elaborates on what happened: "I would line the targets up with a Norden bombsight, and we would bomb from twenty-five hundred feet or less…very low level and high speed. Well, we needed to go high speed, and high speed then was 210-250. This was because the Chinese were very adept at putting the anti-aircraft guns in tunnels or sidetracks, and having them well camouflaged. If you went over that area too closely, they would throw up the camouflage and the anti-aircraft guns were usually on flatbeds. They would pepper the heck out of us. And that's what happened when I got shot up…we stayed there too long.

I got severely wounded, shrapnel in the arm and across the back…We didn't go back to our home base, we landed at Seoul instead because the nose of our airplane was shot off. It was difficult to control but our engines were fine. I stayed in the hospital there for three days, came back to my own base and stayed in the hospital for three more days. After that I went to Japan for seven days of R&R. When I came back, the squadron commander said, 'here are your orders - you're going home.' I said, 'Yes Sir!' And that was all I said, I didn't argue with him."

When he came back to the United States in 1952, Butler flew with the Military Air Transport Service out of Westover Air Force Base in Springfield, Massachusetts. To his surprise, this reserve officer was offered a regular commission and accepted it without hesitation.

During his military career of twenty-seven years, Colonel Butler earned two graduate degrees and was awarded the Distinguished Flying Cross, the Bronze Star, the Purple Heart and numerous Air Medals. After his retirement from the Air Force as a full colonel, he worked for Martin Marietta as an engineer. He also worked on aerospace and telecommunications contracts associated with Fort Meade and NSA. When he retired, Colonel Paul Butler organized the Nation's Capitol Region Chapter of the Distinguished Flying Cross Society and served as its first president.

Notes

Colonel Paul Butler, Distinguished Flying Cross citation, action date: 11 March 1952, the Distinguished Flying Cross Society, San Diego, CA.

Colonel Paul Butler, oral history interview, interviewed by Dr. Barry A. Lanman, 5 December 2002, the Distinguished Flying Cross Society Oral History Collection, the Distinguished Flying Cross Society, San Diego, CA.

Top: Captain Wilbur Coats flew the B-26 on seventeen missions while in Korea. Middle: Captain Coats received a Distinguished Flying Cross in Korea for completing a strategic mission with a severely damaged B-26. Bottom: Coats made the United States Air Force a career and retired as a colonel. He was a founding member of the Distinguished Flying Cross Society. Photographs courtesy of Wilbur Coats

A B-26 Tangles with an Exploding 40mm Shell

Colonel Wilbur L. Coats, USAAF / USAF

"With complete awareness of the condition of his damaged aircraft, Captain Coats continued on his bomb run and dropped one hundred percent of his bombs."_____

As a witness to the bombing of Pearl Harbor, Wilbur L. Coats understood the implications of an ensuing war with Japan. At that time, though, he was not stationed in the American territory as a member of the Army or Navy; he was a civilian employee. After observing the carnage, Wilbur was inclined to join the Army Air Corps on 14 August 1942. He had no delusions about what he was getting into. He wanted to make a difference and this patriotic outlook followed him through World War II, Korea and the balance of his military career.

After completing flight school in July 1943, Lieutenant Coats was trained to fly the B-25 and was sent with a crew to the Pacific. He explained what he did in the 42nd Bomb Group, 13th Air Force, USAAF. "I flew sixty-nine missions in World War II. The maximum was supposed to be fifty-five, but the commander of the base decided he wanted me to stay and they promoted me to Assistant Group Operations officer. So, I flew an additional seventeen missions while I was there and in the Pacific southwest.

Unscathed by combat action in World War II, he returned to the United States and transferred from active duty to the reserves in 1946. During that time, he flew at March Field for more than a year and was then called back to active duty in preparation for a potential conflict with Korea. Coats recounted how he was sent to Korea: "I was flying B-25s at Chanute Air Force Base and I was the pilot for the base commander. They needed some relief for the 452nd Bomb Group in Korea and I was selected to go. At that time, they had a program to train B-26 crews and get them ready to go to Korea. They decided, because I had flown the B-25, that I didn't need to go through this training and sent me directly to Korea.

When I arrived, I checked in with the group commander and he said, 'How much time do you have in the B-26?' "I said, 'None' and he said, 'You didn't go through a training program?' Of course, my answer was, 'No!' The problem was that they didn't have a training program for the B-26 in Korea at that time." To rectify the problem, the commanding officer said, 'I see you're a personnel officer.' His personnel officer was leaving the same day I arrived and he said, 'You're my personnel officer and we'll worry about your flying later.'

Therefore, I spent about five months as the personnel officer and flying C-47s or whatever they had around because I wasn't checked out in the B-26. Finally, a new group commander came in and I said, 'Colonel, I need to get some time in the B-26 or I'll never get out of here.' The rules at that time were you had to have ten months and seventeen missions if you were a 'ground pilot.' So he said, 'Okay, we'll get you checked out.' However, this consisted of a few take-offs and landings and I was shown some of the stall characteristics of the plane. Following that, I was told to solo." Once Coats got the B-26 back on the ground, he received his official papers which cleared him for combat missions.

Coats then flew his required seventeen missions, but number eight was the most memorable. With clarity, as if it were yesterday, Coats explained what happened on 6 August 1952. "The mission was up near Pyongyang at a military supply base. It was a bombing run on a supply depot. We were using 250 pound bombs and trying to knock out their supplies.

It was a night flight, which a lot of the missions were in Korea. And, it was what we called an in-trail flight where you had a section of ten airplanes flying one behind another. I was number five in the rotation. We flew about twenty to thirty seconds apart at night and we flew pretty low - about 1500 feet across the target.

When we approached the target, it was obvious that the supply depot was pretty heavily defended. There were a lot of tracer bullets coming up and some bigger stuff shooting around. Of course, being dark, we couldn't see anything except the tracers. By the time I was coming up on the target, the airplane ahead of me was pulling off and I was lined up to make the bomb drop and 'wamo,' the airplane got hit... the tail punched up and the nose pushed down. Out of reflex, I pulled back on the yoke and put the power on. I just hoped for the best and wasn't aware of how damaged the plane was at the time.

I got down to about 500 feet as I went across the target and released the bombs. I started to gradually climb out...When we got up to about 4 or 5,000 feet, the tail-gunner communicated that he thought we were on fire. He said 'I smell smoke.' And I said, 'Well, do you see any flames?' And, he said, 'No, but I sure smell a lot of smoke.' So I said to the three enlisted crew members, 'Nobody bail out now...Let's just stay calm.' I got up to about 8,000 feet and I could feel the nose was very heavy. I thought, well, I better see how the airplane will control as I pull the power off. So I tried that and it seemed to be alright. It was heavy, but I could control it. So I said, 'We'll continue on - I think we can maybe make it back to base. If not, we'll hit one of the emergency landing strips that are back in the American area.'

We kept going and about an hour and a half later we got back towards the base. Everything seemed to be alright and there was no more report about fire. But then as I called in for emergency equipment and asked for GCA (Ground Controlled Approach) support to help me keep that nose up, one of the crew members in the rear said, 'I really smell smoke - I think the plane is on fire again.' I said, 'Well, we're too low now. Don't jump out. That's the last thing you want to do. We're down to 500 feet and we're going to be landing in a few minutes. When we land be sure you wait until I get the engine stopped.' I didn't want somebody to run forward and through the propeller.

When we landed, everything seemed okay. I shut the engines off and said 'Now get out!' We all took our own ways and got out. I jumped down off of the wing and onto the tarmac. The fire trucks and ambulance were there and all the emergency people. I started running down the runway. And pretty soon somebody came along with a Jeep, tapped me on the shoulder and he said, 'It's okay, son. It's okay.' I looked over and it was the chaplain in this little Jeep. He said, 'Just get in and I'll take you back to operations.' So I did and we went back to operations. Then we had our interview of what happened."

After a few hours of sleep, Captain Coats inspected his plane. To his surprise, there were three men working on the B-26 and Coats could see a huge hole in the empennage of the airplane. At that point he realized just how bad the plane had been damaged by an explosive 40mm shell. When he climbed up on a ladder for a closer inspection, he could put his entire head through the hole. He figured if the shell had hit another eighteen inches towards the tail, the stabilizer would have been destroyed and the plane would have likely crashed.

The pilot said, "After that, I never thought too much more about it...I was busy doing other things. However, about ten days later, the operations officer came to me and said, 'Bill, the commander wants to talk to you.' I went out in front to see what was going on, and he was getting ready to give me a Distinguished Flying Cross...It really never entered my mind that this was a DFC flight, but it turned out it was." The DFC citation included the following language to support that the actions by the pilot did warrant the medal. "With complete awareness of the condition of his damaged aircraft, Captain Coats continued on his bomb run and dropped 100% of his bombs in the center of the target area. Several secondary explosions and two sustained fires resulted from this bomb drop. As a result of this highly successful mission, vital supplies and buildings were destroyed."

Coats' reaction was simple. "I was frankly surprised. I never thought about getting a DFC for the mission...I got the airplane back and I figured that was the important thing. I figured I worked for the Air Force while I dropped my bombs. Once my bombs were dropped, I worked for myself to get out of there and get back to base.

Actually, it meant a lot because of the fact that the airplane was severely damaged and I was able to get it back...I felt at least it showed some capability to fly a crippled airplane and save the crew. So I was rather proud that they did give me the Distinguished Flying Cross for this most harrowing mission."

Captain Coats eventually completed his seventeen missions and got his ticket back to the United States. Once again, he served as a personnel officer and made the decision to make the Air Force a career. Over time, he rose to the rank of colonel and retired in June 1971 after twenty-nine years of service.

As a founding member of the Distinguished Flying Cross Society, Colonel Coats enjoys talking about the B-26 and communicates enormous respect for the aircraft. For him, it was the way in which the B-26 was made, how much punishment it could take and its capability, despite being structurally compromised, in combat to still get its crew back home. The colonel knows he owes his life to the amazing B-26.

Notes

Colonel Wilbur L. Coats, Distinguished Flying Cross citation, action date: 6 August 1952, Archives, the Distinguished Flying Cross Society, San Diego, CA.

Colonel Wilbur L. Coats, oral history interview, interviewed by Dr. Barry A. Lanman, 26 July 2008, transcribed, the Distinguished Flying Cross Society Oral History Collection, the Distinguished Flying Cross Society, San Diego, CA.

Top: The F-51s were nicknamed "'Peter-Dash-Flash" because they often took their targeting direction from "willie peter" white phosphorous markers. Then they dashed in and flashed their ordnance on the enemy.
Middle: First Lieutenant Richard Deihl was photographed with his F-51 sporting the clever name, *The Dealer*.
Bottom: When he came back from Korea he transitioned to jets and taught jet gunnery to new combat pilots.
Photographs courtesy of Richard Deihl

Flying the "Peter-Dash-Flash" in Combat: The F-51 Mustang

First Lieutenant Richard H. Deihl, USAF

"With the F-51, it was all low angle strafe, bomb, napalm and rockets because we could stay on a target longer than the jets." _____

By the time the Korean War began, the P-51 Mustang was already a legend from its exploits in World War II. Transformed into the F-51 for its role in Korea, the aircraft gained nicknames like "Stang, the Ground-Pounder" and "Peter-Dash-Flash." Lieutenant Richard Deihl affectionately called the F-51 all of those names and realized the important role the aircraft played in Korea. The aviator also learned about life while in the cockpit of his F-51 which he called *The Dealer*.

Richard H. Deihl was born on 9 September 1928 in Pico, now Pico Rivera, California. As a child, he grew up during the Depression and lived through World War II as a teenager. A self-professed "bookish kid," he studied a great deal and played tennis rather than football. Deihl understood that in order to get into college he would have to obtain financial assistance and therefore excelled as a high school student.

Rewarded for his efforts, he won a competitive scholarship to Whittier College. However, in the late 1940s, as he progressed through his undergraduate degree, he had to register for the draft. His plan was to get into graduate school before he had to go into the service so he attended the University of California, Berkeley and studied economics. He also decided he wanted to marry his high school sweetheart, Billie, but money was an issue. He had spent all of it on graduate school. Deihl explained how he tried to resolve the dilemma. "Korea had just started…I was concerned about finishing school and being able to get married. So, I checked around to see if there was a way to get a military commission.

To my dismay, all were frozen, as they often are at the very beginning of hostilities. The only thing they had left open was the Air Force cadet program. I had made model airplanes, so I figured I possibly could do that…I joined up with the idea that I would be coming on to active duty some time in six to eight months. I knew what the flight pay was and I figured that would be enough to get married. In essence, I joined the Air Force for money. I guess you could say I was a Hessian. [A mercenary]

I delivered furniture for awhile until my number was called and then joined the Air Force on 2 March 1951. They sent me to James Connally Air Force Base, Waco, Texas, then on to Reese Air Force Base in Lubbock, Texas. I got my wings in March 1952…I got married two days after I got my wings and was gainfully employed. Then, I got orders for Korea and we had about eight weeks of training at Luke AFB in the F-51 before we were sent overseas…

I was sent to the 18th Fighter Bomber Wing, the 67th Fighter Bomber Squadron, 5th Air Force in May 1952. When we got there, they sent us on a couple of training missions…we were guided. I think our first two combat missions were the same as everybody else's in that theater. We went out and bombed some old derelict that was in the harbor. They weren't shooting at us, we were shooting at it and… sometimes we hit it…We were located in K-46, Wonju, Korea. That was in the middle of Korea and we stayed there until the last few months of the tour. Then we moved to K-55 near Seoul.

I flew seventy-six missions – all in the F-51s. By that time they had changed the designation from P-51 in WWII to the F-51. The "P" stood for Pursuit while the "F" was for Fighter. I flew all of my missions in the F-51-Ds. They had the bubble cockpit and a better engine. It was a pretty good plane. In some cases, they were a little old - a little battle weary…They took the P-51 and converted it into a plane for the type of mission in Korea. They beefed up the wings. We carried two 500 pound bombs, four five inch rockets and six fifty caliber machine guns; three in each wing and the others were external stores. They also gave us tip-tanks so we could stay up longer; somewhere between five and six hours. Thus, we could stay on target and get the job done.

The reason they modified the 51s was that our missions were different from the ones in World War II. In that war, the P-51s were primarily accompanying bombers and were high altitude escort. With the F-51 it was all low angle strafe, bomb, napalm and rockets because we could stay on a target longer than the jets…I always get a kick out of talking to the guys who flew jets in Korea. We would be on a target and in came the jets. They would say, 'Oh, we're low on fuel - we've got to get in and off.' So we'd pull off a target, let them 'whoosh' by and drop whatever they were going to drop, and then they had to struggle to get home. We'd go on the target beating it up…We were known as the 'flying ground pounders' of the Air Force." The F-51s were also nicknamed 'Peter-Dash-Flash' because they often took their targeting direction from the 'Willie Peter' white phosphorous markers, dashed in at 450 knots and flashed its ordnance on the enemy."

For the type of mission that the F-51 flew in Korea, the plane had a major limitation. Deihl explained, "I don't believe that the North Koreans knew this, but the F-51 had a weakness in combat. The plane had a liquid cooled engine…If a round of ammunition hit the coolant, the plane would get knocked down in five minutes. That's why it isn't a particularly great design for low angle air to ground missions. It has every other good characteristic except that it can get knocked down by a stray bullet that 'opens' the coolant tank…That was the only thing I was worried about at low level while I was shooting and strafing – that stray bullet. It wasn't like a 'Jug' [F-47] which can bounce off a mountain and be okay."

While the P-51s proved reliable during World War II, maintenance was a major problem for the F-51 in Korea. Bad fuel was the suspected cause of reoccurring engine malfunctions. However, after a great deal of research, the source of the problem was isolated. Lieutenant Deihl added, "They tested the sparkplugs and out of a gross of sparkplugs, a hundred and forty-four, only seven tested OK… Some guy had gotten a great contract with the US and had provided reconditioned sparkplugs. We didn't get brand new sparkplugs like other people, and we lost a few planes because of that. I've always thought I would like to have met that guy with a baseball bat."

On 12 December 1952, First Lieutenant Deihl flew a mission for which he would receive the Distinguished Flying Cross. He explained the event in the following manner. "It was a normal JOC alert mission. JOC alert stands for 'joint operation command' and they have JOC one, two, three, four, five, six, etc.…Maybe there would be fifteen or twenty JOC alerts in a day's operation. A JOC alert normally was four aircraft with four pilots standing by, either in the ready room with their URC-4s, their radios, their flight vests and their G suits, ready to scramble. Or in some cases because there was something very active they knew we were going to be called in a matter of ten or fifteen minutes. We would actually be in the plane, have started the engine and gotten it warmed up, and then turned it off waiting for the call. In this case it was about the fifth or sixth JOC alert. We got called so we took off toward Otanni, near the double bend.

The joint operation command alerts were usually guided by a 'Hammer.' The Hammer was a pilot in an F-51 who was strictly in reconnaissance, or he could be flying a T-6 that was in reconnaissance. They usually had rockets so they could mark a target. We would use that as the reference so they might say, 'Up that, fifty yards to the north. You will see an old burned out tree and that's the beginning of a trench line. Work your way up the trench line until you see a mound, and that's what your target is.' It was that kind of communication - very informal.

We were received by the Hammer and he took us to the mission area. He rocketed what we called 'Willie Peter,' which was white phosphorous, and that was the marker. The North Koreans, after a while, would set off their own white phosphorous markers – maybe even six or seven 'Willie Peters' as a diversion. To counter that, the Air Force got a little smarter and would have different rounds. Sometimes we fired colored smoke. That meant the enemy would have to have a whole inventory of colors to try to confuse the pilots…

On the way to the mission, my number four man developed engine trouble and it was significant. He wasn't sure he was going to make it back, so I sent number three back with him to get him back over the line. They were lucky and did make it back. We were now down from four to two planes and it was a strong point in the enemy line. The American soldiers were either being overrun or in the process of about to be overrun. They called us in on that particular place. [Later, they learned that the plane with engine trouble had bad spark plugs].

When we got there, the panels to mark where the friendly line was were in place. It's a very difficult thing when you have a very fluid line so they used panels to mark the friendly territory…It really helped in this kind of confused, messy type of warfare. It wasn't a nice delineation between good guys and bad guys. That's one of the reasons they used 51s, because we could stay in an area. The Hammer would give us a description of what was going on, who was going where, and then we could take the action, where oftentimes jets just didn't have the fuel to stay on a target.

At that point, we were directed by the Hammer to go in. It was a very hot spot. We made the first run - a bombing attack; a couple of 500 pounders each. Then we made an attack with our five inch rockets, and then we beat up the area with the fifty calibers…you could do a fair amount of damage with each one…you could beat up an area on six or seven passes and do some good.

The Hammer was very complimentary about how effective our mission was and we felt good about it. It was one of those missions where you went back, had your drink at the chaplain's table, and felt that you accomplished something…It was always rewarding when you had a job to do, got it done, and everybody returned safely. That's what this mission was."

The official governmental citation included the following rationale for a DFC: "Locating the target, Lieutenant Deihl pressed his attack through intense enemy ground fire, strafing enemy gun positions and personally scoring a direct hit on the enemy stronghold with his bombs…As a result of this highly successful mission, vital enemy defenses were destroyed, seriously hampering the enemy's potential in that sector. Throughout his entire combat tour, Lieutenant Deihl has displayed excellent qualities of leadership and airmanship in attacking enemy troops, supplies and equipment."

When Lieutenant Deihl was informed that he would receive a Distinguished Flying Cross, he said, "I was delighted…It was a good mission. We didn't lose anybody and we did some good for the guys on the ground." However, while the DFC was an important honor, one other consideration was on Deihl's mind. "At the moment I was counting missions, trying to get home. The December 12th mission was about my fiftieth mission.

We were going to transition into F-86 jets in the 67th Fighter Bomber Squadron. The 18th had already moved into 86s. So I was trying to get enough missions to either return home or to be stepped down so that I would transition in the 86s. My focus was on trying to get missions…I even found myself trying to switch onto missions in other squadrons so that I could get my required number. I finally got my seventy-sixth mission in the latter part of January 1953. However, they made a cutoff by that time. Anybody over sixty missions did not transition to 86s, so I was returned home in March.

They gave me three choices of assignment. My first choice was to teach at the Air Force Academy. I thought that might be interesting since I had a degree in economics. My second choice was to work in Intelligence; that would also relate to my background in economics. However, I received neither placement…Instead I got assigned to Laughlin Air Force Base in Texas. It was a jet training base. And, I had no hours in jets! Therefore, it was an interesting transition…but typically Air Force.

I got there and flew ten hours around the field because student flying was down. It was bad weather, but I had to get ten hours in a jet before I could take those kids up and teach them jet gunnery. Ultimately, it was interesting duty because we played "cops and robbers" there. We set up all kinds of conditions in the field that would simulate actual combat situations. In my opinion, it was excellent training."

About two or three weeks before my four years were up, I had the opportunity to train for the Thunderbirds, which would've been interesting. However, I had a wife, a daughter and a kid on the way…" Thus, in March 1955, Lieutenant Deihl left active duty and was put on in-active status. He remembered how important his Air Force training and experiences were to him. "Once I was in civilian life, the training that I had, the discipline that I had, the understanding of how to focus and how to prioritize, was very important to me.

For about five years, I was a salesman for National Cash Register Company and then I had an opportunity to go into 'selling money' for Home Savings of America – I became a commissioned salesman for them; a loan agent. And, then I convinced them they needed a loan agent supervisor, a sales manager, and that was my biggest sale...

I became involved in a lot of other jobs at Home Savings of America. I wound up working as the CEO of the largest savings institution in the United States for twenty-six years. After that, I became chairman of the holding company and so forth... But all of these things were not done by plan...They were done because opportunities presented themselves and because I had an ability to understand what was important and what was not important, more so than the average guy. Survival is important, many other things are not. My combat experience taught me to be a survivor and taught me to be very, very happy when I got down on the ground, and when my guys were safe. I never forgot that.

The Distinguished Flying Cross meant a lot to me because anytime you're a pilot and you're flying combat, you really don't have a good concept of what the public realizes about what you are doing. That was especially true in Korea because it was right after World War II. People were tired of war and they just didn't want to believe this was going on...It's interesting because so often we talk about failure in Korea and yet I've gone back to Wonju and Seoul, Korea. I saw the good quality of life that the South Koreans have....It would not be like that if the United States had not fought in Korea...The general population really doesn't understand what was sacrificed by the American troops who fought in Korea. By comparison, I remember talking to some Vietnam vets. I heard of the treatment they got when they returned and I much prefer a forgotten war than the kind of reception they received."

While Richard Deihl often ponders the complex contextual perceptions of success or failure in Korea, he clearly understands the significance of the Distinguished Flying Cross. "It is the one thing that I remember the most about my days in Korea. It's wonderful to remember the success [of a mission] where no Americans got hurt. The Distinguished Flying Cross epitomizes extraordinary service. It is something that a combat pilot recognizes and truly appreciates."

Notes

Lieutenant Richard Henry Deihl, Distinguished Flying Cross citation, action date: 12 December 1952, Archives, the Distinguished Flying Cross Society, San Diego, CA.

Lieutenant Richard Henry Deihl, oral history interviews, interviewed by Dr. Barry A. Lanman, 26 April 2005 and 28 July, 2008, transcribed, the Distinguished Flying Cross Society Oral History Collection, the Distinguished Flying Cross Society, San Diego, CA.

Top: Rex Warden flew in World War II and Korea. Middle: In an exchange program with the Navy during 1952-1953, Warden flew the F9F-5 Panther in Korea while deployed on the aircraft carrier USS *Valley Forge*. Bottom: After completing 100 missions in Korea, Captain Warden volunteered to complete thirty more. Photographs courtesy of Rex Warden

Flying the First Jet Fighters in Korea

Major Rex W. Warden, USAAF / USAF

"The jet fighter was new. We were fast and when you came right at them they couldn't hear you…and the enemy wasn't prepared for that."_____

Graduating from high school in 1942, Rex Warden attended the University of Wyoming for a year but abruptly joined the US Army Air Corps in June 1943. He gave a simplistic yet profound rationale for leaving college, "The whole atmosphere in World War II, whether you were a civilian or military, was a very patriotic scenario. Everyone, twenty-four-seven, was doing something for the war effort. My dad was a carpenter building air fields and my mother was working at home and in stores…the country was united, everybody had a flag in the their window." So it was Warden's turn to contribute.

After his decision to become a pilot, Warden recalled his initial training. "They sent us to the college training detachment for three months. The rule was, to be a pilot you had to have two years of college and I had a little over a year at Wyoming, so by going to the college training detachment for three months they said it counted for one year. Thus, I was eligible to go to flight training.

Most of us were eighteen or nineteen years old at that time we went to flight training after classification. Classification was a selection between pilot, navigator and bombardier. I was classified as a pilot and went into primary flight training in Stamford, Texas, flying the PT-19, and our instructors were civilians…I first thought I wanted to be a bomber pilot. I was very impressed with headlines of the B-17s and B-24s, and I thought I would like to do that. But my instructor, Mr. Kibiki, thought I should be a fighter pilot because I apparently reacted well to his teachings for aerobatics and it never bothered me to be upside-down or doing loops and roll maneuvers. The second part of flight training, was called basic training and we flew the Vultee BT-13 aircraft nicknamed the 'Vultee Vibrator.'

The final phase was called advanced. You either went to single-engine or multi-engine advanced, and the fellas who went to multi-engine would become transport or bomber pilots. And fellas who went to single-engine advanced would become fighter pilots…I was sent to Foster Field, Texas for advanced training flying the AT-6, called 'The Texan'."

On 8 September 1944, Warden earned his wings as a fighter pilot and was commissioned as a second lieutenant on a Saturday morning with his fellow classmates. With only one evening to celebrate at the Victoria Country Club, the young officers reported the next morning for P-40 training in their first fighter plane. Warden recalled what he thought would happen next. "I was expecting to go on to a replacement training unit, where you would fly a P-51 or a P-47 type aircraft for overseas duty in Europe or the Pacific…I was really looking forward to that. Apparently, the pipeline was beginning to fill up and they didn't really need replacements right away. To my chagrin, I was ordered to flight instructor training at Randolph Field Texas…that really was a sad deal. I had been trained to be a combat pilot, not a flight instructor."

After training as a flight instructor in the T-6 and serving as an instructor for a short time, Lieutenant Warden took advantage of an opportunity. A request went out to gather a small number of volunteers for overseas duty. Since there were so many pilots interested in the same thing, cards were drawn to determine who would go. Warden drew a king of diamonds, a high card, ensuring he was on the list.

Once underway from the port of embarkation on a C-47, the pilots were told that their orders would be opened thirty minutes into the flight. To his surprise, he was not going to Europe or the Pacific; the orders were for Panama. Of course later, he realized the importance of protecting the Panama Canal, a strategic facility, during WWII. Assigned to the 30th Fighter Squadron, Lieutenant Warden flew the P-39, Air Cobra and the P-38L Lightning; a high performance fighter plane Warden really enjoyed flying until the war ended.

When he returned from Panama in January 1946, the twenty-one year old was once again assigned to Randolph Field as a flight instructor, where he served for a year. During 1947, he was sent to the Air Tactical School for training in squadron leadership positions such as flight commanders and operations officers. With his various qualifications, Lieutenant Warden got a break. He was selected for jet fighter training in the P-80. As a result, however, his wedding plans were expedited. The new bride and bridegroom were married in the chapel at Fort Sam Houston. After a quick celebration with friends they enjoyed a honeymoon on the way. He remembered, "I had recently bought a new 1947 two-door Ford. We put everything we owned in the backseat and headed west to Williams Field, Arizona."

Warden spent the next three months learning to fly the Lockheed P-80 Shooting Star. It was the first jet fighter used operationally by the US Air Force. Once jet qualified, he was ordered to join the 1st Fighter Group, 71st squadron, at March Field, California. He stated, "it was a prestigious assignment with the Air Force's first jet fighter group. One year later, I was ordered to the 49th Fighter Group, based at Misawa AFB, Japan. We helped fighter groups in Japan transition from the F-51 Mustang to the new jet fighters and we were the nucleus of these replacement pilots."

When the Korean War broke out in June 1950, Warden was on the leading edge of combat readiness, however, he was once again delayed from action because he was assigned to train new pilots to fill squadron requirements for the 49th. This time, however, he was more patient and within two months he started flying from Itazuke Air Force Base in southern Japan. He recounted that, "During the first four months, our combat radius was at least 300 nautical miles and we could reach all the way to Wonsan, Korea with large tip tanks. However, by the fall of 1950, our ground forces had fought some terrific battles on the ground, but were pushed back into an area called the Pusan Perimeter.

In many ways the Korean War was very similar to World War II…we had a lot of the same tactics and training because most of us had been in World War II. The leaders, the squadron commanders, the group commander, flight leaders mostly had World War II experience. So you had a tendency to blend in that particular thought process, tactics and strategy, and all of our senior leaders, our generals had all been in World War II…The one big difference – Korea was upgraded with different airplanes – jets."

Flying from Itazuke, Japan over the Korean Peninsula, Warden primarily flew two different types of missions: close support of US soldiers on the ground and interdiction missions designed to disrupt enemy supply lines by destroying targets of opportunity. Both were critical to the ground forces breaking out of the Pusan Perimeter. Warden remembered his missions in support of the troops within this limited area. "We would take-off from Itazuke carrying napalm, five-inch rockets and .50 caliber machine guns, fly about ninety miles across the Sea of Japan and then check in with Melo control, which was the control center in Pusan for target assignment…In order to improve our capability, we would have a fighter pilot from our group embedded, so to speak, with the ground troops. He would have a Jeep and a radio and would be able to talk to the aviation leaders in an effective manner because he was one of them.

So on 19 September 1950, I was checking in with Melo control and I heard this familiar voice - it was Joe Olshefski, a pilot from my flight. He was down there in the Jeep. Well, he heard my voice and you can imagine…he was shouting at me to get over there and help them out [due to the intense combat situation].

It was the 29th Infantry Regiment that was pinned down. They were in a valley bordered by a significant hillside, and were pinned down by enemy fire from troops dug in at the hill top. There were all kinds of trenches in and around the top of the hill. The enemy was effectively firing down at our troops which seriously limited their maneuvering abilities…our job was to clean out the top of that hillside.

Unfortunately, there was a little bit of cloud cover right on top of the mountain, forcing us to come in low and under the clouds, then fly up to attack the enemy positions by launching the five inch (high velocity/high explosive warheads) rockets (four on each aircraft), and strafe the trenches at very close range. Each aircraft was armed with six .50 caliber machine guns…We could see the enemy soldiers running for

106

cover, and being caught in our strafing attacks at such close range. We would then fly up through the cloud cover, let back down through the clouds on the other side of the mountain and come around for a repeat attack.

Apparently, we annihilated the enemy so that our troops could take the hill that evening. The Army regimental commander [on the ground] was so taken with what we had done for him and his troops, he got in touch with the Air Force and said, 'Give that guy a medal.' I'm told that is how I got the Distinguished Flying Cross."

In addition to close support missions, Warden also flew interdiction missions. On these missions he destroyed munitions warehouses, airfields and even a train carrying twelve Russian Stalin tanks near Pyongyang, the capitol of North Korea.

The captain then explained that, "I flew at least twenty missions following the Chinese invasion of North Korea in January 1951. Flying interdiction "jet fighter" missions, against the advancing Chinese infantry crossing the Yalu River, was exemplary of what our own forces were facing. We strafed and bombed them without any significant opposition, yet they kept advancing across the rivers, pushing their little rafts holding their rifles and ammunition, in the blood red waters. The advancing Chinese were right in our gun sights at close range, but we couldn't stop all of them.

One particular mission was a long range bombing mission utilizing four P-80C aircraft each armed with two 500 pound GP bombs. The target was a multi-span bridge over the Yalu River at the very northern tip of Korea. It was a key link in the chain of supplies and reinforcements for the Chinese army. Our orders were very specific, 'Put Steel in the water, but only on the Korean side!' We successfully completed the mission as directed, and during our near vertical dive-bombing maneuvers, we were under heavy anti-aircraft fire from gun emplacements on the Chinese side. They were not even camouflaged.

After dropping one bridge span, on the Korean side, we departed the target area in different directions at low altitudes and high speeds. We met at our pre-arranged rendezvous point while climbing to high altitude for the long flight to home base. Kangye was the capital city of North Korea at that time, and as we flew over the city in a widely spread formation, several bursts of flak exploded nearby and at our altitude, but not close enough to be of any concern. I always felt they just wanted to let us know that they knew we were there! This also supports my personal belief that the tide was beginning to turn in the enemy's favor, eventfully leading to the negotiated settlement dividing Korea into separate nations."

As his one-hundred missions were about to be completed, ending his tour, he volunteered to stay on. His reasons were clear, "I was a flight leader. And flight leaders were critical because we had the experience…we led the missions. That's a little different than being a wingman. So they asked for volunteers to fly more and I volunteered to go to 125 missions.

However, when I got to a 125 they had some critical situations so they asked me to fly some more – and I did five more…I probably would've done more than that, but my wife, who was back in Japan, was pregnant and the doctor had told her she either had to be sent home right away or stay there and have the baby. Somehow the word got down to my group commander and I was summoned to report to operations right away…I thought, 'My God, I just got back from one mission and they are going to send me out again?' So I went down to the operation's tent and my old friend, Tom Queen said, 'Pack your bag. You're out of here tonight. You go and take Jean home.' So I did…after 130 missions from June 1950 to January 1951, I packed my bag and caught a C-47 over to Japan. The next thing you know we're both on a C-54 riding across the Pacific back to the United States."

Upon his return from Korea in 1951, Captain Warden flew F-86 jets at the Air Defense Command in Albuquerque, New Mexico and was later asked if he would volunteer for an exchange pilot program with the Royal Air Force or the US Navy. After volunteering for both, he was selected for the Navy program because he was jet combat qualified and one of the first Air Force pilots back from the war.

Warden commented on the opportunity. "It was one of the best experiences of my life. I was ordered to report to COMNVAVAIRPAC, Naval Air Station North Island, San Diego, on 1 March 1952 for duty with Navy Fighter Squadron VF-51. I trained at Miramar and El Centro. This led to deployment on the carrier, USS *Valley Forge* which would become part of Task Force 77 operating off Korea, in the Sea of Japan. I made forty-three successful launches and recoveries from the *Valley Forge* including twenty combat missions…I became close friends with many of my squadron mates.

With the Navy, I flew the F9F-5 Panther single engine jet fighter during 1952 and 1953. What an experience – for launch, you gave a salute to the catapult officer and bang, in one-hundred feet you're flying at 120 miles per hour. The recovery, landing, took…more skill and bravado!"

In 1954, Captain Warden left the Air Force to spend more time with his family and moved to San Diego, California. However, his civilian job was not really much different from his military career. Warden was hired by the Convair Division of General Dynamics as the Chief production test pilot for the Delta Wing F-102 Delta Daggers and the F-106 Delta Dart Programs. While testing the F-106, he flew above 45,000 feet and at a speed of Mach 2; twice the speed of sound.

After his production flight testing experience in 1959, he served in a variety of mid-level executive positions for both corporate and operating division assignments. In 1973, he was recruited by the Aerojet General Corporation for senior level executive operations assignments, which culminated in his retirement as the corporate chief operating officer (COO) in 1989.

While more than a half-century of time has passed since the flight for which he was awarded the Distinguished Flying Cross, Rex Warden has distinct opinions concerning the importance of the DFC and the rationale for what he did as a fighter pilot. "It was an opportunity to help the troops…They could have lost a lot of men had we not been able to come in to intercede for them. Fortunately we had the weapons, the time and the ability to use them to get the troops out of trouble. And, of course, my wingman, Joe Olshefski who was down there on the ground, was very glad we were there. So we bailed out Joe too, and I really felt good about that."

Warden went on to say, "It was never just about the Distinguished Flying Cross, it was the total military experience…Yes, you're proud of the DFC, but it is how the total military experience impacts your life…It makes you a better citizen…I just tried to do the job I was expected to do."

Recently, Rex Warden participated in a military reunion. Attending was Joe Olshevsky, the forward air controller from the ground who helped coordinate the Pusan Perimeter battle. Alive and well, Olshefski would be the first person to agree that his friend, Rex Warden, most certainly deserved the Distinguished Flying Cross.

Notes

Major Rex W. Warden, Distinguished Flying Cross citation, action date: 19 September 1950, Archives, the Distinguished Flying Cross Society, San Diego, CA.

Major Rex W. Warden, oral history interview, interviewed by Dr. Barry A. Lanman, 16 July 2008, transcribed, the Distinguished Flying Cross Society Oral History Collection, the Distinguished Flying Cross Society, San Diego, CA.

Top: Major Schroeder served with the Marine All Weather Fighter Squadron VMF (N)-513 stationed at Kunsan, Korea. Middle: Schroeder helped pioneer the development and evaluation of searchlight-illuminated, night, close air support assaults against the enemy. Bottom: Lieutenant Colonel Schroeder logged a total of 3,225 hours of flying and completed 200 night fighter combat missions. Photographs courtesy of Chuck Schroeder

A Marine Night Flyer

Lieutenant Colonel Chuck L. Schroeder, USMC

"You didn't know if you were going to come back alive."_____

For Chuck Schroeder, life in Kansas, and his family heritage played a major role in his ultimate decision to join the Marines and become a combat pilot. It was a decision that carried him through World War II and Korea. It would also be a decision that would take him on an extended journey through an entire career as a decorated Marine aviator.

After high school graduation in Russell, Kansas in the spring of 1941, Schroeder was a typical teenager from an agricultural region in the mid-west. He felt far removed from world events and admitted that while he realized a war was going on in Europe, he hadn't paid too much attention to events beyond his home town. However, things were about to change for him. As reality set in and he realized he would most likely be drafted, Schroeder faced a critical decision - enlist or wait to be drafted?

With an uncle who had served in the Marines, Schroeder thought that he might follow in his footsteps, but his mother was strongly opposed to the idea. Schroeder's dad, on the other hand, supported the plan saying, "You will get good training in the Marine Corps and your mother will still be your mother." So Schroeder headed to the local recruiting depot to join the Marines. To his dismay, he found out he was too young to join the Marine Corps, so Schroeder enlisted in the Navy in May 1941 and was sent to Great Lakes Naval Training Center. He then became an aircraft machinist mate.

An additional factor influenced Schroeder's path when considering the military. Having spent summers on his grandfather's farm, he was mesmerized by the biplanes that sprayed the fields. With those images in his mind, Schroeder knew he wanted to fly in the military but he couldn't qualify because he lacked the required two years of college. To Schroeder's advantage, however, the educational requirement for a naval aviation cadet was reduced to a high school diploma by the spring of 1942 due to the dwindling number of candidates with a college background.

Based on the new regulations, Chuck Schroeder completed an application for flight training in the Marine Corps during the fall of 1942 and was accepted. He was then given a discharge from the Navy and ultimately accomplished his original goal of becoming a Marine. On 31 January 1943, after eleven hours in a Stearman PT-17, Schroeder soloed. Interestingly, the aircraft in which he trained was similar to the one that had flown over his grandfather's farm.

Once he completed the required thirty-six week aviation program, Schroeder graduated and became a commissioned officer. Schroeder remembered that when he came back home on leave, "everyone was proud of me for becoming a second lieutenant and a Marine pilot. Even my mother gave in and was proud of what I had accomplished in a relatively short time."

Having progressed to operational training, the new pilot was assigned to fly the *Brewster Buffalo*; a plane that had been removed from operational service subsequent to the Battle of Midway in June 1942. Without equivocation, Schroeder claimed that the Buffalo was the worst aircraft he had ever flown. During the balance of his career, he had the opportunity to fly some of the best airplanes built during the 1940s and 50s and appreciated having state-of-the-art aircraft in combat.

While there is some discussion on how he was assigned to the new Marine Corps night fighter service, it appears he "volunteered" for duty with VMF (N)-531, the first Marine Corps night fighter squadron. He came to the squadron just a few months after it was activated in November 1942, received initial training and flew the PV-1 Ventura. For Lieutenant Schroeder and the other night flyers, combat started in September 1943. But a month later, he was transferred to the second night squadron, VFM (N)-533 flying the same Ventura aircraft, however, he would also be checked out in the Douglass Dauntless and the F6F-3N Hellcat.

On 19 May 1944, Lieutenant Schroeder took off from the deck of the USS *Long Island* and flew a Hellcat to Eniwetok in the Marshall Islands. He stayed there for the next year. However, instead of engaging enemy attacks by long-range Japanese Mitsubishi G4M Betty bombers as planned, he and his fellow pilots received intensive training to fill the void of action.

Thinking back on the experience he remembered, "I was not familiar with flying at night and it took a great deal of skill…I went through night fighter training under Black Mac Mc Gruder. He was a terrific pilot, a lieutenant colonel, and we were just second lieutenants at that time. He made you really work hard and learn. The F6F was a single seat fighter and you had to fly your instruments at night. You had radar too…so you had to learn a lot of new things…Because of Black Mac Mc Gruder, we became noted as pretty good pilots after awhile and we were respected by other pilots who didn't have those night flying skills."

During his tour of duty in the Marshall Islands, Schroeder flew in several combat situations and admitted that it was a frightening experience. "You didn't know if you were going to come back alive." With providence on his side, he always came back and though he never shot down an enemy plane, his night flying skills were useful for a different reason. "In the Pacific, B-24 patrol bombers would go on long range missions and get lost at night…They would send us 'night fighters' out to find them…We would have to be careful and say 'here I am, don't shoot me down' [I am trying to save you]…It was quite scary and a lot of responsibility." At least one B-24 squadron was saved as a result of his ability to find the lost patrol and lead them to safety. While Lieutenant Schroeder didn't receive a Distinguished Flying Cross at this time, he was gratified by the fact he saved so many of his comrades' lives. To Schroeder, that was the best award he could have received.

As he transitioned back to the United States after WWII, Schroeder got his first chance to fly the F7F Tigercat in October 1945. The aircraft quickly became his favorite, eclipsing the Hellcat, Bearcat, Corsair and the Skyraider. He often enjoyed matching his Tigercat against P-51 Mustangs. Schroeder was not only able to out maneuver them but he could accelerate faster and could climb faster than his compatriots in Mustangs. As the word spread of his prowess in the Tigercat, it was difficult to find a worthy competitor.

By December of 1952, Major Schroeder was assigned to the Marine All Weather Fighter Squadron VMF (N)-513, stationed at Kunsan and had the opportunity to fly both the Tigercat and the Skynight for night air support. During this part of the Korean War, the squadron was part of the Marine Aircraft Group 12, 1st Marine Aircraft Wing which was under operational control of the Far East Air Force's 5th Air Force, 3rd Bomb Wing. As a shore-based Marine Corps Squadron, they flew aircraft painted flat black with a very distinctive red "WF" painted on the tail and red numbers on the nose.

VMF (N)-513 carried a majority of the night road reconnaissance and interdiction missions for the 1st Marine Aircraft Wing. The Skynights were also used as night fighter escorts for the B-29 bombing missions carried out over North Korea by the Air Force.

During the spring of 1953, the Marine Corps manned a series of outposts only about ten miles northeast of Panmunjom. The outposts followed the mainline of resistance and were located just below the 38th Parallel. Known as the Nevada Cities, they were coded Vegas, Reno, Carson and Elko. For about a month, they were attacked involving intense hand-to-hand combat as the Chinese planned to gain permanent control of the outposts. A plan was developed to counteract this enemy aggression.

Describing this experience, Schroeder recalled, "We were stationed to support the ground Marines fighting the Chinese and the North Koreans…We were all night fighter pilots, all good pilots instrument trained…The enemy was putting pressure on our Marine ground troops, quite a bit of pressure…the Chinese and North Koreans were pouring troops in and our guys on the ground needed air support at night.

Because the situation had become critical, we had to figure out how we could do this because of the mountains in the dark – you couldn't see them! So, they came up with the idea to use big search lights… They put about four or five of these searchlights along a practice area…and there were only a couple of us who were trained to make these kinds of runs with napalm bombs under the wings. I was the first one… it was kind of hairy, but I raised my hand – I volunteered for the mission along with Lieutenant Thomas F. St. Dennis."

Major Schroeder and Lieutenant St. Dennis practiced daylight and nighttime missions on 7 and 9 April 1953. Then, an ordnance run was made on April 11th to obtain napalm bombs from the Air Force in Seoul. They had to come from Seoul because the Air Force had the equipment to properly mix the napalm, maximizing the effectiveness of the weapons.

On the evening of 12 April 1953, Major Schroeder led the pioneering mission to counteract the enemy and eliminate the threat. Schroeder recounted the three-hour mission. "We took off and headed to the target…we flew about 2,500 feet and ground control would vector us down and tell us when to start the mission. With my radar operator in the back seat, we dropped down between the mountains [with the aid of the search lights] and were low enough that we got some ground fire from the enemy. I estimated we were at about 7 or 800 feet and I got the word to drop my first bomb. I dropped it right on the Chinese and I lit the whole sky with a ball of fire. And I said, 'My God, what happened?' It was a tremendous impact because the whole valley was burning. The Chinese were desperate and they kept shooting at us, but they couldn't get near us…We did this twice and it extended into the early morning hours of April 13th. We just beat the hell out of them and the Chinese retreated…We defeated them that night by air. In effect, we saved the Nevada fire bases.

When I landed, I got word that the general wanted to see me later that morning, and at eight o'clock the general's car was waiting to pick me up at the barracks. As I got to his office, I couldn't believe what I saw. There were generals and colonels in a big circle; including General Maxwell Taylor, the Commanding General of the United Nations forces in Korea. At that point, General Taylor asked me if I would tell them what I had done. I was nervous but gave them an account of the mission. After I finished, General Taylor put his arm around me and said, 'You're getting the Distinguished Flying Cross.' I said, 'Wow! I can't believe it'." General Taylor then asked the Major if he would do it again. So, for seven nights, Schroeder flew similar missions that completely neutralized the enemy attacks.

The official citation elaborated on Schroeder's participation in "the development and evaluation of searchlight-illuminated night close air support assaults against heavily defended and well-entrenched enemy front-line positions, Major Schroeder carried out two low-level bombing and strafing attacks on the carefully camouflaged objective in the face of intense hostile antiaircraft fire. Diving to minimum altitude, he skillfully maneuvered his aircraft through the precipitous terrain and scored direct bomb hits on enemy personnel shelters…By his superb airmanship, courageous initiative and determination, Major Schroeder was largely responsible for the success of two missions that demolished four personnel shelters and inflicted heavy casualties on the enemy."

In all, Major Schroeder completed fifty-four night missions and twenty-four day missions in Korea; some more problematic than others. On a B-29 escort mission while flying a Skynight at about 33,000 feet, the seasoned combat pilot was chased by a MiG-15. Since the Russian plane had a higher ceiling than the Skynight, his adversary picked the engagement and confronted Schroeder with cannon fire. However, the Major had already pre-empted the attack with a diving starboard 180 degree turn and evaded the MiG in the clouds. He then let the jet make a pass and was gratified to see him break off and head across the Yalu River. Due to bad weather, Schroeder even had to make three passes at the runway on low fuel before he could make a successful approach. So drained from the experience, with his legs quivering, he had to be lifted out of the cockpit but was once again on the ground.

Throughout his twenty-year military career, Lieutenant Colonel Schroeder logged a total of 3,225 hours of flying and completed 200 night fighter combat missions. In all, he flew twenty-four different aircraft; the preponderance of which were fighters. While he would have stayed in the military for a thirty year career, because he truly loved to fly, his wife Carol, urged him to retire. Doing so, he made her very happy but in an unexpected twist of fate, she died of cancer shortly after his return to civilian life. Schroeder lamented, "It was hard to overcome…so I decided I'd go back to work again. I went to Columbia University in New York and got a Masters Degree…I got a job with Chase Manhattan Bank, became a vice president and was employed with them for a second career of twenty years."

Retired Lieutenant Colonel Schroeder rarely mentions his military exploits yet is vastly proud of his Distinguished Flying Cross. For this humble aviator, the value of receiving this recognition lies not in receiving public adulation but rather in the personal satisfaction of knowing he played a vital role in protecting American troops during World War II and Korea.

Notes

Lieutenant Colonel Chuck L. Schroeder, Distinguished Flying Cross citation, action date: 12 April 1953, Archives, the Distinguished Flying Cross Society, San Diego, CA.

Lieutenant Colonel Chuck L. Schroeder, oral history interview, interviewed by Dr. Barry A. Lanman, 28 July 2007, transcribed, the Distinguished Flying Cross Society Oral History Collection, the Distinguished Flying Cross Society, San Diego, CA.

Colonel Ken Tollefson, USAF (Ret.). Lt. Col. Charles L. Schroeder, USMC (Ret) F7F-3N Tigercat pilot (DFC), Flying Leatherneck's Log Book, (San Diego, CA: The Leatherneck Historical Foundation), Spring, 2010.

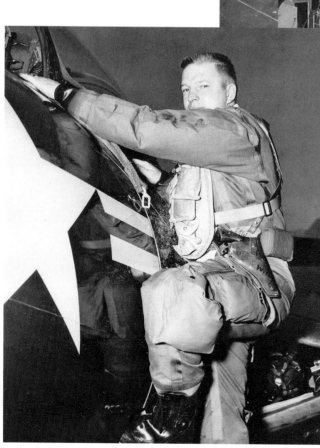

Top: Royce Williams battled seven MiGs for an hour and twenty-five minutes and lived to tell about it. He proudly pointed to the damage sustained in the confrontation. Middle: A Grumman Panther F9F-5 jet aircraft like, the one Royce Williams flew, rested on the deck of a carrier between missions during the Korean War. Bottom: Captain Royce Williams is considered a "MiG Mauler." Photographs courtesy of Royce Williams and the Tailhook Association

The "Silent" MiG Mauler

Captain E. Royce Williams, USN

"I was jumped by seven Soviet MiG-15s…It was one of the longest fighter engagements ever recorded with one American pilot involved."_____

Few terms are as revered by military aviators as "MiG Mauler." It signified a pilot who met up with a Russian MiG in a dogfight and won the confrontation. MiG Maulers were the pilots who came back and created legends as Top Gun instructors, and were the best of the best because they defeated an adversary flying a more advanced jet fighter. Royce Williams wasn't the first MiG Mauler but his exploits were so significant that the newly formed National Security Agency required the mission to be top secret and ordered his silence. Only in the last decade has his legendary dogfight been made public. With this declassification, he has been able to take his rightful place as a MiG Mauler.

Williams had not yet considered what path his life would take while playing in the wide open spaces of South Dakota before World War II. He certainly did not expect to join the Navy in 1943 and retire thirty-three years later as a Captain and an aviator's aviator. However, like a multitude of men coming of age during World War II and graduating from high school, he patriotically joined the Navy as a seaman in 1943, qualified as an aviation cadet and became a pilot by the end of the war. At that point in his career, he was offered and accepted a regular Navy commission and was sent to the University of Minnesota where he received a Bachelor's Degree. He then studied at the Monterey Naval Postgraduate School in Monterey, California.

Highly trained, Lieutenant Williams was poised for combat in Korea. Williams was assigned to Navy Fighter Squadron 781 (VF-781) in Carrier Air Group 102 aboard the USS *Oriskany* in Carrier Task Force 77. The combat assignment was clear; support operations against the North Korean communist aggressors, who had invaded South Korea, and drive them back north towards the Chinese and Soviet borders. Williams, along with his fellow pilots, flew the most advanced Grumman Panther F9F-5 jet aircraft.

Until the latter part of 1952, little aerial combat with MiGs had occurred, thus the Panthers were used in air to ground interdiction and close air support, providing protection for US ground troops. However, for Williams, that would change on 18 November 1952.

The carrier, *Oriskany,* was positioned off the northern coast of North Korea near Chongjin. Navy jets were clearly in striking distance of Soviet aircraft based in Viadivostok, Siberia. The situation was tense – on both sides. The stakes were high and a direct confrontation between the two powers could prove catastrophic. Accounting for the various military scenarios of an aggressive strike by the Soviet Union, the *Oriskany* established a Combat Air Patrol (CAP). The CAP was flown over the carrier as a protection against a surprise attack.

On a bitterly cold November day, with snow and low visibility, radar was required for all inbound and outbound flights, not to mention a rolling deck. Williams flew his first mission of the day over North Korean industrial targets strategically located near the border of the Soviet Union. As part of a large three carrier strike group, Williams participated in multiple bombing runs with minimal anti-aircraft fire. Following the successful interdiction mission all planes were recovered on their respective carriers.

The second mission of the day for Lieutenant Williams was a CAP mission which required him to fly protection over the carrier. The four Panther Jets expected orders to engage and repel any hostile aircraft flying toward the *Oriskany*. While the orders sounded ominous, in reality, no enemy aircraft had ever attempted an engagement near the vessel. Therefore, when Williams launched at 1:00 pm with three other Panthers, he was prepared for a rather boring ninety minutes flying circles around his carrier.

Once in the air the Panthers climbed to more than 12,000 feet reaching clear skies. But the crackle of the radio broke the silence and the complacency of the routine mission. Williams was apprised that bogies were eighty miles north of their position and headed on a course towards the carrier task force. The orders were clear; intercept the incoming aircraft. Lieutenant Williams made first visual contact as he cleared the clouds. The sight was both impressive and daunting. Seven silver MiG-15s well above 35,000 feet glistened in the sunlight as their distinctive contrails signaled a prelude to action. It appeared to be a confrontation of four Panthers with seven MiG-15s.

As the adrenaline started to kick in so did mechanical complications. The flight leader, Lieutenant Elwood experienced problems with his fuel pump and was ordered to fly over the *Oriskany*. Elwood's wingman was also ordered to fly back with him as protection. The odds were now two to seven as Williams and his wingman, Lieutenant Junior Grade Rowlands, continued towards the advancing MiGs. Forty-five miles from the carrier task force, the MiGs passed overhead and banked left as if they had decided to return to their home base in Siberia. Williams continued to shadow the seven MiGs and keep them in sight. However, without provocation, the Russian jets broke sharply back towards the two F9F-5 jets. As they did so, they divided themselves into two groups, made a steep dive and vanished from making vapor trails. Williams' words, "Lost contact," were chilling to the radio operator and his superiors. To the pilot's dismay, he learned that the bogies were no longer on the *Oriskany's* radar.

Williams remembers the events in the following way, "I was jumped by seven Soviet MiG-15's about sixty miles at sea off of Vladivostok, Russia…I have no statistics on it, but air battles normally are very short [three to five minutes] and they usually involve a lot of airplanes, but I was involved in this basically all by myself…It was one of the longest fighter engagements ever recorded with one American pilot involved. I had an hour and 25 minute mission off the *Oriskany*…I guess I was tangling with the MiGs for about thirty minutes or so…I was at full throttle the entire time." A master of understatement, Williams simply commented, "It was a very involved fight."

Due to the differential in numbers of aircraft and aircraft characteristics, the dogfight consisted mainly of hard turns at 26,000 feet. The blink of orange could also be seen by Williams as the MiGs fired at him. After Williams' first shots, his wingman followed a diving and smoking MiG out of the fight, leaving Williams alone to fight with six Russian jets. On two occasions, Williams headed directly towards the attacking MiGs with guns blazing while at other times he fired at a single overshooting MiG. When Rowlands returned, he was of little help because his guns had malfunctioned.

While on the tail of one MiG, Williams realized that he had the enemy on his tail. Calling for help, he evaded the attacker but was hit with a 37mm shell, which exploded into the jet. Williams recalled, "I lost rudder control and I had little use of my ailerons…I only had my elevators fully operating…and the Panther was sluggish. But I was able to dive into the snow storm below and dodge the stream of bullets that followed me down. As I approached our Task Force below the cloud cover, I saw our ships but they fired on me until they realized I was friendly." While the Panther was severely damaged, he had no wish to eject into the Sea of Japan so he kept the jet under control and used emergency procedures to lower the hydraulic deprived landing equipment. The captain of the *Oriskany* lined up the ship for his final approach and after a few nerve-racking moments, touched down on the deck of the carrier with his crippled airplane at an unusually fast airspeed of 170 knots.

With the rapidity of events, it was unclear to Williams what truly took place. "When we got through, I didn't know how well I had done…I was a busy boy and I fired all my ammunition in flight. The Navy was also at a loss to give a full accounting of the incident. However, the agents from the National Security Agency did have an assessment. From their monitoring of the engagement, NSA heard Russian voices, not Chinese or North Korean and they also tracked the MiGs from their take-off near Vladivostok, Russia until the 'remnant' returned. Thus, it was clear that this was a direct confrontation between the two superpowers. NSA was emphatic when they said, 'You can't tell anybody but you shot down at least three MiGs.'

I was then sent to see the President of the United States. Actually, President-elect Eisenhower as it was

November 1952 right after the election. He sat down with his arm around me and we had a chat with several four and five-star generals from the Bradley, Clark and Ridgeway group of World War II heroes. And it was a very nice event. The President-elect's visit to Korea was as a result of a pledge to personally see what needed to be done."

Surpassing the Distinguished Flying Cross, because of the strategic value of the incident and proved that the MiG-15 was now vulnerable in the air and so was the Soviet Union. Lieutenant Williams was awarded the Silver Star. It was the epitome of his career. However, there was one caveat to this amazing event. It was classified as top secret and he was sworn to silence. Even his superiors and his wife were not allowed to know the truth. As far as the government was concerned, the meeting of the two powers was "unofficial" – it never happened. Williams was satisfied that, "we reacted soberly and measured and nothing more came of it, at least that was ever revealed."

When the USS *Oriskany* and the air group completed their combat deployment, they were sent back to the United States. Lieutenant Williams then served in several assignments including a few in Washington, DC. He recalled some of his career highlights between Korea and Vietnam. "I was assigned to a tour with the Air Force flying F-86s, I served as a air weapons instructor, had ship duty and eventually commanded a squadron of Crusaders on an around the world cruise aboard the *Enterprise*…and I had a squadron of F4 Phantoms on the America and was then selected for air wing commander on the *Kitty Hawk* in the Pacific. By that time the Vietnam War was on….The assignment was great because it had all the latest and greatest aircraft – it was a big deck and had a lot of capability."

Williams, a commander during Vietnam, remembered his two most significant missions, the ones for which he received Distinguished Flying Crosses. "There was a bridge between Haiphong and Hanoi called Hidong Bridge. It was a value target and many attempts at destroying it were futile. They'd lost numerous pilots in the effort without any success of dropping the bridge. We had an air wing commander's meeting aboard the aircraft carrier where our task force commander had his command. The admiral said we're going to make a joint effort [between the Air Force and the Navy] to take down the bridge. I raised my hand to speak and said, 'If you don't mind sir, I would prefer taking it as an individual effort instead of jointly with all the other air wings on all the other aircraft carriers out there.' They were pleased to let me do this and I was authorized to do the mission so I went back to my carrier and planned it. I had a lot of training in tactics, both with the Air Force and the Navy and I wanted to try out something new. I sent all of our other aircraft in their normal assignments for the day and I took eight A-6 aircraft and twelve F-4 Phantoms, and we were fully loaded and briefed on everybody's individual target.

We took off on 17 April 1966 and didn't turn on any electronic equipment, radios or anything. Everything was just pre-planned. We rendezvoused below 400 feet and hit the beach at 450 knots or better and just pressed on in fast, popped up, came down and did a job. Then we all went [on] our pre-planned exit routes and returned to the carrier unscathed. I was sent the BDA [bomb damage assessments] at the end and they showed that we had dropped three of the five spans, and had otherwise damaged the area fairly well…I was flying in an F-4 that day and we did quite a job on the surrounding anti-aircraft defenses.

The next mission for which I received a Distinguished Flying Cross, was also during my deployment on the *Kitty Hawk*, about a month-and-a-half after my first DFC mission. I led a group of F-4 Phantoms on an attack of an airstrip at a ship base, north of Haiphong. As we came in, there were several Soviet supply ships unloading their supplies in support of the North Vietnamese and we fairly well destroyed the runways and took out a lot of their defenses…We were given strict orders not to touch the shipping. That was a no no… However, it scared them enough that the ships got underway and went out to sea."

In addition to his missions which warranted DFCs, he also had a few close calls. He added, "I've had some real zingers. I was the first pilot to ever bring a Phantom back with both engines on fire and my back seat guy had to eject…I sneaked this thing back aboard in afterburner with barely enough power… and I did it because you have to get an airplane back to diagnose the problems. Until that time, they had lost sixteen airplanes with everybody jumping out and they never knew what caused the problem. So this gave them something to diagnose and they were eventually able to solve the problem."

He assessed his tour in Vietnam in the following manner: "I had lost a lot of my pilots and air crews and I think it was considered, nonetheless, a very successful deployment…I came back to the next deployment as a naval flight officer…The reason for this was, in years previous, I had broken my back in a plane crash. And they decided that it wasn't really proper for me to be at the actual control of the aircraft as a pilot flying off the aircraft carrier. So I went through a quick schooling, became a naval flight officer and came on the second tour. When I concluded my assignment I was selected to serve next as the Executive Assistant and Senior Aid to DCNO, Deputy Chief of Naval Operations." He continued in that position until Sybil Stockdale, wife of Admiral Stockdale [POW and Medal of Honor recipient], came to town and had lunch with the Secretary of the Navy, Chief of Naval Personnel and his boss. She convinced them to make Captain Williams the coordinator for prisoner of war matters for the Navy Department. Among his final duties, before retirement in 1980, he commanded a ship, the *El Dorado*, served as Chief of Staff for Commander Fleet Air, Western Pacific, held a leadership role as the Assistant Chief of Command and Control Centers CINCPAC and was the Inspector General, CINCPAC.

Captain Williams recently reflected on his military career which included over 4,000 hours of flying and 500 plus traps (carrier landings) on twelve carriers. "I was proud to serve in the United States Navy and during wartime. I think if I'd not gotten involved in it, I would have been disappointed in myself. My dad was in World War I and his sons, my brother and I, were in the rest of the wars…As a young man, I was motivated to become an Eagle Scout because it was an entrance into naval aviation before World War II…I was our community's first Eagle Scout…and I became a naval aviator."

Having served in three wars, received two Distinguished Flying Cross medals, a Silver Star and other commendations and medals, Captain Royce Williams was informed by a friend and ranking government official that his Korean exploit with the MiGs had finally been declassified. After almost five decades, he has been recognized for his aviation prowess and has assumed his rightful place in military aviation history.

Notes

Captain Royce E. Williams, Distinguished Flying Cross citation, action date: 17 April 1966, Archives, the Distinguished Flying Cross Society, San Diego, CA.

Captain Royce E. Williams, oral history interviews, interviewed by Dr. Barry A. Lanman, 26 July 2008 and 19 July 2009, transcribed, the Distinguished Flying Cross Society Oral History Collection, the Distinguished Flying Cross Society, San Diego, CA.

Tillman Brown, "Where are They Now?" The Hook, Winter 2009, 19-23.

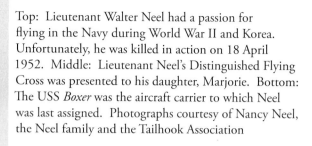

Top: Lieutenant Walter Neel had a passion for flying in the Navy during World War II and Korea. Unfortunately, he was killed in action on 18 April 1952. Middle: Lieutenant Neel's Distinguished Flying Cross was presented to his daughter, Marjorie. Bottom: The USS *Boxer* was the aircraft carrier to which Neel was last assigned. Photographs courtesy of Nancy Neel, the Neel family and the Tailhook Association

With Posthumous Pride

Lieutenant Commander Walter P. Neel, USN

"Killed in action when his plane was hit by enemy fire…He gallantly gave his life for his country."

After the bombing of Pearl Harbor, thousands of young men clamored to enlist in the armed services. Walter P. Neel was no exception. At age eighteen, he left Pasadena Junior College, in Pasadena, California, to join the Navy and fly. Upon completion of flight training, Neel served as a flight instructor for the duration of World War II, never having a chance to participate in combat.

In love with the Navy and flying, he continued his military career during peacetime. However, with the escalation of hostilities in Korea, he was assigned to his first tour of combat duty. Based on the aircraft carrier USS *Boxer*, he was assigned to Air Group 2, Attack Squadron 65, flying the AD-4 Skyraider. As operations officer, he saw combat from 23 March to 18 April 1952. For Lieutenant Commander Neel, it seemed a chance of a lifetime; the chance to experience the action he craved.

After flying numerous missions for about three weeks, the pilot was assigned a bombing and strafing mission on 18 April 1952. From official accounts, Lieutenant Commander Neel demonstrated consistent accuracy as he destroyed twelve enemy supply buildings and fifteen hostile vehicles. He and his squadron also made twenty-four railroad cuts and rendered the enemy's transportation system inoperative in that area. According to R. W. Anderson, Secretary of the Navy, "On one occasion he led his flight in the face of intense and accurate antiaircraft fire in assaults against the vital enemy railroad center at Kowon and succeeded in carrying out two damaging attacks on the assigned target. Regrouping his planes, he initiated a final assault in a gallant attempt to inflict maximum destruction on the railroad center. Killed in action when his plane was hit by enemy fire, the Distinguished Flying Cross citation noted, "Lieutenant Commander Neel, by his superb airmanship, outstanding courage and unwavering devotion to duty, contributed in large measure to the successful completion of many difficult missions and upheld the highest traditions of the United States Naval Service. He gallantly gave his life for his country."

While the story would normally have ended there, his has a unique postscript. When Peggy Jo Neel received the worst possible news about her husband's death, she already had a little girl and was expecting another child in less than a month. With the birth of her second daughter, Nancy, painful memories were suppressed but life slowly returned to normal. Having never known her father, Nancy Neel, grew through her formative years and into adulthood without a desire to learn the details of her father's life; especially his military exploits. However, as she matured, Nancy grew curious about her family's true heritage. Though concerned about enduring painful memories, she was eager to resolve the personal mystery that surrounded the father she never knew.

After graduating from San Diego State College in 1975, Nancy explained, "I held countless jobs before attending the University of California, San Diego for my teaching credential in 1983. While taking a break from one such job, I was offered to dog and house sit for a friend in Idyllwild, California, where I had graduated from a private high school…One evening, after a tiresome trek through the forest with the dogs, I flipped through the available television stations up on the mountain and found an 'oldies' network with a wonderful black and white movie. It was about an American pilot in the Korean War, the wife he'd left behind and the trials of the men on board an aircraft carrier. The actors were all handsome, intelligent and brave. The story was credible, after all, historical. There was some Hollywood stunt flying, lots of winning but also some tragedy. All in all, it was a story that sounded all too familiar. That night, I dreamt intense images from the scenes in the movie and of my father. He somehow asked me why I didn't know him and why I hadn't read anything about him, especially after he had expended so much energy revealing himself through his correspondence. When I awoke the next morning, I was struck by how young he seemed, younger than I was at the time.

I called my mother and told her I wanted to talk with her but I didn't tell her why. Once in San Diego, I had every intention of asking to borrow the letters he sent to her while in Korea, which I wanted to take back with me to read for what remained of the summer. To my surprise, my mother met me at the door of her house and handed me the letters along with a box of documents and artifacts. She had watched the same movie that evening and had a similar dream! Few things in my life have been as eerie as that experience. After sharing with one another the strangeness of it all, I was instructed to take the box and get to know my father…and get to know him I did!"

As Nancy explored the old heirlooms, a treasure trove of documents presented themselves. Among the prized possessions were black and white images of the USS *Boxer*, attack planes like the ones flown by her dad, and a military portrait of a very young and handsome naval aviator. An official letter from the Secretary of the Navy, containing the citation for the posthumous Distinguished Flying Cross, gave her the factual account of his combat experiences and chronicled the last heroic day of her father's life.

While the documents were enlightening, the letters were exactly what she craved and one stood apart from the rest. It was an eight-page letter, written in Neel's script on USS *Boxer* stationary. In the letter, the young aviator stated that he had seen both of the movies that were being shown that night: *A Very Unusual Thing* with Jimmy Stewart and one of Betty Grable's movies. Instead of watching the movies again, he spent his evening penning an in-depth letter to his wife, as he put it, "to my first and only love."

The letter detailed his personal account of life on board an aircraft carrier, his trials and tribulations during combat and dealing with the boredom of waiting for some action. While day-to-day activities were illuminated, it was the stream of consciousness about his aspirations, his hopes and dreams that truly gave insight into the psyche of the man.

Nancy recounted, "I met a very opinionated, gentle, educated, respectful and spiritual young man with a sense of humor…I also learned about his internal conflict with being on missions to destroy the very thing he was trying to protect…life. He questioned the philosophical issues I had hoped he would. Most of all, it revealed the love for his family and his plans for the future." The letter, his last, was postmarked on 6 April 1952, just twelve days before his rendezvous with destiny.

Fifty-seven years after Lieutenant Commander Neel posthumously received the DFC, Nancy joined the Distinguished Flying Cross Society. The feeling of pride could be seen in her eyes along with a sense of peace and serenity. The history that was revealed regarding her father's life, heroism and aerial achievement gave her the best gift of all – the gift of her father.

Notes

Lieutenant Commander Walter P. Neel, Distinguished Flying Cross citation, action date: 18 April 1952, Archives, the Distinguished Flying Cross Society, San Diego, CA.

Nancy Neel, oral history interviews, interviewed by Dr. Barry A. Lanman, 12 March 2008, the Distinguished Flying Cross Society Oral History Collection, the Distinguished Flying Cross Society, San Diego, CA.

Memorable Moments of the Distinguished Flying Cross

Korea

It's wonderful to remember the success of a mission where no Americans got hurt. The Distinguished Flying Cross epitomizes extraordinary service. It is something that a combat pilot recognizes and truly appreciates."

First Lieutenant Richard Harry Deihl, USAF

Colonel James Jabara, USAAF / USAF
First American Jet Ace in US History

During World War II, James Jabara, an American of Lebanese descent, received his wings as a second lieutenant during October 1943. Jabara flew two combat tours in Europe as a P-51 pilot and was attached to the 355th Group of the Eighth Air Force, USAAF. During these tours, he flew 108 combat missions and was credited with destroying 1½ enemy planes in aerial combat and 4 planes on the ground.

During Korea, Colonel Jabara was assigned to the 4th Fighter Interceptor Wing, 5th Air Force, USAF, in December 1950. By January 1951, he had flown five combat missions in F-86 Saberjets and had damaged one MiG-15 enemy jet fighter in aerial combat.

In April 1951, Colonel Jabara downed six MiG-15s in just over two weeks making him the first US jet ace. On a second tour, for which he volunteered, Jabara shot down another nine MiG-15s for a total of fifteen victories.

Colonel Jabara was awarded two Distinguished Flying Crosses in World War II and five DFCs while in Korea. He also received the Distinguished Service Cross and two Silver Stars. [1] In a sad twist of fate, Colonel Jabara was tragically killed in a car accident in Florida in 1966 as he was preparing for a tour of duty in Vietnam.

Captain Gustave F. Lueddeke, USMC
Pioneered the Use of Helicopters For Observation and Rescue Missions

One of the first helicopter pilots cited for bravery in Korea, Captain Gustave F. Lueddeke, Jr. had an astonishing career with the Marine Corps. He served in WWII before becoming one of two Marine pilots to pioneer the use of helicopters in Korea. He earned accolades as a member of the First Marine Division for the rescue of at least eighty soldiers, some behind enemy lines and some out at sea. Among his numerous awards were the Silver Star, two Distinguished Flying Crosses and eight Air Medals.

The Distinguished Flying Cross medals were awarded for flying a combined seventy observation missions between August and November 1950 over hostile, combative territory in an unarmed helicopter. Lueddeke was also among seven helicopter pilots assigned to cover the evacuation of Hungnam in an enormous effort to withdraw the bulk of UN forces from eastern North Korea in December 1950. [2] For the number of lives he saved, Lueddeke received an ace rating. After his service in Korea, the aviator was stricken with polio at the age of thirty-one. Captain Lueddeke was buried with full military honors at Arlington National Cemetery.

Lieutenant Colonel Hans J. "Pete" Petermann, USAAF / USAF
Navigator/Bombardier/Radar Observer

Hans J. Petermann served as a USAAF navigator and a radar observer in World War II. Using those same skills in Korea, he was a United States Air Force navigator, bombardier and radar observer flying B-26 models B and C Invaders from September 1951 to May 1952.

Petermann, a lieutenant at the time, received a DFC in Korea for serving, "as navigator-bombardier of a B-26 attack bomber on the night of 14 October 1951 while participating in aerial flight against an enemy of the United Nations. While reconnoitering the main supply routes north to Pyongyang, North Korea, Lieutenant Petermann sighted a convoy of eight vehicles moving south. An immediate low-level bombing attack was pressed under his expert direction and one napalm bomb was dropped. Two vehicles were observed to burn and explode. Another convoy of twelve trucks was sighted nearby and again Lieutenant Petermann verbally directed his pilot on to the target with consummate skill. Intense and accurate flak was encountered in the vicinity, but Lieutenant Petermann calmly pinpointed their positions thus aiding the pilot in taking evasive action while keeping the trucks under continuous attack. So highly coordinated was this action that three trucks were destroyed by fire and explosions and two more probably damaged. Lieutenant Petermann's exemplary navigational skill and untiring efforts are a credit to himself, his organization, and the United States Air Force."[3] Lieutenant Colonel Petermann retired from the Air Force in 1969.

Captain Henry B. Gibbia, Jr., USAF
Attacked Sixty-Seven Enemy Vehicles in a B-26

Henry B. Gibbia, Jr., a B-26 pilot, was a member of the 90th Bomb Squadron, Light Night Intruder and served in the K-8 section of Korea in 1950-1951. He received a Distinguished Flying Cross on 6 September 1951. The DFC citation recounted, "First Lieutenant Henry B. Gibbia, Jr. distinguished himself by extraordinary achievement while participating in aerial flight. As pilot of a B-26 attack bomber on a night intruder mission over Communist-held Korea, Lieutenant Gibbia took under attack a total of sixty-seven enemy vehicles moving east from Songch'on along the main supply route from Pyongyang to Wonsan, Korea.

Despite a heavy haze in the area which made low-altitude flying extremely hazardous in the mountainous terrain, and intense automatic weapons fire from gun positions in the hills along the road, Lieutenant Gibbia repeatedly made low-level bombing and strafing attacks on the vehicles. As a result of these attacks, seven vehicles were destroyed, twenty-four were severely damaged and use of the supply route was temporarily denied the enemy due to the burning trucks on the road.

As a result of this mission, supplies and equipment vital to the enemy war effort were destroyed; seriously hampering the enemy's war potential. Through his outstanding airmanship, courage and selfless devotion to duty, Lieutenant Gibbia has brought great credit upon himself, his organization and the United States Air Force."[4]

First Lieutenant J. Logan Fagner, USAF
With Fighter Escort, Made a Daring Rescue in a Helicopter

First Lieutenant J. Logan Fagner had grown accustomed to his vulnerable position as a helicopter pilot in Korea. However, he was put to the test on 25 October 1951 when he flew a mission into an area near Taegwang-ni, Korea. Fagner's report to his superiors included the fact that he had observed more than a thousand enemy troops in the vicinity of a downed airman who had parachuted from a disabled aircraft which had burst into flames after being hit by enemy fire.

The documentation from First Lieutenant Fagner's DFC citation re-counted that he, "flew with fighter escort directly to the position. Locating the victim in an area where shells were bursting, Lieutenant Fagner made a fast, low approach, executed a quick stop, and picked up the observer by the use of cable hoist and sling. Lieutenant Fagner then climbed his helicopter to altitude as he reeled the observer in and transported him safely to the nearest Mobile Army Surgical Hospital where the victim was treated for serious burns suffered before parachuting. By his high degree of heroism at the risk of his own life, Lieutenant Fagner has brought great credit upon himself and the United States Air Force." [5]

Lieutenant Harold V. Pepper, USN
F9F Pilot Destroyed Supplies and Equipment to Frontline Enemy Troops

Lieutenant Harold V. Pepper was a pilot in Fighter Squadron 781, which operated off of the USS *Bon Homme Richard*. Their normal missions were attacks on hostile North Korean and Chinese Communist forces. Lieutenant Pepper participated in twenty armed reconnaissance missions on vehicular and rail routes most frequently used by the enemy.

His first Distinguished Flying Cross was awarded for actions ranging from 31 May to 18 July 1951. His DFC citation explained that, "in the face of great enemy anti-aircraft fire he aided his division in the destruction of enemy rail and supply facilities, strafed enemy gun positions, and destroyed numerous enemy vehicular and rail cars in the Changjin, Orori and Hungnan areas."

Pepper's second DFC was conferred for a mission on 2 November 1951. The documentation supporting his medal included the following. "While on an armed reconnaissance mission…Lieutenant Pepper was flying as flight leader of a flight of F9F jet aircraft when he discovered and led his flight against an enemy troop and supply convoy in the enemy held Tanchon area…Lieutenant Pepper persistently attacked this convoy with low-level rocket and strafing runs causing an estimated one hundred fifty casualties among the troops which ran from their troop carriers and exploding and burning eleven of the supply vehicles…The effective destruction of this supply group interrupted a delivery of vitally needed supplies and equipment to the frontline enemy troops."[6] In addition, he was commended for his courage and gallant devotion to duty.

First Lieutenant Lynn E. Thomas, USAF
F-80 Pilot was Hit by Anti-aircraft Battery and Then Silenced his Enemy

First Lieutenant Lynn E. Thomas was awarded the Distinguished Flying Cross for an amazing feat of skillful flying on 9 March 1952. The citation documenting his award recounted that he received the medal, "for exemplary determination, extraordinary flying skill and courage on a combat mission over North Korea. As element leader in a flight of four…F-80 type aircraft, Lieutenant Thomas was entering his bomb run when his aircraft was struck in the right tip tank by a forty…millimeter projectile, severing the tip tank and placing the aircraft in a spin.

He recovered from the spin and spotted the anti-aircraft battery which was continuing to fire at his flight. He then altered his bomb run at the battery, which he demolished with a direct hit, thereby ensuring the safety of the flight. By his skill, determination, and high personal courage, Lieutenant Thomas has brought great credit upon himself and the United States Air Force."[7]

First Lieutenant Donald M. Jones, USAF
Directed a "Bomber Stream" in Obscured Visibility

On 12 October 1952, First Lieutenant Donald M. Jones was a navigator-bombardier on a B-26 mission over enemy held North Korean territory. Despite obscured visibility, he displayed outstanding bombing and navigational skill as he quickly located the pre-briefed target near Yongchong, Korea. As lead ship in a pathfinder night interdiction mission, Jones initiated a series of bombing attacks which resulted in fourteen fires and secondary explosions.

His DFC citation summarized the events which transpired during the interdiction mission. "Orbiting the target, Lieutenant Jones aided in directing the attacks of the following aircraft in such a manner that a large portion of the assigned target was destroyed. He remained in the target area exposed to fire from enemy automatic weapons and the ever-present threat of attack by enemy aircraft until all the aircraft of

the bomber stream had completed their attacks. As a result of this highly successful mission vital enemy supplies and storage facilities were destroyed."[8] First Lieutenant Jones was commended for his skill and his courage under fire. (Jones - right)

Airman Second Class, Joseph E. Riley, USAF
B-26 Gunner Saved his Crew - Twice

Airman Second Class, Joseph E. Riley served as a B-26 gunner in the 452nd Bomb Wing Light of the 5th Air Force. On 10 March 1952, Riley was awarded a Distinguished Flying Cross for actions in the vicinity of Namsi-dong, Korea. During a night interdiction mission, he sighted a large convoy of enemy vehicles and participated in numerous glide bombing attacks. He also assisted the pilot on a series of low level strafing passes. These actions resulted in the destruction of vital enemy supplies and transportation facilities.

While these were noteworthy, his quick reactions and expertise were even more heroic when he saved his crew on two separate occasions. On 29 December 1951, his first emergency situation occurred. The DFC citation recorded that, "while Corporal Riley [USAF rank at the time] was working in the bay area the bomb fell off its shackles and scattered frag bombs all over the bomb bay. Also the bombs were armed because the pins were pulled when they fell and were very sensitive and could trip by the bomb nose hitting anything. Riley requested the bomb doors to be opened, hung on to some service lines which ran along the bomb bay with no parachute on and cleared the bombs. Despite the hazardous condition encountered by Corporal Riley he saved the lives of the remaining crewmen."[9]

Less than a month later on 7 January 1952, a similar situation occurred when an 80 pound incendiary bomb had released from its shackles and came to rest on a 500 pound bomb that would not release from its shackles. To make matters worse, the pin had been pulled. With the bomb doors open, a temperature of minus 35 degrees and no parachute, Corporal Riley was able to release the ordnance and save the entire crew. In all, Joseph Riley, received three DFCs for heroic deeds. (Riley - bottom, center)

First Lieutenant Sam J. Ruvolo, USAF
Displayed Outstanding Navigation and
Bombing Skill

First Lieutenant Sam J. Ruvolo, United States Air Force was assigned to the 17th Bombardment Wing, Light, 5th Air Force and served as a navigator-bombardier on a B-26.

While his day-to-day work was exemplary, he received a Distinguished Flying Cross for extraordinary achievement while on a mission which took place on 22 February 1953. The DFC citation explained that while, "engaged in a night interdiction mission, Lieutenant Ruvolo displayed outstanding navigation and bombing skill. In the vicinity of Wonsan, Korea, a large enemy convoy was sighted. Five bombing attacks were made which caused thirteen secondary explosions and five sustained fires and resulted in the destruction of thirteen ammunition laden vehicles. These attacks were pressed over extremely hazardous mountain terrain despite the ever present threat of attack by enemy aircraft and were continued until all ordnance was expended. As a result of this highly successful mission, vital enemy supplies and transportation facilities were destroyed."[10]   First Lieutenant Ruvolo was also cited for his personal courage and devotion to duty.   (Ruvolo - right)

First Lieutenant Lear H. Simpson, USAF
Night Interdiction Missions in the B-26

On 17 September 1952, First Lieutenant Lear H. Simpson, a United States Air Force pilot, received a Distinguished Flying Cross. The DFC citation recounted his exploits in the air. "Flying as a pilot of a B-26 type aircraft, engaged in a night interdiction mission, Lieutenant Simpson displayed outstanding airmanship and flying skill. In the vicinity of Kowon, Korea, a large enemy convoy was sighted. Seven bombing attacks were made which caused six secondary explosions and one very large sustained fire and resulted in the

destruction of eleven vehicles and a fuel supply area. These attacks were pressed over hazardous mountain terrain despite intense fire from enemy automatic weapons and were continued until all ordnance was expended. As a result of this highly successful mission vital enemy supplies and transportation facilities were destroyed. By his courage and devotion to duty, Lieutenant Simpson brought credit upon himself and the United States Air Force."[11] (Simpson - right)

First Lieutenant Edwin E. Hatton, USAF
Attacked a Train in a B-26

As a B-26 pilot in the United States Air Force, First Lieutenant Edwin E. Hatton was accustomed to various interdiction missions. Many were convoys and other targets of opportunity; however, Lieutenant Hatton received a Distinguished Flying Cross for a mission on 24 April 1952 involving a train.

The Distinguished Flying Cross citation for Lieutenant Hatton certified that, "Hatton displayed outstanding skill and airmanship. Sighting a locomotive and ten boxcars in the vicinity of Kowon, he immediately initiated a series of bombing and low-level strafing attacks, which resulted in the destruction of the locomotive and all of the boxcars.

Despite heavy fire from anti-aircraft weapons, Lieutenant

Hatton continued to press the attack until the complete destruction of the train was assured. As a result of this highly successful mission vital enemy supplies and transportation facilities were destroyed."[12] Lieutenant Hatton was commended for his personal courage, outstanding ability and devotion to duty.

Airman First Class Richard N. Brace, Jr., USAF
Extinguished a Fire on Board his Aircraft to complete the Mission_____

Airman First Class Richard N. Brace, Jr. of the United States Air Force, was a gunner with the 3rd Bombardment Wing, Light, 5th Air Force. Flying on a B-26 attack bomber, Airman Brace participated in many missions, however, one mission proved to be his most defining moment. On 16 July 1953 during an armed reconnaissance mission over the enemy's main supply routes between Sunchon and Pyongyang, Korea, a fire was observed in the air compressor located in the bomb bay and gunner's compartment. Airman Brace's DFC citation commented that, "the fire was rapidly spreading throughout the rear bomb bay and gunner's compartment, and presented an immediate serious threat to the safety of the aircraft and crew.

Airman Brace, without hesitation or regard for his personal safety proceeded to attack the fire in a most efficient manner. After calmly describing the situation to the pilot, he grasped a fire extinguisher, entered the bomb bay, which was fully loaded with high explosives, and extinguished the fire thereby permitting completion of the mission which resulted in the destruction of two enemy vehicles."[13] He was commended for his outstanding courage, quick thinking and devotion to duty.

Admiral Thomas B. Hayward, USN
Skillful Pilot in Korea became Four Star Admiral_____

During World War II, Thomas B. Hayward served as an enlisted sailor. After the war, he attended the US Naval Academy, graduated in 1947 and then became a naval aviator. Hayward flew 146 combat sorties with Fighter Squadron 51 in the Korean War. During that time, Lieutenant, Junior Grade, Thomas B. Hayward was awarded the Distinguished Flying Cross for heroism and extraordinary achievement in aerial flight as a pilot of a jet fighter plane attached to Fighter Squadron 51, based on board the USS *Valley Forge*, during operations against enemy forces on 8 April 1953. Hayward's superiors wrote in the DFC citation that, "leading a four-plane flight in a strike against a camouflaged and heavily defended enemy troop billeting and supply area, Lieutenant, Junior Grade, Hayward skillfully directed a series of well-coordinated attacks in the face of intense and accurate hostile anti-aircraft fire, personally destroying eight buildings and damaging five others.

Subsequently, when the division proceeded on an armed reconnaissance of the Majon-ni-Wonsan supply route, expending their remaining ordnance on camouflaged trucking shelters, he personally destroyed two additional buildings and damaged three others. By his superb airmanship, courage and steadfast devotion to duty, Lieutenant, Junior Grade, Hayward contributed materially to the reduction of the enemy's war-making potential and upheld the highest traditions of the United States Naval Service."[14]

Following his meritorious service in Korea, Thomas Hayward not only flew combat missions from, but later commanded the aircraft carrier USS *America* during the Vietnam War. With superlative leadership skills, he became a of four star admiral and served as chief of naval operations from 1978 to 1982.

Lieutenant Colonel Wallie W. Waltonen, USAF
Interdiction Missions through Mountainous Terrain under Intense Fire_____

Wallie W. Waltonen joined the United States Air Force on 12 May 1950. He had been an engineer in Menominee, Michigan prior to the Korean War but trained as a pilot and was sent to Korea. On 3 May 1953, First Lieutenant Waltonen participated in actions which merited a Distinguished Flying Cross. The account on the DFC citation stated, "Flying as a pilot of a B-26 type aircraft, 17th Bombardment Wing Light, Fifth Air Force, engaged in a night interdiction mission, Lieutenant Waltonen displayed outstanding airmanship and flying skill. In the vicinity of Singo-san, Korea, a large enemy convoy was sighted. Six bombing attacks were made which caused six secondary explosions and four sustained fires and resulted in the destruction of nine vehicles.

These attacks were pressed over hazardous mountain terrain despite intense fire from enemy automatic weapons and were continued until all ordnance was expended. As a result of this highly successful mission vital enemy supplies and transportation facilities were destroyed."[15] Waltonen left the Air Force on 28 September 1953 and flew commercial airlines after his Korean War experiences. (Waltonen - bottom, second from right)

First Lieutenant Bradley Gaylord, Jr., USAF
Reconnaissance and Air Control in an Unarmed T-6 Under Fire_____

First Lieutenant Bradley Gaylord, Jr. served as a pilot in the United States Air Force and was attached to the 6147th Tactical Control Group, 5th Air Force. His role was significantly different from flying bombers on interdiction missions. Lieutenant Gaylord flew unarmed T-6 aircraft and received a Distinguished Flying Cross for the following extraordinary achievement on 27 April 1953. "While on a tactical control mission north of 'Big Nori Hill' on the Western Front in Korea, Lieutenant Gaylord showed great skill in directing a flight of fighter-bombers in an attack on enemy strong-points consisting of two automatic weapons positions, two mortar positions, nineteen bunkers and twelve caves. After making a low altitude reconnaissance of the target area, Lieutenant Gaylord contacted the fighter-bombers and led them to the target.

Despite intense and accurate anti-aircraft and automatic weapons fire, Lieutenant Gaylord remained over the target area at low altitude while directing the four fighter-bombers in their attack runs. Lieutenant Gaylord made a post strike reconnaissance of the target and observed that the strike effectively damaged eight bunkers, four caves, five firing bays and one hundred yards of trench. By his personal courage and devotion to duty, Lieutenant Gaylord has brought credit upon himself and the United States Air Force."[16]

Captain Salvatore S. Sala, USAF
Interdicted the Enemy in "Sub-marginal" Weather and Restricted Visibility

Captain Salvatore S. Sala, like so many of his compatriots, served in World War II and then in Korea. During World War II, Sala flew "over the hump" from India to China as part of the ATC – 4th Group, 59th Squadron, USAAF, between 1942 and 1944. He then became part of the ATC – India Wing from 1944-1945. Surprisingly, he did not receive a DFC for this extremely dangerous flying over the Himalayan Mountains.

However, Captain Sala did receive a Distinguished Flying Cross on 23 April 1953 for a mission while flying a B-26 when he was attached to the 17th Bombardment Wing Light, Fifth Air Force, USAF. While participating in a rather typical interdiction mission for Korea, Sala was recognized in the DFC citation for, "outstanding airmanship and flying skill. In spite of sub-marginal weather and restricted visibility, a large enemy convoy was sighted in the vicinity of Wonson, Korea. Numerous bombing attacks were made which caused several secondary explosions and four sustained fires and resulted in the destruction of seven vehicles and damaged numerous additional vehicles. Despite the present threat of enemy fire and enemy aircraft, Captain Sala was highly successful in completing his mission which resulted in the destruction of vital enemy supply and transportation facilities."[17]

Photographs courtesy of the DFC recipients and/or their families
except for the following:

Page 128:   Southern California Friends of Aces
Page 136:   United States National Archives

Notes

[1] Colonel James Jabara, Distinguished Flying Cross citations, action dates: 22 November 1944, 29 May 1945, 30 April 1951, 4 June, 1951, 26 May 1953, 10 June 1953 and 16 June 1953, Archives, the Distinguished Flying Cross Society, San Diego, CA.

[2] Captain Gustave F. Lueddeke, Distinguished Flying Cross citation, action date: August – November 1950, Archives, the Distinguished Flying Cross Society, San Diego, CA.

[3] Lieutenant Colonel Hans J. "Pete" Petermann, Distinguished Flying Cross citation, action date: 14 October 1951, Archives, the Distinguished Flying Cross Society, San Diego, CA.

[4] Captain Henry B. Gibbia, Jr., Distinguished Flying Cross citation, action date: 6 September 1951, Archives, the Distinguished Flying Cross Society, San Diego, CA.

[5] First Lieutenant J. Logan Fagner, Distinguished Flying Cross citation, action date: 25 October 1951, Archives, the Distinguished Flying Cross Society, San Diego, CA.

[6] Lieutenant Harold V. Pepper, Distinguished Flying Cross citation, action dates: 18 July 1951 and 2 November 1951, Archives, the Distinguished Flying Cross Society, San Diego, CA.

[7] First Lieutenant Lynn E. Thomas, Distinguished Flying Cross citation, action date: 9 March 1952, Archives, the Distinguished Flying Cross Society, San Diego, CA.

[8] First Lieutenant Donald M. Jones, Distinguished Flying Cross citation, action date: 12 October 1952, Archives, the Distinguished Flying Cross Society, San Diego, CA.

[9] Airmen, Joseph E. Riley, Distinguished Flying Cross citation, action dates: 10 March 1951, 29 December 1951 and 7 January 1952, Archives, the Distinguished Flying Cross Society, San Diego CA.

[10] First Lieutenant Sam J. Ruvolo, Distinguished Flying Cross citation, action date: 22 February 1953, Archives, the Distinguished Flying Cross Society, San Diego, CA.

[11] First Lieutenant Lear H. Simpson, Distinguished Flying Cross citation, action date: 17 September 1952, Archives, the Distinguished Flying Cross Society, San Diego, CA.

[12] First Lieutenant Edwin E. Hatton, Distinguished Flying Cross citation, action date: 24 April 1952, Archives, the Distinguished Flying Cross Society, San Diego, CA.

[13] Airman First Class Richard N. Brace, Jr., Distinguished Flying Cross citation, action date: 16 July 1953, Archives, the Distinguished Flying Cross Society, San Diego, CA.

[14] Admiral Thomas B. Hayward, Distinguished Flying Cross citation, action date: 8 April 1953, Archives, the Distinguished Flying Cross Society, San Diego, CA.

[15] First Lieutenant Wallie W. Waltonen, Distinguished Flying Cross citation, action date: 3 May 1953, Archives, the Distinguished Flying Cross Society, San Diego, CA.

[16] First Lieutenant Bradley Gaylord, Jr., Distinguished Flying Cross citation, action date: 27 April 1953, Archives, the Distinguished Flying Cross Society, San Diego, CA.

[17] Captain Salvatore S. Sala, Distinguished Flying Cross citation, action date: 23 April 1953, Archives, the Distinguished Flying Cross Society, San Diego, CA.

Chapter 4

Stories of the Distinguished Flying Cross:

Vietnam

As with previous wars and conflicts, a voluminous amount of literature has been written on the subject of Vietnam. Even the air war has been documented by a number of sources representative of varied perspectives. However, the diverse stories of Distinguished Flying Cross recipients have not been widely recorded until recent times. Even now, more than three decades after the United States withdrew from Vietnam, accounts are still emerging which render additional interpretations of events and produce new contextual viewpoints of the overall conflict.

With less public solidarity of support than in previous wars, young men who wanted to fly still clamored to participate in Vietnam to demonstrate their unwavering loyalty to the United States and its principles. Whether by land or sea, the Army, Navy, Marines, Air Force and Coast Guard all contributed to the overall goal: protecting democracy from the threat of communism.

After years in an advisory role, following the initial air strikes which began with "Operation Pierce Arrow" in 1964, combat strategies improved with experience. American aviators became increasingly adept at jungle warfare throughout Vietnam, Cambodia and Laos as each year passed.

Reminiscent of World War II and Korea, the air war in Vietnam initially relied on propeller-driven airplanes. Forward air controllers served as scouts in small, single-engine craft while planes previously flown in combat were modified for their use in Vietnam. In addition, new aircraft provided assistance for troops in contact with the enemy.

Jet propelled airplanes, faster and more proficient in the 1960s, were produced in all sizes and configurations. Most were designed or modified for a specific purpose as it pertained to combat in Southeast Asia, and each provided an aviation platform capable of delivering highly effective ordnance.

From the emergence of the helicopter in Korea as a tool for transporting wounded soldiers to field hospitals, the new, more robust copters were also able to take on many different responsibilities. They served as transport, multi-purpose vehicles and gunships. Each was destined to gain a reputation as a potent combat asset.

In coordination, propeller aircraft, jets planes and helicopters flew in complex operations to move, protect and extract troops. They also worked together to attack hostile forces, interdict supply routes and destroy the enemy's ability to wage war.

Pilots and aircrews in Vietnam, like their Korean counterparts, fell into two general categories: those who had already tasted the thrill and terror of combat in pervious wars and those with fresh faces who had only logged the minimum number of training hours. For the latter group, the theoretical "unknowns" of combat involved dogfights, fire from the ground and the dangers of SAMs (Surface-to-Air Missiles) that were as daunting as the real experience. However, whether skilled or novice, those who took to the air fought with equal resolve, dedication and loyalty while paying homage to those who came before.

Aviators and aircrew, like most soldiers who returned from Vietnam just a few days off the battlefield, did not come home to fanfare. Instead they faced anti-war protesters. This bewildering sight intertwined with the memories of combat carnage provided a rationale for repression of memories even more deeply than their airborne predecessors. As a source of comfort, the recipients of the Distinguished Flying Cross from Vietnam have their citations and medals as proof of the valor they displayed. Their stories chronicle a heritage of which we can all be proud.

Personal Accounts of the Distinguished Flying Cross:

Venam

"My military experience transformed me...I learned to be part of something bigger than myself. I realized the value of helping others."

CWO-2 Gregory Mac Neil, USA

Top: Lieutenant Cardenas (left) organized the Army Air Corps glider school at Twenty-Nine Palms, California at the beginning of World War II. Middle: Cardenas was the B-29 launch pilot and operations officer for the X-1 supersonic project. Chuck Yeager was launched from the B-29 and accomplished the first successful supersonic flight in October 1947. Bottom: Following orders from President Truman, Cardenas flew the Northrop YB-49, called the "Flying Wing," over the United States Capitol in December 1947. Photographs courtesy of Robert Cardenas

To Bob
Thanks
Chuck Yeager

Glider Pilot, Bomber Pilot, Fighter Pilot and Test Pilot
Brigadier General Robert L. Cardenas, USAAF / USAF

"Friendships that are bound through blood and war can't be duplicated."_____

It was 1925, when at the age of five, Robert Cardenas came to San Diego, California with his parents from their hometown of Merida, Yucatan, Mexico. Without a strong command of English, he soon realized he would face many challenges. "I remember my principal sending a message home to my family advising that no child would graduate from Washington Grammar School until he or she could read, write and speak English. He did it out of pure common sense…The school was comprised of students from China, Japan, Greece, Italy, Portugal and Russia. Their parents mainly worked in the tuna industry; fishing for tuna or canning tuna. The principal knew that if the children couldn't speak to each other, they would form gangs on the playground and discipline would be most difficult."

Consequently, Cardenas became fluent in English and a model student by the time he headed to high school. That educational background and a feeling of self-reliance served him well and gave him the confidence to become a combat pilot, test pilot and senior officer in the military. Such formative lessons also gave him an opportunity few aviators have ever had; the opportunity to fly more than sixty different aircraft.

As a teenager, Cardenas built model airplanes and was fascinated with the gliders that flew by the coast of San Diego. He helped work, and hitched rides, on the gliders before he graduated with honors from high school. In 1939, Cardenas joined the National Guard but a year later, because he had a taste for flying, became an aviation cadet. He almost didn't take advantage of the situation because of the formidable challenge. However, he stuck it out and received his wings in July 1941. Had he not done so, he would have been part of the Bataan Death March with his former unit! Cardenas said, "That's what would've happened to me. So you never know…you have to watch your opportunities as they come and don't turn down something just because it's tough – I learned that an early age."

Following his credo of accepting a challenge, the young second lieutenant, who was content in his assignment at Kelly Field in San Antonio, Texas as an instructor, was queried as to whether he had flown gliders. When he answered in the affirmative, the officer was given orders to help establish the new Army Air Corps glider school at Twenty-Nine Palms, California.

Cardenas stated that, "it was a contractor operated school with winches out on the dry lake bed. There was a tow plane in the hanger but no gliders! I read in the newspaper that the President had named Richard DuPont as head of our National Glider Program and I remembered flying with him out at Torrey Pines, California. So I wrote DuPont a letter in which I told him of my situation. I mentioned that if we could obtain $5000, I might be able to get gliders with instructors. I mailed the letter and two weeks later a C-47 landed on the lake bed and a tall colonel deplaned." The officer turned out to be Colonel Fred R. Dent, Chief of the Aircraft Lab at Wright Field, Dayton, Ohio, and in charge of developing and procuring gliders." While he was less than happy that the lieutenant had written DuPont, he said to Cardenas, "I brought along my check book…get the gliders."

Cardenas' response was as follows: "I made a call to Consolidated Aircraft in San Diego and spoke with Johnny Robinson. I told him that I would give glider pilots $200 a month plus room and board in addition to all the beer they could drink. I also told him that the pilots could fly as much as they wanted if they would bring their gliders…The glider pilots came with their gilders and Colonel Dent stayed." After proving himself, Cardenas was transferred to the Aircraft Lab at Wright Field to help Colonel Dent develop invasion gliders and tow planes for them. Through this process, the CG-4a invasion glider was ultimately developed.

Lieutenant Cardenas got his first combat experience during WWII and did so at his own request – seeking another challenge. This transpired because Colonel Dent received combat orders. Out of loyalty and respect, Cardenas, who had been trained as a fighter pilot, tried to volunteer to serve with Dent in the European Theater, however, the request was declined because all test pilot positions were frozen and could not be reassigned.

Not willing to take no for an answer, the Lieutenant found his way to England and contacted the colonel. After breaking a great deal of protocol and putting Colonel Dent in a precarious position, Cardenas finally convinced Dent to pull a few strings and get him into Dent's unit. However, the cost of these indiscretions would be significant. Cardenas explained the next set of events. "So I wound up assigned to the 44th Bomb Group [USAAF] known as the Flying 8-Balls. Colonel Dent said to me, 'I'm going to fix you…I've got a crew here that just came back from their last mission and the copilot had to hold the pilot back in his seat with his head blown off. They're scared…you did some of the structural integrity when you worked on the B-24, so I'm going to give you that crew'."

"My first flight with that crew was not a mission – it was a just a training flight. I did some aerial stuff with them to prove I could handle the airplane and they gained trust and stuck with me. They only had ten missions completed…if they flew fifteen more, they could go home." When that day came, Cardenas got a big surprise.

"That night at the Officer's Club the navigator came over and he said, 'Captain, we took a vote, the crew and enlisted men too. We want to finish you out…you finished us when we needed you. We want to finish you out.' [Cardenas needed ten more missions before he could go home]. I said, 'Have you lost your mind? They haven't figured these odds out for nothing, you know?' He said again, 'No, we want to finish you out, sir.' With only about fifty percent of aircrews making their twenty five missions, that was a magnanimous gesture."

Captain Cardenas flew four more missions with his comrades, but on his twentieth mission, his luck changed - he was shot down. The irony was that he was not with his loyal crew! Cardenas explained how that came to pass. "Every mission that went out of England had two ships in the whole bomber wave that were command ships and specially equipped…I was the command pilot on a mission that counted as my twentieth…I sat between the pilot and the copilot. Over Germany, we were hit by flak. I knew we were going down…I told the pilot, 'Head for Switzerland. I think you can probably make it before this thing comes apart.' Both engines on the right side were on fire. The wing had a little added dihedral to it. I knew it wasn't going to be long before the wing departed. But one of the things I had to do was go down in the bomb bay and shred all the classified documents. So, I'm down in the bomb bay shredding this stuff and there was an explosion. Kaboom!"

The next thing Cardenas remembered was throwing up in his oxygen mask and floating. The explosion had propelled him out of the plane and opened his chute. Unfortunately he landed on the north side of Lake Constance, which was German territory. Eluding the Germans, he attempted to swim across the expansive lake but started to falter and with great luck was rescued by a Swiss man in a rowboat. From there, he made it from Switzerland to France.

While his thoughts were of survival, he was also concerned about his original crew. Before he was shot down, Cardenas had told Colonel Dent if he ever went down, he wanted for his entire crew to be sent home. It wasn't until after the war that he learned that the colonel had honored his request and sent them home as a group. Still vivid in his mind, Cardenas stated, "any war that you fight, whether it's on the ground or in the air…friendships that are bound through blood and war can't be duplicated…there was a feeling of patriotism in those days…it was your duty.

Surprisingly, Captain Cardenas did not receive a Distinguished Flying Cross for his twentieth mission. While the situation most likely warranted it, Cardenas lamented, "I guess there wasn't anybody around to 'write up' a DFC." It wasn't until much later in his career and in a different conflict that a situation would present itself for such an award.

Back at Wright Patterson AFB in Dayton, Ohio after his return to the United States, Cardenas graduated from the Flight Performance School and was assigned to the Flight Test Division. He flew captured German jets to gather valuable data and conducted jet testing at Muroc, California. By 1947, he was placed in charge of test operations at Muroc and was assigned as the B-29 launch pilot and operations officer for the X-1 supersonic project.

Cardenas related that, "I was the B-29 pilot on all of Chuck Yeager's flights…Flying the B-29 with the X-1 attached was not without hazard. On one flight, the X-1 refused to release from the shackle mechanism and I had to land the B-29 with the X-1 attached (which still contained propellants as Yeager was unable to jettison all of the fuel)…The landing was almost 3-point; had I raised the nose by more than 16 inches, the X-1 would have been damaged, likewise, if the landing had been too hard, the X-1 would have been destroyed." However, with the skill of a surgeon, he protected both planes and the crew from harm. As history records, Cardenas was the pilot of the B-29 on 14 October 1947 when Chuck Yeager made the first successful supersonic flight in the X-1.

Just two months later, in December 1947, Cardenas was designated the Project Pilot and was tasked with making the first flight in the Northrop YB-49 called the "Flying Wing." He was responsible for flying evaluation tests and making recommendations that would impact the government's decision on the purchase of the plane. After the second phase of the performance tests were almost completed in 1948, Cardenas was given an opportunity to finish his engineering degree at the University of Southern California. He left in May 1948 and headed for the west coast with his sweetheart and got married. However, on June 5th he heard a radio report that the Flying Wing had crashed and killed Captain Glen Edwards and his entire crew on a test flight. Immediately, Cardenas was ordered back to the project to determine what had caused the crash.

Following this incident, Major Cardenas flew the YB-49 non-stop from Muroc, California to President Truman's air show at Andrews Air Force Base on 9 February 1949. In doing so, he set a new transcontinental record of four hours and five minutes. Once the plane landed, he was met by President Truman and the Chief of the Air Force. Cardenas remembers the specific words of the President. "General, it looks pretty good to me. I think I'm going to buy some of these."

Of course, Cardenas had already written an evaluation that highlighted the significant flaws of the aircraft. Among them were its stall characteristics. Cardenas elaborated on his one page report. "The aircraft was marginally stable on all three axes and it exceeded the human sensory and response capability because humans are reactive and this aircraft needed a proactive system…Most planes, once in flight, can maintain flight. However, the Flying Wing had to be 'actively' flown every minute. It was a dangerous plane."

While in the presence of Cardenas, President Truman said to the General, "Let's have this whippersnapper fly this thing down Pennsylvania Avenue [to gain congressional funding for the plane]." Reluctantly, Cardenas said, "I bit my tongue and agreed to the president's order…Later, my boss said to me, 'Bob, go fly this thing down Pennsylvania Avenue and don't hit anything!'…and I did."

Pennsylvania Avenue is lined with trees and there were some tall radio towers that were hidden by the trees. The White House is also hidden by trees. I slowed the aircraft to about 350 miles per hour and flew a low pass down Pennsylvania Avenue looking carefully for towers. The next thing I knew, I looked up and the Capitol Dome was straight ahead and I had to pull up to miss it…That may have been the same reason why the terrorists, during 9/11, got confused and had trouble locating the Capitol; causing them to attack the more accessible Pentagon instead." Ultimately, the Air Force rejected the Flying Wing, in part due to the test pilot's final evaluation.

After the YB-49 Project, Colonel Cardenas conducted other fighter and bomber tests at Edwards AFB and Wright Field. He was then assigned to the 51st Fighter Interceptor Group, USAF, as Wing Commander in Okinawa, Japan. Following that experience, he became the Chief of the Aircraft and

Missiles Programming Division in the Pentagon and was later assigned to the US Strike Command in Tampa Florida as Chief of Special Operations. He remembered his unique experiences during this assignment. "I served under General Paul D. Adams who was the CINC of US Strike Command and his deputy was three-star Air Force General Bruce Holloway…In 1962, General Adams called me into his office and said, 'The ignorant Minister of Defense of India has split his Forces to the West and East, leaving the middle wide open for the Chicom's to come over the Himalayas, thru Nathu La pass, and link up with troops from East Pakistan (who were Communist) located only sixty kilometers away.'

In 1960, Red Erickson of the CIA brought the Dali Lama out of Tibet into Sikkim through Nathu La pass using Kampa tribesmen. In 1962, General Adams sent me to the same place to help in the defense of the pass using some of the same tribesmen. With the assistance of my contact in the area, Maharajah Kumar of Sikkim (who was a Sandhurst graduate and an RAF pilot), I gave input in the development of successful unconventional air re-supply at those altitudes [14,000 feet] and fierce wind currents. I felt that I was in a Steve Canyon comic strip."

Other adventures followed which are still classified but it appears he was equally successful in these endeavors because General Holloway arranged for Cardenas to command the legendary 18th Tactical Fighter Wing, in Vietnam starting in 1964. This also provided Colonel Cardenas a chance to fly the F-105 Thunderchief over North Vietnam.

Cardenas' recollections were vivid about taking over the unit. "I was sent over to command the 18th Tac Fighter Wing. Some very illustrious people had commanded that unit before me. I arrived there… and, I could fly the airplane; that was no problem. I was not particularly a fighter pilot. I'd come from bombers…Of course, the guys were interested in knowing what sort of a guy they inherited. So Robby Risener, a Top Gun of the outfit said, 'You know, they're not going to accept you until you let me set up a wing shoot.' [a mock combat contest]. So there was dive bombing, aerial, over the shoulder delivery, etc. and I tied him on one, he beat me on one, debatable on the other…But the most important thing I did for the men was give them leadership.

As I analyzed their missions, I noticed they were flying three-hour missions in the F-105 day after day after day, and with fuel tanks. So at the operations meeting I said, 'Why do you fly three-hour missions in the 105 when you're a fighter?' And the answer was, 'we've got to fill out the flying time chart. We have to meet our hours.' Therefore, I just ordered all tanks dropped from then on and they flew one hour missions. That was before the Gulf of Tonkin.

This got the men ready for combat but we couldn't fly out of Okinawa so we kept one squadron in Korat, Thailand. I devised a "daisy chain." I used to fly with the 67th Squadron, so when their turn came to go to Korat, I would go to Korat with them. I kept a second squadron in Okinawa glued to the cement - they stood nuclear alert because the F-105s were capable of carrying nuclear weapons and we had a nuclear mission. So that squadron was not flying. They were on alert. The third squadron was in training to go to Korat…When the squadron in Korat finished combat, they came back and sat on the nuclear pad, and the one that came off the nuclear pad went into training, etc. Thus, a daisy chain was instituted and it was an effective use of pilots and aircraft."

Finally recognized for his combat skills and leadership, Colonel Cardenas was awarded a Distinguished Flying Cross on 8 May 1965. The citation noted his "extraordinary achievement while participating in aerial flight as a combat strike pilot, flight leader, mission coordinator and as Wing Commander…Colonel Cardenas demonstrated diligence and perseverance far exceeding that expected of an aircrew member in a hostile environment. His aerial actions resulted in significantly great contributions, both to the morale of his entire wing, and the effectiveness and success of the United States Air Force in Southeast Asia. His exceptional initiative in combat, and application of professional knowledge, served as an inspiration to all who served under him and reflect great credit upon himself and the United States Air Force."

In 1968, Cardenas was promoted to Brigadier General and became the Vice Commander of the 16th Air Force based in Spain. It was during this assignment that General Cardenas was a member of a three-man delegation who negotiated with Muhmar Quadafi concerning the United States withdrawal from Wheelus AFB and the desert range in Libya.

General Cardenas' last assignment, (1971-1973) was with the Joint Strategic Target Planning Staff, JSTPS. In this position, he assisted the Chairman of the Joint Chiefs in selecting a list of nuclear targets in case such weapons were unleashed by an aggressor.

After his retirement from the Air Force, General Cardenas received numerous awards and has been recognized by a wide range of prestigious organizations. Among the honors, he was inducted into the Air Commando Hall of Fame and the Aerospace Walk of Honor. He was also made a "Distinguished Alumnus" at the USAF Test Pilot School at Edwards Air Force Base.

Along with myriad charitable activities and civic responsibilities during retirement, General Cardenas spends valuable hours talking with young people all over Southern California and shares his life-long wisdom. "I learned some significant lessons at a young age…I didn't start flying because I dreamed of the things I was going to do. I didn't know they existed. I came up by chance, working for Consolidated, wound up running a glider school with Richard DuPont, which in turn got me to Wright Field, which in turn got me into flight testing…The lesson: work hard, get good grades but most of all, take advantage of the opportunities…Don't let something go by because you think it's too tough. Just like when they said, 'Cardenas, you're going to go command the 18th Tac Fighter Wing.' I could've spoken up and said, 'Hey, I'm basically not a fighter pilot.' But I didn't – I said 'I'll give it a whirl.' I guess I would've even joined a space crew, but I have fillings in my teeth and that kept me from being considered for the space program.

After school presentations involving inspirational stories and words of wisdom, he often receives letters from students. Cardenas was particularly taken by one young person's response. "I got a letter that was a classic. I gave a talk at Brookville High School in Imperial Valley, California…This letter was from a sixteen-year-old. He said, 'I got your message…I was going to graduate and be a farmer - I am going to be a farmer, but I'm also going to be a scientist. I'm also going to be an engineer and I'm going to grow food and feed the world."

It appears that General Cardenas' legacy will include glider pilot, bomber pilot, fighter pilot, test pilot and inspiration for the next generation who will hopefully seize the abundant opportunities America has to offer.

Notes

General Robert L. Cardenas, Distinguished Flying Cross citation, action date: 8 May 1965, Archives, the Distinguished Flying Cross Society, San Diego, CA.

General Robert L. Cardenas, oral history interview, interviewed by Dr. Barry A. Lanman, 19 July 2009, transcribed, the Distinguished Flying Cross Society Oral History Collection, the Distinguished Flying Cross Society, San Diego, CA.

Top: Flying the A-4, Chuck Sweeney was awarded three Distinguished Flying Crosses in one week during the summer of 1972. Middle: Commander Sweeney retired from the Navy in 1980 with over 4,300 flight hours and 757 carrier landings. Bottom: As president of the Distinguished Flying Cross Society, Sweeney sat in the cockpit of an A-4 painted with his squadron's colors and emblems (VA-212 – the "Rampant Raiders"). The plane also carried the name of Commander Frank Green, the pilot he replaced in Vietnam. The aircraft resides in the San Diego Air & Space Museum. Photographs courtesy of Chuck Sweeney and the San Diego Air & Space Museum

The Summer of "72"
Three Distinguished Flying Crosses in One Week
Commander Charles "Chuck" Sweeney, USN

"I didn't realize it then but the summer of 1972 was a very pivotal time in my life."_____

Charles "Chuck" Sweeney never intended to fly. He grew up in Philadelphia, Pennsylvania and graduated from St. Joseph's University, after which he became an engineer working in the defense industry on the atomic powered bomber and a large antenna to record Russian Missile tests. Although Sweeney entered the United States Navy in 1958, he did so as an aeronautical engineer. It wasn't until his tour of duty at Patuxent River, Maryland that he became interested in flying and was encouraged to pursue this newfound passion by Jim Lovell and other test pilots. Their recommendation for him was to go into carrier aviation.

After flight training, Sweeney's first tour was flying S-2E aircraft from the USS *Yorktown*. He even got to fly in the Tonkin Gulf, performing maritime surveillance, immediately after the first strikes against North Vietnam were launched in 1964. Following that tour, he received a Master of Science degree in Aeronautical Engineering at the Naval Postgraduate School in Monterey, California and commented that, "as they were looking for cannon fodder in Vietnam I volunteered to transition to A-4 jets."

In reflecting on the experience he stated, "I didn't realize it then, but the summer of 1972 was a very pivotal time in my life. I was the Operations Officer in VA-127 stationed at NAS Lemoore, California and as a LCDR in the US Navy, it was a great billet. I was flying the A-4 Skyhawk which was a true pilot's airplane as it was tough, small, agile, responsive, easy to maintain and had a low operating cost. The Easter Offensive had escalated the war in Vietnam and we were responsible for training replacement pilots for the A-4 Skyhawk squadrons on board the aircraft carrier USS *Hancock*. We were working very hard to meet the changing requirements as pilots were killed, captured or rotated back. I got to know all of the new pilots extremely well as I was flying with them every day. One particular pilot was Commander Frank Green who was scheduled to be the Executive Officer in VA-212 on the USS *Hancock* flying the A-4F attack aircraft. I became friends with Frank and he said that I was lucky to be on shore duty with the war escalating and squadrons suffering heavier losses. I still had 18 months of shore duty left so I thought the war would be over before I went back to sea duty. Shortly after that Frank deployed to VA-212 off the coast of North Vietnam along with other replacement pilots.

One morning in mid-July I received a phone call from the Bureau of Naval Personnel in Washington telling me that Frank Green was MIA after a night bombing mission in North Vietnam. Since I was the most qualified senior A-4 pilot in the squadron, I was given immediate priority for night carrier landings on the USS *Enterprise*, and ten days after the call, I was on my way as the Executive Officer of VA-212 off the coast of North Vietnam.

I adjusted quite quickly to flying combat missions again instead of training pilots how to fly them, and it seemed like old home week since I knew all the pilots not only in VA-212 but in the other two A-4 squadrons as I had helped train most of them. The flying was great since I was getting two to three hops every day and many of the restrictions that had hampered us for so long were removed.

Late in the afternoon of 6 September 1972, I launched from the USS *Hancock* as the Division leader of a flight of four A-4F aircraft. My wingman was Lieutenant Tom Follis from VA-164 and Lieutenant Will Pear and Lieutenant Ray Winn from VA-212 were in the other section. Our mission was to hit any lucrative targets that we could find in our assigned area in North Vietnam just south of the Than Hoa bridge and as we approached the coastline the two sections split as briefed. Lieutenant Pear reported finding several trucks and while making a bombing run was hit by several 23mm AAA rounds. His aircraft was on fire as he climbed and headed for the water followed by his wingman. I turned towards them as I could easily see the A-4 with huge flames shooting out the back, looking like a giant Roman candle against the darkening sky. About that time his engine quit but he stayed with the failing aircraft until he got about two miles off shore and ejected at 1900 feet. Lieutenant Winn stayed low to keep him in sight and I climbed to altitude with my wingman to alert the Search and Rescue (SAR) forces and act as the on-scene commander. I had more assets volunteer to help than I could reasonably employ so I picked assets from my Air Wing since I knew their capabilities, especially in a critical combat situation. It was always difficult running a rescue from the tight cockpit of a single seat, single engine aircraft but we trained to do it and overcome the obstacles. I assigned missions to the various aircraft that I had selected including the SAR helo escort, flak suppressors, tankers, combat air patrol, etc.

Lieutenant Pear's ejection went extremely well and was fascinating to watch as I saw the entire ejection sequence. The ESCAPAC seat worked perfectly from the canopy being jettisoned, through seat ejection, pilot/seat separation and automatic chute opening...Will got out of his parachute while being dragged through the water and managed to get into his raft successfully. The fear factor set in as the wind and high seas were moving him toward the heavily defended beach and the dwindling light was also a significant factor. The wind also had a positive side as it had kept all the fishing boats on the beach. The SAR helo from the duty SAR destroyer in the Gulf came under fire as he passed an island on his way to the rescue area so I instructed the escorting A-4s to mark the site and hit it after the rescue was accomplished. While orbiting, the enemy figured out who was coordinating the rescue and when I flew a little too close to the coastline, I came under heavy AAA fire. I assigned flak suppressors to hit two of the sites when the helo was making the pickup.

The helo flew over the downed pilot and dropped a smoke about 1000 yards past him and I figured he was a professional who knew what he was doing but it looked strange to me. The helo came around and as he was making his hover for the pickup, a coastal defense gun bracketed the smoke light with several rounds before my wingman, who had been dispatched as a flak suppressor, spotted the site and blasted it with two bombs to silence it completely. The pick-up went very quickly and two AAA sites were destroyed during the rescue.

I reported a successful pick-up and while the helo was leaving the scene, I decided to hit the one remaining site that had tried to take me out. As I was approaching the roll in point, an extremely authoritative voice came up on the SAR frequency and it sounded like God was speaking. The voice said 'Flying Eagle 312, this is Jehovah, report all chicks feet wet.' Jehovah, a very appropriate name, was the personal call sign of the two-star admiral, CTF77, in charge of the task force in the Tonkin Gulf and he wanted me to verify that everyone was safe. I debated whether to continue on and drop my bombs or just return with them. However, feeling a personal vendetta against the AAA site, which is not always smart, I continued my approach, rolled in, dropped my bombs and destroyed the site with several secondary explosions. After I got back over the water, I finally reported 'All chicks' feet wet.'

Lieutenant Pear was the last A-4 pilot to be rescued in the Vietnam War and was quite happy to avoid the 'Hanoi Hilton,' but he also reported that the brandy on the SAR destroyer was not very good. All in all it was a great day as he was successfully rescued with everyone doing their job very professionally just as we trained, and several AAA sites were destroyed including the ones that had fired at the helo. I was awarded my first DFC for this mission which went far smoother in actual combat than it ever did during training.

The helo crew consisting of the pilot, Lieutenant Commander Frank Koch, the co-pilot, Lieutenant Gene Gilbert, the swimmer, Tim McCarthy, the second crewmember, Miguel Melendez and the hoist operator, Gary Tremel, were the real heroes of the rescue. Frank Koch and Tim McCarthy were awarded DFCs while the other three were awarded Air Medals. [For more information on Lieutenant Commander Frank Koch see his story which appears later in this chapter.]

Several days later, on 12 September 1972, I was selected to lead an 'Alpha Strike' of thirty-five aircraft from the USS *Hancock* against an AAA repair and storage site at Cap Mai which is northeast of Haiphong (near Hon Gai) and thirty-five miles from the Chinese border. There were no known active SAM sites in the immediate target area but that was never a sure thing as they moved the SAMs around frequently. There were numerous AAA sites protecting the target area but no worse than many targets we had already faced. I was fortunate to have a great handpicked team of pilots to help me plan my first big strike in actual combat as the strike lead. I had planned numerous strikes and lead them in training but this was the real thing.

The strike consisted of twenty-two A-4 attack aircraft, twelve F-8 fighter aircraft and one E-2 command and control aircraft. The weather was not expected to be too bad for that time of the year and so the day's fun commenced on time. As usual, with this many aircraft being launched in short order, some aircraft didn't make it but the spares filled in dutifully and I had to reshuffle a few assignments which is 'fun' in the small confined cockpit of the A-4. But we all rendezvoused quickly and pushed toward the target on time. En route I realized the cloud cover would preclude us from doing our pre-planned run in and realigned the strike to take advantage of a clear area. As we were approaching the target area the enemy radars started pinging us and then we got the call that MiGs were in the air and were headed our way. I pushed ahead with the attack aircraft and flak suppressors and let the fighters do what they do best which is to protect us and kill the MiGs. About that time we were approaching roll in and the AAA became pretty intense but then the flak suppressors did their job to silence the guns while we did our bombing run. We did a pretty good job on the target and thankfully nobody was hit and everyone made it back to the carrier safely. Fortunately, or unfortunately depending on your viewpoint, the MiGs decided not to engage our fighters and went back to their base unscathed. For doing the job that I was trained to do I was awarded my second DFC.

The very next day, 13 September 1972, I was the division leader of four A-4s on another 'Alpha Strike' but this was against a major rail yard and trans-shipment point near Hanoi that was heavily defended by multiple active SAM sites and numerous AAA sites. This time my division was being tracked by several SAMs coming up at us and I had to time the violent defensive maneuvers so that the SAMs would miss and explode harmlessly above us. To do this maneuver we had to head away from the main strike force. I finally caught up to the strike as they were about to commence the attack. As I looked at the area I realized my assigned target was underwater and no longer a viable option so I quickly picked out another target. I told my division about the change and we commenced our attack while avoiding the AAA. We were able to track the target, a loaded train, well and placed most of our bombs on the cars and got numerous secondary explosions and sustained fires. Pulling off target, we met more AAA and a few SAMs but everyone made it back safely to the carrier. For this mission I was awarded my third DFC, all within one week. My last mission in Vietnam was against the Than Hoa bridge and I thought it was appropriate to finish the Summer of '72 by going after one of North Vietnam's most famous and heavily defended targets. One more time the magnificent A-4F Skyhawk brought me back to the carrier unscathed and it was a great feeling to be headed home in one piece."

Sweeney's love for the A-4 was evident. "The A-4 Skyhawk was the only modern carrier-based aircraft that did not require folding wings to reduce deck space requirements. The small size was an attribute that I appreciated when flying combat against heavily defended targets. The A-4s formed the backbone of the naval aviation attack community in the 60s and 70s, making 112 combat squadron cruises, more than any other squadron type in the Vietnam air war. More A-4s were lost in Vietnam combat operations from August 1964 until January 1973 than any other naval aircraft during that war – a total of 266 Skyhawks were lost. However, this figure is somewhat misleading as Skyhawks suffered only a .002 loss per combat sortie, the lowest of all combat types and a true indication of its heavy usage. The Skyhawks flew in some of the most significant strikes of the war including the Than Hoa bridge, Hanoi thermal power plant, defense of Khe Sanh, Kep MiG airfield, downtown Hanoi and Haiphong, to name a few."

Commander Sweeney retired from the Navy in 1980 with over 4,300 flight hours and 757 carrier landings and returned to a career in aeronautical engineering. However, a unique experience in 1983 served as a defining moment for him and provided closure for his Vietnam experience. As he visited the San Diego Air & Space Museum for the first time since a horrendous fire destroyed the original museum, he couldn't believe his eyes. Before him was an A-4 not only painted with his old squadron's colors and emblems (VA-212 – the "Rampant Raiders") but the name on the side was Commander Frank Green; the pilot he had replaced in Vietnam. The aircraft was dedicated to Commander Green as a lasting tribute to all of the Missing in Action (MIA) or Killed in Action (KIA) personnel from the Vietnam conflict.

Chuck Sweeney currently serves as the President and CEO of the Distinguished Flying Cross Society. He recently stated that, "I feel proud and at the same time humbled that I was awarded three DFCs. Since joining the DFC Society, I have been overwhelmed by the heroic deeds performed by the DFC recipients of every era. War is not a video game, it is life and death and if people aren't willing to die for our country, the USA won't exist for very long. Almost all of our members feel they were just doing what they were trained to do and that the other members are the heroic ones. They are all fantastic but quiet heroes who don't talk about their actions very often but have outstanding stories of heroism to tell if you can get them to open up."

Notes

Commander Charles "Chuck" Sweeney, Distinguished Flying Cross citations, action dates: 6 September 1972, 12 September1972 and 13 September 1972, Archives, the Distinguished Flying Cross Society, San Diego, CA.

Commander Charles "Chuck" Sweeney, oral history interview, interviewed by Dr. Barry A. Lanman, 26 April 2005, transcribed, the Distinguished Flying Cross Society Oral History Collection, the Distinguished Flying Cross Society Oral History Collection, the Distinguished Flying Cross Society, San Diego, CA. .

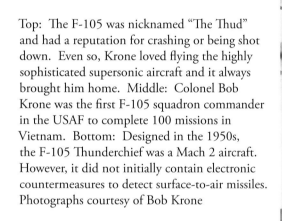

Top: The F-105 was nicknamed "The Thud" and had a reputation for crashing or being shot down. Even so, Krone loved flying the highly sophisticated supersonic aircraft and it always brought him home. Middle: Colonel Bob Krone was the first F-105 squadron commander in the USAF to complete 100 missions in Vietnam. Bottom: Designed in the 1950s, the F-105 Thunderchief was a Mach 2 aircraft. However, it did not initially contain electronic countermeasures to detect surface-to-air missiles. Photographs courtesy of Bob Krone

One-Hundred Missions Flying a "Thud"

Colonel Robert M. Krone, USAF

"Thirty-five percent of our F-105 pilots never got to a hundred missions. They were either shot down, MIA, KIA, or ended up as a prisoner of war."_____

During peacetime in the aftermath of World War II, Robert Krone completed high school and attended the University of Southern California's ROTC program. When he graduated in 1952, he also received a commission as a second lieutenant in the United States Air Force. Being a pilot was not a passion or even the slightest interest. However, the next set of events would set the course for the balance of his life.

Krone remembers thinking, "I had not planned on doing any flying…when I was sent off to San Antonio for initial orientation I think my superiors had a plan…they roomed me, a young, brown-bar second lieutenant with a lieutenant colonel test pilot…So for several days, this test pilot would come back and tell me stories. By the time I had finished the three week orientation I said, 'I'm going to be a pilot!' The rest is history – I became a combat pilot and I stayed in the Air Force for twenty-three years.

As an experienced F-105 pilot in November 1965, Krone and his unit, the 469th Tactical Fighter Squadron, was sent to Thailand. It was the first tactical fighter squadron to be permanently assigned from the United States to fly over North Vietnam.

Colonel Krone remembers the camaraderie between the pilots. "The interaction of the pilots of the 469th was incredible…We ended up being the most experienced group of pilots because we had all flown the F-105 for a year or two before we deployed. We deployed as a unit and had a high degree of expertise. We averaged 400 hours in the F-105 with each other when we got to Vietnam.

We didn't have to do much briefing. We could just get out and fly. We knew what we were going to do. For a fighter pilot, that is probably the most satisfying part of flying. There we were, one pilot in each jet, a complicated hunk of machinery, a complicated mission, and yet there's all this teamwork and cooperation that goes on between the flight members for every flight. It's a unique team experience.

The feeling is hard to explain. That teamwork is critically important for mission accomplishment and for keeping up morale when you sustain losses, which we did. Overall, it was the best flying any of us ever had. We had fun flying home from missions because we could 'paint the sky' with no rules. We could fly low level over Thailand and look in the hootches. The Thai Government and the Royal Thai Air Force were so cooperative. Our F-105s flew out of two Thailand bases: Korat and Tahkli."

Adding to the combat experience for Colonel Krone was the aircraft he adored. "The F-105 Thunderchief was my favorite airplane…It was actually designed in the 50s and got operational in the early 60s…and was a very interesting innovation for America's aerospace. The F-105 was the first fighter bomber built with an internal bomb bay. We carried a fuel tank in the bomb bay.

They called the F-105 a Mach 2 airplane. All of us flew it at least once at Mach 2.1, but you could never fly supersonic when it was loaded with bombs, rockets and everything else that you had to take into combat in Vietnam. So our normal speeds were under supersonic, but we would frequently go supersonic when we got rid of our ordnance; if we were hunting a MiG, or if we wanted a supersonic ride back home. The airplane was just marvelous…

In the early Vietnam combat days, the F-105 had a major limitation. It didn't contain electronic counter measures to detect surface-to-air missiles…the Chinese had helped the Vietnamese develop the most effective air defense system America had ever faced. So our squadron, being the first, took some heavy losses until the electronic counter measures came in – we just had to sense when the missiles were coming up at us and that didn't always work. We lost pilots to SAMS.

The F-105 got its nickname, the Thud, when it first came out in the early 60s. Other pilots taxiing by it in their F-84s or F-100s would look up and say, 'the only thing that's good for is going thud!' Soon, the term stuck and the F-105 pilots used the term affectionately.

Like all combat planes, it did have problems in the beginning, but by the time it went to Vietnam it was a workhorse. Eighty-five percent of combat missions over North Vietnam between 1965 and 1968 were carried out by the F-105. I flew the F-105 for all of my hundred and twenty-five missions without one ground abort. I had one air abort with a hydraulic system failure but, that is phenomenal for any airplane in a combat situation…it was an Air Force jewel.

By early 1965, the United States Air Force decided that pilots, flying in the north, would have to do one hundred missions to complete a tour. Over the south, the pilots would stay for twelve or thirteen months and go home, regardless of how many missions. They based that policy on risk. It was a very high risk environment flying in the north, so a hundred missions was a tour. But those were a hundred 'counters', so if your mission was to Laos or South Vietnam it didn't count…Most of the Ho Chi Minh Trail was actually in the 'count' zone, but some of it was in Laos. We did a lot of flying seeking Ho Chi Minh Trail activity because our primary mission was against the logistics capabilities for the north to move to South Vietnam.

The hundred missions was our Thud pilots' obsession. We spent all of our time planning, flying, debriefing, or story telling…That filled our lives seven days a week. Since we were short of pilots, days off were few…We carefully logged every counter on the Operations board. Captain Tony Gangol, after his thirty-fifth mission, would stride into Ops and say, 'There ain't any way to get 100.' For too many there was no way…

There were too frequent sad days because thirty-five percent of our F-105 pilots never got to a hundred missions. They either were shot down, MIA, KIA, or ended up as a prisoner of war…I wrote the Commander of the USAF Los Angeles Lookout Mountain Film Lab in January 1966 with the message, 'We're fighting a war over here and no one's filming it.' He was a friend since I had worked with the Lab when they filmed our Operational Tests of the F-105s new boom-recepticle air refueling system at George AFB in 1963…When he brought a film crew to Thailand to film the F-105 combat story later in 1966, they titled it, 'There is a Way.' And, for sixty-five percent of Thud Pilots, there was a way."

Like most combat pilots, certain missions are imprinted in their memory, never to be forgotten. Of his hundred and twenty-five missions, Colonel Krone has his own list of special missions. "My first Distinguished Flying Cross was in December of '65. We got there in November. I happened to be flying the first actual Wild Weasel mission. The Wild Weasels were the ones who were dedicated to attacking the SAM sites. So Gary Willard was there with his F-100 Wild Weasel airplanes and I was the commander of the strike flight of four F-105s. The weather was bad and no missile sites 'painted' us; but that mission on 22 December 1965 initiated the USAF Wild Weasel Program. It contained the highest risk missions of the Vietnam War. Wild Weasel crews suffered continual losses, became famous throughout the war and were all highly decorated. That was the first of my four Distinguished Flying Cross missions."

During a hundred "counters," some missions were naturally more problematic than others. For Colonel Krone, the missions involving bad weather were always more difficult. "Now for the F-105 in 1966, with some rare exceptions, we had to see the ground to hit a target… one of the most challenging missions for me was associated with President Johnson's hope of reaching a peace settlement with the North Vietnamese. So, by December 1965, he called a halt to the bombing and sent Henry Kissinger to talk with the North Vietnamese on the anticipation that a resolution could be found…Well, it was almost a month later and it was clear that the North Vietnamese weren't at all interested in peace. They wanted to win the war and they were using that time to rebuild.

The war in the south was still going on, but we were essentially North flyers…so we were not doing much flying. Near the end of January 1966, the first frag order (timely instructions) came in. 'Get ready - You're going to start missions again.' We were ready to go but were experiencing lousy weather. I mean, the weather was down to the deck. For three days we briefed, and the missions were canceled. However, on the evening of January 30th we got a frag order from Saigon that none of us had ever seen before. It was orders for the next day involving all F-105s in both wings at Korat and at Takhli and it said, 'You will fly these missions regardless of weather.'

When Captain Bud Millner, Captain Wally Belew, Captain Fred de Yong, Lieutenant Jerry Driscoll and I read that message at 0400 in the 469th Operations Room, we suddenly got very serious about mission planning. We would be Elm Flight - 5 F-105s. A total of sixteen F-105 flights were scheduled from Korat and Takhli RTAFB that day split between morning and afternoon flights. Takhli RTAFB was our sister base 350 miles to the west in Thailand. Under these extreme weather conditions, my flight of five Thuds took off from Korat in Thailand. We flew over South Vietnam, let down over the Gulf of Tonkin to be underneath the radar. We were at 500 hundred feet over the water and still in the soup.

Bud, Wally, Fred and Jerry were flying close formation and I was on radar. These pros could fly in tight and still crosscheck their own instruments. Our target happened to be on the east coast of North Vietnam. I could see it on the radar. We had it all briefed. I had said, 'Okay, seven miles out we will start a pull up to six or seven thousand feet. When we see the target we'll roll in.' That's a standard attack maneuver. However, the weather was still lousy. My other brief was, 'if we get up to 6 or 7,000 thousand feet and we don't see the target, we'll have to abort…We'll just keep climbing and head back home.'

As we climbed up in the clouds, I had my thumb on the button to call an abort, when all of a sudden, it just opened up. There it was. There was the target - ships in a river outlet in North Vietnam. Just like a slide show. Instead of saying, 'Abort!' I said, 'Number one in.' And Wally Ballou, who was from the south and had a wonderful drawl, said, 'And they're shooting!' We were all laughing on the way down. Fred DeJong was acting as photo chase, so he got the photography. We hit the target, got out, felt pretty good about it until we were on top going home again and suddenly we were hearing on the radio, 'We lost two 105s.'…The weather was so bad and the pilots were valiantly trying to get the target but could not… turned out, when we got home we found out we were the only flight to have hit the target that day and President Johnson went back on TV and announced resumption of bombing North Vietnam. So, that was the most challenging flight I ever led. All of us received decorations."

While some missions stand apart because of their difficulty, other missions merit recognition because of their strategic value. The Bac Jiang Bridge was one such target. Colonel Krone stated, "The Bac Jiang Bridge was my mission for which I received the Silver Star. It was one of the big bridges in the Hanoi area and, of course, our main mission was to try and keep the materials of war from coming out of China into Hanoi and down south into South Vietnam. So the bridges were high priority and we kept after the Bac Jiang Bridge day after day, losing airplanes on every mission. I just happened to be leading a sixteen-flight mission that put the bridge out of commission…, at least for awhile. The interesting thing, which I didn't realize at the time, but learned when my wife, Sue, and I made a tourist trip to Hanoi in 2004, was that Mr. Eiffel designed that bridge in 1900. Of course, he was the same architect who designed the Eiffel Tower…The bridge was later rebuilt and exists to this day."

While Colonel Krone's second and third Distinguished Flying Cross citations were significant, the events leading to his fourth DFC were particularly interesting. They took place on 31 May 1966. "This was a JCS mission - when the Chairman of the Joint Chiefs, Robert McNamara, would meet on Tuesday with President Johnson and they would pick the JCS targets. The JCS targets were always the tough ones, usually around Hanoi. Well, on this date they picked the Yen Bai Railroad Yards and Military Warehousing. It was my ninety-ninth mission.

Now, as commander I had put in a policy that said, 'when you get to ninety-seven missions we're going to try and give you milk runs.' We believed that successfully completing ninety-seven missions qualified a pilot to be given a high probability of reaching the magic one hundred. However, for the 31st of May, Major Jimmy Jones, the 469th Ops Officer, came to me and said 'Bob, I don't have a lead for this flight.' And I said, 'Alright, put me on.' So I ended up leading this one to Yen Bai. Now Yen Bai is where Ho

Chi Minh was born. It was on the Red River going northwest up to China, and it was a huge military marshalling center. It was a prime target; heavily defended. I remember thinking that if I were going to be shot down on my ninety-ninth mission, it might as well be at Ho Chi Minh's hometown. We had about twenty-four F-105s from Korat and Tahkli. This was a big gaggle and I ended up leading it. We lost two F-105 pilots, as we usually did on those JCS targets, but the mission was a significant success. For this event, I received my fourth DFC.

On my 100th mission, 3 June 1966, it turned out I was going to be the first USAF squadron commander to reach the hundred counters. There had been four commanders previously shot down… There were three shot down before we arrived including our squadron commander, Bill Cooper, on 26 April 1966 – which is why I became the squadron commander. So, the Air Force realized that they were going to have a commander who actually made it to one hundred. For the first time they sent a film crew over to Korat to photograph the whole day of me getting out of bed, briefing, pre-flighting the airplane and flying the mission…It was an important milestone and it was important for the morale of the pilots still flying over the north…That day I finished my tour and joined the group of Thud Pilots who became the 'lucky ones'."

In the decades since his last combat flight, Colonel Krone has pondered his role in the Vietnam War, the overall importance of the war and the collective lessons learned. In many respects, for Colonel Krone it was the event of a lifetime that defined his character and gave him professional direction. He received a Ph.D. and became an expert on a variety of military and space related issues.

As for his analysis of Vietnam, he believed that, "the eleven years the United States spent fighting communism in Vietnam did a number of very important things… First and foremost, it helped in the demise of communism, accelerated the fall of the Berlin Wall, the collapse of the Soviet Union and winning the Cold War. Vietnam also kept communism from spreading into the rest of Asia because they were so involved in Vietnam." Krone further states, "I think these perspectives, which are increasingly being shared by historians, are helping Vietnam veterans appreciate their contributions and helping the public revise some negative beliefs."

The Vietnam experience, followed by thirty-five years of university teaching and administration as well as working with Vietnam POWs and space organizations, led Colonel Krone to become founder and Provost of the new Kepler Space University. Using his fifty years of experience, Colonel Krone is leading discussions, publishing and teaching about the Law of Space Abundance where space offers unbounded resources for human needs. Colonel Robert M. Krone concluded by saying, "The Kepler Telescope is searching for Earth-like planets. The Kepler Space University is searching for adventure-sharing scholars. We believe that innovative governance for space settlements can be a model for peace on Earth…I believe true victory is winning without war."

Notes

Colonel Robert M. Krone, Distinguished Flying Cross citations, action dates: 22 December 1965, 31 January 1966, 8 May 1966 and 31 May 1966, Archives, the Distinguished Flying Cross Society, San Diego, CA.

Colonel Robert M. Krone, oral history interview, interviewed by Dr. Barry A. Lanman, 19 July 2009, transcribed, the Distinguished Flying Cross Society Oral History Collection, The Distinguished Flying Cross Society, San Diego, CA.

Colonel Howard Plunkett, F-105 History, unpublished paper, Archives, the Distinguished Flying Cross Society, San Diego, CA, 1.

Top: Captain Withuhn (top row, right) saved his AC-119G from destruction when he dislodged a flare with an ignited fuse which had hung up in the automatic flare launcher in the back of their airplane. Withuhn flew 207 missions and was awarded one of the first 200-mission patches of the "Left Turn Club." He also received two Distinguished Flying Crosses and a Bronze Star. Bottom: The AC-119G Shadow was an aircraft designed to replace the AC-47. It flew at night and protected ground troops in trouble. Photographs courtesy of Bill Withuhn

Navigating the "Shadow" as a Member of the "Left Turn Club"

Major William "Bill" L. Withuhn, USAF

"It's a moment of self-discovery for a lot of people in combat They find out what really matters."

When Bill Withuhn was five, his dad was not around the house to play catch or teach him to ride a bicycle. Even so, Withuhn idolized him and knew his dad was helping win World War II as an Army officer in the Pacific. The treasured photographs and "V" letters had a tremendous impact on the impressionable young boy. Instilled with a sense of public service at an early age, Withuhn yearned to walk in his father's shoes, but in the Air Force rather than the Army.

In 1963, Withuhn graduated from the University of California at Berkeley. Fresh out of ROTC he entered the United States Air Force as a distinguished graduate and regular officer. However, he did not realize his dream of being a fighter pilot. At six foot, four inches, he was too tall and his eyesight was not quite perfect. He decided that if he couldn't be in the front seat, he didn't want any part of flying. He noted, "I would fly a desk for awhile at the Western Transport AF Headquarters, Military Air Transport Service, Travis Air Force Base, located in California." Eventually, Lieutenant Withuhn was given the opportunity to attend navigation school and he accepted the challenge, after getting married in 1964.

Stationed at James Connally AFB, Texas in 1965, Withuhn realized he had a strong proclivity for the exacting skills of a great navigator. He graduated at the top of his class, receiving the USAF Air Training Commander's Trophy. He subsequently chose an assignment at Dover AFB in Delaware, as a worldwide navigator on the C-133A. Withuhn explained what happened next. "In 1967, I filled out a form requesting a Southeast Asia duty station…before long I got a letter assigning me to the Air Commandos. I said, 'Oops what's this?' Well, a little while later they changed the name to Special Operations, and I trained for nearly a year in the AC-119G. It was called the 'Shadow'."

Once in Vietnam, Captain Withuhn was initially assigned to the 71st Special Operations Squadron in Nha Trang and was then re-assigned to the 17th Special Operations Squadron in Nha Trang and Tuy Noa. The Shadow missions in Vietnam were flown exclusively at night, from sundown to the pre-dawn hours, and defended troops in contact with the enemy on the ground. It was a form of night-combat in Vietnam that was the exception rather than the rule.

The AC-119G Shadow was built by Fairchild and was a replacement for the AC-47 "Spooky." The Shadow carried a crew of eight including two pilots and two navigators. Compared to its sister plane the AC-119K, it did not have two small jet engines, had much less sophisticated electronic equipment and no radar of any kind. In addition, the ceramic armor that was planned for the plane was deleted in production because of excessive weight. It was a basic piston-powered aircraft with few amenities, yet the crews who flew them became dedicated to the Shadow because it was perfect for the mission of close coordination with troops and Special Forces on the ground when under attack.

The Shadow flew in a tight left-hand circular orbit between 1,500 and 3,500 feet above the action. One of the navigators, in the left-front doorway, tracked the targets with the night observation sight (NOS), while the pilot in the left seat aimed the plane's fixed mini-guns by means of a special cockpit gun sight mounted directly to the pilot's left. The ability to stay on the target, until the enemy troops retreated or were neutralized, was the specialty of the AC-119G. The four 7.62mm miniguns could each fire up to 6,000 rounds per minute – up to a total fire of 24,000 rpm in short bursts. That made for a formidable source of suppression.

To expose the enemy, the Shadow had two effective pieces of equipment: a pneumatically powered flare-launcher, which held twenty high-intensity parachute flares, and a powerful xenon-arc spotlight gimbaled in the open rear left-hand doorway. It quickly became evident that the spotlight was not only effective in exposing the enemy but it served to disorient them as well. By 1969, the Shadow was confirmed by Army Rangers, Special Forces and Marine intelligence officers as the Air Force's most intimidating night weapon. Just the sound of an AC-119G approaching could cause the Viet Cong to flee from a potential attack.

On 11-12 May 1969, after flying the Shadow in combat for just three months, Captain Withuhn was involved in a mission for which he would receive his first Distinguished Flying Cross. In a unique set of circumstances, a citation was not presented with the medal because part of the mission was of a "sensitive nature." In the vicinity of DaNang, his aircraft was notified of the highest priority contact to the west, followed in rapid succession by several more contacts, one after another. It was a hectic night. After refueling and re-arming twice in eleven hours, the crew landed after first light, knowing that every one of the enemy attacks had been repulsed.

While he flew a vast number of other missions, one other flight at night stood apart from the rest. It was on 7 September 1969 near Tuy Hoa City. Later, Withuhn explained the events that threatened his life and the lives of his entire crew. "We'd been called by the coordinators in Saigon to go over to a firebase that was under attack…Our version of the aircraft was strictly for troops in trouble on the ground. On this particular night, it was a firebase and it was lit up like two in the afternoon. There were flares all over the place, tracers flying around. You could actually see some of the enemy units coming toward the perimeter, so we rolled in and began firing our mini-guns. We turned on our big xenon arc spotlight and started to kick out our own flares, all in coordination with the ground commander.

A few seconds after initiating our penetration, a flare hung up in the automatic flare launcher in the back of our airplane. Of course, it's a very hazardous situation. These flares are primarily magnesium. When they go off they'd take the whole back of the plane with it in a 3000-degree incineration…Also, if we went out of commission, our troops below us in the firebase would be over-run. I got permission from the aircraft commander to go back and help; a gunner [Technical Sergeant Clayton Hedge] went with me. We quickly tried to figure out a way to get the flare out of the tube…I got a big long stick that was kept for that purpose, and gingerly pushed this sucker because you don't know if it's going to go off or not. We got it out of the tube - and then it hung up on the arming lanyard and was banging around on the back of the plane with sparks showing that the fuse had already ignited. During that kind of a moment you don't think about anything…you just do what's called for.

I had this long stick and without thinking, swung out in the air stream—I remember it almost taking my helmet off…and I got a point of leverage down where the lanyard was connected to the flare launcher and just ripped it. It fell away and immediately ignited…I just called on the radio and said, 'AC [aircraft commander], we're clear of the flare.'

We went back to work and were gratified that we drove off the attackers within about twenty minutes. And, I don't think you get the shakes or anything of that sort until you're actually back on terra-firma - at four in the morning in this case…" For this act of heroism, involving split-second decisions, Captain Withuhn was awarded a second Distinguished Flying Cross. It was an event in his life that solidified his character.

Through these experiences on the AC-119Gs, Withuhn also gained a new respect for the role of a navigator. "I had a sense of being up there with the 'big boys'…I found it intense and satisfying, because of the equality and total commitment of the whole crew, working so tightly together…In effect, the two navigators, one up in the flight deck and one on the night targeting scope, basically ran the tactical mission. The flight-deck navigator talked to all of the coordinators, talked to all the ground commanders on the secure channels, and directed the operations…Clearly, the navigator on the flight deck – observing through the AC-119's big cockpit windows [which stretched well back along the plane's sides], seeing the whole combat scenario unfold below, keeping exact track of the plane's location and that of our ground guys in the darkness, and talking to the ground commanders – had the best situational awareness. That gave me a tremendous feeling of satisfaction, and I was proud of my contribution … I was proud to be part of a group saving so many American lives, a group that 'Denied Him the Dark,' ['him' being the VC or NVA], which became the slogan of the Shadows." In the early 1970s, the 17th Special Operations Squadron was awarded the Presidential Unit Citation.

In addition to his exploits in the air, Captain Withuhn distinguished himself on the ground as the voluntary civil affairs officer for his squadron. "We actually created quite an operation in our off-duty time. I got about a half-dozen men to help me rebuild parts of a school in a little town just outside the base…and then we raised money for a scholarship program. We also obtained much needed items for the children in the local orphanages."

Remembering this experience he said, "Those things were not without risks - I got shot at a couple of times because I was out in unprotected territory. Many people thought I was absolutely nuts…but it was gratifying to make wonderful friendships and make a difference in the lives of children. One of the friendships developed was with a civilian in Nah Trang who was the Boy Scoutmaster for the troop of Vietnamese kids in the city of Nah Trang. Years later, in 1975, I researched the names of the 'boat people' who escaped Vietnam but I never saw his name or the names of others who I had known. I have always wondered where they went and what happened to them…"

For these remarkable humanitarian efforts beyond the call of duty, Withuhn was awarded a Bronze Star. For the Captain, however, it was not about a medal or recognition; it was about doing something positive for other human beings while participating in combat.

By the end of his tour in Vietnam, this navigator had flown 207 missions and was awarded one of the first 200-mission patches of the "Left Turn Club," a very unofficial bunch, so named for the left-hand firing orbit of the AC gunships.

After Vietnam, Withuhn obtained the rank of major and even learned to fly a light aircraft. Withuhn crossed the Atlantic and the Pacific dozens of times and flew to every continent. He retired from active duty in 1972 and then completed twenty years of service in the Reserves.

In civilian life, Withuhn earned an MBA with distinction at Cornell University, and after a career as the senior vice president of a group of newly created regional and short line railroad companies operating in five states, he joined the Smithsonian Institution in 1983. During his twenty-six year tenure with the Smithsonian, Withuhn served as a project manager or curator for ten major exhibitions.

An introspective person, Withuhn continues to analyze his role and the role of others in combat. In many respects, his feelings are remarkably similar to his original thoughts while in Vietnam. The former Shadow navigator stated, "I think there is something that happens to every soldier, every airman, every sailor in a combat situation … the political context and the military context of what you're doing at that moment just goes away. The only thing that matters is your buddy. And, in my case, it was often a disembodied voice of some guy on the radio with an accent from Indiana or Ohio or Florida … It's a unique feeling that takes over entirely, and it's a moment of self-discovery for a lot of people in combat. They find out what really matters."

Notes

Major William L. "Bill" Withuhn, Distinguished Flying Cross citation, action date: 7 September 1969, Archives, the Distinguished Flying Cross Society, San Diego, CA.

Major William L. "Bill" Withuhn, oral history interview, interviewed by Dr. Barry A. Lanman, 20 June 2003, transcribed, the Distinguished Flying Cross Society Oral History Collection, the Distinguished Flying Cross Society Oral History Collection, the Distinguished Flying Cross Society, San Diego, CA.

Top: This F-4 with the distinctive falcon emblem of VMFA 334 was a formidable combat aircraft during the Vietnam era. Bottom: As a young lieutenant, Robert "Bob" Frantz flew combat missions in Vietnam and continued to actively fly in the United States Marines for nineteen years, attaining the rank of lieutenant colonel. Photographs courtesy of Bob Frantz and the Flying Leatherneck Museum

Conducting Air to Ground Support in a F-4J Phantom

Lieutenant Colonel, Robert "Bob" L. Frantz, USMC

"One missed step on our part and you've lost your Marines on the ground... you just had to fly by the seat of your pants."_____

Few young boys practice bombing runs during the summer. However, Robert "Bob" Frantz, with a prophetic calling, did just that. On the lakes of Minnesota, his best friend's uncle would take him for rides in a Piper PA-18 Super Cub on floats. Beside Frantz, in the tiny airplane, was a bucket of speared fish that he would hurl one-by-one at buoys on the water as if they were bombs destined for a military target. Thus, Frantz learned a great deal about estimated dive bombing factors while playing. When he became a Marine F-4 Phantom pilot, conducting bombing missions in Vietnam was second nature to this adventurous aviator.

Frantz attended the University of Minnesota, completed NROTC and was commissioned in 1966 as a second lieutenant in the Marine Corps. Hubert Humphrey actually presided over the commissioning ceremony as the senator lived in the same community and personally knew the family. After infantry training in Quantico, Virginia, the new Lieutenant attended flight training and because of his high class ranking, was selected to fly the new F-4Js before he headed for combat.

Frantz loved the F-4J Phantom II, a multi-purpose two-seater jet. With its twin engines, it was capable of Mach 2 (twice the speed of sound) and could carry up to 16,000 pounds of bombs, rockets, missiles and guns. In addition, the jet contained highly functioning radar and missile systems used by the radar intercept officer, who was located in the backseat.

In late 1968, Lieutenant Frantz was assigned to Chu Lai, Vietnam with Marine Fighter/Attack Squadron 334, Marine Aircraft Group 13, 1st Marine Aircraft Wing. The squadron was known as the "Falcons." It had twelve aircraft and, depending on rotations, fifteen crews.

Frantz recounted his initial involvement with VMFA 334. "I was the first replacement pilot in the squadron. When I got to my assigned hooch, there were two occupied beds and one bed that had a lot of personal effects laid out neatly. The roommates said that the pilot just got killed. So you can imagine how I felt as his replacement and then having my CO eject a couple of days later. It was also during the Tet Offensive and we were being shelled on the base quite often.

I immediately flew combat missions on my first flight and I fit in really well with the squadron. However, a replacement pilot who came after me flew into a mountain so they put the new guys after that through orientation flights.

The 'Falcons' flew mostly close air support missions for the Marines, but there were also many air-to-air missions. We were shot at frequently but you really couldn't tell from the cockpit except when they had 57mm anti-aircraft guns. Then, you could see the puffs of air bursts. One time the forward air controller told me to 'get the hell out of there - the whole world is shooting at you.' So, I immediately pulled straight up in full after burner. I could actually see rounds decelerating around me..."

After nearly 100 missions and a promotion to captain, Frantz experienced one of his most challenging situations. "We were just north of Chu-Li in Vietnam and conducting a close air support mission on 11 July 1969. As we arrived, we saw that a forward air controller (in an OV-10) was already on site and he briefed us.

The situation involved a Marine recon unit that was trapped on the ground and completely surrounded by North Vietnamese regulars. They were running low on ammunition and were in desperate need of help. The plan was to extract them from there...They were positioned in an outcropping of some rocks, so the target was well defined.

We were briefed and were tasked to make single runs with our two aircraft all around the perimeter of their defensive position and to drop our ordnance within 50 meters of the troops…And so we broke up and started our runs on the target. It was rather unusual because each run would be a single run. That would be twelve runs apiece. And we had to keep working our way around the defensive perimeter.

We started out dropping our 500 pound Snake-Eye bombs and then Napalm. So we put the bombs right in there, 50 meters from the 'friendlies' in a 360 degree perimeter…Of course, it was a very tense situation because you're dropping ordnance so close to the 'friendlies.' You have to be extremely accurate. One missed step on our part and you've lost your Marines on the ground…A 500 pound Snake-Eye going off at a hundred and fifty feet from the friendlies is a rather big event for them, so they were told to keep their heads down and that we were coming in. It was a very complex situation.

We dove in at low altitude and released our bombs at about 500 feet off the ground…At the same time the forward air controller told us how to re-establish our pattern for the next round. And, of course, the radar intercept officer in the back monitored our dive angle and air speed to help make adjustments for the mark, as well as to keep track of the wingman and the forward air controller, the terrain, and the weather. In other words, he kept our situational awareness at all times because I was so intensely involved in what I was doing; looking through that gun sight and flying the plane.

This was not the standard mission because we were trained to make a single run in on the same heading. On this mission, each run was on a different heading with terrain considerations and not much time to set up. You just had to fly by the seat of your pants… It's also physically demanding. In twelve runs you're pulling a lot of G's in the aircraft and you're 'jinking' around (maneuvering sharply at random) to avoid the ground fire coming up [to] fire at you.

My first reaction was that this mission represented unbelievable teamwork between me and my wingman, between our 'backseaters' and the forward air controller. And, then I thought about the Marines on the ground who trusted us to deliver that ordnance so close to them and this was heavy ordnance.

Out of all my missions, I distinctly remember this one after more than forty years. It was unique and as we left the target area, we were informed that the Marines were being extracted safely by helicopter…So that was a very satisfying experience."

For their acts of heroism, Captain Frantz, his wingman and the two radar intercept officers were awarded the Distinguished Flying Cross medal. Corroborating his personal account of the event, Frantz's Marine Corps citation stated, "…a previous extraction attempt had been aborted because of intense enemy fire. With complete disregard for his own safety, Captain Frantz commenced his attack against the North Vietnamese Army soldiers and, despite a heavy volume of hostile fire, relentlessly pressed his assault during numerous low-altitude runs. Although turbulent winds constituted a constant threat to accuracy, due to his superb airmanship, he delivered his ordnance on target unerringly, thereby enabling the team to be extracted from its critical position. Captain Frantz's courage, superior aeronautical ability, and unwavering devotion to duty in the face of grave personal danger inspired all who observed him…"

Throughout his entire tour in Vietnam with the "Falcons," Captain Frantz flew just under 200 missions and felt lucky that he was never hit and didn't experience any major mechanical problems in flight. Some of his friends in other squadrons were not as fortunate in their Phantoms.

When VMFA 334 rotated out to Japan in the summer of 1969, Captain Frantz was required to stay in Vietnam to finish his thirteen month tour. He was assigned as a legal officer for a Marine Air Base Squadron until he was sent home.

With the relative peace following Vietnam, this experience proved the only chance Frantz had to exercise his combat prowess. As time progressed, the fighter pilot was promoted through the ranks to lieutenant colonel and flew Phantoms and other jets for nineteen of his twenty year military career. Two years after his retirement in the spring of 1987, Frantz put on a different uniform and became a United Airlines pilot. For the next sixteen years, he flew various Boeing aircraft from the 737 to the 777 and the

Airbus A-320. In a combined total of thirty-six years of military and commercial flying, Robert Frantz accumulated over 15,000 hours in the air.

In a third career, Frantz completed his Ph.D. and is a professor specializing in business administration and on-line education. He also serves as President and CEO of Kepler University where he is able to integrate his volunteer work in Africa developing technology infrastructure and educational delivery through distant learning. Concurrently, he served on the Distinguished Flying Cross Society Board for ten years and held positions as president and chairman of the board.

The soft-spoken retired Marine does not talk about his exploits, except in the company of his compatriots or if he is asked to speak on behalf of the Distinguished Flying Cross. He simply states that, "My Distinguished Flying Cross is displayed on a shelf in my office. In itself, it doesn't have that much significance…except for the memories of the experiences I had in the Marine Corp…the memories of the friends I made in the Marine Corps…the people we saved…and the people we lost. So, to me, it is kind of a memorial."

There was one event that has stuck in his mind and is as vivid as his DFC mission. It was a chance encounter when he was flying as a commercial pilot. While in Kansas City on a lay-over, he had the opportunity to attend a luncheon at a VFW convention. There, he met a Marine who had been on the ground in Chu-Li at the same time Frantz had been conducting the air to ground support. The Marine bought Frantz a drink for saving his life. To Frantz, that meant more than the medal sitting on his shelf.

Notes

Lieutenant Colonel Robert "Bob" Frantz, Distinguished Flying Cross citation, action date: 11 July 1969, Distinguished Flying Cross Society, San Diego, CA.

Lieutenant Colonel Robert "Bob" Frantz, oral history interview, interviewed by Dr. Barry A. Lanman, 20 June 2003, transcribed, the Distinguished Flying Cross Society Oral History Collection, the Distinguished Flying Cross Society Oral History Collection, the Distinguished Flying Cross Society, San Diego, Ca.

Top: Captain O'Neil flew the first model Cobra – AH-1G. The assault helicopter carried fifty-six rockets and 4,000 rounds of ammunition. Bottom, left: Michael O'Neil struck an action pose for the camera while in Vietnam. He embraced his combat role as a Cobra pilot. Bottom, right: O'Neil was combat ready in his Cobra. He served with the First Air Cavalry Division, USA. Photographs courtesy of Michael O'Neil

Cobras, Corvettes and Cambodia
Captain Michael E. O'Neil, USA

"I was in the front seat of the first Cobra to go into Cambodia at treetop level."_____

For most teenagers, it takes many years to find a true calling. To borrow a phrase, life can be a long and winding road. However, Michael E. O'Neil knew exactly what he wanted to do; join the United States military and serve his country. Flying Huey Cobras would allow him to live out his dream.

With O'Neil's passion, it wasn't a surprise to his friends and family when he joined the Navy directly after high school graduation. However, he often needed to explain his atypical service record. "I served four years in the Navy as an enlisted man and then six years in the Army as a commissioned officer…I came up through the ranks.

Aviation appealed to me when I was about twenty-one years old. That's when I realized that the Vietnam War was really heating up and I wasn't happy with my enlisted status at that time. The government was soliciting for helicopter pilots, so I figured I'd sign up…The training for me as a commissioned officer was fun when I went through flight school. I had an extra thousand dollars a month tax-free, so it seemed like all of us officers had new Corvettes and other fast cars. It was a fun lifestyle.'

The other fast vehicle that Captain O'Neil loved was the Huey Cobra Helicopter. He explained why saying, "The Cobra was referred to as the AH-1 Snake. 'AH' stands for assault helicopter. That's the nomenclature. They have many different variations. I was on the first one, the model G. So I flew the AH-1G." O'Neil liked the Cobra because it was faster than the UH-1H Huey (Utility Helicopter) which carried troops and it could stay over a target for up to two hours before refueling…With its width of just thirty-six inches, it was a narrower target than the 100 inch wide UH-1 Huey. In addition to its speed, the attack helicopter was armed with 2.75 inch rockets, 7.62 mm miniguns, 40mm grenade launchers and a 20 mm Gatling gun. Thus, O'Neil had up to 56 rockets, over 4,000 rounds of 7.62 mm ammunition, 300 40 mm grenades and 750 rounds of 20 mm at his disposal in combat situations. The Cobras had the SCAS (Stability Control Augmentation System) that made it the first helicopter flying gunship platform. Its computer compensated for airspeed, wind direction, and altitude and placed the ordnance on target while using the cross-hair, heads-up display.

Trained as a Cobra pilot and sent to Vietnam, Lieutenant O'Neil wanted to make sure he flew the Cobra in combat and recounted the process by which he left nothing to chance. "As an officer, when you got to Vietnam, you could actually apply for different units. That was one of our benefits. I went to what they called the 91st Replacement Center in Long Binh. Once I got there, they said, 'Okay, where do you want to go?' Well, I asked around…'Who is getting all the action?' They told me, 'The First Air Cavalry Division is where you want to go,' because I wanted to fly Cobras. I wanted to do what my specialty was. They give me three choices on the application. I put down 1st Cavalry, 1st Cavalry and 1st Cavalry - I went to the First Cavalry.

I went to a Gun Company, flying Cobras, and I stayed with the First Cavalry my full tour in Vietnam. However, I did serve in two different units. In my first unit, we did combat assaults. We did five to eight combat assaults a day. I would go in and cover the troop ships. We called them Slicks [HU-1H Huey]. The helicopters, as they were carrying the troops, would go in, in formation and drop off the troops. I would go into the LZ [landing zone] one minute before the drop-off firing my guns and rockets as suppressive fire to cover the troop ships, hopefully eliminating any bad guys before they could shoot our guys, and then escort the troop carriers back to pick-up more troops. I did that for six months.

Three months into his tour in Vietnam, Lieutenant O'Neil had an opportunity of a lifetime. He was chosen to participate in an assault into Cambodia. To that point, Cambodia was off-limits from a political standpoint. However, for a period of 60 days, starting on 1 May 1970, the First Air Cavalry Division led the charge into the stronghold of the Viet Cong. Lieutenant O'Neil explained the memorable day.

"It was 1 May 1970 - That was when the First Air Cavalry Division had its incursion in Cambodia. I was with Delta Company 227th…It was quite a day. We started off with over 200 troop carriers. They were side by side. They were on the ground. Just picture this - 200 of them, side by side in 'double trouble' formation, with about eight to ten troops in each carrier. There were twenty-three Cobras, the gun ships, which were escorting them, so they were along both sides. On the mission of the day, we rose up, all of the helicopters at once, and that is how we proceeded with the incursion in Cambodia. We had combat assaults. We had strategic areas, landing zones, already mapped out exactly where we were going.

It just so happened that I was in the first lead Cobra helicopter with my CO, so that was really exciting. I was in the front seat of the first Cobra to go into Cambodia at treetop level. It was a tremendous feeling because it was the first time we had been in Cambodia and we knew that the enemy was pretty bountiful. This was where they actually had all their caches and they had their headquarters in Cambodia. So, we went in. The orders of the day were 'you will not fire unless fired upon.' That was always the mission statement. So as we went over the first village I remember looking down. I was probably a hundred feet above the village. All of a sudden my CO in the backseat said, 'Taking fire.' I had never seen anything like that in my life. I could see all the helicopters; they just started firing and just decimated everything along the way…whatever you saw shooting at you. So I suppressed enemy fire along the route.

When we came back and shut down we all looked at our aircraft and most had bullet holes in the rotors or in the sides. But we were oblivious to that until we shut down because during the mission we did hot refuels - we never shut down. It was the longest day I remember flying – twelve hours.

My reactions were simple. At twenty-five years old, it was exciting. We were doing what we had trained to do and we were actually going in after the enemy into locations where they had the cache. It really felt good to engage the enemy in their *rear* area. I think the one word was excitement…

After our mission in Cambodia, they found out that we had captured more arms in Cambodia in those sixty days than they did throughout all of the Vietnam War in Vietnam. It was the largest enemy cache of arms that they ever found. I feel good to be able to say that I was there and a part of it.

When I first heard about receiving a medal, I found out that they put me up for a Silver Star and they asked me 'Would you rather have the Silver Star or the Distinguished Flying Cross?' Being an aviator, I said, 'I will take the DFC.' So, I had a choice - I really did. I chose the DFC because, to me, that was an aviator's award – and I was proud to be an aviator.   I felt honored to receive the Distinguished Flying Cross."

The words describing O'Neil's meritorious actions on the Distinguished Flying Cross citation captured the significance of his role in this massive attack. "Michael E. O'Neil, First Lieutenant, United States Army, an AH-1G Cobra helicopter pilot with the D Company, 227th Aviation Battalion, 1st Air Cavalry Division, operating in Vietnam in 1970, for heroism while participating in aerial flight evidenced by voluntary actions above and beyond the call of duty in the Republic of Cambodia. First Lieutenant O'Neil distinguished himself by valorous action on 1 May 1970 as a gunship copilot when called upon to place suppressive fire on enemy positions along a route of flight and in the vicinity of a landing zone."

O'Neil is also proud of his DFC citation because it was so unique. "I think what is very unusual with my DFC, it says I received it 'in the Republic of Cambodia,' it actually says that on my citation. We were only in Cambodia for sixty days, so there weren't that many of us who actually received a DFC for actions in the Republic of Cambodia. That's why it really means a lot to me.

Three months after he received his DFC and was promoted to the rank of captain, O'Neil experienced one more profound life event. This time, it was personal rather than an event in combat. Like many other young soldiers who were away from their wives for a tour in Vietnam, he received a "Dear John" letter. His wife wanted a divorce and sought custody of their young son. Some officers, who were attorneys, offered advice. "They said, 'Look, eighty-percent of the guys over here are getting divorced.' It is a very high ratio but that is what happens in combat.' They also said, 'You can't go home for that, but if you wanted to fight for custody of your child we can let you go home for thirty days.' And, I said I did, so I actually went home for thirty days, took my wife to court in Alabama, came back to Vietnam and served the rest of my tour…While I was back in Vietnam, I received word that I won custody of my son, and after my tour, if I lived, I could pick him up; which I eventually did. We have been together ever since and he is now forty years old."

In the second part of his tour, the unit transformed itself into part of the 1st of the 9th Cavalry, which was a highly recognized unit in Vietnam. "I was with F-Troop and we did what was called 'Hunter-Killer Teams.' This strategy was brought forth by the 1st of the 9th Cavalry…The hunter would be the LOH helicopter and fly right at treetop level and serve as a scout. LOH is the nomenclature and it stands for Light Observation Helicopter. It would carry one pilot. It was small and looked egg-shaped. [The LOH were built by Hughes and given the name Cayuse after a Native American tribe.] The LOH would follow the trails…

I would be at 1,500 hundred feet in my Cobra, circling. Just think of a buzzard/vulture…And, I'm in direct contact with the LOH, the scout pilot. Once the scout pilot found the enemy, he would throw smoke down; red smoke, yellow smoke, whatever he had. He would then veer off to the right or left, and once he did that he would say 'Enemy's sighted.' I would then roll in, expend my ammo and try to terminate the enemy. After my attack, the scout pilot would go in, assess the battle damage and then we would move on and do it again…

It was a very strategic concept and the LOH were well put together helicopters because they did get shot down quite often but the pilots would usually survive. We would do the "Hunter-Killer Teams" for eight to ten hours a day.

While Cobra pilots dealt with life and death situations on a daily basis, there were amusing opportunities to reduce the stress of combat. Captain O'Neil is fond of telling his flechette rocket story. "Flechette rockets are designed to explode and send out sharp metal objects that look like six-penny nails; which could go through triple canopy jungle. The flechette rocket puts one 'nail' within every twelve inches (a square foot) in an area the size of a football field, and they were widely used as a weapon on the Cobras.

On one battalion combat assault, I flew over a valley with a wide open area. I looked down and realized I was flying over a pond. I estimated this pond had about 500 ducks in it. Not being a game hunter prior to the military, I thought, 'I have to do this.' So, I rolled over and fired a pair of flechette rockets. At 500 hundred feet, the optimum bursting radius, two big red puffs of smoke came over the pond and the nails were released. At that time, ducks flew out but I estimated I killed about three hundred and fifty ducks in one shot, so I thought I was definitely the world's greatest duck hunter! Besides, the 'friendlies' had plenty of food for awhile."

In February 1971, with over 1100 hours of combat flying, Captain O'Neil came back to the United States once again. This time he had an unexpected welcome on his final return. "I came back with four other US Army captains. Of the five captains, three of them were Army nurses. Once we landed at Travis Air Force Base in California, all of us had on the uniforms that we wore in Vietnam; our flight suits, or nurse's uniforms. And, at that time in 1971, to fly back to our home we would go on commercial airlines. If we put on our dress uniforms we could fly for half price. That was the deal. So the five of us caught a taxi and went to the San Francisco Airport.

When we got there, we changed our uniforms and decided to meet in the center of the airport foyer. We wanted to have a last drink, say goodbye and go on our way. After I changed my uniform and walked out in the foyer, I looked around in the center and there were probably about thirty people in a big circle and I heard some voices and some shouting…The nurses were in the center of the circle and there were two "hippies" calling the nurses "baby killers."

I walked up behind them and reached in my satchel that contained a souvenir enemy rifle and bayonet. I pulled out the bayonet and grabbed one guy by the collar and held it to his head... He had this look of absolute fear on his face. And the person across from him, the other 'hippie,' just looked – he didn't know what to do.

I told them to get on their knees and they better say that they're sorry. So, they apologized to the nurses. All the other people, the civilians, didn't know what was going to happen. Of course, I knew that I wasn't going to kill them. I just wanted to scare them. I gave them a parting kick in the side and put my bayonet away. They were left on the ground crying, and we all went and had a drink. So, my return from Vietnam does stick in my mind."

In many respects this was not an uncommon homecoming for the men and women returning from Vietnam. It points out the difficult transition for military personnel of that era. Having participated in an unpopular war, these soldiers, unlike their predecessors, returned from the battlefield to civilian life to face American protesters angry at them, American foreign policy and skeptical of the federal government itself. However, to this day, Captain O'Neil has justified his reaction in assisting the nurses he saw verbally assaulted by protestors.

Since he left the Army in 1972, Captain O'Neil has had the opportunity to put the entire Vietnam experience in context. "You're doing your job. You're doing your duty for your country, for your fellow soldiers. But I believe time has to pass so you can fully understand the ramifications of what you've done... From my combat experience, I have learned that persistence pays off. If you're persistent and you have faith in what you do and you don't listen to all the negative voices around you and you just keep a positive attitude – persistence pays off. And I believe that that outlook has served me well over the years. I think with the military, you can do whatever you want to do - the limitations are only in a person's mind. I believe that I'm proof that you can do and go where you want to go...I mean, I've accomplished a great deal – I went back to college and received a degree. And, it was just because I wanted to do it." In his role as a successful real estate broker in San Diego, California, the values of positive thinking and persistence have obviously served him well.

Since camaraderie was an important part of his time in Vietnam, he joined the Distinguished Flying Cross Society in 1996 and worked through the ranks of leadership to become its president and CEO. Currently, as the President Emeritus of the DFCS, he understands the value of this organization for military personnel such as himself. The decorated, disabled veteran makes his point by saying, "Camaraderie in Vietnam was important but I think the camaraderie that we feel, sharing our experiences in the DFCS, is even more meaningful than the actual time in combat...Maybe time has dimmed this perspective but I believe that talking with people who have shared these unique life situations is a form of catharsis. Our association enriches our lives and we in turn work hard to give something back to society and to preserve this history for future generations."

While Captain Michael O'Neil no longer pilots a Cobra gunship and no longer has his vintage Corvette, he always drives to Distinguished Flying Cross events in a shiny, new sports car containing the most advanced technology. You can tell that speed and control of a sophisticated piece of equipment is still in his blood. The glint in his eye, when he steps out of his latest machine, is just about the same as it was when he used to climb out of his AH-1G after combat.

Notes

Captain Michael E. O'Neil, Distinguished Flying Cross citation, action date: 1 May 1970, the Distinguished Flying Cross Society, San Diego, CA.

Captain Michael E. O'Neil, oral history interview, 12 December 2009, interviewed by Dr. Barry A. Lanman, 12 December 2009, transcribed, the Distinguished Flying Cross Society Oral History Collection, the Distinguished Flying Cross Society, San Diego, CA.

Top: Lieutenant Phillips was part of Project TRIM during his tour in Vietnam. Middle, right: Phillips flew the TRIM AP-2H configured gunship which contained some of the most sophisticated electronics of the Vietnam era. Middle, left: During his free time, Phillips participated in building a school for Vietnamese children. Bottom: Lieutenant Reed Phillips on a mission over Vietnam. He flew commercial jets after his retirement from the Navy as a captain. Photographs courtesy of Reed Phillips

Developing and Evaluating High Tech Night Sensors in Combat

Captain Reed M. Phillips, USN

"It was just a reaction. I laid on the grenade launcher and slammed up the jets."

After graduating from Burien High School in Seattle, Washington with the class of 1956, Reed Phillips acquired his initial work experience at Lou's 19 Cent Hamburgers. That provided him with a dose of reality and taught him the values of hard work. Having progressed to the "Flying A" gas station and then on to Ernie's Mobile gas station, where he served as the night manager, Phillips learned the art of leadership and teamwork. Those skills prepared him for the Navy where his career took flight.

Concurrent with his part-time work, Reed started college at the University of Washington in Seattle during the fall of 1956 and graduated with a degree in Mechanical Engineering in the fall of 1961. In addition to his studies as an engineer, he was accepted into the Naval Reserve Officer Training (NROTC) at the university and participated in two midshipman cruises before he completed his studies.

With his undergraduate degree completed and a commission as a reserve officer in the Navy, Reed had to make the next set of life decisions. He loved the sea and yet he had a strong desire, since the fourth grade, to become a commercial pilot like his step-father. The decision ultimately became clear: he would become a naval aviator.

In January 1961, Ensign Phillips started Navy Flight School at Pensacola, Florida and completed his training as a Naval Aviator by May 1962. He related vivid memories of his training. "The T-28 was the basic training aircraft after initial instruction in the T-34…Once the basic training phase was completed at Pensacola, our last phase was carrier qualification. After practicing Field Carrier Landing Practice (FCLPs), our instructor, a marine colonel in charge of the carrier qualification program, made the decision as to whether or not we were ready to car qual (carrier qualify)…You would take off all by yourself and fly to the ship, check in and make two 'touch and go landings' on the ship followed by six 'arrested' landings. It was such an experience for me to be in the aircraft alone and complete the mission successfully with great confidence…I got my Navy wings in May 1962."

As his naval career progressed, Phillips integrated his initial education as an engineer and completed the U S Naval Postgraduate School in October 1966. He then worked at the Naval Test Center, Patuxent River, Maryland and became part of the Weapons System Test (WST) Division of the Naval Air Test Center at Patuxent River. During this assignment, he became part of Project TRIM (Trails, Roads, Interdiction and Multi-sensors). In this capacity, he worked on sensor testing for the AP-2H airplane from Lockheed and in June 1967, witnessed a solo AP-2H aircraft acceptance flight at Edwards Air Force Base, California.

In early 1968, Lieutenant Phillips received orders for Vietnam. He left Alameda, California on 9 March 1965 and flew to Naval Air Station Barbers Point, Hawaii. Once there, he island hopped to Midway Island, Wake Island, Guam and then landed at Cam Ranh Bay, Vietnam on 15 March 1968. He was assigned to VAH-21 (heavy attack) Navy Squadron at NAF (Naval Air Facility), Cam Ranh Bay with detachments at DaNang.

Reed explained his overall mission and the aircraft he flew. "Military intelligence documented the North Vietnamese [Viet Cong] were using night operations for attacks and supply logistic movement. Our mission was to suppress this effort. The number of sensor contact and artillery/small arms fire we received while airborne verified these facts.

The TRIM AP-2H configured gunship definitely influenced our missions in Vietnam and provided valuable military intelligence…The night sensors were a new technology not previously available. Our missions were successful in demonstrating the value of infrared sensors developed by Texas Instruments and Hughes. Thus we were evaluating two models.

As far as the aircraft itself, it was a gunship and was an outgrowth of World War II bombers with two large Wright reciprocating engines producing 3,700 hp. In addition, two Westinghouse turbo compound jet engines were available to produce 3,400 lbs of thrust for takeoff and combat missions. The aircraft would be flown at low-level (1500 feet) with the jets in idle. The APQ-116 terrain avoidance radar was utilized on all combat missions that required both reciprocating and jet engines at full power when needed. To make the aircraft harder to detect and target, the planes were painted in a very effective tri-color gray pattern…Metal shrouds were fitted over the exhaust stacks to reduce the visual and thermal signatures emitted from the engines. For additional protection, armor plating was fitted around the engine oil coolers and the main hydraulic panel, and around the fuel valves and propeller feathering pumps.

The bottoms of all crew seats were armor plated and there was extra protection in the forward and side areas of the cockpit. The wings were also fitted with self-sealing fuel tanks and the tanks were stuffed with polyurethane foam material. Nitrogen was used to purge the tip tanks of fuel vapors when they had been emptied. A final protection was a bailout chute, installed on the forward flight deck. A pull on the emergency release handle would fire explosive charges that would blow 3x3 foot panels through the flight deck and the lower fuselage. The advanced model of the AP-2H was the #4 Buno 145902 which had the most sophisticated safety devices and sensors.

The AP-2H combat configuration had a crew of seven: pilot (designated combat aircraft commander), co-pilot (coordinated all communications pertaining to flight and crew functions), bombardier (BN - primary sensor operator), navigator (usually a junior pilot - responsible for correct route selection and also to assist the bombardier with sensor target selection), plane captain (a senior enlisted mechanic in charge of aircraft maintenance; various crew members reported to him the status of their respective aircraft systems), radio operator (UHF, HF, and all radio communications) and ordnanceman (manned dual 20mm cannons with a night observation scope mounted in the tail turret to protect the rear of the aircraft as it departed the target). After 9 February 1969, two 7.62mm miniguns were added with a crew complement increase from seven to nine.

To perform the nighttime interdiction mission, the AP-2H had to find the targets and destroy them quickly and efficiently. The primary weapons for this task were wing-mounted bombs, 500 pound Mark 82s and 250 pound Mark 81s, both fitted with snake-eye fins and daisy-cutter fuses, and Mark 77 napalm canisters. The planes were fitted with wing-mounted Gatling guns and pintle-mounted guns firing from the aft crew stations windows. To counter ground fire directly below, 84mm grenade launchers were installed in the bomb bay at various firing angles. That was a brand new gun at the time and is now installed in the AC-130 gunships. It would fire almost 1,000 rounds per minute per barrel, resulting in almost 8,000 total rounds a minute. The Mark 81, Mark 82, and Mark 77 were loaded on the four wing stations to accommodate various missions. Our senior ordnanceman designed a delayed fuse on the 500 pound Mark 82 so that when the Mark 82 and Mark 77 napalm were dropped together they would explode. At low level that was awesome! It was very effective with fire and shrapnel against an enemy convoy.

The BN would normally operate the primary sensors: the LLLTV (Low Light Level Television) and the FLIR (Forward Looking Infrared). Both sensors were mounted in a chin fairing just beneath the nose of the aircraft and co-aligned. Both systems were tied to an automatic bombing system that could be manually locked on a target. The system would solve the attack problem and release selected weapons.

The target lock-on system was displayed on the pilot's (left seat) attitude gyro with guidance for him to fly to the target for auto release of selected weapons. Also, both the bombardier and navigator on the flight deck had dual displays for the LLLTV and FLIR, and could compare the electro-optical and thermo images while searching for targets. In addition, there was also a DLIR (Downward Looking Infrared) for post flight analysis and four ECM Jammers.

I flew sixty-one combat missions, seven of which were flown from VAH-21 detachment at DaNang, VNN, and I worked with more than twenty technical representatives from various electronic and weapons manufacturers stationed at Cam Ranh Bay. We evaluated equipment to see what worked the best under real combat conditions. Because of this testing and development role, our briefings were fairly long and we would launch with all night missions."

One challenging experience for then Lieutenant Phillips was on a mission north east of Ton Son Nut (Saigon). He recalled, "My aircraft was hit with small arms fire in the rear of the aircraft. The plane captain (senior enlisted mechanic) ran to the rear of the aircraft and discovered that the relief tube heater was on fire and he extinguished the fire with his hands. The 20mm tail turret had used almost all of its ammo and this definitely saved the aircraft…Once on the ground, we found many holes in the aft section of the plane."

While this experience was harrowing, his most significant mission was flown on 20 January 1969. Phillips remembers it in detail. "We flew that particular mission out of Cam Ranh Bay and it was a single-plane, low level, night strike against a heavily defended supply storage facility along the Kinh Cai Beo Canal in Kien Phong Province, Republic of Vietnam…We were getting ready to go home and I was training my relief.

He had flown three missions from the left seat (pilot's seat) and I, as the copilot, was in the right seat to give him command experience…This mission was briefed as having fairly good intelligence, which came from the Navy and the Air Force. While the intelligence was about three days old, it seemed like a good mission…

I could tell the pilot in training was very nervous about being the actual pilot on this mission. In addition, my entire crew was new. I said to the pilot in training, whose nickname was Tex, 'Why don't you let me fly this one? You're really doing a good job at this stage of the turnover. I'll fly in the left seat and you fly in the right seat.' Well, he liked that idea, so that's the way we flew this mission.

We'd launched about one-thirty in the morning and tried to get our IP (Initial Point - pre selected grid coordinate point to update the computer) somewhere around 3:00 am. We did that and flew about 160 miles over enemy held territory. I descended to 1500 feet as we were approaching our IP. As we came in to our IP we had to update our computer—we had to be below 2,000 feet in order for the computers to work. We had pre-briefed and when we reached the IP, the plane captain laid down in the nose with night goggles, wearing a flak vest for protection, and gave us a mark and that updated our computer.

As we were making our approach, we were fired on by two fifty caliber automatic weapon sites with tracers. Of course, we hadn't known they were there and I was about 1,500 feet. I said, 'Oh my gosh!' It was just a reaction…I laid on the grenade launcher and slammed up the jets, which raised the nose up sharply and then I lowered it as we came on top [at a higher altitude]. I remember the BN said all he did was cover his face with the scope because he thought that was the end…when he saw all those tracers coming up on his scope.

We then shot straight down, and we saw this thing blow up…It was an ammo dump storage facility. The explosion raised and rocked the airplane. It also silenced the weapon sites. Because this was not our target, we continued to our intended target and dropped our ordnance.

This particular ordnance load was a little different. We simultaneously dropped a 500 pound Mark 77 napalm, a 500 pound Mark 82 iron bomb and 200 40 mm grenades on our target. Then, we came back around to our IP and strafed the entire area with approximately 300 rounds of 7.62 mm at altitudes as low as 400 feet; meeting only light resistance in return.

I think the surprise on that mission was that we received a lot of fire as we updated our computer. It's different when somebody's shooting at you. The adrenaline takes over…Your briefings and your training also takes over when you get into a situation like that and you just react. At any rate, we achieved our mission and didn't get shot down; we didn't even get hit that night."

For this mission, Lieutenant Reed Phillips received the Distinguished Flying Cross once he returned to the United States. However, many thoughts went through his mind as he got ready to depart Cam Ranh Bay on 1 February 1969. He prized the working relationships developed between his fellow officers, his crew and the technical representatives. He understood the personal growth that the experience had provided and the camaraderie that had grown through the bonds of combat.

Upon leaving, Phillips was even more resolute about his support for the Vietnam War than he was before he came. He justified his position by saying, "My true thoughts always considered our vital mission in Vietnam…During the TET Offensive in 1968, all of us felt that we were winning the war. We were privy to the intelligence chatter from the Navy, Air Force and Marines – all that we did with the F-105s in Korat, Thailand and our B-52 strikes from Guam, we were convinced we were on our way to victory. My own opinion was that if the communists took Vietnam, the next would be the Philippines and so on…I think the only thing that stopped our eventual progress was Watergate, politics and attitudes against the war…So, it wasn't as easy to leave as I thought it would be…"

While Lieutenant Phillips had been highly trained for his role in Vietnam, he was totally unprepared for his re-entry to the United States and the growing anti-war sentiment. "I came back to Alameda, California and I was getting out [of] the Navy to fly for TWA, Trans World Airlines. I was shocked to see the look on high school students' faces when they saw me in my Navy uniform in an ice cream shop. If looks could have killed, I would have been dead. I didn't realize that the animosity was so prevalent…To them I was the 'scum of the earth'…"

So greatly affected by this and other similar situations, he declined to attend the inspection ceremony to personally receive his Distinguished Flying Cross. In fact, it would take some time before he put the events of that era in perspective and realized the importance of the medal and the words on his DFC citation.

For more than two decades, Phillips served on either active duty or in reserve status and retired in 1992 as a Navy captain after thirty-two years of service. During that time he also flew B-707s, B-727s, and the Lockheed L-1011 for TWA as a commercial pilot. Both civilian and military aviation was a thrill for Reed and he revered every moment he was up in the air. He also revered the time he spent with his stepdad since they could share their satisfaction and love of flying.

As a former vice-president and a board member of the Distinguished Flying Cross Society, Reed Phillips has had a substantial amount of time to think about what the DFC means to him and his family. He emphatically tells people his perspective.

"It's not so much an award for me. Instead, what I would like to pass on to my grandchildren is the message that their grandfather was one of those individuals who was willing to fight for his country and his principles…I had no hesitation about Vietnam. I thought there was a good cause and I supported it. I want them to know that all my buddies were willing to give their lives to fight for their country.

My children ask me, 'Gee Dad, would you go to Iraq?' I tell them, 'I'd go in a minute!' I compare the attitudes during Vietnam with the attitudes of today. I see our veterans serving in two wars with back-to-back combat tours…We need to commend and care for them and their families in a more thorough way than in the past. We need to revere their sacrifice for this country. I hope we never lose that commitment to freedom."

Notes

Captain Reed Phillips, Distinguished Flying Cross citation, action date: 20 January 1969, Archives, the Distinguished Flying Cross Society, San Diego, CA.

Captain Reed Phillips, oral history interview, interviewed by Dr. Barry A. Lanman, 20 June 2003, transcribed, the Distinguished Flying Cross Society Oral History Collection, The Distinguished Flying Cross Society, San Diego, CA.

Top: Considering his Native American heritage, John Meyers'
ancestors participated in every conflict throughout American
history. However, he was the first family warrior in the air.
Middle: Meyers served as a forward air controller in Vietnam.
He extended his tour of duty to support his fellow aviators.
Bottom: Along with combat experience in Vietnam, Colonel
Meyers served in Desert Storm. Throughout his career he
was awarded the Distinguished Flying Cross seven times.
Photographs courtesy of John Meyers

A Native American Warrior in the Air

Colonel John V. Meyers, USA

"It wasn't the medals. It was the memories."
"It was the relationships that can only be forged under fire."_____

When people ask John Vance Meyers why he joined the military, he responds with a glint in his eye and the hint of a smile, "I was *invited* to join the Army." Referring to being drafted on 12 June 1966, Meyers had no intention of making the military a career. "I fully intended, when I was drafted, to do my two years, do them honorably and come home." From the numerous medals and awards proudly displayed in the basement of his home, he did more than an honorable job for three decades.

His heritage and family traditions may have had something to do with Meyers' ultimate career choice and success. "My mother was Cherokee and my father was Cahuilla, from California." Since the arrival of the Europeans, the American Indian community has had warriors in every conflict including both sides of the Revolutionary War and the Civil War. "As far back as our family research has been explored we have had family members that served in the Confederacy as well as the US Army during the Civil War; my grandmother's brother was a Marine in World War I; my father served in the Navy during World War II; his brother, my uncle was an Army veteran of the European campaigns. He was captured during the Battle of the Bulge and spent the remaining months of the war as a 'guest' of the Germans. Another uncle served in the Army during the Korean War. I guess I am a continuation of that tradition with one exception…I am the only aviator."

As with his induction in the Army through the draft, Private Meyers did not see himself as a pilot. Instead, he wanted to jump out of planes so he volunteered for Airborne Advanced Infantry Training (AIT). After basic training at Fort Bliss, Texas he was sent to Fort Gordon, Georgia to complete Airborne AIT. "I was twenty-five years old when I got drafted, so I was always the old man in training. I had a first sergeant who strongly encouraged me to go to Officer Candidate School so I applied. I wanted infantry and put it down for all three choices, but the Army sent me to Field Artillery OCS." Upon graduation in June 1967 as a new lieutenant, Meyers still wanted to complete his Airborne Ranger training but could never get a slot because all of the training slots went to West Point Graduates and ROTC Distinguished Graduates. "So out of total frustration, and wanting to do something special, I applied for flight school and was accepted."

I reported for fixed wing training at Fort Stewart, Georgia and, to tell you the truth, I almost busted out - fear of flying. And I almost busted my solo ride, but I managed to pull it off…Having conquered that first bit of fear, I got better and better. After graduation they shipped me over to Vietnam."

The Army aviator was initially assigned to the 185th Reconnaissance Airplane Company (RAC) flying O-1 Birddogs out of Buon Ma Thout in support of Studies and Observation Group (MACVSOG) Command & Control South (CCS) conducting covert strategic reconnaissance, and interdiction missions along the Ho Chi Minh Trail in Laos and Cambodia (at the time a Top Secret mission; much of that history remains classified). In actuality, the mission involved radio relay and became quite routine and boring. Due to the lack of action, he managed to get reassigned to the 219th RAC headquartered out of Pleiku. Meyers was then sent to Kontum to lead a Flight Section in support of Command & Control Central (CCC) one of the SOG mission forward operating bases (FOB). The area of operations (AO) was due west of Kontum in the tri-border area which included a large portion of northern Cambodia stretching south to CCSs AO and included an equally large portion of southern Laos extending north into Command & Control North's (CCN) AO.

Meyers described some of the types of missions they flew. "As part of our daily support activities we went in and selected the LZs (Landing Zones) to be used for insertions and extractions of the three to five man Special Forces recon teams. We provided command and control coordination for the insertions and extractions, monitored the progress of the reconnaissance teams, received and forwarded situation reports (SITREPS) to the CCC Operations Center.

The Ho Chi Minh Trail was a hostile environment heavily populated with AAA anti-aircraft batteries strategically employed throughout the area of operations (AO), which included 12.7 machine guns, 37mm and 57mm guns. We could always count on fire from an AK-47 and occasionally from an RPG. When the bad guys, North Vietnamese Regulars, (NVA) discovered the recon teams we served as forward air controllers and routinely brought the teams out under heavy ground fire. Under these circumstances, the Air Force fighter pilots always honored our marks when we marked targets, and set up the engagement. Normal protocol required an Air Force (AF) FAC to set up the air to ground engagement of enemy targets in close proximity to friendly troops. When the teams were within range of Army Field Artillery (FA) we routinely adjusted this fire within fifty meters of the team. Hot extractions were very common occurrences.

When our recon teams came in contact with the enemy, often times the AF and Army gunships were several minutes away. In these cases we would provide as much cover for the team as we had available. For example; four white phosphorous marking rockets; hand grenades dropped from the aircraft; and firing our CAR-15s out the window. The pilots I flew with were some of the most courageous men I have ever known. They would never leave a deployed team without air cover even when they were the only cover available or leave a member of the team that became separated. In order to provide this close support, we flew right on the trees; sometimes bring part of the trees back in our landing gear.

While we weren't supposed to fly below 1,500 feet, we did so as a common practice for survival. You couldn't really see anything with any detail at that altitude and 1,500 feet was also optimum for the enemy to engage your single-engine Cessna L-19/0-1 Bird Dog, flying at a maximum cruise speed of seventy-five miles per hour.

We tried to fly all of our missions with a low and a high ship. The low ship was on the trees and the high ship had one mission, and that was to watch the low ship in case he took fire and to coordinate evasive action efforts. If the low ship did go down, there was an immediate call for evacuation. We'd be able to get in there real quick and get the downed crew out.

When we weren't directly supporting the teams with the command and control (CC), and forward air control (FAC), sometimes all we did was go out there and just hunt…We hunted the North Vietnamese regulars…and some of us got good at hunting…We used ourselves as bait in order to draw them out. You also learned how to read their camouflage…in that environment it doesn't take very long for cut vegetation to turn…The leaves will stay green, but they will look different in the sunlight than everything else that's growing around them.

There were some experimental activities that we engaged in as well to liven things up a bit. For example, we'd take C-4 and put it in a box of six-penny nails, have these EOD guys rig the thing up with a timed fuse and we'd try to figure out how to drop it out of the plane to get optimum explosion. Most of us thought we were indestructible and the answer to combat aviation.

They couldn't keep me out of the cockpit…it was exciting; I was an adrenalin junky. One of the psychologically acquired burdens of this mission was that you never wanted to leave. That was because once you became close to the people you were supporting, they depended on you and you were a part of this very unique 'Warrior Family.' I had stayed twenty months in the country before I rotated back, not the usual twelve. I extended to stay there and fly those missions. I was accused by one of my company commanders of having a death wish. To tell you the truth, I didn't think there was a bullet that could be fired at me that could get me at that particular time in my life.

We lived on the compound with the Special Forces troops, and that particular compound was divided up into four distinct sections: American Special Forces, Vietnamese Rangers and various indigenous mercenaries such as Vietnamese Montagnards and Chinese Nungs.

It was really interesting and a real nonconformist group of people…But they were dedicated to one another in a very special way to ensure that the mission succeeded…and that we did our best to get everybody out. Some reconnaissance teams were sent in to do a prisoner snatch as a source of intelligence; probably the most dangerous of SOG missions. Once the snatch was made, we would have to bring him out immediately. Sometimes, a real hot gun fight would result in order to get the team and prisoner out. This would involve bringing in the gunships and A1Es and 'fast movers' to assist.

We were basically responsible for the care and well-being of the reconnaissance teams that we deployed in Northern Cambodia and Southern Laos. Many of the missions turned out to be regular gunfights; not so often with the insertion, but many times with the extractions of those teams.

Combat is a deadly game. For those that have come to thrive in that environment, it's the same mentality or buzz that people get from bungee jumping, parachuting, free-falling; pushing everything out there to the edge. When you've got a reconnaissance team on the ground in trouble, sometimes you're their first line of defense and you've got those four little rocket tubes, maybe some hand grenades and maybe a CAR-15 that you shoot out the window just to hold the bad guys away from your buddies until you can get the rescue ships there and the gunships there. You're basically covering…'six' of the guy[s] you drank with the night before. You're not going to let them down."

With 1,500 combat hours of flying, Meyers clearly admitted, "Those missions have all become blurred together…How do you separate that? At one point, I received three Distinguished Flying Cross medals in the same ceremony and I was written up in a news article. Those were the first three DFCs." Meyers would ultimately receive a total of six Distinguished Flying Crosses and two Bronze Stars.

"The only nomination for in country action that I received was a nomination for a Silver Star that was down graded to a DFC. I was temporarily assigned to the Hawkeyes at Quy Nhon that was centrally located on the coast…Charlie Ryan, my Platoon Leader and I flew a reconnaissance mission just northwest of Phu Kat Airbase. Phu Kat Airbase sat inland from Quy Nhon about five or six kilometers and north about the same amount. The runway generally ran southeast to northwest. It was located on a plain and there were mountains to the north and the upper plain, which went west to Pleiku.

I was flying illegally down on the deck and I happened to look out of my right window and saw a camouflaged 12.7 gun emplacement. It sat on a big elevated tripod and the VC dug something that looks like a Mexican hat – a big ditch in a circle and they would leave the center and put the tripod on the center so that the gunner is actually in the ditch and he can fire from this position and not be all that well exposed. He's got a 360 field of fire for anti-aircraft. Well, this gun was sitting about two to three kilometers off the end of Phu Kat. The airbase accommodated all of the F-100s and I think, for a while, F-105s, and F-4s.

They were just setting up and they were trying to get it camouflaged when I saw the gun and everything else. LZ Eagle, which was the 101st Airborne Division's command post, was just over the hill from us, and we initially called in gunships. They came in and they worked the place over. Charlie and I, with our eight rockets, scattered the covey; we then called in for a reaction force, from Camp Eagle, and they sent a platoon from the 101st to clean up . The platoon captured the gun and some secret documents. Charlie Ryan and I were both awarded the Distinguished Flying Cross for that action."

After John Meyers was rotated back to the United States, he served in the 82nd Airborne Division but got riffed because he didn't have a college education. He then joined the South Carolina Army National Guard and went to Wofford College on the GI Bill. Upon graduation, he worked for the Bureau of Indian Affairs and transitioned from National Guard to the United States Army Reserve 80th Training Division.

From that assignment, he went to the 352nd Civil Affairs Brigade, received a battalion command, and was activated for Desert Storm. "As a result of qualifying for my Special Forces Tab in 1988, I went over as the 7th Corps Artillery's Senior Special Operations Officer. In that capacity, during the shooting part of that war, I did all of the target preclusions and airspace management. I also monitored the progress and the activities of the Special Forces teams that were forward deployed so we wouldn't inadvertently target them."

Once the assignment in Desert Storm ended, Meyers was selected to attend the National War College. Considering there was only one chair in each class for an Army Reserve officer, his acceptance was both an honor and a privilege, and he graduated in the class of 1994. Colonel Meyers completed a combined Active and Reserve Military career spanning some thirty-one years of service having commanded at every level; from Battery, to Battalion, to Brigade. Among other honors, he was inducted as a member of the US Army's Field Artillery Officer Candidate School Hall of Fame. Meyers' public service also included significant appointments with the Departments of Defense, Housing & Urban Development, Labor and Indian Affairs. In the private sector, he served as the President and Chief Operating Officer of Native American Industrial Distributors, Inc.

On his retirement from the military, John Meyers was meritoriously appointed as the Army Reserve Ambassador from the State of Maryland, which carried the honorary rank of major general. In that role, he communicates the Army Reserve's mission to the public. He also assists families left behind from deployed soldiers and helps families with burial issues. However, he explained his most cherished part of the duty: "The most rewarding part of my ambassadorship is the Welcome Home Warrior Program where we actually take part in welcoming home the soldiers. I carry the Challenge Coins with me and I 'coin them' and say, 'thank you.' And you don't know what it does for their morale…We didn't get that welcome home from Vietnam. Now, we did better in Desert Storm. We had the big parade in Washington D.C. and so forth…that was really odd because those of us who had participated in both wars just couldn't get over the difference between the two experiences."

As Colonel Meyers reflects on his life, he has many thoughts on the value of his time in the military, especially his combat experiences. "When I started early in my career, I was basically incorrigible, and then somewhere along the line I guess I grew up and decided I was going to really put forth a sincere effort to be a professional soldier…

My uncle would never talk to me about WWII – until I got back from Vietnam. Then we sat down and we talked about it because there was this understanding that can't happen unless you experience some of the same things…There's this brotherhood…'The family of warriors.' If there's anything good that comes out of combat and out of that experience, it is the tendency to erase some of the things we stumble over continually, like race, class and now that we've got women in combat, gender issues."

Realizing that the family legacy continues, Colonel Meyers proudly talks about his son, who is a West Point graduate, a veteran of Kosovo and currently serves as an assistant professor at the Point. With a pending assignment most likely in Afghanistan, another generation is fulfilling the family tradition.

When asked about his seven DFCs and Bronze Stars, he responded: "For years, I didn't think about it and now I realize the real significance…It wasn't the medals. It was the memories…It was the relationships that can only be forged under fire."

Notes

Colonel John Vance Myers, Distinguished Flying Cross citation, action date: 9 February 1970, Archives, the Distinguished Flying Cross Society, San Diego, CA.

Colonel John Vance Myers, oral history interview, interviewed by Dr. Barry A. Lanman, 8 July 2009, transcribed, the Distinguished Flying Cross Society Oral History Collection, The Distinguished Flying Cross Society, San Diego, CA.

Memorable Moments of the Distinguished Flying Cross

Vietnam

"Combat in Vietnam was basically like watching a motion picture right in front of my very own eyes."

Captain Bob Jackson, USA

Captain James L. Champlin, USAF
Directed Fighter and Tactical Sorties as a Forward Air Controller

As an O-1E, Bird Dog pilot, Captain James L. Champlin's job was to fly slow and low over the dense jungles of Vietnam to spot Viet Cong, direct air strikes and support the ground troops. Champlin received a Distinguished Flying Cross with a citation that stated, "while participating in aerial flight as a Forward Air Controller near Bong Son, Binh Dinh Province, Republic of Vietnam on 30 January 1966...Captain Champlin, in support of friendly ground forces, made repeated passes through heavy anti-aircraft fire to draw the fire away from the friendly forces and expose the hostile forces' positions. He then expertly directed six fighter sorties against these positions while continuously under deadly ground fire and completely routed the attack."

His second DFC, 1st Oak Leaf Cluster, serving as a forward air controller was awarded on 6 May 1966 also near Bong Son, Binh Dinh Province, Republic of Vietnam. "On that date, in support of friendly ground troops who were pinned down by heavy fire from a battalion size hostile force, Captain Champlin made several low passes through intense anti-aircraft fire to harass and contain escaping hostile troops, pinpoint their positions, and relieve fire from the friendly forces. He then directed two tactical close air support sorties on these positions under heavy ground-to-air fire, killing fifteen hostile troops and regaining the offense that the United States forces needed."[1]

Staff Sergeant Aaron D. Farrior, USAF
Pararescue Technician Saved Many Under Fire

Staff Sergeant Aaron D. Farrior was awarded the Distinguished Flying Cross for extraordinary achievement while participating in aerial flight as a helicopter pararescueman over Southeast Asia on 7 March 1966. On that date, he made a successful rescue and recovery of an American pilot whose aircraft had been shot down.

His second DFC in 1966 involved, "three desperate attempts to rescue an American pilot who was forced to bail out of his disabled aircraft over hostile territory... Farrior's aircraft was raked by hostile fire. Because of the battle damage to his rescue helicopter, Sergeant Farrior was forced to withdraw from the area.

His third and fourth DFCs, also in 1966, were

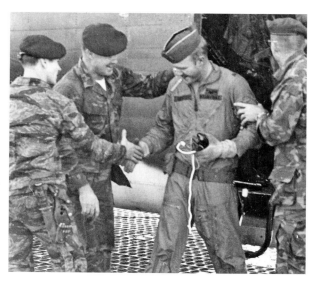

188

awarded for participating in aerial flight as a HH-3E Pararescue Technician in Southeast Asia. His third DFC was awarded for recovering a pilot while his fourth DFC was conferred for recovering two Air Force pilots from an extremely hostile area. The citation for his fourth DFC described the scene as follows: "Despite automatic weapons fire directed at his helicopter, Sergeant Farrior exposed himself in the open doorway while skillfully directing a precarious hover down into the trees to place the fully extended hoist cable within one survivor's reach."[2]   Both pilots were rescued.

Throughout his time in Southeast Asia, Sergeant Farrior was engaged in over 440 hours of actual combat time. Most of his missions were spent over North Vietnam or Laos and involved rescues which were extremely close to either Hanoi or the Chinese border. Without regard for his own personal safety, Sergeant Farrior saved the lives of countless pilots and crew.   (Farrior - right)

Captain Dean Jones and Captain Wayne Jones, USAF
Twin Brothers Received Distinguished Flying Crosses

Captain Dean Jones received a DFC on 11 June 1967 while serving as a forward air controller near Duc Pho, Republic of Vietnam. The citation read as follows; "Captain Jones directed Combat Air Support aircraft in support of friendly forces who were under intense fire from a large and aggressive hostile force. With tenacity and courage, Captain Jones directed a large volume of Combat Air Support aircraft onto the target and coordinated the activities of army aviation and friendly artillery. The maximum possible amount of fire power was brought…"

Captain Dean Jones' second DFC was received on 29 September 1967 for locating and neutralizing the enemy with, "precise and devastating air support missions. His courageous actions saved several friendly lives by enabling a rapid medevac helicopter evacuation of the critically wounded.[3]

Jones' twin brother, Captain Wayne Jones served as an AC-47 pilot near DaNang, Republic of Vietnam and protected the Marble Mountain Air Station on 4 March 1968. As the base came under hostile rocket attack, the DFC citation recounted that, "Captain Jones' timely and professional reaction to the attack was credited with halting the attack, disrupting the hostile battle plan, destroying much of the hostile forces' war waging materials inflicting heavy casualties on the attacking personnel and eliminating further threat of attack to the friendly forces and materials of Marble Mountain Air Station."[4]   (Dean Jones – left and Wayne Jones – right)

Master Sergeant Alexander Underwood, USAF
Re-enlisted on His 100th Mission

Master Sergeant Alexander Underwood served in the Air Force for twenty years between 1959 and 1979. However, the most challenging time for him was his duty in Thailand during 1965 and 1966 when he served as a flight engineer/ECM operator. Assigned to the 25th TAC Reconnaissance Wing, USAFE at Takhli Airbase, he flew forty missions over North Vietnam and then completed another sixty missions over North Vietnam as part of the 6460th TRS at Takhli Airbase.

Master Sergeant Underwood received a DFC on 29 June 1966 during an extremely hazardous mission while under hostile fire from unfriendly forces.[5] Believing in his service to the United States, Underwood re-enlisted on his last mission over North Vietnam and stayed in the Air Force until his retirement in 1979.

Sergeant Pat Stouffer, USAF
Aerial Gunner on a "Puff the Magic Dragon"

In September 1966, Sergeant Pat Stouffer was assigned to the 4th Air Commando Squadron stationed in Bien Hoa, Vietnam. Stouffer, a twenty-one year old native of San Diego, served as an aerial gunner on AC 47's flying night missions for the defense of fire bases against the enemy throughout War Zone C.

The planes Stouffer served on had been used in World War II and Korea before they were modified for their role in Vietnam to carry a formidable 21,000 rounds of 7.62mm ammunition and forty-five flares. At nighttime, the flames, tracers and roar of their mini-guns made the plane look like a mythical creature from the ground. Thus, the AC-47s were nicknamed "Puff the Magic Dragon." As a way to keep ever vigilant during missions, Pat stated "We had a standing rule - if you made a mistake during a mission, you bought the crew a case of beer, so no minor infractions went unnoticed."

Sergeant Stouffer was awarded a Distinguished Flying Cross for a mission conducted on 7 August 1967. Despite adverse weather and heavy anti-aircraft fire, Stouffer repelled several waves of enemy forces and saved the lives of American soldiers at a Special Forces camp in Tong Le Chon.[6] Completing a total of 179 combat missions during his tour in Vietnam, Sergeant Stouffer summed up his combat experience by saying "from these life and death situations, we all learned the meaning of team work and I grew up in the air over Vietnam."

Lieutenant Dave E. Clement, USN
Rescued Survivors from the Burning USS *Forrestal*

Lieutenant David E. Clement was awarded a Distinguished Flying Cross for heroism involving an explosion and fire which occurred on the USS *Forrestal* during 29 July 1967. Clement, a UH-2A Seasprite rescue helicopter pilot was highly commended for the following actions by the Navy in his DFC citation. "While Lieutenant Clement was flying plane guard for the *Forrestal* a tremendous fire broke out on the air flight deck of the *Forrestal*. Several people were blown over the side of the aircraft carrier by explosions. At the very beginning of the fire, Lieutenant Clement immediately flew to the position astern of the ship to pick up survivors in the water.

Braving flying debris and explosions that violently shook his aircraft, he skillfully hovered his overweight helicopter to rescue four badly burned survivors from the water. He delivered the four people to the flight deck of the nearby USS *Oriskany* (CVA 34), returned to the *Forrestal*, picked up an additional survivor from the water, and delivered this survivor to the forward flight deck of the *Forrestal*. He then made two additional landings on the still burning *Forrestal* to deliver medical personnel and supplies from the *Oriskany*. The landings aboard the *Forrestal* were all extremely hazardous because of the enormous fire, debris and explosions which continued to occur. His courageous and selfless action was in keeping with the highest traditions of the United States Naval Service."[7]

Chief Warrant Officer 2 Gregory Mac Neil, USA
Made a Daring Helicopter Rescue While Under Fire

Gregory Mac Neil joined the United States Army in January 1966. While in Army Flight School, he learned to fly UH-1 "Huey" type helicopters. Mac Neil was ultimately sent to Vietnam in 1967 with B Troop, 3rd Squadron of the 17th Air Cavalry as a "slick driver" for the first six months of his tour of duty. Slick drivers were Huey pilots who carried troops to and from combat operations. Shortly after the Tet Offensive began in 1968, Mac Neil was transferred to A Troop, 7th Squadron of the 1st Air Cavalry and transitioned to the OH-6A "Loach" flying as a "Scout".

On 27 April 1968, Chief Warrant Officer 2 Mac Neil was returning from a mission when he heard a call for help to rescue wounded soldiers involved in a firefight. He volunteered to go into a very small opening of a heavily wooded area for which he was awarded the Distinguished Flying Cross. The citation stated that, "Chief Warrant Officer Mac Neil distinguished himself while serving as a member of an aero-scout team, during an evacuation of wounded American soldiers. An American ground unit was pinned down by a large insurgent force and was sustaining casualties. Though he encountered heavy

191

enemy automatic weapons fire, he made a one hundred foot vertical descent into the landing area to perform the mission. He demonstrated great skill and professionalism in maneuvering his aircraft around the numerous obstacles endangering his flight path. Chief Warrant Officer Mac Neil thus was responsible for saving the life of a seriously wounded soldier."[8]

In a recent interview, Mac Neil explained that, "My military experience transformed me...I learned to be part of something bigger than myself. I realized the value of helping others." Greg Mac Neil is currently a member of the Board of Directors for the Distinguished Flying Cross Society.

Chief Warrant Officer 2 Dannie C. King, USA
Inserted Friendly Infantry Near Tra Cu

Chief Warrant Officer 2 Dannie C. King flew the UH-1C as part of the 240th Aviation Company (Assault Helicopter) in the Republic of Vietnam from 1969-1970. King was awarded a Distinguished Flying Cross for, "heroism while participating in aerial flight evidenced by voluntary actions above and beyond the call of duty. Warrant Officer King distinguished himself by exceptionally valorous actions while serving as pilot aboard an armed helicopter supporting an insertion of friendly infantry near Tra Cu [near the tip of Parrot's Beak where Cambodia points in close proximity to Saigon].

He began identifying enemy positions for the aircraft commander. When one of the lift ships was forced to land with severe damage, the aircraft commander initiated a false orbit to mislead the enemy and Warrant Officer King was continually pointing out sources of enemy fire. Later in the day as the aircraft commander initiated rocket runs on the bunker, Warrant Officer King began directing the fire of the door gunners onto enemy positions so the aircraft commander could successfully complete the runs while taking minimum aircraft damage. As night and hazardous weather moved into the area, Chief Warrant Officer 2 King continued to pinpoint enemy fire and initiate evasive maneuvers to avoid collision with the other aircraft operating in the general area."[9]

Dannie King is currently the president of the Lindbergh Chapter of the DFCS. He was also included in Ruth Mayer's painting about the Distinguished Flying Cross (see Chapter 7).

Chief Warrant Officer 4 Jack J. King, USA
Flew Chinooks Under Hostile Conditions_____

While piloting a CH-47 Chinook Helicopter on 14 March 1967, Chief Warrant Officer 2 Jack J. King participated in a mission for which he received a Distinguished Flying Cross. The combat action took place near Bong Son, Republic of Vietnam. The heroic measures taken by the aviator were recorded on his DFC citation. "When the safety pins were pulled prematurely on two fifty-five gallon drums of tear gas, one of the drums exploded inside Chief Warrant Officer King's aircraft. The entire cockpit was immediately filled with the gas. Although nauseated and temporarily blinded, Chief Warrant Officer King... maintained a level altitude while flying the helicopter. Because of the extreme distortion produced by his gas mask, the pilot was unable to land the aircraft. After the gas cleared to some degree, Chief Warrant Officer King took the controls and executed a successful emergency landing...ensuring that the injured personnel were placed on a medical evacuation helicopter, Chief Warrant Officer King joined in the defense of the contaminated aircraft. His display of personal bravery and outstanding flying ability is in keeping with the highest traditions of the military service..."[10]

Only a month later, Chief Warrant Officer 2 King received a second DFC for a combat support mission along Highway 506 Valley, in the Republic of Vietnam. Disregarding impossible conditions, he flew his helicopter down a steep hill at treetop level to pick up infantrymen. He then flew at low altitude and airspeed for ten miles so the soldiers could be unloaded. He was lauded for his personal bravery and outstanding flying ability. King retired as a chief warrant officer 4.

Major William R. Bradfield, USAF
A Forward Air Controller Received Three DFCs_____

Major William Bradfield served in the United States Air Force from 1964 to 1985 and was awarded three DFCs medals throughout his military career. Flying the O-2 as a forward air controller in the Republic of Vietnam, then Captain Bradfield was first awarded a DFC for a mission on 22 April 1968 which involved the direction of tactical aircraft in support of friendly troops who were pinned down by automatic weapons. With his unarmed aircraft, Bradfield was able to resolve the emergency situation on behalf of his fellow soldiers.

Bradfield received a second DFC for a mission which occurred on 24 April 1968. The DFC citation stated that, "Captain Bradfield flew a vitally important mission into the A Shau Valley to seek out and destroy hostile firing positions. Due to his professional airmanship and disregard for his own safety, friendly forces were able to move into the valley and secure it."

Demonstrating continued bravery and heroism on 7 July 1968, "Captain Bradfield flew to the aid of a friendly company which was surrounded and pinned down by a large hostile force. Captain Bradfield successfully directed tactical airpower against the aggressor, who constantly fired at his small aircraft. Because of his superior airmanship, the friendly company was relieved of the hostile pressure and was able to gain the offensive."[11] For this mission, Bradfield received his third Distinguished Flying Cross. Bill Bradfield is currently Chairman of the Board for the Distinguished Flying Cross Society. (Bradfield - left)

Colonel George Henry, USAF
From Street Gang to Electronic Gooney Bird Missions_____

As a young African-American growing up in a rather poor St. Louis neighborhood, George Henry became resourceful at an early age. Known as "Hank," he joined a street gang but quickly realized that was not the lifestyle for him. One older and stronger person in town realized Hank's potential interest in aviation and put the word out on the street that he could leave the gang and was not to be touched. Hank's guardian angel was none other than enigmatic boxer Sonny Liston.

In the Air Force, Henry fulfilled his dream, became an aviator and was sent to Vietnam where he flew the C-47 "Gooney Bird." Henry conducted "electric gooney missions" which involved flying in a circular pattern around an enemy teletype signal and pinpointing the transmission so that the target could be struck and neutralized.

Colonel Henry stated, "The first time in combat is a life-altering experience. When you see the red balls of enemy fire coming up at you, out of your side window, you know you have to take evasive action – and quick."[12] In all, Henry flew 150 missions and received a Distinguished Flying Cross for saving numerous American lives by rendering the enemy ineffective. After his retirement in 1983, Colonel Henry served as the head of the speakers' bureau of the East Coast Chapter of the Tuskegee Airmen.

Major Ben Games, USAAF / USAF / USA
Flew Fixed-Wing and Helicopters in Three Wars_____

Commissioned in December 1943, Ben Games served in the Army, the Air Force and the National Guard. He started flying the B-24, B-29, P-40, P-51 and the P-61 during WWII while serving in the USAAF and then transitioned to the F-80, F-94 and F-86 during the Korean War as a member of the USAF. In Vietnam, "Gentle Ben" as he was known flew Army helicopters including the UH-1 and the CH-47.

In the position of special projects officer, Major Games brought his wife, Helen M. Games, to Vietnam and she actually flew with her husband on some missions. Thus, she became known as "Whirly

Girl." CW3 Games was awarded the DFC for a flight on 8 November 1969. When his helicopter sustained direct fire near landing zone Vivian, Games was able to direct the craft away from populated areas. Despite the fact that the helo was engulfed in flames, he stayed onboard until the crew was safely evacuated.

Games flew 737 combat hours and in addition to the Distinguished Flying Cross, was awarded the Bronze Star and thirteen Air Medals throughout his career as a major and chief warrant officer 4 in the Army and a Major in the Air Force.[13]

Lieutenant Colonel Edwin W. Johnson, USAF
Flew Unarmed Reconnaissance Missions

Within a short period of time, Lieutenant Colonel Edwin W. Johnson, United States Air Force, experienced significant action as a RF-4C aircraft commander while serving in Vietnam and was awarded three Distinguished Flying Crosses. His first DFC was received for a flight over hostile territory on 13 March 1970 in order to obtain vital intelligence. In doing so, he penetrated an extremely sophisticated air defense network to photograph hostile activities. A second DFC was conferred for a similar act of bravery on 28 March 1970.

While participating in a mission over North Vietnam on 21 July 1970, Lieutenant Colonel Johnson once again flew an extremely hazardous, unarmed reconnaissance mission through one of the most heavily defended areas of Southeast Asia. Despite intense hostile ground fire, he maneuvered his aircraft to fly directly over all objectives and obtained outstanding photography of high interest sites and several anti-aircraft positions. Lieutenant Colonel Johnson was awarded his third Distinguished Flying Cross for these vital actions.[14]

Major John E. Appel, USAF
255 Combat Missions in F-4D
Phantoms

Major John E. Appel, an F-4D Phantom Aircraft Commander, received a Distinguished Flying Cross on 25 May 1970. The citation stated that Major Appel was assigned to attack anti-aircraft artillery positions which posed a serious threat to friendly air operations. Despite intense and accurate anti-aircraft fire, Major Appel delivered his ordnance precisely on target, destroying three hostile anti-aircraft artillery weapons.[15]

During 1971, he received three additional DFCs: the first for destroying three separate targets, the second for conducting an air strike on revetted anti-aircraft artillery sites, even though he was struck by defending ground fire and the third for bombing and destroying a heavily fortified storage and supply complex.

Major Appel flew 255 combat missions. Twenty-one of those missions were flown over North Vietnam. John Appel is currently the vice president of the Distinguished Flying Cross Society. (Appel - holding ladder)

Major Gordon L. Bocher, USAF
Survived a Mid-Air Explosion on a Gunship

Gordon L. Bocher was preparing his dissertation to complete his doctorate at Ohio State University when he decided to join the Air Force on 2 January 1968. After being commissioned, he was diagnosed with thyroid cancer and was retired with 100% disability against his wishes. However, he was allowed to rejoin the Air Force under a special program for cancer rehabilitated victims and subsequently volunteered to serve in Vietnam as a navigator

with the 15th Special Operations Squadron "Spectre" flying AC-130A gunships from Thailand.

On 18 June 1972, his aircraft was hit with a surface to air missile causing the plane to explode and the right wing to fall off. In a stroke of luck, the explosion catapulted Bocher away from the burning plane and he parachuted into the jungle where he hid for fourteen hours before being rescued by an HH-53 "Super Jolly Green" Helicopter. Only two other members of the fifteen man crew survived.[16]

After the incident, Captain Bocher assisted in writing evasive tactics which resulted in no further damage to gunships when fired upon throughout the balance of hostilities in Vietnam. Ultimately, Bocher was awarded two Distinguished Flying Cross medals, a purple heart and several other commendations for his heroism and devotion to duty.

Captain Larry Yarham, USN
A-6 Pilot Received Two DFCs

As an A-6 pilot for the Navy, then Lieutenant Larry Yarham flew off of the USS *Kitty Hawk* while attached to Attack Squadron 52. Missions during April and August 1972 would prove to be two of his most challenging experiences in combat.

On 16 April 1972, the events of the day were recorded in Yarham's Distinguished Flying Cross citation. "In the darkness of early morning, Lieutenant Yarham conducted a single plane, all weather strike on a surface-to-air missile site, thereby silencing the site and creating a diversion for enemy defenses to allow a massive strike to hit another target largely unopposed. The mission was executed at night in the face of determined intense and formidable enemy defenses and surface-to-air missiles. Lieutenant Yarham displayed [un]daunted courage, superb airmanship and unwavering devotion to duty…".

On 28 August 1972, Lieutenant Yarham initiated another single plane attack against a surface-to-air missile installation deep in enemy territory. However, he diverted from his assigned target and executed a daring bomb attack against a surface-to-air missile installation which had launched two missiles at his aircraft. During his egress, Yarham was able to observe the destruction of the missile site. Lieutenant Yarham was awarded his second DFC for this exemplary display of combat airmanship.[17]

Captain Larry Yarham is currently the President of the A-6 Intruder Association and recently retired as a Director for Northrop Grumman.

Lieutenant Commander Frank C. Koch, USN
Rescued Downed A-4 Pilot

Navy helicopter pilot, Lieutenant Commander Frank C. Koch received a Distinguished Flying Cross while flying as a Helicopter Aircraft Commander of an HH-3A armed combat rescue helicopter when he was attached to Helicopter Combat Support Squadron 7, Detachment 110 embarked on 7th Fleet carriers in the Tonkin Gulf. The citation stated, "On 6 September 1972, Lieutenant Commander Koch was aboard the USS *Gridley* (DLG-21) when word was received that [an] A-4 Skyhawk had been downed by anti-aircraft artillery fire. Within minutes Lieutenant Commander Koch had his combat rescue helicopter airborne and enroute to the rescue area. Receiving vectors in the air, Lieutenant Commander Koch learned that the survivor was within two miles of the coast of North Vietnam and that the wind was blowing him toward the beach. Lieutenant Commander Koch elected to transit dangerously close to the island of Hon Me to save valuable time.

Upon entering the rescue area, splashes from coastal batteries were observed along with anti-aircraft artillery fire. Lieutenant Commander Koch made a high speed approach to drop his swimmer and moved away from the survivor to "drop smoke" as a diversionary tactic. When signaled by the swimmer that he and the downed pilot were ready for the pick-up, Lieutenant Commander Koch quickly brought his combat rescue helicopter into a hover overhead and hoisted them aboard."[18] *Note:* The rescued survivor was Lieutenant Will Pear. For more information on Lieutenant Pear, see the story of Chuck Sweeney which appears earlier in this chapter.

Colonel Anthony Adessa, USA
Distinguished Combat Aviator and Leader

Colonel Anthony Adessa was a consummate aviator and leader who demonstrated his prowess on and off the battlefield. After previous combat experience, Adessa was assigned to Camp Radcliff located in Vietnam. There, he developed an extensive training program for air traffic controllers so that they were more effective in combat emergencies. His understanding of airmobile warfare and his personal combat experience made his programs a success and improved the record of mission success. For these meritorious actions, Adessa received his first Distinguished Flying Cross on 21 July 1970.

His second DFC was awarded while serving as an aircraft commander on a search and rescue mission in the flooded Binh Dinh Province of Vietnam where thousands of Americans and Vietnamese were stranded and drowning on 28 December 1970. During the rescue, his citation documented that, "Lieutenant Colonel Adessa saw two American soldiers on top of a truck which was nearly submerged in treacherous flood waters…after several attempts, he hovered in a dangerously small opening to successfully extract the exhausted men." Adessa then traveled to another area and rescued twenty-five more men that day.

Lieutenant Colonel Adessa received a third Distinguished Flying Cross under combat conditions while serving as aircraft commander of a utility helicopter in Vietnam. Volunteering to help repel a large enemy force on 23 March 1971, Adessa made several passes at the enemy marking their positions for the armed helicopters. After five hours of being exposed to intense fire, the enemy forces retreated into the mountains and thus a large number of American lives were saved.[19]

With thirty years of collective combat and leadership experiences during eight commands, Anthony Adessa retired as a colonel.

Captain Art Overman, USAF
EC-47 Pilot Supported Friendly Ground Forces

Captain Arthur W. Overman was awarded the Distinguished Flying Cross for extraordinary achievement while participating in aerial flight as an EC-47 pilot in Southeast Asia on 10 July 1973. His DFC citation explained that, "Captain Overman flew an extremely hazardous mission through adverse weather conditions and through the constant threat of hostile ground fire and attack. In spite of this, he superbly accomplished this highly intricate and hazardous mission in support of friendly ground forces. Through his personal bravery and energetic application of knowledge and skill, he significantly furthered the goal of the United States Air Force in Southeast Asia.

The professional competence, aerial skill, and devotion to duty displayed by Captain Overman reflect great credit upon himself and the United States Air Force." [20]

Art Overman served on the Board of the Distinguished Flying Cross Society.

Captain Charles E. Southwick, USN
F-4B Pilot - Prisoner of War for Six Years

Charles E. Southwick joined the Navy, became a pilot and flew FJ-3 Furies and F-8 Crusaders in fighter squadrons from 1955 to 1964. Following these aviation experiences, Southwick served in the Bureau of Naval Personnel and tolerated desk duty for the next two years. By 1966, he returned to the cockpit flying the F-4B and was sent to Vietnam.

Southwick received a DFC for a mission on 14 May 1967. As leader of a three-plane, flak-suppression element during an air wing, coordinated strike against the heavily defended Than Hoa Bridge, North Vietnam, Southwick

accomplished his objective but was shot down. The aircraft crash landed on mud flats southeast of the bridge and Southwick was captured. The Lieutenant Commander then endured six years of captivity until he was released on 4 March 1973. The F-4B was eventually transported to Hanoi where the wreckage resides today.

He stated that he was able to endure captivity because, "I was raised an American…and I was released from captivity as a direct result of the overwhelming involvement and support of the American people… and our President, Richard M. Nixon. I will never be able to adequately repay the American people or our President." Southwick was promoted to Captain before he retired.[21]

Photographs courtesy of the DFC recipients and/or their families.

Notes

[1] Captain James L. Champlin, Distinguished Flying Cross citations, action dates: 30 January 1966 and 6 May, 1966, Archives, the Distinguished Flying Cross Society, San Diego, CA.

[2] Staff Sergeant Aaron D. Farrior, Distinguished Flying Cross citation, action date: 7 March 1966, Archives, the Distinguished Flying Cross Society, San Diego, CA.

[3] Captain Dean Jones, Distinguished Flying Cross citations, action dates: 11 June 1967 and 29 September 1967, Archives, the Distinguished Flying Cross Society, San Diego, CA.

[4] Captain Wayne Jones, Distinguished Flying Cross citation, action date: 4 March 1968, Archives, the Distinguished Flying Cross Society, San Diego, CA.

[5] Master Sergeant Alexander Underwood, Distinguished Flying Cross citation, action date: 29 June 1966, Archives, the Distinguished Flying Cross Society, San Diego, CA.

[6] Sergeant Pat Stouffer, Distinguished Flying Cross citation, action date: 7 August 1967, Archives, the Distinguished Flying Cross Society, San Diego, CA.

[7] Lieutenant Dave E. Clement, Distinguished Flying Cross citation, action date: 29 July 1967, Archives, the Distinguished Flying Cross Society, San Diego, CA.

[8] Chief Warrant Officer 2 Gregory Mac Neil, Distinguished Flying Cross citation, action date: 27 April 1968, Archives, the Distinguished Flying Cross Society, San Diego, CA.

[9] Chief Warrant Officer 2 Dannie C. King, Distinguished Flying Cross citation, action dates: 1968-1969, Archives, the Distinguished Flying Cross Society, San Diego, CA.

[10] Chief Warrant Officer 4 Jack J. King, Distinguished Flying Cross citation, action date: 14 March 1967, Archives, the Distinguished Flying Cross Society, San Diego, CA.

[11] Major William R. Bradfield, Distinguished Flying Cross citations, action dates: 22 April, 24 April and 7 July 1968, Archives, Distinguished Flying Cross Society, San Diego, CA.

[12] Colonel George Henry, Distinguished Flying Cross citation, action date: 1968, Archives, Distinguished Flying Cross Society, San Diego, CA.

[13] Major Ben Games, Distinguished Flying Cross citation, action date: 1966, Archives, Distinguished Flying Cross Society, San Diego, CA.

[14] Lieutenant Colonel Edwin W. Johnson, Distinguished Flying Cross citations, action dates: 13 March 1970, 28 March 1970 and 21 July 1970, Archives, Distinguished Flying Cross Society, San Diego, CA.

[15] Major John Appel, Distinguished Flying Cross citation, action date: 25 May 1970, Archives, Distinguished Flying Cross Society, San Diego, CA.

[16] Major Gordon L. Bocher, Distinguished Flying Cross citations, action dates: 18 June 1972 and 6 February 1973, Archives, Distinguished Flying Cross Society, San Diego, CA.

[17] Captain Larry Yarham, Distinguished Flying Cross citations, action dates: 16 April 1972 and 28 August 1972, Archives, Distinguished Flying Cross Society, San Diego, CA.

[18] Lieutenant Commander Frank C. Koch, Distinguished Flying Cross citation, action date: 6 September 1972, Archives, Distinguished Flying Cross Society, San Diego, CA.

[19] Colonel Anthony Adessa, Distinguished Flying Cross citations, action dates: 21 July 1970, 28 December 1970 and 23 March 1971, Archives, Distinguished Flying Cross Society, San Diego, CA.

[20] Captain Art Overman, Distinguished Flying Cross citation, action date: 10 July 1973, Archives, Distinguished Flying Cross Society, San Diego, CA.

[21] Captain Charles E. Southwick, Distinguished Flying Cross citation, action date: 14 May 1967, Archives, Distinguished Flying Cross Society, San Diego, CA.

Chapter 5

Stories of the Distinguished Flying Cross:

Recent Decades

*S*hortly after the hostilities subsided in Vietnam, the Distinguished Flying Cross celebrated a half-century of recognizing aerial achievement and heroic actions during periods of war and peace. As time passed and aviation approached its centennial, the aircraft and the aircrews who flew them entered another new era of sophistication, as evidenced by the integration of "smart" weapons and elaborate computerized systems.

Since the latetr part of the 1970s, a multitude of tensions have erupted requiring United States military engagements around the globe. "Operation El Dorado Canyon" and "Operation Just Cause" reverberated from the 1980s and emphasized America's resolve to fight terrorism. However, actions involving countries like Lebanon, Panama and Libya were dwarfed by "Operation Desert Storm" which took place in 1991 after Iraq invaded Kuwait. It was a confrontation of dramatic proportions that produced a prodigious cadre of aerial heroes who received the Distinguished Flying Cross.

As 20th century military actions came to a close in 1999 with "Operation Allied Force," which took place in the Federal Republic of Yugoslavia, "Operation Enduring Freedom" in 2001 and "Operation Anaconda" in 2002 foreshadowed the ever-expanding roles aviation would assume during military confrontations. Few contemporary engagements, though, have rivaled the size and scope of "Operation Iraqi Freedom" in 2003. At present, Iraq and Afghanistan are the focal points of conflict which require the use of aviators and aircrews for the protection of American interests at home and abroad.

The military engagements that have occurred during recent decades have had their own distinct characteristics, and the war on terrorism necessitated unprecedented cooperation among the military services, yet peacetime acts of heroism have continued too, which demonstrate the time-honored traditions that extend back to the inception of the DFC. The willingness of aviators and aircrew to risk their lives to save others during natural disasters such as Hurricane Katrina and other cataclysmic events reinforced the concept that American military pilots and aircrew were ever vigilant in accomplishing the human and superhuman missions presented to them.

There are many similarities between these recent decades and the previous wars and conflicts involving aviation, but there are also distinct departures from the past. One such change has been the inclusion of women as combat pilots and aircrew; the culmination of a dream for women since the days of the WASP during World War II. Another profound advancement has been the inclusion of people of color; especially those flying aircraft and assuming leadership roles. Though slow to transpire, ultimately the vision of Executive Order 9981 is being realized.

When one views a contemporary pilot standing next to the most advanced aircraft, it is initially difficult to find commonalities with pioneering aviators who flew biplanes and wore silk scarves. Although upon reflection, it is the tradition of duty and honor of the aviator that truly matters - not the sophistication of the equipment. In that spirit, as the Distinguished Flying Cross has recently been pinned on the uniform of a diverse population of aviators and aircrew, the stories of aerial heroism have truly reflected contemporary America.

Personal Accounts of the Distinguished Flying Cross:

Recent Decades

I look at the line of pilots who have received the DFC, and it's extremely humbling to look back...and realize you're part of that group, you're part of that history. It's just incredibly humbling."

Lieutenant Colonel Kim Campbell, USAF

Top: Captain Ng was awarded a Distinguished Flying Cross in 1980 and another in 1984. Both medals were conferred for saving crews of sinking ships. Middle: As a young aviator, Jimmy Ng flew various Coast Guard helicopters including the HH-3F SAR. In addition to the DFCs and several other awards, Captain Ng was selected as Helicopter Aviator of the Year in 1980 by the Association of Naval Aviation. Bottom: As evidenced by this photograph, the Coast Guard and his family were the two most important aspects of his life. Photographs courtesy of Jimmy and Joy Ng

Alaskan Rescues on a "Wing and a Prayer"

Captain Jimmy Ng, USCG

"Jimmy was keenly aware of the fact that the people in each and every case were real individuals, with families and people who loved them. He never took any case lightly."
Joy Ng

When a Distinguished Flying Cross is conferred, the citation accompanying the medal usually recounts the saga of a military confrontation with an enemy force. The experiences of Captain Jimmy Ng, recipient of two Distinguished Flying Crosses, follow this traditional pattern. However, the "enemy" that Captain Ng routinely battled, as a United States Coast Guard pilot, was the weather and his ability to overcome the forces of nature in order to rescue individuals in imminent peril on the high seas.

Jimmy Ng grew up in an Army family, spending most of his childhood in the Northwestern part of the United States. With the military engrained in his personality, it was logical for him to enter the United States Coast Guard Academy. Ng graduated in the Class of 1972.

His first assignment after graduation from the Coast Guard Academy was aboard the Coast Guard Icebreaker *Staten Island*. It was the perfect assignment for a "salt," a man who felt more at home on the water than on the land. He loved going to sea, piloting ships and the adventure of the multi-faceted icebreaker missions.

In 1973, Ng married Joy Ellen Healey. It was his wife who pointed out to her young ensign husband that ice breakers go out for six months at a time while Coast Guard helicopters only go out for six hours at a time. Being the highly educated Coast Guard Academy graduate that he was, and recognizing that he enjoyed spending time with his wife more than he loved going to sea, the ensign concluded that he should apply for flight training.

After he received his wings at the Naval Air Station Pensacola and was simultaneously conferred a Masters Degree in Aeronautical Systems from the University of West Florida, Joy Ng stated that "much to his delight, he found that he loved flying even more than he loved sailing ships!"

After completing a tour in Oregon, Ng spent almost eight years serving at Air Station Kodiak, "it didn't take us long to fall in love with Alaska and decide that this is where we wanted to be forever. We hunted, hiked, fished, made friends, and got involved in the community...and we commercially fished for halibut for seven years. Commercial fishing had a profound impact on Ng's approach to flying search and rescue. He understood what the fishermen were up against, why they were doing what they were doing, and, in many cases, where they probably were. He had a keen sense of weather and currents that was instrumental in the many successful rescues he completed. Those were the days before survival suits... Ng was instrumental in getting survival suits into the hands of both the local fishermen in Kodiak and the Coast Guard. In fact, we opened a small marine safety business and sold safety gear at a discounted price so people like us and other fishermen in Kodiak could afford to have that kind of safety equipment."

While Lieutenant Ng had been involved in many rescues during his initial years of flying helicopters, one incident would prove to be the most challenging to that point in his career. During August of 1980, one of the worst typhoons of the season raged through the seas of Alaska. On August 17th, Lieutenant Ng had already made two rescues before 1,800 hours. However, the third call of the day involved a distant rescue of a ship's crew facing imminent demise if they did not receive immediate assistance. Lieutenant Ng knew that he could not do it alone; it would require the combined skills and the daring of a veteran crew. Fortunately for Ng, the people he most trusted with his life were available: copilot Lieutenant Michael B. Garwood, flight mechanic Drew E. Bratt and AT1 James H Ellis.

The case involved the *Teresa Lee*, a 185 foot US merchant vessel/processor with twenty-two crewmen... most of whom were college kids. The ship was floundering with a broken rudder in thirty to forty foot waves, sixty five miles northwest of Port Heidan, Alaska. Lieutenant Ng and his crew, in their HH-3F SAR helicopter, took off from the Coast Guard Air Station at Kodiak along with a HC-130. With seventy knot winds, severe turbulence, less than a quarter-mile visibility and 300-500 foot cloud ceilings along with heavy rain as the sky darkened, conditions could not have been more problematic.

Through contact with the *Teresa Lee*, the crew of the HC-130 learned that the ship was taking on water, leaking ammonia below deck and the skipper projected they would sink in about five hours. Relaying this to the helicopter, Lieutenant Ng flew as fast as he could in order to cover a distance of two hundred miles. "As we made our way to the *Teresa Lee* we crossed into Becharof Lake, flying at about 500 feet because of the poor visibility and obscured ceiling due to the thick haze of the storm. The winds and turbulence increased and about halfway across the lake, I noticed the water in front of us exploding in great splashes… I veered to the north to go around a water spout extending from the lake surface up into the haze – Spooky!

Prior to crossing the shoreline of Bristol Bay, I briefed the crew about high wind and sea hoists. I told Bratt to plan on tying two trail lines together…using all the weight bags and possibly the aircraft anchor to get the lines down to the vessel…The surf along the shoreline was awesome…it rolled over the normal beachline well into the tundra area of the shore. I have never seen the ocean more impressive…the surface of the ocean was like meringue.

Once radio contact was established, we informed the ship of the potential procedures for the rescue and discussed a suitable hoisting area. The commander of the ship was not very optimistic that hoists could even be attempted…I realized that if a hoist was even possible in these conditions, it would require all the skill that our crew could possibly provide. I tried to make it very clear that anyone in the crew had the option of canceling the mission. I told them that I would not second guess their decision….After much soul searching and thought, the entire crew decided to risk our lives for the lives of the twenty-two crewmen. We also decided to take the calculated risk of not wearing our wetsuits in order to be better able physically to help the people on board the *Teresa Lee*."

When the helicopter and its crew arrived in just under three hours, the *Teresa Lee* was being battered by the waves as she wallowed in circles because of her damaged rudder. Lieutenant Ng advised the skipper to go dead in the water when he came around to the north. They also discussed the real possibility of the vessel capsizing and the skipper made a passionate plea to have his crew evacuated. Two pumps were then sent down to counteract the water that was continuing to pour into the ship.

The obstacles impeding the rescue by hoists were numerous. Steel cables, a fifty foot king post and a radio longwire were the physical impediments on board ship while mountainous thirty to forty foot waves made the vessel a moving target. In order to get to the hoists, the crew had to crawl along the deck holding onto lines and rails. It was a miracle that no one was washed overboard.

Lieutenant Ng later wrote, "As we tried to make a hoist, with the helo semi-stopped, the wind would drop and we would surge forward as if shot out of a cannon…I had the window open and wipers going for better visibility…It was a matter of routine to put my head out the window in order to maintain visual reference with the ship. I had never seen or heard about, nor could I have imagined, a worse hoisting situation!"

While dealing with fatigue and the elements, the helicopter crew finally hoisted seventeen sailors to the safe confines of the helicopter and, with low fuel lights on, departed for the nearest shore. On the way to the shoreline, it seemed as if all difficulties had been abated, however, one more emergency presented itself. The cockpit filled with dense smoke and flames arose from behind the control panel. After several tense moments, it was determined that a wiper motor had malfunctioned and the problem was alleviated. He stated in his After Action Report, "I really believe that the crew of 1471 accomplished a phenomenal mission. Bratt and Ellis [crew members] did a super human job…and I cannot adequately express how much invaluable assistance Lieutenant Garwood provided [as copilot]. However, the Lord deserves all the credit for our actions and for holding the aircraft together." Lieutenant Ng also reflected, "Looking at the situation, some might have thought that the rescue attempt was foolhardy, however, the seventeen sailors who were saved did not share that assessment." The Coast Guard also agreed. For their actions, copilot Lieutenant Michael B. Garwood, flight mechanic Drew E. Bratt and AT1 James H. Ellis were awarded individual Air Medals. Lieutenant Ng was not only awarded the Distinguished Flying Cross but was also selected as Helicopter Aviator of the Year in 1980 by the Association of Naval Aviation.

With such a harrowing experience behind him, it would seem unlikely that "lightning" would strike a second time. However, in just four short years, Lieutenant Ng would be called on once again to put his life on the line in order to save others. On February 25, 1984 Jimmy Ng, now a lieutenant commander, was dispatched from the Air Station at Kodiak for a rescue of the *Mia Dawn*'s crew. Similar to the *Teresa Lee* rescue, Lieutenant Commander Ng was faced with sixty-eighty knot winds, whiteout conditions and extreme turbulence. Despite inoperative loran and radar, the fifty-six foot fishing vessel was located in whiteout conditions at the base of a 200 foot cliff. The *Mia Dawn* had capsized on a reef and was covered with ice. The wind was so strong that the rescue basket sailed aft just below the tail rotor. It had to be pulled down to the boat by a line attached to the aircraft anchor. Three sailors were eventually hoisted into the rescue helicopter. The vertical turbulence was so severe that both engines and gearbox were over-torqued numerous times. After completing the hoists, the aircraft began an instrument departure into the snow and severe turbulence. Passing 2,000 feet, Ng passed the controls to his copilot as he had been overcome by a severe case of vertigo. Lieutenant Cheek assumed control, completed the ascent and flew the helicopter back to Sand Point, Alaska. The C-130 crew that met the helicopter crew described them as pale and stoic on the deadhead flight back to Kodiak. They had come close to death and they knew it.

Knowing Ng better than any other person, his wife understood her husband's feelings about the rescues for which he received Distinguished Flying Cross citations. "I can't say that the cases for which he received the DFCs had a profound impact on Jimmy. I also can't say that they 'were business as usual.' Jimmy took every case very seriously and he had many, many cases. There were two cases in particular that seriously impacted Jimmy. The first occurred in October of the first year we were in Kodiak. Friends of ours (two pilots and their five year old sons) went fishing. Their boat capsized and they sat on the over-turned hull for seven hours until Jimmy found them. By then, the weather had deteriorated and it was a very difficult case. I remember the wife of one of the guys calling Ng to say that her husband was overdue. Ng happened to have duty and he went to look for them. He had fished with these guys before and knew where they might be. Finally, Ng found them when he spotted the tiny flint spark from a wet lighter that the guys tried to light when the helicopter came near. One of the five-year-old boys died of hypothermia… the dads couldn't get him out from under the over-turned boat. They talked to him through the hull until he died…Ng received an Air Medal for that case. The other case with profound impact on Ng was the death of his best friend, Pat Rivas, who was killed when his helicopter crashed while trying to rescue a fisherman from a floundering boat in bad weather. Ng found Pat on the beach.

I think these two cases helped to make Ng keenly aware of the fact that the people in each and every case were real individuals, with families and people who loved them. He never took any case lightly, and he never begrudged going out after people in trouble. As commanding officer, Ng often made contact with the families during the rescue operations when he wasn't flying. I know that together we attended many funerals, even of people we had never met before."

Following his tour in Kodiak, Jimmy Ng was promoted to captain and served as the administrative officer at Air Station Cape Cod, operations officer in the Caribbean and executive officer at Air Station Borinquen, Puerto Rico. Captain Ng then returned to Alaska in 1992 to become the commanding officer of Air Station Sitka. After his second tour in Alaska, Captain Ng graduated from the Industrial College of the Armed Forces at the National Defense University in Washington, DC and then served as deputy director, International Affairs, United States Coast Guard Headquarters. Once again, Captain Ng returned to Alaska in 1997 to become the commanding officer of Air Station Kodiak. He transferred to the Kodiak Integrated Support Command in 2000, where he served as the commanding officer until his retirement in May, 2002.

Throughout his military career, Captain Ng flew many different helicopters as well as the fixed wing HC-130H. Along with his two Distinguished Flying Crosses, Captain Ng received the Legion of Merit, two Meritorious Service Medals, an Air Medal and four Coast Guard Commendation Medals. He was also honored with several national and international awards including the Aviation/Space Writers Association's Helicopter Heroism Award, the Kossler Award from the American Helicopter Society and the Coast Guard Foundation Award.

In retirement, Ng, Joy and their family have made Alaska their permanent home. He has concurrently served as the director of community affairs and foundation for the Providence Kodiak Island Medical Center as well as being the technical director of Kodiak Operations for COLSA Corporation, which is involved in the rocket launch industry.

In concluding her thoughts on her husband's outlook concerning all his rescues over the years, Mrs. Ng was most emphatic about one point. "Jimmy is quick to say that it wasn't him, but his crews that accomplished these missions." She also reinforced the fact that Ng is a man of great faith. "I know that it is his dependence on God that has given him such success…and kept him alive all these years. He will tell you that the scripture we claim as our life guidance is Psalm 139: 9 - 10. "If I rise on the wings of the dawn, if I settle on the far side of the sea, even there your hand will guide me, your right hand will hold me fast.'"

Notes

Captain Jimmy Ng, Distinguished Flying Cross citations, action dates: 17 August 1980 and 25 February 1984, Archives, the Distinguished Flying Cross Society, San Diego, CA.

Captain Jimmy Ng, After Action Report, Crewmembers from the M/V *Teresa Lee*, by the CG 1471

Joy Ng, personal written reflections, April 2008.

Top and middle: Both Rob Weber and the A-6 Intruder were tested in combat on 15 April 1986 during Operation El Dorado Canyon. Both performed in an outstanding manner. Bottom: Rob Weber sits in the captain's chair of the USS *John F. Kennedy* while making command decisions. Captain Weber and his father received Distinguished Flying Crosses, four decades apart. His daughter is a third generation naval officer. Photographs courtesy of Rob Weber and the Tailhook Association

Operation El Dorado Canyon: The Libya Raid

Captain Rob Weber, USN

"My Dad was a naval aviator and so was I....He served on the *Coral Sea* and so did I. And, we both received Distinguished Flying Crosses."_____

Early in life Rob Weber had a few career paths in mind. He wanted to be a fireman, a naval aviator or Matt Dillon. While the image of being a fireman faded, he accomplished his goal of becoming a naval aviator. Matt Dillon, the gun-toting sheriff in the classic television series Gun Smoke, was forgotten as soon as Dillon realized he had far more firepower at his disposal in his A-6 Intruder attack aircraft. Both Weber and the A-6 would be amply tested in combat on 15 April 1986 during Operation El Dorado Canyon.

While Weber had served as a Navy pilot during the Vietnam era, he deployed to the Mediterranean and flew RA-5C Vigilantes. Therefore, he did not have an early opportunity to experience combat. After the hostilities concluded in Vietnam and a period of relative peace ensued, the commander along with his fellow military aviators trained for every conceivable situation, and for the eventual day when their skills would be required.

By the mid-1980s, tensions around the world had again escalated, requiring all branches of the US military to step-up their preparedness. One significant foreign relations concern was Libya and Muammar Gaddafi. Under his rule, Gaddafi had a grandiose vision of creating a Great Arab Nation comprised of all North Africa. To that end, he developed terrorist training centers. The killings at the Rome and Vienna airports during December 1985 were just a few of the violent activities supported by Gaddafi's regime.

In January 1986, Gaddafi once again took provocative action by proclaiming a "Line of Death" across the Gulf of Sidra. He warned that Libyan forces would destroy American ships and planes if they crossed the line. In Operation Prairie Fire, 45 US ships and 200 planes intentionally crossed the line with the support of 3 aircraft carriers and Los Angeles-class attack submarines below the surface. On 24 March 1986, the Libyans fired several surface-to-air missiles (SAMs) at American targets. Fortunately, jamming devices diverted the missiles from doing any harm. The American forces were able to damage and/or destroy several of the enemy vessels. Fifty-sixty Libyans were killed with no American casualties. President Reagan personally congratulated the airmen and sailors of the 6th Fleet.

American sentiment had strongly supported action by the military; however, many people also believed that additional retaliation would transpire. Gaddafi did not disappoint when, on 25 March, he ordered his embassies to carry out terrorist activities against Americans. In a massive rally in Tripoli, he declared war on the United States and a few days later, the bombing of La Belle Discotheque in Berlin caused the death of an American soldier. The stage was now set for a showdown between the two nations.

Intelligence reports clearly determined that Libya had been responsible for the terrorism and that other such actions were being planned. As a result, President Reagan supported military operations to end the terrorism and actively participated in the planning of the raid. US Attorney General, Edwin Meese, recalled that, "the President had maps all over the floor of the Oval Office...in order to select potential targets."

Rob Weber remembered that a mission was imminent and explained his role as a Commander leading up to what would be called Operation El Dorado Canyon. "We had been conducting Gulf of Sidra operations, freedom of navigation ops and ops north of what Libya called the 'line of death' for about six months during the Navy deployment on the *Coral Sea*. In fact, a few weeks prior to El Dorado Canyon, there were some threats by Libyan patrol boats and aircraft. Our carrier battle group actually had some air-to-surface and surface-to-surface engagements with the Libyans...So there were long-standing tensions and we had been planning contingencies for several months.

In conjunction with that planning we met with the senior leadership at EUCOM headquarters in Stuttgart, Germany, regarding how the Navy would approach a combat situation and how we would al support the Air Force. On the Navy side, our senior leadership in the 6th Fleet and the Navy European Command had completed an initial concept before they brought us up to Stuttgart for a meeting with deputy commander of EUCOM, who was an Air Force four-star. We then had an opportunity to expl what we would do and how we would do it if they sent us into Libya.

By April 1986, the *Coral Sea* was in its last port call in Malaga, Spain and ready to head home. However, when the Berlin discotheque was hit and President Reagan made the decision to strike Libya, were retained in the Mediterranean even though we had conducted our last operation. We were told to start refining our plan…We were given the targets.

Basically, the Air Force would come down from England to strike targets in Tripoli with their F-111 and EF-111s. The Navy carriers, USS *America* and USS *Coral Sea*, would provide the major strikes on Benina Airfield and Benghazi. The *America* would send six A-6 aircraft from VA-34 into downtown Benghazi while eight A-6s from VA-55 aboard the *Coral Sea* would hit the Benina Airfield…It would be a simultaneous strike…Meanwhile, the *America* Battlegroup would also provide support to the Air Forc strike package hitting Tripoli.

I was told by the carrier air wing commander that I would be the overall strike leader of *Coral Sea*'s package into Benina Airfield. In actuality, we wound up with six A-6s because two didn't achieve full mission readiness following our launch. Of course, there were a large number of support aircraft… including F/A-18 Hornets, EA-6B Prowlers, E-2C Hawkeyes, an EA-3B "Whale" and combat SAR helicopters…We decided to do a 'chain strike' in the target area (one jet after another), which you normally wouldn't try more than once, but the Navy hadn't done a strike in many years and…we figure we could get away with it on the first try…you wouldn't have to come in from multiple directions tryin to deconflict aircraft in a very complicated night operation requiring low altitudes to keep under their radar until the last minute…

It was an ideal plan for a Navy guy, and it was why carriers offer wonderful flexibility. We were allo to pick the carrier's launch point…far enough out from the target to allow an undetected launch and rendezvous, but close enough in to minimize, or eliminate, the need for tanking. So we elected to launc from a 150 miles north of Benina and Benghazi at night with a large strike package…

I thought, 'this is a hell of a time to go into combat for the first time and you're the Squadron CO. How will you respond? How well will you perform?' I was the son of a naval aviator who had been in t Battle of the Philippine Sea. You wonder how you will react and if you will overreact…

It was clearly challenging…once you lit off the engine and started taxiing to the cat, you say to yours 'Okay, we've got a lot to accomplish…Get it right.' And then you trust your training and preparation, you just get back to the fundamentals, back to checklists, back to procedures, and back to good basic airmanship. You just do the job for which you were trained.

The first wave of the strike package was about twenty-five airplanes. We sent in two waves: the mai wave and the backup support wave, to protect returning strike aircraft and in case we had a combat SAR situation…We did everything without communications. That included the launch. Everything was meticulously planned and kept as simple as possible to enhance execution and success. It was completel comms-out and we all rendezvoused, the entire strike package, at different altitudes and different sectors around the ship, but all below the long EW radar horizon of Benina and Benghazi.

As we departed the ship and commenced our route to the target area, we started descending, descending, descending…While we were still feet wet [flying over water] headed in, we approached clos and closer to their radar. We were running at an altitude of about two hundred feet as we crossed the beach line.

Flying in, we knew the location of many missile sites that we wanted preemptively taken out. In fac one of them was on my coast-in point. There was a SA-6 site that we were going to have to go right ove and we didn't have a choice about that. We wanted to make sure that thing didn't come up.

I remember seeing preemptive HARMS (High-speed Antiradiation Missiles) being shot off-axis by the F/A-18 Hornets from about thirty miles out. It was a very clear night with great visibility. No overcast, no clouds and there wasn't much moonlight. As I was fifteen miles feet wet, an explosion went off ahead of my nose. Of course, as I said, I'd never been in combat before and when you watch all the combat movies, there's noise all the time. Well, everything was quiet. It was silent. The only thing you heard was your own airplane. It was like watching everything with the sound turned off, which I thought was kind of eerie.

By now, we were going as fast as we could…The A-6 is a very high-drag airplane. You've got a big fat wing and a big bulbous nose and loaded up with all that high-drag ordnance. We did much of the early transit at 360 knots, which is typical - six miles a minute. But as we neared the coast, it was time to ramp up the speed. I think we kicked it up to 420 knots, and then near the target we just went for it, close to 500 knots, once we knew we had our safe separation between the six aircraft in the chain.

No doubt we surprised them. I remember we could see the lights of the town, we could see the lights of the airfield while we were still feet wet, as we crossed the beach line and still had fifteen to twenty miles to go. You could see it better and better. They even had their rotating field beacon on…all the airport lights were on.

As we got closer to the target, we elevated to 500 feet so that we could properly fuse the ordnance…it needed time to arm before it hit the ground…Two aircraft were using high drag general purpose bombs and four aircraft were using APAM (Anti-Personnel/Anti-Material), which is similar to Rockeye. It's a cluster weapon that had a pretty good incendiary feature.

We basically flew right up the runway and down the main ramp. The airfield was oriented east and west. We came in from the east in a six aircraft chain. We were about forty-five seconds to a minute apart so that we could do our low altitude deliveries. Thus, the subsequent guys in the chain were assured all the bombs ahead of them had already gone off and the frag envelopes had collapsed before they crossed the target…

Our targets were the MiG-23s at the ends of the runways on hot-pad duty and those parked on the ramp. They also had some planes in maintenance hangars alongside the ramp. And each guy in the strike had a different pattern…Our plan used the cluster weapons against the exposed MiGs on the ramps and at the ends of the field because you could lay down a lot of bomblets in each canister and each little flechette can do a pretty good job of going through the fuselage and wing of an airplane, hopefully starting large fires. Two of our planes went after the aircraft in the hangers. They used Mark 80 Series high drag Snake Eyes with delayed fuses so they would go through the roof of the hangar and then blow up inside.

The Air Force over in Tripoli, with the F-111s, was tossing 2,000 pound laser-guided bombs. That was their expertise – their key mission. We were often asked, 'Why aren't you using bigger, heavier weapons that would also make observable craters in the concrete?' The reason was that we got better coverage with cluster weapons against exposed MiGs on the ramps – we could hit more with our ordnance and we could burn more of them up…

It gave us confidence that we were ingressing undetected when the airfield was totally illuminated and the city looked quiet and normal for the middle of the night. The fact that all the runway lights were on, the taxiway lights were on, was confirmation that we had totally caught them off guard.

I ran right down a ramp that was parallel to one of the taxiways. The airfield was a joint civilian-military airfield. On the ramp I was bombing, where the MiG-23s were, there was also a 727 passenger plane all lit up and parked at the far end by the terminal…. When objects on the ground start to disappear under your nose when you're at 500 feet, they're still fairly far out ahead of you, but I was concerned that I still had ordnance coming off my jet when that 727 started going under my nose…I thought to myself, 'Oh, My God – I don't want to hit a plane with civilians.' But, in fact, we had plenty of clearance.

Thank goodness everything was okay and the bombs went where they were supposed to go. I was just inexperienced in combat and this was the first time I'd ever dropped a long stick of bombs in anger.

I remember as I pulled off target, I was supposed to extend just a little bit and then was going to break hard right and proceed just to the west of Benghazi. All of a sudden, I saw a red light, co-altitude and directly ahead and I thought, 'Damn - there's an undetected MiG out there!' It looked just like a red anti-collision light as it blinked. And then I looked at it a little harder and all of the sudden I realized it wasn't moving and was a red light on the top of an uncharted radio tower. It was really sticking out. The only call I put out that night was, 'Off target, look out for a tall radio tower on your nose.' Happily, the balance of the trip back to the *Coral Sea* was without incident. I think I was back at the ship in less than two hours.

Once we had a chance to make an assessment, we realized there had been no combat damage to any of our Navy aircraft. The A-6s were all fine from both groups, and all the support aircraft were intact. It was really picture perfect!"

The total appraisal for the combined Air Force and Navy operation showed that United States used forty-five airplanes, dropped three-hundred bombs and launched forty-eight missiles. Sadly, the Air Force lost two pilots in an F-111 during the ten minute ordeal; however, the enemy suffered significant losses in terms of military hardware, property and human life. The point had been made.

With the silencing of the weapons, President Reagan made a television address to the American people and stated, "I said that we would act…to ensure that terrorists have no sanctuary anywhere…Tonight, we have." Once again, the American citizens resoundingly supported the actions of the President even though most realized that this was just one chapter in the story of terrorism.

Shortly after the Libya strike Weber was transferred to the A-6 Fleet Readiness Squadron as the commanding officer, but it was months before he was informed that he would receive the Distinguished Flying Cross. When the medal was presented, a variety of thoughts went through his mind. "In one way it was a surprise to get a DFC because nobody shot at me…the tail-end pilots in my flight saw a better show then I did. But it was a complex mission and we executed it very, very well. It was the Navy's first combat strike in quite awhile…so it meant a great deal to me personally. I was also pleased that I was not the only one who received a DFC. Several medals were awarded for our mission."

Moving through the ranks, Weber became an executive officer of an aircraft carrier, a CO of an underway replenishment ship and then the commanding officer of the carrier USS *John F. Kennedy*. He later retired in July 2000, which ended a thirty-one year career with the Navy. As he reflected on his service to his country, he also thought about his unique family connections. "My Dad was a naval aviator and so was I. He was a flight instructor at Corpus Christi, Texas, where I was born, and so was I. He served on the *Coral Sea* and thirty-two years later so did I. And, we both received Distinguished Flying Crosses." But the parallels didn't end with two generations. Captain Weber's daughter, also born in Corpus Christi, is now carrying on the Weber naval tradition as a surface warfare officer.

When the decorated aviator is asked about his exploits over Libya a quarter-century ago, he states, "I'm really proud of what our squadron was able to accomplish collectively…The squadron and the air wing was a well-oiled team – not just the A-6s but all of the team, in the air and on the carrier. It was a well-orchestrated ballet – a ballet that awesomely accomplished its mission."

Notes

Captain Rob Weber, Distinguished Flying Cross citation, action date: 15 April 1986, Archives, the Distinguished Flying Cross Society, San Diego, CA.

Captain Rob Weber, oral history interview, interviewed by Dr. Barry A. Lanman, 2 March 2010, transcribed, the Distinguished Flying Cross Society Oral History Collection, the Distinguished Flying Cross Society, San Diego, CA.

"The Raid on Libya," Eighties Club, The Politics and Pop Culture of the 1980s [http://eightiesclub.tripod.com/id313.htm]. Accessed February 2011.

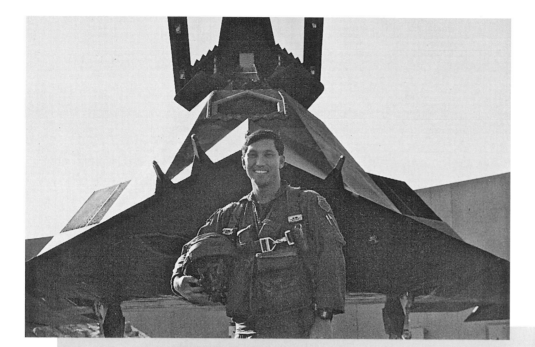

Top: Lieutenant Colonel Joe Bouley bombed the Baghdad Nuclear Complex during Operation Desert Storm on 17 January 1991. Middle: Bouley and his squadron pose in front of the F-117A Stealth fighter at Khamis, a Royal Saudi airbase in the mountains north of Yemen. Bottom: While serving his country, Bouley came across a letter from a female addressed to "Any pilots?" He answered the letter and they were married three months after he returned home. Joe and Sara have been married for almost two decades. Photographs courtesy of Joe Bouley

Thirty Stealths Execute "Wolfpack"

Lieutenant Colonel Joe Bouley, USAF

"17 January 1991 – A date I won't soon forget"_____

Joseph R. Bouley was born in Fukuoka, Japan on 7 January 1955, the eldest child of Wilfrid Bouley, an Air Force veteran of Korea and Vietnam. A few years earlier, Wilfrid met Minori Naraki while he was stationed in Japan and they were married. Ultimately the couple had six children. Throughout his military career, Chief Master Sergeant Bouley traveled with his family around the world from base to base in the line of duty. Thus, Bouley spent his entire childhood growing up on military bases. While he had ambitions of becoming an Air Force officer, flying was not something he had always wanted to do. However, fate intervened when he received a four-year AFROTC pilot candidate scholarship. As Lieutenant Colonel Bouley says, "…the rest was history."

By 1977, Bouley was a Distinguished Graduate of the University Nebraska-Lincoln AFROTC program and he entered undergraduate pilot training in 1978 at Williams AFB, Arizona, graduating in 1979. Over the next six years, he flew the OV-10A Bronco with the 19th Tactical Air Support Squadron, Osan AB, Korea; served as an air liaison officer attached to the 2nd Brigade, 2nd Infantry Division, Camp Hovey, Korea; transitioned to the A-10A Thunderbolt II, flying with the 18th Tactical Fighter Squadron, Eielson AFB, Alaska, and was also a member of the four-man Alaskan Air Command GUNSMOKE 83 worldwide air-to-ground gunnery meet team.

Additional assignments included service as the Chief of A-10 Weapons & Tactics, instructor pilot and flight examiner with the 25th Tactical Fighter Squadron, Suwon AB, Korea. He also became a 1985 Distinguished Graduate of the USAF Fighter Weapons School at Nellis AFB, Nevada and a 1990 graduate of the Armed Forces Staff College, Norfolk, Virginia. Upon graduation, Major Bouley was assigned to the 415th Tactical Fighter Squadron, Tonopah Test Range, Nevada, flying the F-117A Stealth fighter. He served as the Squadron Chief of Mission Planning and Assistant Operations Officer and was deployed to Khamis Mushayt, Saudi Arabia, from August 1990 to April 1991, participating in Operations Desert Shield and Desert Storm.

Although a seasoned military aviator with extensive training, Major Bouley was about to experience his most memorable and challenging flight. "17 January 1991 – a date I won't soon forget. That was the day I would fly my first combat mission after nearly fourteen years of 'practice' in the Air Force. This would also be the mission where I would be awarded the DFC – a truly memorable night!

My unit, the 415th Tactical Fighter Squadron 'Nightstalkers,' consisting of 24 F-117As, had deployed to Khamis Mushayt, Saudi Arabia, 20 August 1990, after a fifteen hour nonstop flight from Langley AFB, VA. We refueled every hour to keep our tanks topped off in case we had to divert along the way. But we all made it to Khamis; a Royal Saudi F-15 base high in the mountains north of Yemen. This would be our home for the next eight months. It was very boring to say the least! To remain 'politically correct' with our hosts, there was General Order Number One which stated no alcohol, no girlie magazines, no mingling with the populace, etc. Bottled water was plentiful, but any can of soft drink was worth its weight in gold. We had no field kitchen, so we relied on Pakistani cooks from the base chow hall to attempt to cook western meals, package them up and transport them to our little section of the base. We would get the meals hours after they had been made. A lot of us just grabbed MREs to eat.

On the morning of 16 January 1991, the word came down from CENTAF HQ in Riyadh in a simple message: 'Execute Wolfpack.' H-hour was 0100Z, or 0300 local, 17 January. The order actually both surprised and relieved us. Surprised - because we thought the Allies wouldn't bomb downtown Baghdad right away, thinking back to Vietnam where we didn't take the war to Hanoi from the get-go. Relieved -

because we had been sitting in the desert for five months waiting...The whole Wing was pumped up and we were only a few hours away from flying missions to the north.

The 37TFW would have thirty Stealths in three separate waves of ten hit Iraq that first night. One wave would attack in the early morning hours, starting at 0250 hours. A cruise missile attack would follow a few minutes later. A second and third Stealth wave would follow the cruise missiles. Army Apaches, led by AF Spec Ops Pave Low helicopters, would actually fire the first shots in anger against border radar sites, to allow the non-stealthy follow-on waves of fighters a clear path. By the time these shots were fired, the F-117s were already deep into Iraq.

Careful consideration was made throughout the war to avoid hitting the Al Rasheed Hotel in downtown Baghdad – we wouldn't want to interrupt Peter Arnett's CNN broadcasts! The only problem was that this hotel was smack in the middle of all the prime strategic targets, making it difficult to deconflict timing and run-in lines on the attack routes. Losses were projected by the Pentagon to be 10% - three Stealths.

My targets that night were the North Taji command bunker, located in the northwest corner of Baghdad, and the Osirak nuclear reactor, located in the southeast corner. I was to drop a GBU-27 2,000 penetrator bomb on the bunker and a GBU-10 2,000 general purpose bomb on the reactor. The Osirak was the same reactor the Israelis bombed in 1981, now rebuilt.

We flew in pairs with a KC-135R tanker comms-out to the Iraqi border, and then at a designated time we would just leave as singletons on our particular runs. The missions were five to six hours long – two hours to the border, about two hours in Iraq, then two hours home. I crossed the border and ten minutes later spotted, using my infra-red system, two Iraqi MiG-23s on patrol. I just watched them fly by, but was thinking what two easy kills they would be if I only had something other than bombs loaded up. As I flew west of the city, sporadic AAA tracers sprayed the sky, with an occasional missile plume going up. Baghdad was easy to spot – it was the only area lit up like the Fourth of July. There were tracers all over the sky, going in all directions. Several SAMs arced their way skyward.

My 'cockroach,' as we lovingly called the F-117s, descended to a lower attack altitude of 8,900 feet on its planned computed run, now putting me into the heart of the barrage AAA. There would be no "jinking" to avoid the AAA/SAMs – the F-117 autopilot would fly the run on a line, while I concentrated on finding the target and releasing the bomb. This was a little disconcerting for an old A-10 pilot used to constantly moving his jet through the sky. This time I would have to just sit and take whatever came. I hoped that both the pre-planning and this 'stealth' stuff would pay off, but if I got hit, well, I got hit! I found the Taji bunker and dropped the laser-guided bomb (we self-lased) with the cross-hairs squarely on the top center. The bomb went in, penetrating several feet before exploding. I immediately climbed to 14,000 feet for the short run from the northwest to the southeast of the city. I think I was too busy looking for my next target to notice all the AAA, though I could see it all through my peripheral vision.

The Baghdad Nuclear Complex consisted of three big reactors – the Osirak, the Isis and the Russian, plus a large cluster of research buildings and labs. I easily found the Osirak, hard to miss with such a huge 'IR' signature. I released the GBU-10 into the center of it and watched it explode. I immediately began an egress climb, then turned south toward the border.

My first combat mission had gone well, I thought. I felt totally drained from it all, but was glad I had found and hit my targets. All the years of training paid off for me, and I would fly twenty more missions in the next forty-two days. The good thing was that our unit had no losses the first day and we would fly nearly 1,300 missions without a loss or even a scratch! We were very fortunate. We brought everyone home when it was all over. Mission accomplished!"

After Desert Storm, in August 1991, Major Bouley was reassigned as the Operations Officer, A-10 Division, USAF Fighter Weapons School. Bouley then transferred to the USAF Reserve in 1992, and was assigned as an Air Operations Officer and Crisis Action Team member, J-3 Directorate, US Pacific Command, Camp H.M. Smith, Hawaii. He retired from the USAF Reserve as a lieutenant colonel in

January 2000.

The military played one additional role in Lieutenant Colonel Bouley's life. Though he had been previously married before Desert Shield, fate once again intervened. Sara Caldwell of Fayetteville, Arkansas, was finishing her degree at the University of Texas-Austin and decided to write a military man fighting in combat. She wrote an "any serviceman" letter, which was given to Bouley because she wrote "Any pilots?" on the outside of the envelope. She requested an aviator for a pen pal because she was a private pilot herself. Once the connection was made, they wrote each other for eight months, met when he got back to the United States and were married less than three months later. Bouley said, "it was funny because everyone in my Stealth squadron gave our relationship only six months. That was over eighteen years ago!"

Bouley currently resides in North Salt Lake, Utah with Sara and their six children, and has been a pilot for United Airlines since 1992. Looking back on receiving the DFC, Lieutenant Colonel Bouley said that, "...when people find out I have a DFC, they want to know everything and are 'wow'ed' that I got it flying the Stealth. I'm honored to have received the medal, but I tend to focus more on the relationships I have with the guys in my squadron. While I keep in touch with fellow aviators from all of my old units, the ones who were with me in combat are the most special. We have an extremely tight bond with one another that will never be broken."

Notes

Lieutenant Colonel Joe Bouley, Distinguished Flying Cross citation, action date: 17 January 1991, Archives, the Distinguished Flying Cross Society, San Diego, CA.

Lieutenant Colonel Joe Bouley, personal written account, unpublished, the Distinguished Flying Cross Society Oral History Collection, the Distinguished Flying Cross Society, San Diego, CA.

Top: A Chinese jet collided with Lieutenant Shane Osborn's EP-3E causing an international situation. Only by visual inspection of the aircraft can the enormity of the damage be appreciated. Middle: The entire crew of the EP-3E flew back home on a chartered airplane after being released by the Chinese. The flight was a joyous celebration of freedom. Bottom: Lieutenant Shane Osborn was honored for his heroism when he returned to US soil. Photographs courtesy of the United States Navy

The Hainan EP-3E International Incident

Lieutenant Shane Osborn, USAF

"...my scenario, we had out of control flight...We lost over eighty-five hundred feet in an inverted dive."

Few Navy pilots have ever had the opportunity to see a J-8 fighter jet, from the People's Republic of China, up close while in flight. Lieutenant Shane Osborn not only had that experience, he also had a J-8 collide with his airplane and lived to tell about it. The next eleven days after the accident put Lieutenant Osborn in the center of a tense international standoff. His anonymity was lost but his actions in the air and on the ground propelled him to the status of a national symbol.

Shane Osborn was born in South Dakota in 1974 but spent his formative years in Nebraska. From his perspective, he was born to fly and remarked, "Becoming a pilot had been my ambition for as long as I can remember. In fact, flying formed my first vivid memory...Dad took me flying with our neighbor, a sheep farmer named Lyle Brewer, who flew his bright yellow Piper J-3 Cub from a pasture near our home." The Civil Air Patrol also made a major impression on Osborn and he focused on obtaining his private pilot's license. An interlude with high school sports, music and a car crash were the only things that slowed down his dream.

After many applications to service academies, Osborn was finally offered a four-year Naval Reserve Officers Training Corps (NROTC) scholarship to any university that offered the program. The University of Nebraska was his ultimate choice and at the end of four years he heard the best words he could have imagined from his commanding officer, "You got your pilot slot...You're going to Pensacola." In October 1997, he finished his primary training but did not get an advanced slot flying jets. Instead, he headed for intermediate and then advanced training. When he received his wings, he was type-rated in a TC-12 Huron and then trained as a P-3 pilot.

Osborn described the plane he would ultimately fly as a command pilot. "The P-3 and its EP-3E electronic reconnaissance variant was a big plane with a wingspan just short of 100 feet and an overall aircraft length of almost 105 feet. The tail stood as high as a three-story building...Its four turbo-prop engines, miles of wiring, hydraulic plumbing and electronics, made the plane one of the most systems-intensive in the American military inventory." The plane cruised at 180 knots and was normally flown at an altitude of 24,000 feet.

In addition to his aviation training he had one hurdle to complete; SERE (Survival, Evasion, Resistance and Escape School). Little did he realize how important this training would be in less than four years.

Lieutenant Osborn was then assigned to the World Watchers of Fleet Air Reconnaissance Squadron, VQ-1, the Navy's largest operational squadron. The missions involved electronic reconnaissance in three distinct regions of the world: Bahrain on the Arabian Gulf (to support Operation Southern Watch – the No Fly Zone in southern Iraq); Ecuador, (to support antinarcotics endeavors) and Okinawa, Japan (to provide Chinese reconnaissance). Lieutenant Osborn was first assigned to Bahrain then on to Ecuador. After additional flight training and education pertaining to geopolitical policies, Osborn was sent to Kadena Air Base on Okinawa as mission commander.

To put these reconnaissance missions in perspective, Osborn stated, "the Russians did these kinds of missions, the Iranians did them from time to time, and when we had other countries' aircraft patrolling our coast, we intercepted them as well...However, it was 2001 and President George W. Bush had just taken office and the United States was getting ready to sell destroyers to the Taiwanese along with missile weapons systems. These actions had the Chinese upset and they were doing some 'saber rattling'...So the Navy brought in carrier groups and stepped up reconnaissance missions to see what was going on in the

South China Sea...

We'd always been intercepted [by the Chinese] but these series of events led to more threatening maneuvers - more hot-dogging, so to speak and the length of intercepts tripled. A few weeks prior to my incident, we had an intercept that lasted over thirty-five minutes." Some jets, as a form of harassment, flew within 50 feet of the EP-3Es and then rocked the slower aircraft with jet wash when they blasted away. While protests had been made about this dangerous flying, the close intercepts continued.

On Sunday, 1 April 2001, 26-year-old Lieutenant Shane Osborn was the aircraft and mission commander of an EP-3E Aries II flying a routine reconnaissance mission off the coast of China. The mission began like many others with a predawn launch from Kadena Air Base. During the nine-hour flight, the aircraft was scheduled to head down the Asian coast to the South China Sea and conduct a signals intelligence gathering mission in international airspace northeast of the Chinese island of Hainan.

Lieutenant Osborn and his crew of twenty-three were intercepted, as usual, once the Chinese radar identified them. A pair of J-8 Finback fighters were sent to check out the American aircraft about seventy miles from China in international airspace. However this time, one of the Chinese fighter jets came too close and suddenly collided with Osborn's plane. The EP-3E's propeller cut the J-8 jet in half. The fighter's front section smashed into the EP-3E and tore off the radome which contained the Big Look radar, leaving a gaping hole in the nose of the aircraft.

Osborn explained what happened. "In my scenario, we had out of control flight... I had my nose torn off. There was an explosive decompression...We lost over 8,500 feet in an inverted dive [in thirty seconds]. My aileron had a hole through it. My tail was torn apart and the number one engine was out with a wind-milling prop, at about sixty-seven percent, causing drag.

Once I got the plane out of the dive...it took full elevator, full right aileron and full right rudder to hold the airplane level. I was literally at maximum power with the 'cherry lights' just to hold altitude...I didn't have the ability to make small minute corrections. It literally tore my shoulder apart holding this airplane up like this for the thirty-five minutes." After locating the closest airfield, they made an unauthorized emergency landing, without airspeed data or flaps, at the Lingshui Air Base on Hainan Island. Once on the ground, the entire crew was taken to Chinese military barracks where they were detained and questioned.

Osborn recounted his concerns, thoughts and interpersonal-conflicts during the days when he and his crew were detained on Chinese soil. "There were really two issues that I was worried about: Protecting my crew and making sure I didn't mess up during the hours and hours of interrogations...I didn't want the wrong words used on tape to compromise our honor or the country's secrets.

The Chinese were not intimidated by the United States, so I wanted to be strong and firm, and not allow them to interrogate my crew. I never expected it to work [for awhile] when I said, 'No, you can't interrogate the rest of the crew.'... I also knew that as long as I was sitting in that chair I was doing my job, and that my job was to make sure I protected my crew to the best of my ability, not compromise our secrets, our integrity, and also not come off as too confrontational. I didn't want to put their backs up against the wall. That culture is very directed towards saving face, so I didn't want to be confrontational with them because I knew that wasn't going to do the crew or me any good.

I understood there were different rules in this type of captivity and that the Geneva Convention didn't apply. So I wasn't limited to name, rank and serial number, but I certainly didn't want to give them anything more than that. I didn't want to tell them where my crew was from. I certainly wasn't going to let them know the specialties of my crew. I did let them know that we were a very tight unit...I wanted to show the Chinese officials right away that this was a big crew of twenty-four people, but we knew each other well.

That was the hardest part of captivity - the fact that you don't have any control. So I worked hard to not give them anything, and then over time compromising...For about a day and a half, I just quit talking and the crew went on a hunger strike. And, so we pushed them into letting me see my crew at meals. I'd get an update on how things were going. That would recharge my batteries; getting to see the scared crew that you're responsible for, and then going back into the interrogation. It came to the point where they would let General Sealock, who was the US attaché to China, come in and he'd get to see us for ten minutes. He had been a pilot…and we'd speak in pilot code."

From the discussion with General Sealock, Lieutenant Osborn deduced that he was going to have to let the Chinese eventually talk with his crew. After six days of saying no to this demand, the strategic game then centered around Osborn's ability to negotiate how the interrogations were going to transpire. He spent another day and a half negotiating the terms. "They knew they had me, but I wasn't going to give it to them…the compromise was that the interrogations would last ten minutes, there would be no cameras or recording devices in the room, and the most important thing was the fact that there would never be fewer than two crew members in the room…it's strength in numbers. If your buddy is sitting next to you and you're both catching hell, it's a lot better than being alone…

By day eight or nine, the Chinese knew that they were not going to get anything useful out of the crew. This situation was now an international negotiation between the heads of state…The bid for the Olympics was coming up that summer and the Chinese were trying to get the Olympics in Beijing. There was no way they would get the Olympics if they were still holding us prisoners.

In addition, the Chinese were trying to get into the World Trade Organization and get most favored nation trading status from Congress…which was a huge economic benefit for China, as for us…so there were things I knew were happening that would help this situation get resolved. However, I never thought we'd get out of there in eleven days.

The Chinese knew they caused the accident. However, they were trying to blame me the whole time. They wanted me to admit that I rammed their aircraft, killed their pilot…that I was a murderer. They made it known that I should be tried and put in a prison camp…They actually had me convinced for a few days this would happen. However, once they realized they weren't going to get an admission out of me, they tried to work on the US and get an apology to save face…Nothing was ideal, but the crew held together and the training paid off in the end.

Ultimately, this incident was solved by two mid-level government agency representatives basically meeting in a park, sitting on a bench and hashing this out. It sounds kind of like something you'd see in a movie, but it's true…We were released on 11 April 2001." The aircraft was unceremoniously returned to the US in boxes several months after it had been "inspected" by Chinese officials.

As with most international incidents, public opinion on how the situation was handled varied. Some people "second-guessed" Lieutenant Osborn's decision to land on Chinese soil and potentially divulge secrets to a rival power. Lieutenant Osborn defended his actions in a vehement manner. "The squadron SOP, Standard Operating Procedures, in no way stated that I should ditch the airplane [in this type of situation]. The decision for me was quite simple. We aren't at war with China. We do quite a bit of trade and we have good relations…it's not the same scenario as it had been with North Korea.

Anybody that's seen the EP-3E knows there's a big dish underneath. There's a lot of drag…You could not successfully ditch that plane in the ocean even if everything else was working well. The dish underneath would catch [the water], cause a cartwheel and flip the plane upside-down. And, remember, we had out of control flight.

I couldn't get the fuel dumped. I was about fifteen to twenty thousand pounds overweight for a regular landing, let alone a no-flap or a ditch. All these factors made it pretty easy to decide. It was a matter of, 'do I want to kill everyone on board or not?' That's why we have an emergency destruction plan. This aircraft was the last of its kind. It was due, two weeks later, to get completely stripped out and upgraded in Texas, so it was the oldest stuff we had. I always tell people, you know, if they want to reverse engineer the stuff we had on there, they're more than welcome to. It will set them back thirty years.

Most of the complex equipment, the top secret material, were the laptops and things we brought on board. That's why I activated the emergency destruction checklist and they took care of it in the back.

They got rid of that stuff, chopped it up and made it unusable…

Everyone in my chain of command agreed [with my decision] all the way up to the President of the United States. I talked to them personally, including the head of the National Security Agency. To conclude his justification for his actions, Osborn often asks the rhetorical question: "What would have been the political implications if the United States had lost twenty-four servicemen and women as a result of the actions by the People's Republic of China?"

During his convalescent leave, one of the Chairmen of the Joint Chief's staff informed Lieutenant Osborn that he and his crew were going to receive medals at a ceremony that coincided with the Andrews Air Force Base Air Show. Osborn later found out he would receive the Distinguished Flying Cross while the balance of the crew would be given Air Medals.

While Lieutenant Osborn considered this a great personal honor, he was disappointed that his master chief, engineers and copilots did not receive DFCs since they had all worked together as a team. He commented, "It definitely wasn't a one-man show up there, and they were critical in keeping this airplane up in the sky."

Never expecting to be an author, Osborn wrote *Born to Fly: The Untold Story of a Downed American Spy Plane*, which was released in 2001. He did so to chronicle the story in his own words and to set the record straight from his perspective. The book was personal in nature and gave an inside look at the international incident, the complexities of the situation and the decisions made based on those variables.

To fulfill his emerging political aspirations, Osborn left the Navy and went back to Nebraska, the state in which he was raised. He decided to run for the office of Nebraska State Treasurer. He won the 2006 election with seventy-six percent of the electorate.

Through his term as treasurer he focused on creating transparency with regard to the finances of Nebraska. In a bold move that set a financial example for his fellow Nebraskans, Osborn reduced the size of his overall staff and froze the salaries of his top staff members. These actions resulted in impressive statistics to back up his sound financial policies.

Surprisingly, Osborn announced in the fall of 2009 that he would not seek another term as State Treasurer. While not elaborating on his specific plans, sources from Rush Limbaugh to the Wall Street Journal eluded to the fact that he might run for a Senate seat in 2012.

No matter what transpires in Shane Osborn's future, the Hainan Incident will always be a guiding force for the pilot turned politician. He philosophically stated, "I can tell you now that I'm in politics… having gone through the Hainan Incident makes life a lot easier…it puts things into perspective."

Notes

Lieutenant Shane Osborn, Distinguished Flying Cross citation, action date: 1 April 2001, the Distinguished Flying Cross Society, San Diego, CA.

Lieutenant Shane Osborn, oral history interview, interviewed by Brennan Willard and John D. Willard V., 31 July 2007, transcribed, the Distinguished Flying Cross Society Oral History Collection, the Distinguished Flying Cross Society, San Diego, CA.

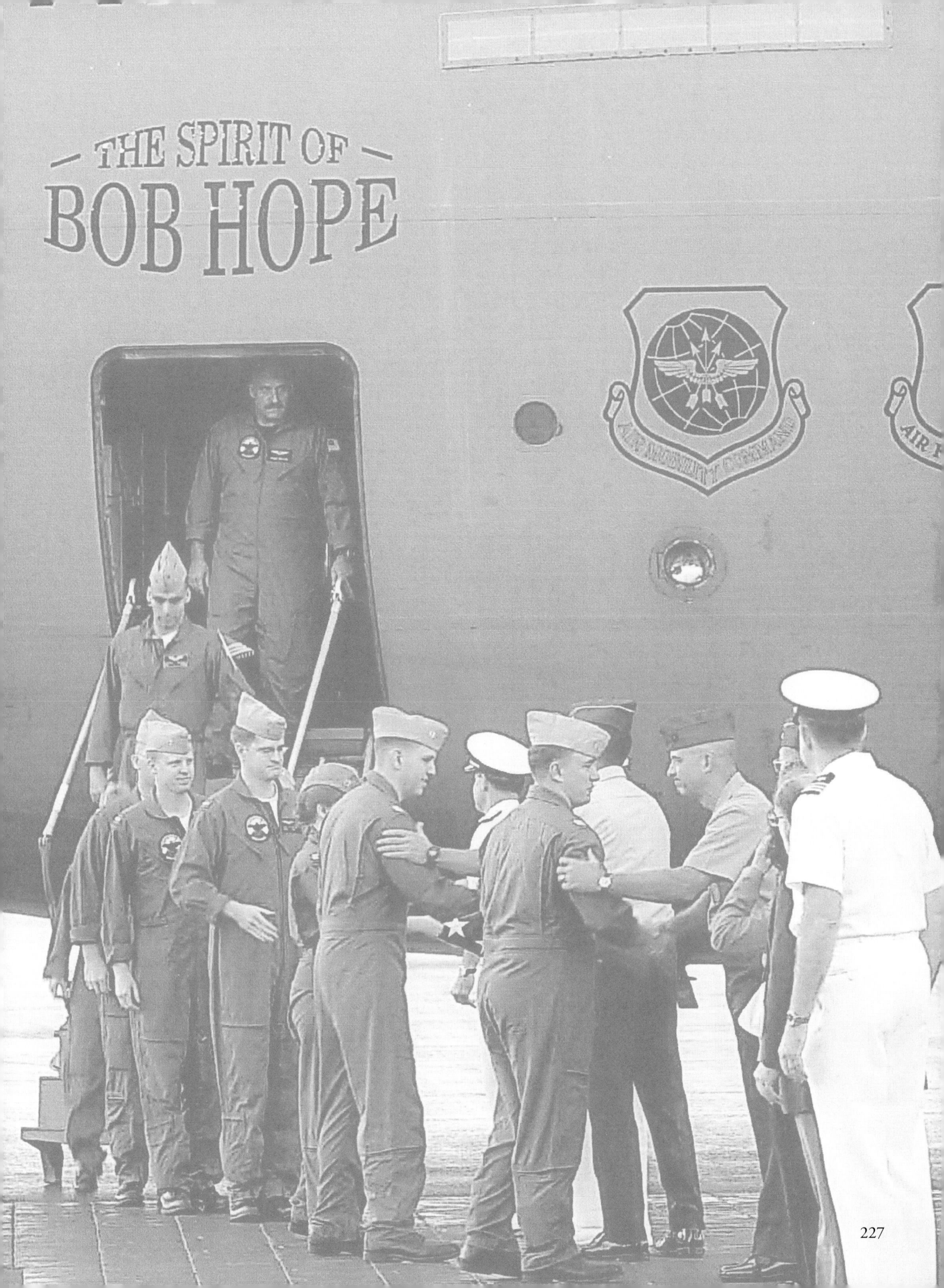
THE SPIRIT OF
BOB HOPE

Top: Lieutenant Colonel Scott Campbell received three DFCs in four days while flying in Afghanistan. It is believed that Campbell and his wife are the first married pilots to receive Distinguished Flying Crosses. Middle: Campbell's A-10 was refueled mid-air on the way to a mission in Afghanistan. Bottom: Lieutenant Colonel Scott Campbell, Lieutenant Colonel Kim Campbell and their son Colin Reed Campbell are a proud USAF family. Photographs courtesy of Scott Campbell and the United States Air Force

"Warthog" Pilot Controls Chaos in Afghanistan

Lieutenant Colonel Scott C. Campbell, USAF

"Every year at our Flying Tiger reunion, we get together with the likes of Tex Hill and our brothers before us in World War II and Vietnam. They did things that were far greater than what I did."_____

When Scott Campbell decided to attend the United States Air Force Academy and become a fighter pilot, he never envisioned receiving three Distinguished Flying Crosses – especially not in four days! He also did not foresee that he would marry a fighter pilot who would receive this prestigious aviation honor as well.

Born in 1973 in upstate New York, Scott Christopher Campbell graduated from the United States Air Force Academy and was commissioned on 31 May 1995. As part of an exchange program with the Navy, he completed the first part of his primary pilot training at the Naval Air Station at Whiting Field, Florida. There, he flew T-34s with the Navy. For the second part of his training, he was tracked by the Air Force for fighter/bombers and sent to Vance AFB to fly T-38s. When he received his wings, Campbell was assigned to Pope AFB where he primarily flew the A-10 Thunderbolt II; also known as the "Warthog."

Campbell then acquired advanced training at the United States Air Force Weapons School before he was assigned to Osan Air Base, Korea where he served as the Chief of Weapons and Tactics for the 25th Fighter Squadron. Following that tour, he was sent back to Pope Air Force Base and assigned to the 74th Fighter Squadron as a flight commander in the squadron. Almost immediately, the squadron was deployed forward to Ahmed Al-Jaber Air Base in Kuwait for a scheduled rotation during Operation Southern Watch, enforcing the no-fly zone over Southern Iraq. In particular, the squadron's mission was combat search and rescue support. Campbell stated, "I served in two roles deploying forward as the Chief of Weapons and Tactics for the squadron as well as the flight commander because the individual who was the chief of weapons and tactics had to stay behind from that deployment…but was later deployed after 'Anaconda' was over."

From Scott's perspective and crystal-clear memory, he noted, "The DFC missions are pretty easy to recall as they happened consecutively over the course of four days, so they were one right after the other. The total period of time was 4 March through 7 March 2002."

The sortie for which he was awarded his initial DFC involved the first flight of A-10s into Afghanistan in support of Operation Enduring Freedom. In specific, he provided protection for the 10th Mountain and 101st Airborne Divisions on the ground in close contact with Al-Qaeda and Taliban forces. At that time the 332nd Air Expeditionary Wing at Al-Jaber was conducting simultaneous Southern Watch operations as well as Operation Enduring Freedom over Afghanistan. The A-10s were specifically tasked to conduct Southern Watch.

While it had been quiet from an air perspective over Afghanistan since the heavy bombing of Tora Bora, during December 2001, a new operation was being devised at the beginning of March. It appeared that the Army was preparing a large scale assault into the Shah-i-Kot Valley in Afghanistan which involved a division size unit which required air support. Captain Campbell and his compatriots were initially informed that the A-10 squadron would not be involved in this major operation. The squadron was disappointed, to say the least, because they had been sitting on alert and had not seen much action in Iraq. However, the situation changed, placing Captain Campbell at the epicenter of the action.

"The operation had kicked off on the 2nd and had taken a turn for the worse on the 3rd of March, when a helicopter was shot down on what would eventually be known as Robert's Ridge (Takur Ghar). This stranded Ranger Quick Reaction Forces and some Special Ops Forces that were up there in an attempt to rescue the SEAL who was lost from their helo.

I was informed that I would lead the first "2-ship" into Afghanistan the next morning and that the rest of the mission planning cell would take care of preparing all of our materials and maps for the next day. I was then ordered to go sleep and get my required pilot rest, which was kind of tough to do considering the excitement level.

The first thing I wanted to do was just dive into reading all of the 'spins', you know, the special instructions. The Rules of Engagement (ROE) for Afghanistan were far different from Iraq…I went to my wingman, Lieutenant Colonel Edward Kostelnik—call sign K-9, and told him what was going on. Both of us figured by morning this would probably be all called off. We tried not to get too excited. But sure enough, after a little bit of sleep, things had continued to go badly during the night in Afghanistan and the game was still on for us to go and launch.

The trick to this, of course, was that we were stationed in Al-Jaber and Afghanistan was a good ways away. We couldn't fly directly there based on Iran being in the way. We would have to fly along the Gulf, up through Pakistan and into Afghanistan, which for the 'pointy-nosed fighters,', was about a three-hour trip. For the 'Hog' it was going to be a five-hour flight just to get over the top of the battle area.

From the intelligence, it was controlled chaos…it appeared that the friendlies were everywhere and the enemy was everywhere…There was no line of good guys on this side and the bad guys on that side. We were also told that we were launching but weren't told our point of recovery (landing). So, we threw gear together and launched knowing we had no idea where we were going or how long we would be there. To refuel, we met our tanker over the Gulf which dragged us all the way into Afghanistan – about three air refuelings just to get there."

By the time the A-10s arrived, they were losing daylight and Captain Campbell realized they would be fighting between peaks 12,000-13,000 feet high with valley floors at 8,000 feet. Coupled with heavy ordnance, their job was exceptionally daunting considering the normal regulations. Campbell explained their orders. "Before we stepped, our group commander told us, 'Just go in there. I know you guys haven't read the spins and don't know the ROE like the back of your hand. Just go in there, employ smartly, employ tactically and don't worry about any of the black and white rules…If you do what's tactically smart, I'll take care of the rest.' So that was reassuring.

Once in the air, due to the conditions, we ultimately elected to roll in and put a couple of white phosphorous rockets down – some Willie Pete. I then had K-9 roll in and put the first 500 pounder down which was right on target….However, at that point, we started hearing a lot of additional communication on our strike frequency from other aircraft we weren't working with or coordinating with at the time… there were a lot of things we weren't aware of that were around us in the dark - in the same piece of air space… So at that point we stepped back as the immediate target was sequestered and silenced. I found out about a week later from a buddy of mine that I'd ended up pulling off one of my runs about 300 feet off the nose of a AC-130 Gunship that I never saw because it was completely blacked out"

In actuality, A-10s, AC-130s, helicopters and a B-52 were not in coordination and the situation was chaotic at best. This presented a scenario that might lead to mid-air collisions and accidental strikes on the American ground troops. At this point, Captain Campbell assessed the overall situation and made a momentous decision; he would de-conflict the air space.

"We took charge of the battle space as forward air controllers. Thus, we kept all the aircraft apart from one another, reducing the chances for mid-air collisions and fratricide. During that time-frame we also conducted a strike against a 200-300 strong force Al-Qaeda-Taliban group with my two-ship of A-10s, and as a forward air controller brought in two F-18s to strike that target. It was one of the largest forces struck during Operation Anaconda.

The mission had been over eleven hours – but all totaled, I was in the jet for fourteen hours. It was the longest sortie I had ever flown." The harrowing long mission was not culminated by a simple landing at a supporting Air Force Base. With minimal information, Scott had to find and land at a sensitive air base in Pakistain using night vision googles for the first time since the base was completely blacked out for security purposes. "The next morning, we woke up and launched again. Originally the agreement was that we were only going to fly the A-10s in and out at night under the cover of darkness, but we broke the rule right from the start just because they needed support in the area. So we launched again about mid-afternoon.

My second and third Distinguished Flying Crosses were a lot less exciting, per se. I would actually not even fire a shot or drop a bomb which was kind of strange for me.

The second DFC event, the 6th of March 2002, was in support of a high value target. It was unknown which target or who it was. All we knew was that it was in support of a special operations unit that was taking control of a high value target and doing a sensitive site exploitation on a neighboring site for intelligence, or neighboring areas with intelligence gathering requirements; and then providing close escort on the special operation's helicopters as they brought their high value targets or high value individuals back to their base...I guess it had more importance than my knowing, but that was the event for which I received my second Distinguished Flying Cross.

My third sortie, for which I received a Distinguished Flying Cross was the next day, the 7th of March. It was a night mission in support of 10th Mountain, 101st Airborne and Special Operations Forces. The weather had turned really bad and it was hampering a lot of the close air support that was being provided (and not a whole lot of fun in the mountains). I had a young wingman with me, Captain 'Frag' Hayden, whose old man had been an A-10 commander in Desert Storm. Frag was on my wing...at this point on the air tasking order we were being denoted as the forward air controller and having control of the AO.

So if there was a forward air controller in the area, AWACS would turn control of the entire battle space, as far as where the employment was going on, to the forward air controllers. There were a couple of F-16 guys out of Al-Jaber who were also forward air conrollers-airborne (FAC-As). They were doing a tag-teaming with us, covering that as much as we could, because we were packing so many airplanes into such a small air space. The real threat was us running into each other. We had some Strike Eagles, some F-16s, F-18s...we had a B-1 on station and a number of Predators.

That night, we did mostly command and control, de-confliction and forward air controlling, hitting some small targets and then, at the tail-end of the evening...we struck the 'Rat Line'...The 'Rat Line' was believed to be the main line of supplies or line of communication for the enemy from Khowst into this valley. At this point, it was more of their escape route and at this phase of the operation what we were trying to do was block them...So, in coordination with AC-130 gun-ships, my wingman 'Frag' and I rolled in – we had six Mark 82 airbursts a piece. I ripped six and my wingman ripped six - we also put about 700 rounds of high explosive incendiary down. Twelve 500 pounders and 700 rounds of 30mm pretty much took care of that job and eradicated the target. At that point, we were out of gas and headed back to Pakistan.

While I was in Afghanistan, I was happy that the 74th Fighter Squadron of A-10s, was able to get involved in the fight because it was our kind of fight. It was what the airplane was built to do. It was close air support. That's where we were meant to be... and we were able to get in the fight and do a lot of good.

During the events, I didn't think much about it because I was so busy, just continuing to stay ahead of the game, get more information on what was going on. However, after the fact, the event that brought it home for me was when we moved forward to Bagram. I think everybody realized that was the right place to have our jets. I got a call from one of my old commanders, deputy group commander, Lieutenant Colonel Muck Brown. His son was a soldier in the 10th Mountain. While he was retired, he figured out what the A-10s were doing in Afghanistan. He said that, 'the first night you came in there, the company under attack was my son's company. He was on the ground there.' It brought it full circle for me, especially being that Muck was one of the guys who trained me, brought me up as a young instructor and sent me to Weapons School. So that was pretty awesome.

Currently, Lieutenant Colonel Scott Campbell is commander of the 358th Fighter Squadron at Davis-Monthan AFB in Arizona. Even when he comes home, he "talks shop" because his wife, Lieutenant

Colonel Kim Campbell, is an A-10 pilot and was awarded the Distinguished Flying Cross for her flying in Iraq (Lieutenant Colonel Kim Campbell's story is included in this chapter). As far as the Campbells know, they are the only husband and wife pilot team who have received Distinguished Flying Cross medals. While their time apart has been a challenge, they speak the same language when it comes to their work and their careers. They also share a passion for the Air Force and flying the A-10. In 2008, the Campbells celebrated the birth of a baby boy named Colin Reed Campbell. Time will tell if he becomes a third generation Air Force Academy graduate.

In assessing the medals he has received for military aviation exploits, Campbell stated, "I think looking back on the Distinguished Flying Crosses, it was awesome for me because, at the time, I was in one of the hallowed units in the Air Force, the 23rd Fighter Group - the Flying Tigers. Every year at our Flying Tiger reunion we get together with the likes of Tex Hill and our brothers before us in World War II and Vietnam. They did things that were far greater than what I did. It was very humbling to be in that crowd and in that company... It's an honor to be able to associate myself with aviators of that caliber."

Notes

Lieutenant Colonel Scott Christopher Campbell, Distinguished Flying Cross citations, action dates: 4 March – 7 March 2002, Archives, the Distinguished Flying Cross Society, San Diego, CA.

Lieutenant Colonel Scott Christopher Campbell, oral history interview, interviewed by Chuck Sweeney, 19 November 2008, transcribed, the Distinguished Flying Cross Society Oral History Collection, the Distinguished Flying Cross Society, San Diego, CA.

233

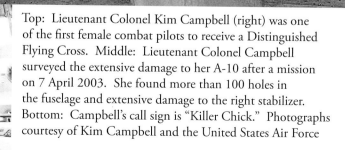

Top: Lieutenant Colonel Kim Campbell (right) was one of the first female combat pilots to receive a Distinguished Flying Cross. Middle: Lieutenant Colonel Campbell surveyed the extensive damage to her A-10 after a mission on 7 April 2003. She found more than 100 holes in the fuselage and extensive damage to the right stabilizer. Bottom: Campbell's call sign is "Killer Chick." Photographs courtesy of Kim Campbell and the United States Air Force

"Killer Chick" Brings Wounded Bird Home

Lieutenant Colonel Kim Campbell, USAF

"I got a letter on a napkin from an Army troop saying,
'Hey, thanks for saving us that day.'"

By the fifth grade Kim Campbell knew what she wanted to do when she grew up - attend the United States Air Force Academy and become a fighter pilot! While some children make such statements, they often change their minds. However, Campbell never waivered from her original career path. The fact that her father was a graduate of the Air Force Academy might have had an influence on her interest in aviation but Campbell always knew she belonged in the air. "I started flying when I was sixteen, as a birthday present from my parents. I soloed in a Cessna and was lucky enough to be able to do it at an early age and continue on with it."

With unwavering intrinsic motivation, Campbell accomplished the first part of her dream when she graduated from the Air Force Academy and was commissioned in May 1997. "As soon as I graduated, I went off to do a graduate school program as part of the Marshall Scholarship in the United Kingdom. I spent two years there and once I returned from graduate school, I went to pilot training at Columbus Air Force Base in Mississippi, selected the A-10 and went on to follow-up training in the T-38. I qualified in the A-10 at Davis-Monthan Air Force Base.

My first A-10 assignment was at Pope Air Force Base, North Carolina, as part of the 23rd Fighter Group, 75th Fighter Squadron and, following that assignment, I was selected to go to Nellis Air Force Base as part of the 422 Test and Evaluation Squadron where I served as the A-10 division commander. After assignments in the United States, Captain Campbell was assigned to the 75th Expeditionary Fighter Squadron stationed at Al-Jaber Air Base in Kuwait. I was a wingman as part of the squadron." She was known by her call sign "Killer Chick" or "KC."

On 7 April 2003, Campbell faced the most significant challenge of her aviation career. "I was flying a close air support mission in support of Operation Iraqi Freedom. We were tasked to support some ground troops near downtown Baghdad. The weather that day was less than desirable. There were clouds probably up to 20,000 feet and down to maybe about 10,000 feet, but we got a call from a Forward Air Controller on the ground, a joint terminal attack controller, saying that they were taking fire. It was a 'troops in contact' situation and they requested immediate assistance. We made it over the target area very quickly, got down below the weather, and then almost immediately saw that we were taking fire, surface-to-air fire. We could see puffs of smoke coming up around us, bright flashes. We could also see fire going across the river. It was in Northern Baghdad, across the Tigris River.

Our friendly troops were on the west side, members of the 3rd Infantry Division, and then members of the Iraqi Republican Guard were on the east side of the river. We were taking fire as soon as we got down below the weather, but quickly found the target, identified the friendly location, and were able to put 30mm [fire] down on the enemy location, as well as some high explosive rockets. We were able to silence the fire that was targeting our friendly troops. But on my last pass, after I was coming off target, I felt and heard a large explosion at the back of the aircraft. There was no doubt in my mind—I knew immediately that I had been hit by enemy fire.

I didn't know exactly what had hit me or how it had happened, but I knew that I was hit and I knew it wasn't good. I looked down at my caution panel and noticed that, most alarming to me, there were several lights flashing and an instant loss of all my hydraulics. The jet was also not responding to any of my control inputs. At this point I was lower and slower than I'd like to be since the jet was not responding. I only had one real good option. I knew that I could eject if I needed to, but I had the option luckily, in the A-10 to switch into a backup system which is called manual reversion. I was able to flip that switch which allowed me to control the aircraft mechanically, just with a system of cranks and cables, and thus I was able to get the aircraft under control and start climbing out and away from Baghdad.

I told my flight lead at the time that I had been hit. We started maneuvering, first, to get over friendly forces in case I had to eject so I could hopefully come down in their location as opposed to the enemy location where we had just been firing weapons. Then we started to climb up, out and away from Baghdad. I didn't know how long I would have in the jet. It wasn't responding very well, but we were hoping we'd at least be able to get out of Baghdad. As we started going through all of the emergency checklists, my flight lead came up alongside me and took a look at the jet, he said, 'Well, you've got hundreds of holes in the fuselage and tail, and a football-size hole in the right horizontal stabilizer.' I didn't know what to expect, but that certainly didn't sound great to me. I was lucky because I was flying the A-10 which was designed to take these kinds of hits, and I was still flying.

The airplane flew extremely well [in its condition] and we were able to actually fly the aircraft all the way back to Kuwait. I made it back to Al-Jaber Air Base and successfully landed the damaged aircraft."

As with any fighter pilot in this situation, instinctual behaviors take over from all the training. Emotion and personal thoughts were reflections done on the ground after the emergency abated. When asked what was going through her mind when she realized she was hit by enemy fire, Campbell responded: "My immediate thoughts were that this could turn out really badly…I knew that if I ejected in Baghdad over the Iraqi Republican Guard, things probably wouldn't go well, and so I was incredibly thankful the jet worked as advertised. You know, it all happened very quickly, but I still remember being just incredibly thankful the system responded the way it did, that our maintainers had done their job, and that the jet worked exactly as it was supposed to in that emergency situation. I was thankful I was flying an A-10."

For this combat action, Captain Campbell was awarded the Distinguished Flying Cross. "It was extremely humbling to receive the DFC. Looking back at it, I was just doing my job. My job as an A-10 pilot is close air support and to help those guys out on the ground, and that's all I was doing. It took so many people to make that happen. I mean, the maintainers made sure the aircraft could fly, the guys on the ground were doing their job, so really it was just very humbling to be awarded such a high honor and to be categorized with other DFC recipients for something that I felt was just me doing my job."

As time passed, Campbell, who is now a Lieutenant Colonel, had an even more reflective perspective about her DFC. "It's been five years now and I look at the line of pilots who have received the DFC, and it's extremely humbling to look back in history and realize you're part of that group, you're part of that organization, you're part of that history. It's just incredibly humbling."

While being a female combat pilot is rare in its own right, Campbell is also unique in many other respects. Lieutenant Colonel Kim Campbell is married to Lieutenant Colonel Scott Campbell who also received DFCs in an A-10 for his combat experiences in Afghanistan. To their knowledge, they are the only husband and wife pilot team who have been awarded this high military honor.

Campbell stated, "We have a unique perspective in that we have the ability to share our experiences and truly understand what each other has gone through…Being married to another military member means you're always working to try to get assignments together. We both really enjoy flying the A-10 and we both would like to stay in the military. It's always a challenge but it's one that we knew we were getting into when we started. And this just makes it that much more fun.

Recent parenthood has also added another dimension to Campbell's rather complex life. "Your priorities change when you have children, but at the same time Scott and I really enjoy what we do. It's a great environment and community in which to raise a child. The military gives a sense of family and a sense of service. It's something that Scott and I are going to love to share with our son."

Lieutenant Colonel Campbell is currently the commanding officer of the 355th Operations Support Squadron at Davis-Monthan Air Force Base, Arizona where she is responsible for all operations that support the 355th Operations Group and the 355th Fighter Wing. Making additional comments on her Distinguished Flying Cross and her combat career thus far, "Killer Chick" stated, "When I look back at my time so far, flying the A-10, the DFC mission was probably one of the situations I'm most proud of, for several reasons. That mission was working and supporting the ground troops, and I think that's the most important thing we do as A-10 pilots; support the guys on the ground. I can think of a few other situations with close air support, combat search and rescue, and just making sure our guys get out safely. They weren't necessarily awarded with a DFC or anything like that, but I got a letter on a napkin from an Army troop saying, 'Hey, thanks for saving us that day.' And that, quite honestly, meant more to me than a Distinguished Flying Cross ever would."

Notes

Lieutenant Colonel Kim Campbell, Distinguished Flying Cross citation, action date: 7 April 2003, Archives, the Distinguished Flying Cross Society, San Diego, CA.

Lieutenant Kim Campbell, oral history interview, interviewed by Chuck Sweeney, 19 November 2008, transcribed, the Distinguished Flying Cross Society Oral History Collection, the Distinguished Flying Cross Society, San Diego, CA.

Top: Using make-shift materials for a flagpole, Captain Armando Espinoza flew the American flag whenever the opportunity presented itself. Middle: In April 2003, Captain Espinoza (right) and his crew rescued a large number of Marines and several Iraqi civilians. The action was recorded by the cameras of Oliver North (left). Bottom: Espinoza flew the CH-46E Sea Knight helicopter during the mission for which he received a DFC. Captain Espinoza accepted the DFC on behalf of his entire crew. Photographs courtesy of Armando Espinoza

Casualty Evacuations Over Baghdad

Captain Armando Espinoza, USMC

"Sir, this is what we have been waiting for – this is it, right here!"_____

On live television, broadcast around the world, audiences were captivated by the images of the massive aerial assault known as "Shock and Awe." Directed towards Baghdad and other Iraqi targets on 22 March 2003, the United States and its allies initiated their campaign to seize control of Iraq. Over the next few weeks, the fighting intensified as Operation Iraqi Freedom progressed. History recorded that this process was a long and costly ordeal. It also recorded the scores of heroic actions by the United States military; this is but one of those stories about Baghdad.

Armando Espinoza was born in Mexico and became a naturalized citizen of the United States. In 1987, he enlisted in the Marine Corps, went to boot camp in June 1987 and became an infantryman with Bravo Company 1st Battalion 7th Marines stationed out of Camp Pendleton, California. In support of Desert Storm and Desert Shield, he was deployed with the Battalion in 1990 and 1991 and experienced combat as an enlisted Marine. When his tour of duty was complete, he was discharged and was accepted to the University of Arizona. In his freshman year, he was offered an aviation contract. By 1995, Espinoza completed basic officer training and then continued on to flight school in Pensacola, Florida. Given his desire to fly helicopters, he was then sent to New River, North Carolina and was trained on the large double-bladed CH-46E helicopter. Upon graduation, Armando became a first lieutenant and joined HMM 268 in Camp Pendleton, California.

Until 11 September 2001, training and exercises were conducted in a routine military manner. Things changed, however, with the terrorist attacks on the World Trade Center, the Pentagon and the hijacking of a fourth commercial airliner. By February 2003, Espinoza had been promoted to captain and received word that US forces were going into Iraq. By March he was ready for his first combat experience as an aviator. Espinoza was attached to the Marine Medium Helicopter Squadron 268, Marine Aircraft Group 39, 3rd Marine Aircraft Wing, and was assigned to fly the CH-46E Sea Knight helicopter.

He described the situation this way, "It was the first night of the war, 19 March, when we had a very unfortunate event happen in our squadron. We were in support of the 42nd British Commando Unit and were supposed to insert troops at the Al Faw Peninsula just on the southern part of the Gulf. The third aircraft that lifted off crashed and killed sixteen American and British Royal Commandos. My job in the squadron, at that point, was aviation safety officer, and I was supposed to be the tenth CH-46 on the mission but we never took off – the mission was aborted. We were up all night and we had a lot of SCUD alerts going on, so we were fatigued. Many things were not going in our favor, but since it was the first combat mission for most of us, we knew the importance of what we were expected to accomplish. Eventually, we got the word from the general to execute. And it was never a doubt in our mind that our leaders were making the right decisions – it was just a bad night to be flying."

Much to Captain Espinoza's dismay, as aviation safety officer, his principal role had changed from combat pilot to aviation investigator. So he drove to the crash site and for the next week headed the investigation of the deadly accident. Captain Espinoza stated, "So I saw the first week of the war on CNN, just like everybody else...I never got to fly. Sensing my frustration, the commanding officer from the squadron finally said, 'Okay, you need to get out and fly.' And, of course, as aviators that's what we want to do. We want to fly. So, he said 'Put the investigation aside for a day. You're going to get some flight time.' And I said, 'alright sir, sounds good. I need to get my mind off everything that's been going on here.' So we flew just a couple of routine missions, picking up and dropping off supplies. The division was already moving and pressing forward, so we were starting to deliver supplies, ammunition, water,

MREs, whatever the Marines needed forward."

On 10 April 2003, Captain Espinoza was ordered to provide multiple day and night casualty evacuation missions in support of the 1st Battalion, 5th Marines' attack into Baghdad. He flew in tandem with Major Donald Presto's helicopter. It was the experience for which he had trained since the first day he entered boot camp.

"As we got to the LZ (Landing Zone), you could see Baghdad and it's just black smoke...Baghdad was on fire but strategically. It wasn't the schools and mosques. It was strategic buildings that the Air Force, the Navy, the Marine pilots and the jet pilots had gone in there and targeted. I don't care what anybody says. I was there! So, it was a sight to see."

Captain Espinoza vividly remembered the situation before they left the ground for the first time. "We strapped in and turned the birds up...I had four crew members: my copilot, Chris Grahamn, Sergeant Joe Morralis, "Doc" Bernette and Corporal Olkenson; five of us in all. I looked back at my crew and said, 'We are going into Baghdad and if you don't want to go with me, nothing will be said. Just step out of the aircraft and I will pick you up on the way back.' They just looked at me like I was crazy and said, 'Sir, this is what we have been waiting for – this is it, right here!' I responded, 'that is what I wanted to hear' and we took off."

Since the lead aircraft, under the command of Major Presto experienced radio problems, Captain Espinoza was given the lead and the call sign Grizzly 40 and quickly found out that no rotary wing escorts were available for the flight into Baghdad. In fact, they were radioed that all Cobras and Hueys had been restricted from flying into Baghdad. So after a moment to process the situation, Espinoza got back on the radio and said, "Okay, let me get this straight. You're sending a section of CH-46s, who have two door guns on them, four between the two aircraft, into Baghdad alone without any rotary wing escorts? The response was, 'Grizzly 40, that's affirmative'...my cryptic one-word response was 'Outstanding...'

Once under way, I instructed my copilot, Captain Chris Graham, to fly the bird as low and as fast as he could while I navigated. It was just smoke and burning buildings, and I had tanks off to the left shooting at buildings. I had Marines going into buildings. There was a lot going on and it was very confusing. When we got the call to pick up injured Marines and knew we could possibly save their lives, there was never a doubt in anybody's mind that we were not going in...we were going!

Coming up the Euphrates River we had the map out and you could pick out the identifiable features in Baghdad like the bridges. As we counted the bridges I talked to the FAC (Forward Air Controller) and I said, 'Do you have us in sight?' After they popped smoke and I identified the area, we came around to the south, broke in and Chris did a fabulous job getting us in there [on the ground] for the first time. Major Presto, who was behind me, came around and there was nowhere for him to land. There was debris all over the LZ and just enough room for one aircraft to fit in there. We put our ramp down and we were just sitting there. We were helpless...We were just sitting there in the cockpit waiting for the casualties to get loaded up into the back of the aircraft. And I remember sitting there in the cockpit and looking over to my right-hand side and there's a gunnery sergeant who's got his knee blown off... you could tell he'd had a pretty intense evening and morning, and he walked in the aircraft himself but only after his men were taken care of...these guys were amazing...Marines did this all the time.

So we loaded up a few of the casualties and all of a sudden, the Marines who were front security hit the deck and commenced firing. As Major Preston wasn't able to land he just hovered there. At the same time, Sergeant DiMartino, who was running the right .50 caliber machine gun, started to engage enemy targets on the rooftop. After that, everything kind of settled down...the Marines got everything under control and it was time for us to go.

As I took off, I looked back into the tunnel of the helicopter. The CH-46 is a tandem-rotor aircraft, so it's pretty long and there's blood all over the inside of my aircraft and that's the first and only time I looked back on those Casevac calls. I remember getting on the intercom and talking to Doc Burnett while we are flying out of there, taking small arms fire and my door gunners are shooting out of the doors. I asked Doc,

'How are the casualties doing?' I had no rotary wing escort. I had casualties in the back and we were all fatigued and I'm worried about the guys in the back. Doc Burnett got back on the intercom and said, 'Sir, fly the plane! I'll do my job, you do yours,' and he was right. I didn't need to worry about what was going on back there. I needed to worry about navigating, getting ourselves out of Baghdad to start with and then getting the Marines into the LZ so the medical people could take care of them.

So we flew back to the 7th Surgical Center and as soon as we landed it was just like the TV show MASH. The ambulances were coming out, corpsmen were running out and taking those guys in and that's all we saw of them...our job was done and we flew back.

What I didn't say was that Oliver North was on Major Presto's aircraft and his producer was on our aircraft. So they filmed some of the action and they helped us. They actually loaded up injured Marines. At one point we transported an entire Iraqi family of seven, some were injured and one of the ladies was pregnant. I think it was the third or the fourth run...and we wanted to keep the family together. So even though we're combat Marines, like General Mattis, the division commander, always said, 'You have to win the hearts and the minds of these people.' It was just the kind of thing Marines did, and are still doing and will continue to do to preserve that nation."

Throughout the day, Captain Espinoza flew from 0500 hours in the morning to 2200 hours that evening with only two hours of rest in-between five trips. Landing multiple times under enemy fire, they loaded casualties, provided suppressive cover and conducted evasive maneuvers on route back to the medical evacuation points. In all, the two helicopters rescued twenty-eight Marines and the family of seven Iraqi nationals.

Once back in the United States, Captain Espinoza put the experience into perspective. "The bond you have between the enlisted crew and the officers in aviation is unique. On the 'ground side' it is different but in the air, you are a crew. If I do something wrong, it could get them killed and if they do something wrong in the back, it is my life too. Thus, you develop a very special bond that is unique in the military. With that unique bond in mind, I received a Distinguished Flying Cross along with Major Donald J. Presto. The copilots and the crew members did not receive DFCs. Receiving this honor was bittersweet. Therefore, I accepted the medal on behalf of all of us."

Notes

Captain Armando Espinoza, Distinguished Flying Cross citation, action date: 10 April 2003, Archives, the Distinguished Flying Cross Society, San Diego, CA.

Captian Armando Espinoza, oral history interview, interviewed by Dr. Barry A. Lanman, 16 April 2005, transcribed, the Distinguished Flying Cross Society Oral History Collection, the Distinguished Flying Cross Society, San Diego, CA.

Top: This rescue was one of countless actions taken to save civilian lives during Hurricane Katrina in 2005. Middle: Lieutenant Commander Mark Vislay was awarded a Distinguished Flying Cross for his extraordinary achievement during aerial flight from 29 August to 6 September 2005. Bottom: Lieutenant Commander Vislay, was one of approximately fifty aviators and aircrew who received Distinguished Flying Crosses during Katrina. Photographs courtesy of Mark Vislay

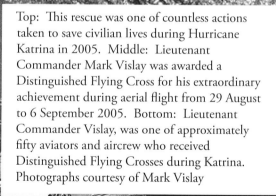

Urban Rescues During Hurricane Katrina

Commander Mark Vislay, Jr., USCG

"The briefings were literally, 'Mark, there's your helicopter and your crew.' We went out there and did what we were trained to do."_____

On 29 August 2005, a category five hurricane named Katrina took aim at New Orleans. The intensity of its winds created a twenty to twenty-five foot storm surge, levies failed and a disaster of epoch proportions occurred. For Mark Vislay, Jr. Hurricane Katrina tested his ability to conduct urban rescues and defined this valiant aviator as an individual who displayed courage and devotion to duty in the highest tradition of military service.

In 1994, Mark Vislay graduated from the United States Coast Guard Academy and was assigned duty on the USCG Cutter *Boutwell* based out of Alameda, California. After selection for flight school at the Naval Air Station Whiting Field, located in Milton, Florida, he spent sixteen months in training and then received his wings as a Naval Aviator. Following his initial instruction, Vislay took a transition course and became a Coast Guard aviator flying the HH-60 Jayhawk helicopter. His first aviation tour was in Clearwater, Florida, followed by Air Station Sitka, Alaska in 2002. In 2005, the young aviator received an assignment to Aviation Training Center in Mobile, Alabama.

Then a lieutenant commander, Vislay explained the transition to Mobile. "We moved in July…and I had a golf trip planned. So I left my wife and twelve-month old son in a house that was still in the process of renovation…and I went on this golf trip to Dolphin Island, Alabama with six of my close friends. We were all members of the same graduating class. I remember it was Saturday night and we were going to drive back to Mobile on Sunday, which was August 28th…At that time Katrina was in the Gulf, but had been downgraded to a Category 1 or 2 hurricane. We called our wives and I remember going to bed concerned, but not overly concerned. Then, on Sunday morning at 5:00 am, one of my buddies came into my room and said, 'We've got to go – Katrina is now a Cat 4 and building to Cat 5. We need to go home.'

On the way to Mobile, the traffic was horrible and we knew something was going on here…My wife and I weren't from this area nor had we ever experienced a hurricane of this magnitude. I didn't have boards to cover the windows of my house…and I wasn't really prepared." During the drive home, Vislay called the base and was given an option to decline the first wave of missions. While he did so at first, thinking of his ill-preparedness and the inability of his wife to now evacuate, he called the scheduling officer back within fifteen minutes and said, "Hey, if you guys really need me, I'll do it." They replied, 'we have three other pilots, all have wives who are eight and nine months pregnant - so would you mind doing it?', and I said, 'Absolutely.' So that's how I was chosen to HUREVAC a helicopter away from danger, away from harm's way and preposition for Search and Rescue efforts."

The lieutenant commander got home, packed a bag and made arrangements for his family's safety. Within hours and without directly asking, Vislay had several Coast Guard pilots boarding-up the house. Additionally, his closest friend, Commander Christopher Conley, along with his pregnant spouse elected to ride out the entire storm with Vislay's family.

Vislay explained what happened when he got to the Aviation Training Center in Mobile. "It was pretty hectic…and I was in command of an HH-60 helicopter…All of a sudden the decision was made to leave. We got in the aircraft and headed west to Shreveport, Louisiana while the rest of the Hurrevac aircraft went east to Jacksonville…Once we got there, I called my wife and she said, 'Here we go, it's about to hit'.

We tried to get some rest…and I called my wife several times throughout the night. The next morning, the decision was made to make preparations to head back and we were put on alert as news of the Hurricane's devastation was coming in…so we were on alert…Before losing all cell coverage which was to be expected, my wife informed me that she and my son were okay…We were then told to head back immediately via New Orleans to come in behind the hurricane for a damage assessment. The adrenalin was pumping. But I knew everything was okay at home so I was ready to do my job… being a helo pilot, executing hoist ops as necessary and saving people."

After logistical planning for damage assessment, reports showed the range of devastation and the immediate need to rescue people. However, Lieutenant Commander Vislay was tasked to pick-up the head of FEMA at the Superdome. At that point, Vislay made his feelings known when he insisted, "There are better assets to obtain and continue damage assessment operations. I need to rescue people - and the head of FEMA immediately agreed as did the Coast Guard Captains on board from Shreveport for the assessment flight. We dropped them off and started hoisting people off roofs…I was one of the first… That was Monday, the day the storm hit."

For the next five days, Vislay flew a total of 44.3 hours and accomplished approximately thirteen sorties. He explained the main focus of his efforts. "We would hoist and rescue people and take them to dry land…like the "Cloverleaf" [a highway cloverleaf on high elevation which served as an interim evacuation point] or an airport…I worked with Hueys, Army 60s (Black Hawks)…46s were working and even 53s…It was pretty amazing to see all of those helicopters.

What made things work was our aviation standardization program and superb training initiatives…The Coast Guard gives people the tools…We get the autonomy to use those tools – to make the right decisions. The briefings were literally, 'Mark, there's your helicopter and your crew.' We went out there and did what we were trained to do!

Night flights were fatiguing but even during the day you couldn't see each other. A bright orange helicopter was our counterpart; an HH-65, you think you could pick it out…but I must have flown over three of them when I was around a hundred feet and they're at thirty feet hoisting, and that's only seventy feet of separation…a little scary. Your heart starts to pound pretty fast in that situation. But at night the other helicopters had their lights on. You could always pick them out. Hoisting was a lot more demanding at night but aircraft separation was easier…However, I guess it doesn't make up for the power lines you couldn't see and the trees and the other dangers out there…I don't think I ever lifted up my night goggles other then to take a break. I never hoisted at night without goggles—a technique I acquired and believe in from rescue operations during a tour in Sitka, Alaska.

During the day, we deployed and recovered by every means possible – sometimes using creative methods that weren't in our flight manual… For one rescue, there were three guys sitting on top of a truck filled with water and surprisingly there was a very strong current. They were barely holding onto the truck…at the same time, my crew in the back of the helo was shouting to us that there were people on a building roof. One of the guys was panicking. waving his shirt, and obviously pointing at a hole in his roof. We saw the people and at the same time there were other individuals on another roof; they looked in really bad shape and had an infant with them. So we started in and triaged the situation… My rescue swimmer said, 'Where do we go first?' Well obviously the guys in the truck needed our attention first because they we're going to end up back in the water. We maneuvered over to the truck and quickly deployed the swimmer…he was amazing and quickly analyzed the situation to determine the proper rescue method which led to recovery of both survivors by basket pick-up. We brought our swimmer, Petty Officer Jason Leahr, part way up, kept him on the hook and maneuvered over towards the roof of the building before deploying him on the roof. At that point the older man, who had been waving at us, told us there were two infants in the building along with his wife, who was unconscious in the attic. He thought she was dying. Fortunately, she was just severely dehydrated from heat exhaustion…but still in real bad shape.

There was also an individual in the building with a broken arm. That's where all the different methods of rescue came up. We ended up recovering them by deploying the basket directly into the hole in the roof. It's daunting and unnerving, when you lose sight of your hook and the swimmer…I remember we had two in the helicopter, then we brought the lady up next, and we had some room so we went back for the two children. The next thing I knew, the swimmer said, 'Let's keep going!' and I said, 'No, it's time to stop, that's it…Tell them we'll be right back.' So, Petty Officer Leahr started to come up…and when I saw him on the hook, he was holding an infant, just by physical grip - a technique only used for emergencies because nothing was connected to the survivor. As I watched the swimmer bring the infant up, it hit me hard to think my son was only twelve months old, just like this infant, and here the swimmer was holding this baby with just a physical grip. It made me really feel for the people we were rescuing and their unbelievable situation…I remembered talking with the swimmer afterwards and he said, 'I just had to get that baby out of there because the baby looked in real bad shape.' We brought all of those people to dry land…I think we rescued about forty people that night and I've never been more exhausted in my life with those sets of hoistings.

In another situation, this guy jumped over a fence…He was wading through the water and he was half naked. He only had underwear on and he was bleeding and later claimed he had a gunshot wound. He jumped into the basket; he was obviously being chased. I remember the flight mechanic saying, 'Mr. Vislay, what do we do, what do we do?' I said, 'Hoist him up.'…So we hoisted him up. We finished clearing this house before leaving. We took him to the Cloverleaf and notified the authorities before we got there. He was met by a couple of highway patrolmen as we landed…that was Wednesday. The next day we cleared 107 people from the roof of a Days Inn. We just sat there and hoisted for about three hours taking people from the Days Inn over to a dryer place."

Lieutenant Commander Vislay remarked, "We weren't specifically trained for urban rescue the way I think a lot of us call it. Until Katrina I'd never landed on top of a J.C. Penney's before. You know, I never hovered right next to the penthouse of a hotel and pulled people off a hotel. But that's what we did – we used the tools we already had, and the training and the crew…I think we're exceptionally trained because of the standardization of our training. What we harp on in the Coast Guard is standard common tactics, techniques and procedures…everybody is trained the same. We can fly and interact with each other when the situation demands. We can also improvise and adapt to a situation; overcome the problems and complete the rescue.

The other asset is our people, the exceptional men and women who make up our aircrews. They are also the people who fix our planes and fly on our planes. Our flight mechanics who are in the back executing hoisting operations are the same individuals who fix the aircrafts - they are superb. That just gives me a 'warm fuzzy' every time I fly to know the aircrew has a vested interest in how well they repair the aircraft because their butts are in the back of the helicopter…They are really good at what they do. They're the best."

Throughout the entire week of initial rescues, the physical challenges were enormous. However, the emotional component also had an impact. Vislay commented that, "My initial reaction, when we got on-scene in New Orleans, was shock. It was incredible…what I was looking at, the flooding, people on roofs – it was beyond description.

And, this may sound bad but there was an excitement level of wanting to rescue people…knowing every day you were going to go out on a mission, that you were actually going to conduct operations, have a positive impact and save lives; it was exhilarating and it kept you going! As tired as I was throughout the ordeal, I don't think I ever felt that fatigued. I did though when I stopped after a 10-hour day and tried to get some sleep. But three hours later I was ready to go…Just a little rest, something to eat and I was ready… You wanted back in there so bad, but couldn't due to crew rest minimums. However, you wanted to continue to fly and that was for about the first five days.

When you picked someone up and you saw a guy back there giving you the thumbs up sign or when a person smiled at you, it felt really good. I remember turning around one time when I wasn't flying and this kid was crying, the mom was crying and the dad was trying to consol them both. I had a Snickers bar, a few bottles of water, a Gatorade and some unit patches. I just started handing them to the kid and I got the kid to laugh. The mom was appreciative and thanked me. It was a fantastic feeling... just knowing we were saving them and getting them out of harm's way. Afterwards, I flew Senators around and talked to them and told them the stories. I never thought I'd see and talk to our Commandant or get to talk to Senators Warren, Frisk, Kennedy and Lieberman."

Back in ATC Mobile, Lieutenant Commander Vislay realized the personal and professional value of the Katrina experience. "I'm sure every CG pilot has lessons learned on dealing with a victim, a situation or how you might want to approach a rescue, but I would offer some advice to fellow pilots in training. Remain calm, remember your training, continue to do what you were taught, strive to be the best, learn all you can and take your training seriously. Make it realistic and be creative with your training - develop and think about different situations and scenarios. Think about all these things in advance so when a situation happens, you're prepared ...to test yourself to be the best.

From the standpoint of the HH-60 Jayhawk helicopter, what we do here to meet new capabilities [at Aviation Training Center Mobile] is to make changes to our flight manual and procedures; which is the right thing to do. However, I don't think there's ever been talk of updating or changing our flight manual on how we do procedures based on what we learned from Katrina. We just said, 'Our Training program works...so let's not try to fix or change our training strategy...just pass on the experience. When Hurricane Rita hit, we knew what was going to happen and how to react."

On 17 March 2006, Lieutenant Commander Vislay was awarded a Distinguished Flying Cross for his extraordinary achievement during aerial flight from 29 August to 6 September 2005. The citation highlighted his various sorties and explained that Lieutenant Commander Vislay flew rescue missions in winds exceeding fifty knots. The citation also stated he was personally responsible for the rescue of 167 storm victims, ninety-six of whom were taken to safety from a Days Inn roof.

Petty Officer Leahr, the Rescue Swimmer (formally termed an Aviation Survival Technician), also received a Distinguished Flying Cross for his gallant participation in the hurricane from 30 August to 3 September 2005. While he mainly flew as part of Vislay's crew, he also served with other pilots as well. Leahr was cited for accumulating twenty-seven hours of flying time and participating in numerous missions in a hazardous urban disaster environment. Some of the missions specifically mentioned in the DFC citation were: "On the night of 30 August, Petty Officer Leahr provided a life saving rescue breathing to two patients simultaneously during MEDEVAC from Baptist Memorial Hospital, saving both survivors...He demonstrated incredible strength and determination by lifting a 300 pound survivor out of an attic and onto a roof...On 3 September, Petty Officer Leahr deployed to a hotel rooftop where he found himself amidst a scene of utter chaos with an angry and hostile crowd. He quickly volunteered to search the building for survivors. Courageously, he methodically searched each blacked-out floor, ultimately locating an additional seventy survivors. Petty Officer Leahr's performance in the face of extreme danger ultimately guaranteed the rescue of over 300 survivors. Petty Office Leahr's actions, skill and valor were instrumental in the rescue of 151 storm victims."

The impact of Hurricane Katrina has been measured in myriad ways. In many respects, Katrina was like a Dickens novel...The best of times and the worst of times. From an economic analysis, the disaster cost an estimated ninety billion dollars. In human terms, 1,836 people perished during the storm and its aftermath. However, the loss of life would have been substantially higher had Lieutenant Commander Vislay, Petty Officer Leahr and their fellow Coast Guard aviators, swimmers and aircrew not arrived immediately on the scene.

For these actions in extreme emergency circumstances, it is estimated that over fifty officers and enlisted personnel of the Coast Guard received Distinguished Flying Crosses, a prolific number of awards, for their actions during Hurricane Katrina. Individuals like Lieutenant Commander Vislay were a beacon of light and a model for military operations under such horrific circumstances. Currently as Chief Operations Training & Performance US Coast Guard Force Readiness Command, Mark Vislay Jr. provides leadership as a commander and is ready to act when called.

Notes

Commander Mark Vislay, Jr., Distinguished Flying Cross citation, action date: 30 August – 3 September 2005, the Distinguished Flying Cross Society, San Diego, CA.

Petty Officer Jaason M. Leahr, Distinguished Flying Cross citation, action date: 30 August – 3 September 2005, the Distinguished Flying Cross Society, San Diego, CA.

Commander Mark Vislay, Jr., oral history interview, interviewed by William Thiesen, LANTAREA Historian, 9 May 2006, Aviation Training Center, Mobile, US Coast Guard Historian Office, USCG Exhibit Center, Forestville, MD.

Memorable Moments of the Distinguished Flying Cross

Recent Decades

"I keep in touch with fellow aviators from all of my old units, the ones who were with me in combat are the most special. We have an extremely tight bond with one another that will never be broken."

Lieutenant Colonel Joe Bouley, USAF

Commander Edward Keith Andrews, USN
Led a Twenty-Six Aircraft Strike Near Beirut Lebanon_____

After receiving his first DFC, in Vietnam, Commander Edward Keith Andrews was awarded a second Distinguished Flying Cross, "for extraordinary achievement while participating in aerial flight on 4 December 1983 as a pilot of an A-7E aircraft in Attack Squadron FIFTEEN (VA-15), embarked in USS *Independence* (CV-62). As the commander of Air Wing SIX, Andrews led a twenty-six aircraft strike against several targets near Beirut, Lebanon.

Under conditions of intense enemy anti-aircraft fire and over forty surface-to-air missile firings, he continued the attack and precisely delivered ordnance which destroyed a crucial command and control battlefield radar site. He demonstrated exceptional courage and airborne leadership off target by calling numerous missile avoidance maneuvers to other aircraft in a flight and in particular was directly responsible for saving a wingman from being hit by a missile which then impacted his aircraft.

Even though sustaining crippling damage, he exhibited superior airmanship in controlling the wildly gyrating aircraft until he was able to safely eject over water. Commander Andrews' outstanding leadership, heroic actions in the face of personal risk, and unselfish devotion to duty reflected great credit upon himself and were in keeping with the highest traditions of the United States Naval Service."[1]

Major General Clay T. McCutchan, USAF
Saved Forty Lives During Operation Just Cause in Panama_____

During "Operation Just Cause," Major Clay T. McCutchan served on board an AC-130A and was stationed at Howard Air Force Base in the Republic of Panama. While exposed to extreme danger from hostile anti-aircraft artillery fire on 20 December 1989, the major displayed a selfless act of courage and received a Distinguished Flying Cross. The citation granted from the President of the United States detailed the events of his mission. (Clay T. McCutchan - second from left)

"On that date, while exposed to extreme danger from hostile anti-aircraft artillery fire, Major McCutchan's professionalism and attention to detail directly impacted on the success of air operations during Operation Just Cause and in the saving of over forty American lives."[2]

Two years later, major McCutchan received a second DFC for his heroism while in Kuwait on 26 February 1991. His second medal carried a citation stating,

"During this period, Major McCutchan demonstrated the highest degree of courage, perseverance, and aerial skill while flawlessly accomplishing an intense, high-risk combat interdiction mission across heavily defended enemy lines in support of the ground assault phase of Operation Desert Storm. His crew led a daring, three-gunship assault which contributed to the quick capture and decisive defeat of enemy forces in the area. At great risk to their own safety, they skillfully inflicted significant damage on numerous enemy combat transportation assets and personnel. The professional competence, aerial skill, and devotion to duty displayed by Major McCutchan reflect great credit upon himself and the United States Air Force."[3]

In relation to the McCutchan's family heritage, Clay's father, James R. McCutchan, had been awarded a DFC during WWII for flying fifty combat missions from bases in China as a pilot of fighter type aircraft.[4] The two men shared this special bond.

Major Richard L. Pauly, USAF
Endured SAMs and Fought the Elite Medina Armored Division

Major Richard L. Pauly distinguished himself by extraordinary achievement while participating in aerial flight as an A-10 fighter pilot in Kuwait on 2 February 1991. His superiors provided extensive details of a mission which proved Pauly's heroism and led to the award of the Distinguished Flying Cross. The citation included the following statements.

"Major Pauly displayed outstanding airmanship and courage under extremely hazardous conditions, while employing his aircraft against a heavily defended Iraqi radar site. Despite encountering accurate antiaircraft artillery and infrared surface-to-air missile fire that hit the cockpit of his aircraft, the flight successfully disabled this high value target, and Major Pauly was able to successfully land his crippled aircraft. The professional competence, aerial skill, and devotion to duty displayed by Major Pauly reflect great credit upon himself and the United States Air Force."[5]

Less than a month later, Major Pauly once again demonstrated valor and was awarded a second DFC for a mission on 27 February 1991. The official record recounted that, "Major Pauly displayed outstanding airmanship and courage, under extremely hazardous conditions, while employing his aircraft against elements of the elite Medina armored Division of the Republican Guards Forces Command, which were actively engaged with units of the United States first Armored Division. Despite automatic weapons and heavy antiaircraft artillery fire and reported surface-to-air missile launches, Major Pauly successfully employed MK-20 Rockeye Cluster Munitions and the A-10's 30mm cannon against second echelon armor arrayed against and firing upon elements of the Second Brigade, first Armored Division. This was done under extremely poor weather conditions. The outstanding heroism and devotion to duty displayed by Major Pauly reflect great credit upon himself and the United States Air Force."[6]

Vice Admiral Lewis W. Crenshaw, Jr., USN
A-6E Pilot Conducted a 600 Mile Strike Against Enemy Forces in Iraq

Commander Lewis W. Crenshaw, Jr. was presented a Distinguished Flying Cross for, "heroism while participating in aerial flight as a Naval Flight Officer of an A-6E aircraft while serving with Attack Squadron 85 embarked in USS *America* (CV 66) on 25 January 1991. Commander Crenshaw launched, as the lead of a 600-mile night-coordinated attack against the artillery production facility near Habbaniyah, Iraq. The strike aircraft encountered intense anti-aircraft artillery fire during the entire forty-five minute flight over enemy territory. Entering overlapping surface-to-air missile envelopes, Commander Crenshaw successfully led his strike group through five separate missile engagements and continued prosecution of the target through a broken overcast. Defeating radar-guided anti-aircraft artillery shells exploding in the formation, his precision radar attack culminated in direct hits on the storage facility. The attack, confirmed by Forward Looking Infrared video tape and national assets, destroyed the plant's artillery production capability and severely damaged the enemy's ability and will to sustain war. Commander Crenshaw's aggressive leadership, superb airmanship, and courageous devotion to duty in the face of hazardous flying conditions reflected great credit upon himself and were in keeping with the highest traditions of the United States Naval Service."[7]

Major Leslie P. Matheson, USAF
Electronic Warfare Officer Led a Three Gunship Assault

Major Leslie P. Matheson, an AC-130A electronic warfare officer, participated in a heroic act on 26 February 1991 while serving in northern Kuwait. The specific actions of that day were recorded in his Distinguished Flying Cross citation.

"Major Matheson demonstrated the highest degree of courage, perseverance, and aerial skill while flawlessly accomplishing an intense, high-risk combat interdiction mission across heavily defended enemy lines in support of the ground assault phase of Operation Desert Storm. His crew led a daring, three-gunship assault which contributed to the quick capture and decisive defeat of enemy forces in the area.

At great risk to their own safety, they skillfully inflicted significant damage on numerous enemy combat transportation assets and personnel. The professional competence, aerial skill, and devotion to duty displayed by Major Matheson reflect great credit upon himself and the United States Air Force."[8] Along with Major Matheson, the entire crew received DFCs for the success of this vital mission. (Matheson - top, far right)

Captain Terry V. Morgan, USA
Aeroscout Pilot Flew Deep into Enemy-held Kuwait to Accomplish Mission_____

Captain Terry V. Morgan, an Army pilot, participated in Operation Desert Storm. On 27 February 1991, he flew his most heroic mission and received a Distinguished Flying Cross for his actions above and beyond the call of duty. Morgan's DFC citation explained his actions while flying an OH-58 Aeroscout when he was attached to Headquarters Company, 4th Battalion, 1st Aviation Regiment, 1st Infantry Division (mechanized).

"While under enemy fire and adverse weather conditions, he repeatedly contributed to the destruction of enemy vehicles and flew deep into enemy-held Kuwait. His demonstrated bravery and fighter skills were above and beyond the call of duty. His flawless execution was key to the total success of the unit mission, the destruction of Iraqi ground forces and the Liberation of Kuwait. Captain Morgan's superb performance was in keeping with the proudest traditions of the military service and reflects great credit upon himself, the 1st Infantry Division (mechanized), and the United States Army."[9]

Petty Officer David M. Yoder, III, USCG
Risked his Life to Save Three Crewman of a Sinking Vessel_____

Petty Officer David M. Yoder, III, a Coast Guard Aviation Survivalman, was commended for extraordinary heroism while performing a vessel rescue on 12 December 1993 while serving aboard a HH-60J helicopter. The rescue involved three crewmembers from the sailing vessel *Malachite*, east of Elizabeth City, North Carolina. The Distinguished Flying Cross citation included the following documentation. "Petty Officer Yoder observed the beleaguered vessel surfing down 30-foot raging seas, her sail in ribbons, and her rigging torn and sailing in the wind.

Recognizing that *Malachite's* crew would not survive the night, Petty Officer Yoder volunteered to deploy into the perilous seas. With the first survivor in tow, he swam toward the rescue basket and was battered by a rogue wave which tore off his mask and snorkel. Repeatedly, as he shoved the dazed survivors into the basket, he was left dangling as the seas dropped out beneath him, then smashed against the basket. Because of the pilot's difficulty in maintaining a steady hover, the basket was frequently torn from his grasp.

After each pick up, Petty Officer Yoder swam back against tremendous resistance to reach the others. Near exhaustion, he loaded the last survivor, then, just as he hooked up, a huge wave buried him, then flung him violently as it passed. At that moment, the stainless steel rescue cable parted halfway through its diameter. Fortunately, the remaining strands held. Petty Officer Yoder's actions, skill, and valor were instrumental in the rescue of three victims."[10]   (Yoder - second from right)

Colonel Terence "Tom" Henricks, USAF
First Space Shuttle Pilot/Commander to log over a 1,000 Hours

Colonel Terence "Tom" Henricks served as an Air Force aviator flying F-4s then eventually became a test pilot at Edwards Air Force Base in California. In that capacity, he flew thirty different types of aircraft accumulating more than 6,000 flight hours. In addition to his skills as a pilot, Henricks performed 749 parachute jumps and obtained a Master Parachutist rating.

In 1986, Henricks became a NASA astronaut and flew on four shuttle missions: STS-44, STS-55, STS-70 and STS-78. The flights took place between 1991 and 1996. On two of the missions, he served as the pilot and on the other two he was the commander.

Colonel Henricks was awarded a Distinguished Flying Cross for his third flight; STS-70 which was launched from the Kennedy Space Center in Florida on 13 July and returned on 22 July 1995. Throughout the flight, he made 142 orbits of the Earth, conducted a range of experiments and deployed the sixth and final NASA Tracking and Data Relay Satellite. Colonel Henricks was the first person in space to log over a 1,000 hours as a space shuttle pilot/commander.[11]

Commander Jeff McCullars, USA / USCG
Flew Helicopters for the Army and the Coast Guard

Commander Jeff McCullars enlisted in the US Army in 1980 and upon being promoted to E-5 he was selected for Army flight training after which his first aviation assignment was flying Hueys for the Pershing II missiles support in West Germany. This was followed by a UH-60A transition and deployment to Panama.

Nearly ten years later, he left the Army and began a career as a commercial helicopter pilot. During that time he also joined the local Army Reserve UH-1 MEDEVAC unit in Lafayette, Louisiana. McCullars applied for and was accepted to the US Coast Guard as a Direct Commission Aviator (DCA). His assignments included CGAS Clearwater (HH-3F), CGAS Kodiak (HH-60J), ATC Mobile (HH-60J) and NAS Whiting Field (TH-57 and T-34). Commander McCullars' major projects included flight testing and deploying the Coast Guard's HF-ALE aircraft communications system and the design team for the new MH-60T glass cockpit. He was also a member of the investigation team for the only Coast Guard HH-60J crash.

Several of his cases have been featured on Discovery Channel and Storm Stories. Among Commander

McCullars' highest decorations were the Distinguished Flying Cross, two Air Medals, the Coast Guard Foundation award for Heroism West Coast 1997 and the Coast Guard Foundation award for Heroism East Coast 1999.[12]

Lieutenant Colonel William B. O'Connor, USAF
Stealth Fighter Pilot Contributed to the Success of Operation Allied Force_____

Lieutenant Colonel William B. O'Connor, a stealth fighter pilot for the Air Force, served in the 8th Expeditionary Fighter Squadron, 31st Expeditionary Operations Group, 31st Air Expeditionary Wing stationed at Aviano Air Base, Italy during 1999.

While on a flight over the former Federal Republic of Yugoslavia on 14 April 1999, O'Connor's actions warranted a Distinguished Flying Cross. The DFC citation documented his selfless devotion to duty.

"Lieutenant Colonel O'Connor executed one of several coordinated strike missions deep into the heart of the Serbian integrated air defense system. With complete disregard for his personal safety, Lieutenant Colonel O'Connor prosecuted his attack and braved a barrage of surface-to-air missile launches and anti-aircraft artillery fire. Despite the presence of intense enemy air defense activity directed at his aircraft, Lieutenant Colonel O'Connor executed a highly successful attack resulting in the precision-guided weapon destroying the target. Lieutenant Colonel O'Connor's flawless aerial skill and coolness under pressure while attacking a key Serbian military facility directly contributed to the historic success of the Operation Allied Force air campaign."[13]

Chief Warrant Officer 4 John Nix, USA
Flawless Execution of a Mission During Operation Enduring Freedom_____

On 19 October 2001, Chief Warrant Officer 4 John Nix participated in aerial flight under combat conditions and displayed gallant actions. For the heroism displayed, Nix was awarded a Distinguished Flying Cross with a citation that included the following statement.

"While conducting joint combat operations against an enemy of the United States of America…Chief Warrant Officer Nix's display of personal courage contributed to the flawless execution of the unit's

missions while supporting Operation Enduring Freedom. Throughout the operation, he displayed great personal courage and complete disregard for his personal safety."[14]

Note: Because the details of this mission are still classified, the specific actions of Chief Warrant Officer 4 Nix cannot be divulged. However, his service is recognized and appreciated by the Distinguished Flying Cross Society.

Lieutenant Colonel Andra V. P. Kniep, USAF
Two DFCs in Two Days in 2002

Captain Andra V. P. Kniep received two Distinguished Flying Crosses in two days while participating in aerial flight as an A/OA-10 forward air control, airborne and flight lead, 74th Expeditionary Fighter Squadron, 332d Air Expeditionary Group. The combat missions for which she received the DFCs were located in Afghanistan on 5 March and 6 March 2002.

On 5 March, the DFC citation explained that, "flying as Cherry 01, her professional skill and airmanship enabled her to successfully engage and destroy enemy vehicles and an infantry force concentration while working in close proximity to friendly ground forces." Working with unmanned aerial vehicles and aircraft bombing preplanned targets, she deconflicted the airspace and provided close air support and scored direct hits on targets with a number of confirmed enemy vehicles destroyed and infantry casualties.

The DFC citation continued to say that, "after a second refueling, she led her flight to a night recovery at a remote, unfamiliar, classified location to complete the 7.9-hour deployment sortie. By inflicting heavy losses on Taliban and al Qaeda forces, Captain Kniep saved coalition lives and advanced the United States goals in the war on terrorism."

On the next day, 6 March 2002, Captain Kniep took control of Operation Anaconda airspace and directed a devastating attack on enemy forces. She developed a plan to clear the airspace and prevent fratricide between eleven strike aircraft and three unmanned aerial vehicles. The DFC citation related that Captain Kniep, "skillfully controlled F-15E, F-16, B-1 and B-52 strikes employing scores of weapons to destroy a weapons cache, multiple vehicles and troop concentrations with punishing hits…Captain Kniep's superb control of a highly congested target area saved coalition lives and advanced the United States' goals in the war on global terrorism."[15]

Lieutenant Colonel Brian M. Kennedy, USMC
Flew the AH-1W "Super Cobra" in Operation Iraqi Freedom

Brian M. Kennedy became an officer through the NROTC program in 1989 and received his wings in 1991. The next year, he participated in Operations Deny Flight/Provide Promise and Sharp Guard in Bosnia-Herzegovnia. He was also deployed to Guantanamo Bay and Haiti. In many respects, all these assignments prepared Kennedy for his combat duty in Iraq.

Major Kennedy received the Distinguished Flying Cross as flight lead of an AH-1W Cobra helicopter attached to Marine Light Attack Helicopter Squadron 269, 3rd Marine Aircraft Wing, I Marine Expeditionary Force in support of Operation Iraqi Freedom from 20 March to 14 April 2003. His DFC citation stated that, "Major Kennedy performed courageously as a primary flight lead during seventy-one combat missions. He routinely led his flight at night and during the harshest of conditions to support I Marine Expeditionary Force's rapid advance into Baghdad, Iraq. Conducting close air support missions in support of the British 7th Armored Brigade in Al Basra, Major Kennedy's section successfully engaged numerous Iraqi units, which proved critical to the maneuver of British forces in their successful bid for the city.

While deftly guiding his section through air defense artillery and small arms fire, his flight destroyed the final un-located theater ballistic missile system capable of delivering weapons of mass destruction against Allied Forces in Kuwait. Acting as a Forward Air Controller (Airborne), Major Kennedy coordinated more than thirty strikes against fortified Iraqi weapons caches of the Special Republican Guard which helped eliminate enemy defenses west of Tikrit."[16]

Major David R. Goodell, III, USMC
Secured Initial Bridgehead Across the Tigris River During Operation Iraqi Freedom

Major David R. Goodell III was awarded the Distinguished Flying Cross for heroism while participating in aerial flight as flight leader, Marine Light Attack Helicopter Squadron 169, 3rd Marine Aircraft Wing, I Marine Expeditionary Force in support of Operation Iraqi Freedom on 2 April 2003. The official citation supporting the award of a Distinguished Flying Cross stated the following:

"Having provided Close Air Support to 1st Marine Division units for six hours in low light level conditions, Major Goodell led his flight from the Forward Arming and Refueling Point prior to sunrise to support the advance. Arriving on station and finding Regimental Combat Team 5's lead armor element halted in a vulnerable position along a canal, Major Goodell immediately directed his flight to a secure route. Relaying crucial information concerning traffic ability and threat status, he provided armed reconnaissance for the tank's advance toward the regimental objective of An Numaniyah. Using all elements of his flight, he quickly detected and identified a coordinated enemy ambush site within the city.

Under heavy enemy fire, Major Goodell decisively directed his flight, using precision weapons and multi-axis, close-in rocket and gun attacks to destroy over seven armored vehicles and approximately twenty enemy personnel. His quick and highly effective actions enabled Regimental Combat Team 5 to rapidly advance through the objective city of An Numaniyah, across the Tigris River, and secure an initial bridgehead across the Tigris River for I Marine Expeditionary Force's continued offensive operations toward the capital city of Baghdad."[17] He was also honored for superb airmanship, inspiring courage and loyal devotion to duty in the face of hazardous flying conditions.

Lieutenant Colonel Donald J. Presto, USMC
After Shock and Awe, Oliver North Documented Casualty Evacuation Missions_____

Major Donald J. Presto served as a section leader of a two plane section of CH-46E SeaKnight helicopters while attached to Marine Medium Helicopter Squadron 268 Marine Aircraft Group 39, 3rd Marine Aircraft Wing, 1st Marine Expeditionary Force in support of Operation Iraqi Freedom. On 10 April 2003, shortly after "Shock and Awe," Oliver North and his film crew were imbedded with the two plane section to document the early stages of the military action and subsequent rescue operations.

For this day of multiple missions, Major Presto was awarded a Distinguished Flying Cross along with his wingman, Armando Espinoza. In addition to Oliver North's cameras, Presto's DFC citation documented the heroic deeds.

"Major Presto performed courageously in the conduct of a casualty evacuation mission in the vicinity of Baghdad in support of Regimental Combat Team 5. He maneuvered his section into one of Baghdad's most heavily defended areas and through numerous small arms and rocket-propelled grenade attacks in order to evacuate critically wounded Marines. After he positioned his section on the ground to load the wounded, the ground unit's forward air controller warned him about enemy sniper fire. He lifted his aircraft into a high hover and positioned it broadside to the snipers and directed the crew chief to return suppressive fire. This action ceased enemy fire and allowed the safe evacuation of the wounded Marines."[18]

Note: Major Presto along with Armando Espinoza is featured in Ruth Mayer's painting of the Distinguished Flying Cross described in Chapter Seven.

Captain Joseph T. Bertagna, USMC
Protected a Convoy Under Attack Using Aiming Symbology_____

Captain Joseph T. Bertagna received a Distinguished Flying Cross while serving as a pilot of an AV-8B Harrier, attached to Attack Squadron 513 of the United States Marine Corps located at Central Command, Bagram, Afghanistan. The DFC citation for a mission on 19 July 2003 provided documentation for the award of the medal in support of Operation Enduring Freedom.

"Assigned to escort a ground convoy in eastern Afghanistan, Captain Bertagna arrived on-station to find the convoy was under attack by enemy forces. Flying over the enemy at a very low altitude, he acquired the enemy at dangerously close range of 200 meters from ground forces. Precisely positioning his aiming symbology, Captain Bertagna employed his 25mm cannon into the enemy's position. He immediately re-attacked and emptied his cannon into an additional enemy position. He then assumed duties as the on-scene commander for a helicopter borne medical evacuation. Captain Bertagna used his targeting pod to locate a suitable landing site for the medical evacuation aircraft. By his superb airmanship, inspiring courage, and loyal devotion to duty in the face of hazardous flying conditions, Captain Bertagna reflected great credit upon himself and upheld the highest traditions of the Marine Corps and the United States Naval Service."[19]

Chief Warrant Officer 2 Eric B. Fox, USA
Defeated a Taliban Ambush During Operation Asbury Park

While serving as an Apache helicopter pilot during Operation Asbury Park, a part of Operation Enduring Freedom, Chief Warrant Officer 2 Eric B. Fox was cited for bravery under fire and heroism while participating in combat against Taliban fighters. Awarded a Distinguished Flying Cross, the Warrant Officer's documentation recounted his deeds on the day of 8 June 2004.

"Under great risk and threat of mortal danger from anti-coalition militia supported by Taliban fighters… Chief Warrant Officer 2 Fox's actions enabled a United States Marine Corps ground unit to defeat an established ambush against their convoy during Operation Asbury Park. His expert use of the AH-64A Apache helicopter as an aerial weapons platform and his calm demeanor under extreme circumstances throughout both engagements not only saved him and his crew, but saved the United States Marine convoy from destruction in an ambush from three sides. Chief Warrant Officer 2 Fox's valorous actions are in keeping with the finest traditions of military service and reflect great credit upon himself, Task Force Diamondhead, Task Force Wings, Combined Joint Task Force 76, and the United States Army."[20]

Petty Officer Jason A. Shepard, USCG
Made Daring Water Rescues in Alaska and New Orleans

As a United States Coast Guard Rescue Swimmer, Petty Officer Jason A. Shepard was accustomed to jumping out of helicopters and making rescues. Two situations demonstrated Petty Officer Shepard's heroism and devotion to duty.

While stationed in Alaska, Shepard was aboard a HH-60J helicopter on 12 December 1996. His Distinguished Flying Cross citation told the story of his bravery, not in battle with enemy forces but in a battle against Mother Nature.

"Petty Officer Shepard was engaged in the search and rescue of two survivors from the Fishing Vessel Oceanic, which sank twenty nautical miles west of Craig, Alaska after encountering mechanical problems in heavy seas…Once on scene, Petty Officer Shepard diligently searched the massive twenty-foot seas for forty minutes, remarkably located three persons floating in the frigid thirty-eight degree water…Battling massive seas, Petty Officer Shepard reached the unresponsive victim, but despite a herculean effort, was unable to get the victim aboard the helicopter."[21] However, the two men were saved as the helicopter made it to safety with only five minutes of fuel remaining in the tank.

Again, using his incredible skill and strength during Hurricane Katrina on 30 August 2005, Shepard performed an amazing rescue in the city of New Orleans. His second DFC citation explained how he rescued a couple and their six-month-old baby from the top of a car surrounded by rising flood waters. After this rescue, Shepard noted that there were a large number of people stranded on surrounding roof tops. The citation went on to say that, "with heroic perseverance and complete disregard for his own safety, Petty Officer Shepard swam from house to house through the floodwaters, navigating jagged debris and industrial waste. Upon reaching the flooded homes, he fought his way through tangled debris, sometimes scaling walls to climb his way to each rooftop to reach

survivors."[22] At the end of the day, Shepard was credited with saving sixty-two storm victims.

Chief Warrant Officer 3 Lori Hill, USA
Helicopter Pilot Sustained Injuries in an Iraqi Battle and Brought the "Bird" Home_____

Chief Warrant Officer 3 Lori Hill, with the 2nd Squadron, 17th Cavalry Regiment, was piloting a Kiowa Warrior en route to the city of Al Muqdadiyah, Iraq on 21 March 2006. When the lead chopper came under heavy fire, Hill drew the attack away from the first helicopter and simultaneously provided suppressive fire for the troops engaged with the enemy on the ground. While performing these actions Hill's aircraft was hit, damaging her instrumentation and causing the loss of hydraulic power. Hit two more times and wounded in her right heel and ankle, she was still able to control the damaged helicopter. The DFC citation stated, "despite her wound, as well as the severe damage to the aircraft, CW3 Hill safely performed a run on landing without hydraulics to a 300-foot refueling pad, saving the lives of the crew as well as the aircraft. CW3 Hill's bravery, courage under fire, and rapid assessment of the enemy situation saved the lives of countless coalition forces and serve as a testament to her heroism."[23]

For her selfless bravery under fire, Chief Warrant Officer 3 Lori Hill was presented a Distinguished Flying Cross by Vice President Richard Cheney at Fort Campbell, Kentucky on 16 October 2006. In the spirit of Amelia Earhart and the WASP of WWII, she was lauded as a modern female hero of the United States Army during the ceremony.

Chief Warrant Officer 4 Brent S. Cole, USA
Sacrificed his Life to Save a Fellow Pilot

As part of Task Force Wolfpack, Task Force Pegasus and the International Security Assistance Force, Chief Warrant Officer 4 Brent S. Cole was faced with an emergency situation and rose to the occasion. It was an action for which he was posthumously awarded a Distinguished Flying Cross.

On 22 May 2009, while flying a mission in Afghanistan, W-4 Cole demonstrated gallant airmanship and ultimate courage. His DFC citation explained the series of events which transpired. "While piloting a critical escort mission, his AH-64D Apache Longbow attack helicopter experienced an engine malfunction. Due to his exceptional skills as a pilot-in-command, chief warrant officer 4 Cole flew his disabled aircraft, fully loaded with Hellfire missiles, rockets, and 30mm ammunition, into a controlled crash that saved the life of his front-seat pilot. Chief Warrant Officer Four Cole's heroic actions are in keeping with the finest traditions of Army Aviation."[24]

As a result of Brent's untimely death in combat, his wife Vanessa issued a statement which characterized her personal thoughts. "He was a loving, dedicated husband and father who adored his family to the highest degree. As a military officer, he was a consummate professional who always led by example and was revered by his peers and leaders alike. His loss is devastating to the family, Army Aviation and to our country…he will forever remain deep in our hearts." These sentiments echo the feelings of all family members who have lost aviators and aircrew while serving their country.

Photographs courtesy of the DFC recipients and/or their families except for the following:

Page 250: Tailhook Association
Page 260: United States Army

Notes

[1] Commander Edward Keith Andrews, Distinguished Flying Cross citation, action date: 4 December 1983, Archives, Distinguished Flying Cross Society, San Diego, CA.
[2] Major Clay T. McCutchan, Distinguished Flying Cross citation, action date: 20 December 1989, Archives, Distinguished Flying Cross Society, San Diego, CA.
[3] Major Clay T. McCutchan, Distinguished Flying Cross citation, action date: 26 February 1991, Archives, Distinguished Flying Cross Society, San Diego, CA.
[4] First Lieutenant James R. McCutchan, Distinguished Flying Cross citation, action date: 1944, Archives, Distinguished Flying Cross Society, San Diego, CA.
[5] Major Richard L. Pauly, Distinguished Flying Cross citation, action date: 2 February 1991, Archives, Distinguished Flying Cross Society, San Diego, CA.
[6] Major Richard L. Pauly, Distinguished Flying Cross citation, action date: 27 February, 1991, Archives, Distinguished Flying Cross Society, San Diego, CA.
[7] Commander Lewis W. Crenshaw, Jr., Distinguished Flying Cross citation, action date: 25 January 1991, Archives, Distinguished Flying Cross Society, San Diego, CA.
[8] Major Leslie P. Matheson, Distinguished Flying Cross citation, action date: 26 February 1991, Archives, Distinguished Flying Cross Society, San Diego, CA.
[9] Captain Terry V. Morgan, Distinguished Flying Cross citation, action date: 27 February 1991, Archives, Distinguished Flying Cross Society, San Diego, CA.
[10] Petty Officer David M. Yoder, III, Distinguished Flying Cross citation, action date: 12 December 1993, Archives, Distinguished Flying Cross Society, San Diego, CA.
[11] Colonel Terence "Tom" Henricks, Distinguished Flying Cross citation, action date: 22 July 1995, Archives, Distinguished Flying Cross Society, San Diego, CA.
[12] Commander Jeff McCullars, Distinguished Flying Cross citation, action date: 5 December 1996, Archives, Distinguished Flying Cross Society, San Diego, CA.
[13] Lieutenant Colonel William B. O'Connor, Distinguished Flying Cross citation, action date: 14 April 1999, Archives, Distinguished Flying Cross Society, San Diego, CA.
[14] Chief Warrant Officer 4 John Nix, Distinguished Flying Cross citation, action date: 19 October 2001, Archives, Distinguished Flying Cross Society, San Diego, CA.
[15] Captain Andrea V. P. Kniep, Distinguished Flying Cross citation, action dates: 5 and 6, March 2002, Archives, Distinguished Flying Cross Society, San Diego, CA.
[16] Major Brian M. Kennedy, Distinguished Flying Cross citation, action dates: 20 March – 14 April 2003, Archives, Distinguished Flying Cross Society, San Diego, CA.
[17] Major David R. Goodell, III, Distinguished Flying Cross citation, action date: 2 April 2003, Archives, Distinguished Flying Cross Society, San Diego, CA.
[18] Major Donald J. Presto, Distinguished Flying Cross citation, action date: 10 April 2003, Archives, Distinguished Flying Cross Society, San Diego, CA.
[19] Captain Joseph T. Bertagna, Distinguished Flying Cross citation, action date: 19 July 2003, Archives, Distinguished Flying Cross Society, San Diego, CA.
[20] Chief Warrant Officer 2 Eric B. Fox, Distinguished Flying Cross citation, action date: 8 June 2004, Archives, Distinguished Flying Cross Society, San Diego, CA.
[21] Petty Officer Jason A. Shepard, Distinguished Flying Cross citation, action date: 12 December 1996, Archives, Distinguished Flying Cross Society, San Diego, CA.
[22] Petty Officer Jason A. Shepard, Distinguished Flying Cross citation, action date: 30 August 2005, Archives, Distinguished Flying Cross Society, San Diego, CA.
[23] Chief Warrant Officer 3 Lori Hill, Distinguished Flying Cross citation, action date: 21 March 2006, Archives, Distinguished Flying Cross Society, San Diego, CA.
[24] Chief Warrant Officer 4 Brent S. Cole, Distinguished Flying Cross citation, action date: 22 May 2009, Archives, Distinguished Flying Cross Society, San Diego, CA.

Chapter 6

In a Class by Themselves

*T*he award of a Distinguished Flying Cross is a prestigious honor which has elevated aviators into a distinctive category. It was recognition that stood alone, and for most individuals, the presentation of the medal was their moment in history. However, beyond the attainment of a DFC, some pilots were thrust into prominence because of their participation in a mission of major historical importance. In addition to those who gained notoriety for a single event, there were pilots who flew in harm's way repeatedly and received numerous medals.

Along with combat and rescue missions for which the Distinguished Flying Cross was awarded, an inspired group of aviators were recognized as visionaries who were responsible for innovations and inventions. Their creative endeavors had an impact on improving aircraft, weapons systems, communications, navigation and most importantly, techniques which won battles and saved American lives.

Almost six decades after the art of flight was mastered, exploration of space began. Starting with seven original astronauts, the quest to journey beyond our atmosphere began with a sequence of small incremental ventures. Due to the extremely dangerous nature of their missions, many of the early pioneers were awarded a Distinguished Flying Cross. With each flight that followed, select astronauts were recognized for their aerial achievement and heroism in space, although some of these fearless human beings had already received aviation medals and awards prior to their exploits in space, for either their combat heroism or their role as test pilots.

Once DFC recipients made their final military landing, they often progressed to new challenges. Many who were still motivated to contribute to the United States entered government service. Among the ranks of local officials, state legislators, governors, congressmen and high ranking appointees are a surprising number who have performed heroic acts which merited the red, white and blue ribbon of the DFC. Only one person, however, earned a Distinguished Flying Cross and achieved the position of Commander in Chief; George Herbert Walker Bush, the Forty-first President of the United States.

Public office is only one of the ways in which those who have received the DFC have chosen to use leadership skills acquired in the military,. Numerous DFC recipients have opted to make their mark in the private sector as well. From banking, finance and law to manufacturing and real estate, individuals who excelled in the air have also demonstrated an ability to excel in the world of business.

Americans love to be entertained. They attend movies, live performances and sporting events. To the surprise of their adoring fans, a unique group of aviators has been decorated with the Distinguished Flying Cross and then obtained celebrity status after serving their country. An even smaller number of individuals achieved fame prior to their aerial exploits and then returned to the spotlight as civilians.

As one reviews the eclectic nature of the representative individuals who comprise the chapter, "In a Class by Themselves," it becomes clear that these are iconic figures who are recognized and admired. In the final analysis, though, it is not just about a single person of note; it is about the collective contributions of all the men and women who share the honor of the Distinguished Flying Cross. Together, they are a dynamic force that symbolizes the best America has to offer.

This rare photograph of Marine Ace, Joe Foss and Charles A. Lindbergh, was taken by Lieutenant Colonel Noble Newson, Jr., USMC, in the Pacific during World War II (all three Distinguished Flying Cross recipients). For Foss, the meeting was an experience of a lifetime as Lindbergh was his hero. Newsom carried the snapshot in his wallet for several years. According to the Distinguished Flying Cross Society, this photograph has never been published.

In this patriotic image, Captain Gene Cernan (the last man on the moon) saluted the American Flag during the Apollo 17 mission.

Captain Eugene Cernan received the 2007 Lindbergh Spirit Award which is presented every five years. It was a tribute which has connected the Distinguished Flying Cross recipients through the decades.

Lieutenant George Herbert Walker Bush, USN, named his airplane *Barbara* after his girlfriend, Barbara Pierce. They were married in January 1945.

Lieutenant Bush flew TBM torpedo bombers in the south Pacific during World War II.

President George Herbert Walker Bush

Distinguished Navy Pilot became Commander in Chief_____

While a student at Phillips Academy in Andover, Massachusetts, George Bush learned of the attack on Pearl Harbor and decided he wanted to join the military to become an aviator. After graduation, he enlisted in the Navy, on his eighteenth birthday, and began pre-flight training at the University of North Carolina at Chapel Hill. Once his flight training was completed, he was commissioned as an ensign in the US Naval Reserve on 9 June 1943. He was, at the time, the youngest naval aviator of that era.

Ensign Bush was then assigned to Torpedo Squadron VT-51 as photographic officer in September 1943. His squadron, part of Air Group 51, was based on the USS *San Jacinto* in spring 1944. The *San Jacinto* was part of Task Force 58 which participated in several major air battles throughout WWII. On his return from a mission in June 1944, Ensign Bush was compelled to make a forced water landing. Bush and his crew were rescued by the destroyer, USS *Clarence K. Bronson*. A month later, Ensign Bush and another pilot received credit for sinking a small cargo ship.

Once operations commenced against the Japanese in the Bonin Islands, Bush was promoted to lieutenant junior grade. On 2 September 1944, he participated in a mission to attack Japanese installations on Chichi Jima. For that mission, he received the Distinguished Flying Cross. The event was explained on his citation: "He led one section of a four plane division which attacked a radio station. Opposed by intense anti-aircraft fire, his plane was hit and set afire as he commenced his dive. In spite of smoke and flames from the fire in his plane he continued in his dive and scored damaging bomb hits on the radio station, before bailing out of his plane. His courage and complete disregard for his own safety, both in pressing home his attack in the face of intense and accurate anti-aircraft fire, and in continuing in his dive on the target after being hit and his plane on fire, were at all times in keeping with the highest traditions of the United States Naval Service."[1]

After his parachute hit the water, Lieutenant Junior Grade Bush anxiously waited for four hours in his inflated raft while several fighters protected him from the air until he was rescued by the submarine, USS *Finback*. While on the submarine for almost a month, Bush participated in the rescue of other pilots. Upon his return to the *San Jacinto* in November 1944, Bush was again involved with operations in the Philippines. However, by the time the *San Jacinto* returned to Guam, the squadron was replaced and sent back to the United States due to the high rate of pilot casualties.

Throughout his combat experience, Lieutenant Bush was credited with 1,228 flight hours, 126 carrier landings and 58 combat missions. Along with the Distinguished Flying Cross, he received three Air Medals and the Presidential Unit citation awarded to the *San Jacinto*.[2]

Due to his extensive combat experience, Bush was sent to Norfolk, Virginia and assigned to a training wing for new torpedo pilots. Later, he served as a naval aviator in a new torpedo squadron, VT-153. When the war concluded, he was honorably discharged in September 1945 and then attended Yale University.

As history has recorded, George Herbert Walker Bush entered politics and was elected to two terms in the House of Representatives before being named Ambassador to the United Nations. After serving as the director of the Central Intelligence Agency, Bush went on to hold the office of vice president when Ronald Reagan chose Bush as his presidential running mate in 1980. Nine years later, George H. W. Bush became the Forty-first President of the United States. His son, George W. Bush, followed in his father's footsteps as the Forty-third President upon his election in 2001. Reflecting on his WWII experiences, President George H. W. Bush described combat as one of the most dramatic times of his life, which left him with a "sobering understanding of war and peace." [3]

General Benjamin O. Davis, Jr., USAF

Commander of the Tuskegee Airmen

Benjamin O. Davis, Jr. learned what it was like to be a military officer at an early age as he observed his father in the Army. When they lived in Wyoming, Benjamin O. Davis, Sr. was a lieutenant in an all-white cavalry unit. He eventually attained the rank of general. With his family heritage, it seemed natural for the younger Davis to follow in the footsteps of his father.

After attending the University of Chicago, he entered the United States Military Academy at West Point and graduated in 1936. Davis was the fourth African American to graduate from the Academy. Though he was initially rejected by the Army Air Corps because of his race, Davis completed Advanced Flying School and was the first officer to receive his wings at Tuskegee Air Field in Alabama.

Colonel Benjamin O. Davis commanded the Tuskegee Airman during WWII.

During the summer of 1942, he was promoted to lieutenant colonel and was named the commander of the 99th Pursuit Squadron which was the first all African American air unit. After more than a year in this assignment, Davis took command of the 332nd Fighter Group, a larger unit preparing for combat in Italy. During his command, the Tuskegee Airmen flew over 15,000 missions and shot down at least 111 enemy planes.[4]

Lieutenant Colonel Davis led many missions in P-47 Thunderbolts and P-51 Mustangs. He received a Distinguished Flying Cross for a bomber-escort mission to Munich, Germany on 9 June 1944. The official citation from the USAAF included the following description of the mission: "En route, the bomber formation was attacked by approximately one hundred enemy fighters…Colonel Davis so skillfully disposed his squadrons that in spite of the large number of enemy fighters, the bomber formation suffered only a few losses…His aggressive spirit and determined leadership caused his men to rout the enemy fighters and emerge with five victories."[5]

After WWII, Colonel Davis assisted in developing the United States Air Force plan for integration based on President Truman's Executive Order in July 1948. With the help of Colonel Davis' efforts, the Air Force was the first service to become racially integrated.

Davis also served in Korea as commander of the 51st Fighter-Interceptor Wing and was later assigned to a variety of high level positions until his retirement as a three-star general in 1970. On 9 December 1998, Benjamin O. Davis, Jr. was advanced to the rank of general, US Air Force (Retired).

After WWII, Davis was a driving force in the racial integration of the USAF.

Lieutenant Aleda Lutz, USAAF

First Female to Receive a DFC in Military Action

Aleda Lutz was born in Freeland, Michigan on 9 November 1915 and attended Saginaw General Hospital School of Nursing after high school. Following graduation in 1937, she gained traditional nursing experience. However, she took part in a new military concept, aerial evacuation, after enlisting in the Army Nurse Corps in February 1942.

As part of the 802nd Medical Air Evacuation Squadron, Lieutenant Lutz flew on converted C-47s which were used as flying ambulances, equipped with medical supplies, capable of carrying up to twenty-two patients from the front lines to base hospitals. It was the first unit to do so in any theater of war. Since the medical planes were flying in and around the battles, they were frequently escorted by fighters.

When the Allies entered North Africa in February 1943, she was sent to Tunisia to evacuate wounded troops from positions near the front lines. After Tunisia, she took part in campaigns in Sicily, Naples and Rome. When southern France was invaded by the Allies in 1944, Lieutenant Lutz was transferred to France.

Lieutenant Aleda E. Lutz had a Veterans Hospital named in her honor.

Lieutenant Lutz attended to patients on a C-47 flying ambulance.

On 1 November 1944, the Army nurse was aboard a C-47 airborne ambulance caring for eighteen patients being transported from the front lines to a hospital in Italy when the plane encountered severe weather. Unfortunately, the plane crashed near Lyon, France and all aboard were lost. Lieutenant Lutz was not yet twenty-nine years old at the time of her death. Throughout her military career, she had completed 196 missions and led the squadron in the number of missions flown and the total number of flight hours overseas. She impressively cared for more than 3,500 injured soldiers.[6]

For her service beyond the call of duty, the Distinguished Flying Cross was posthumously awarded to 1st Lieutenant Aleda E. Lutz on 28 December 1944. She was the first military woman to die in a combat zone in WWII and the first woman awarded the DFC in a military action. Lieutenant Lutz also received four Air Medals, the Red Cross Medal and the Purple Heart. An Army hospital ship was named after her in 1945 and to further honor her memory, a VA medical facility, in Michigan, was named for her. [7]

Commander Hamilton "Mac" McWhorter, USN

Double F6F Hellcat Ace

Hamilton "Mac" McWhorter experienced combat as a Navy lieutenant for the first time in November 1942 as part of "Operation Torch" during the invasion of North Africa. When he returned to Virginia with his squadron VF-9, on the carrier USS *Ranger*, they were the first to receive the new F6F Hellcat in August 1943.

While he was not the first in his squadron to score a victory with a Hellcat, on 5 October 1943 during a raid on Wake Island, he did shoot down an enemy fighter with a single burst from his guns. This action earned him the nickname "One Slug."

Lieutenant McWhorter ultimately flew eighty-nine combat missions and stated that Rubaul was his most memorable. On 11 November 1943, thirty Hellcats tangled with fifty Zeros and he downed three enemy planes that day. McWhorter described what it was like to get hit by enemy fire. "Imagine you're in a metal shed and someone throws rocks against the outside. That's what it sounded like

Lieutenant McWhorter downed twelve enemy planes.

when machine gun fire ripped into my Hellcat." After the battle, the lieutenant realized that the raids on Rubaul proved that carrier task forces could operate within the range of Japanese land-based bombers.

On 19 February 1944, the twenty-two year old was credited with downing two Zeros and he became the first carrier pilot and Hellcat pilot to achieve the status of double ace. He would add two more victories by 13 May 1945 as part of VF-12 flying against the Japanese home islands.

As part of VF-9, McWhorter flew the F6F Hellcat. He was a double ace.

"Mac" received five DFCs for combat missions ranging from 11 November 1943 to 10 May 1945.[8] The aerial combat took place in Rubaul Harbor, New Britain, the Marshall Islands, the islands adjacent to Japan and in the vicinity of Tokyo. When WWII ended, McWhorter stayed in the Navy, retiring as a commander in 1969. For the next two decades, he trained civilian pilots and enjoyed every minute of being aloft.

Major General James Stewart, USAF

A Movie Star who Wore the Stars of a General

Most movie fans know that James Maitland Stewart starred in more than sixty films and was considered one of the finest actors during the golden age of Hollywood. However, only the aficionado, well versed in his military career, would know that the movie star also wore the stars of a highly decorated general.

By 1935, Jimmy Stewart was a contract actor with MGM. He starred in films such as *You Can't Take It With You* and *Mr. Smith Goes to Washington*. Even in the 1930s, Stewart combined motion pictures and flying. As he gained prominence in movies, he also acted on his passion for flying. In 1935, he received his private pilot's license and often flew from California to his home town in Pennsylvania by navigating along railroad tracks. Becoming more proficient, Stewart earned his commercial rating in 1938 and flew in a cross-country race as a copilot in 1939. Foreseeing the need to train pilots for the approaching war, the actor along with other Hollywood celebrities purchased Thunderbird Field in Glendale, Arizona. Prophetically, the airfield became part of the United States Army Air Forces and trained over 10,000 pilots by the end of the war.[9]

Jimmy Stewart was a highly decorated aviator during World War II. He was as comfortable in the air as he was in front of a movie camera.

Determined to be a military pilot and fly in combat, Stewart overcame several obstacles and served as the operations officer for the 703rd Bomb Squadron, 445th Bombardment Group of the 8th Air Force in Tibenham, England and was subsequently transferred to the 453rd Bombardment Group. There, he flew as a lead pilot in B-24 Liberators.

The official record indicated that Stewart flew twenty combat missions over enemy territory which included bombing raids to Berlin, Brunswick, Bremen, Frankfurt and Schweinfurt. For these and other actions, he was twice awarded the Distinguished Flying Cross, the first on 20 February 1944 and the second on 27 May 1944.[10] Stewart also received Air Medals and the French Croix de Guerre with Palm.

In four years, Stewart rose from private to colonel, and demonstrated that he could be an effective bomber pilot and command level officer. With this success, he decided to stay in the military and transitioned to the USAF Reserves after the war. In 1946, after a long absence from Hollywood, Jimmy Stewart starred in *It's a Wonderful Life*. The immediate success of the film demonstrated that he had not lost his skills and charm as an actor. While he made many successful movies in the following decades such as *The Philadelphia Story, Harvey, Rear Window* and *Vertigo*, the star continued his Air Force Reserve duties and was promoted to brigadier general in 1959. Over time, Jimmy Stewart received the Distinguished Service Medal and ultimately the Presidential Medal of Freedom. He was also promoted to the rank of major general by President Ronald Reagan.

First Lieutenant John Edwards, USAAF and First Lieutenant Donald Kilburg, USAAF

Led Castle's Raid to Success on Christmas Eve, 1944_____

On Christmas Eve of 1944, during a heavy onslaught by German ground forces that the press called the Battle of the Bulge, the United States Army Air Forces planned a mission that involved 2,046 B-17s and B-24s protected by 800 fighters. It was the greatest air armada ever assembled. The targets included German airfields and other strategic locations.

The 487th Bomb Group, part of Brigadier General Frederick W. Castle's 4th Bomb Wing was selected to spearhead the entire operation. Castle, himself the recipient of four DFCs, made the decision to be air leader for the mission with Lieutenant Robert W. Harriman piloting the lead plane. John "Pappy" Edwards flew with Captain Mayfield Shilling in the right seat as deputy air leader. They positioned their aircraft to the right of Castle's aircraft. Donald Kilburg was the bombardier of Edward's plane and both were equipped with the Path Finder Force (PFF) radar system.

Lieutenants, John Edwards (left) and Donald Kilburg in Cambridge, England during 1944.

Once the aircraft departed from the fields of West Anglia, England, they crossed to Europe in an orderly fashion; however, as they flew south of Liege, Belgium, pandemonium erupted. Nazi fighters attacked the lead formation while ground fire targeted the massive invasion force. Eyewitnesses, including John Edwards, recalled seeing the lead plane sustain multiple hits and then fall from the formation with General Castle aboard.

Edwards then assumed the position of lead plane and Shilling was the new air leader who refocused the formation after the Nazi attack was finally repulsed. As they reached their first target, an airbase at Babenhausen, the aircraft was turned over to bombardier, Don Kilburg. On his command the formation dropped 325 tons of bombs. Other targets were Luftwaffe airbases, railroad yards, roads, communication centers and bridges vital to Germany's ability to wage war.

The plane carrying Edwards and Kilburg was riddled with flak and cannon holes but returned the crew back to England in time to celebrate Christmas. Both men received the Distinguished Flying Cross for heroism and leadership.[11] General Castle was posthumously awarded the Congressional Medal of Honor. As a result of Castle's Raid and other successful military actions, the Germans only lasted another four months before they surrendered.

After General Castle's aircraft crashed, Edwards and his crew took control of the mission as the lead plane.

Colonel Francis "Gabby" Gabreski, USAF

America's Two-War Ace Received Thirteen DFCs

Although Francis Gabreski had a desire to fly, he was advised in 1938 that he didn't have "the touch" to be a pilot. He ignored that assessment of his talents and eventually enlisted in the US Army Air Corps, received his wings in March 1941 and was sent to Hawaii. During the attack on Pearl Harbor, Gabreski made an attempt to intercept the Japanese but by the time he was able to get his P-36 in the air, the enemy had departed.

In honor of his Polish heritage, Gabreski suggested that he serve as a liaison officer to the Polish squadrons of the RAF. The idea was approved and he was transferred, in 1942, to the 8th Air Force in England where he flew twenty missions with the Polish, but only once saw combat.

During February 1943, Gabreski became part of the 56th Fighter Group, USAAF, and flew P-47s with the 61st Fighter Squadron. By summer 1944, Gabby had amassed twenty-eight victories, which surpassed Eddie Rickenbacker's record from WWI, and made him the leading ace in the European Theater. This

Colonel Gabreski was awarded thirteen DFCs.

record remained for the duration of the war.

On his last mission, Lieutenant Colonel Gabreski was forced to crash land in enemy territory where he was eventually captured and imprisoned until his liberation by Soviet forces in April 1945. After WWII, Gabreski became a test pilot at Wright Field and left the military to work for Douglas Aircraft but he was recalled by the USAF in April 1947. He was promoted to the rank of colonel in 1950. Gabreski was sent to Korea and flew jets in combat where he downed an official six and a half MiGs, thus becoming a jet ace.

Throughout his entire career, Gabreski was awarded an astounding thirteen Distinguished Flying Crosses during the two wars; eleven during WWII and two while he was in Korea.[12] Current Distinguished Flying Cross Society records indicate that Colonel Gabreski and Captain Robert "Duke" Peacher, USN, may hold the record for receiving the largest number of Distinguished Flying Crosses.

"Gabby" proudly displayed his twenty-eight victories.

Brigadier General Joseph Foss, USMC / SDANG

Marine Top Ace – Twenty Six Victories in Forty-Four Days

As an eleven-year-old growing up in Sioux Falls, South Dakota, Joe Foss like so many others, was inspired by Charles Lindbergh. So it was no surprise that Foss became a Marine pilot in 1942. He was sent to the Pacific and was stationed at Henderson Field in Guadalcanal. There he became the executive officer of VMF-121 and flew Wildcats.

Foss downed his first enemy Zero on 13 October 1942, and over the next seven days he shot down five more enemy Zeros and an enemy bomber. For this impressive combat record, Captain Foss was awarded the Distinguished Flying Cross. The medal was personally presented by Admiral Halsey. By 19 November 1942, the combat pilot had accomplished his twenty-third victory. That included the day he became the Marine Corps' first "Ace in a Day," on 25 October 1942. Fewer than two weeks after his last victory, he was credited with leading a mission that repelled a large force of Japanese bombers and fighters from destroying his base. His defense was so compelling that Henderson Field never came under direct attack again.

Captain Joseph Foss shot down five enemy planes in one day.

Foss received a DFC and a Medal of Honor.

Under the captain's leadership, his group of aviators became known as the "Flying Circus" for their acrobatic maneuvers. The Flying Circus was credited with an astonishing, combined total of seventy-two victories. During his combat tour of the Pacific, Foss met his inspiration, Charles Lindbergh. It was an event the Marine would never forget.

In addition to the Distinguished Flying Cross, Foss also received the Medal of Honor from President Roosevelt.[13] After WWII, Joe Foss became a colonel, served in Korea and then helped establish the Air National Guard in South Dakota before retiring from the Guard as a brigadier general.

Foss was always known for his positive thinking. He was famous for saying, "I always had the attitude that every day will be a great day." This zest for life also carried him through his civilian endeavors. Foss served in the South Dakota State Legislature from 1948 to 1953 and then as Governor from 1955 to 1959. He was also a Commissioner of the American Football League and head of the National Rifle Association.

Lieutenant Colonel Jerry Coleman, USMC

World War II, Korea and the New York Yankees

On his eighteenth birthday, Jerry Coleman enlisted in the Navy and joined the V-5 program. At pre-flight school, Joe Foss, the celebrated Marine Corps ace, inspired Coleman with his tales of combat. These stories motivated Coleman to become a Marine aviator. He was commissioned in April 1944 and over the next twelve months, Coleman flew the Douglas SBD Dauntless dive bomber out of Green Island, a tiny island in the Solomon Islands, as a member of the VMSB-341.

Coleman confessed, "I never sank a carrier as I'd envisioned as a high school senior, but I flew fifty-seven missions in the battles for the Solomon Islands and the Philippines." Coleman received a DFC during a period of combat near the Philippine Islands which occurred between 4 and 13 March 1945. He received a second DFC for military operations from 29 April to 16 May 1945.[14] Coleman then said in a matter-of-fact way, "When the Japanese surrendered, I returned home and resumed my baseball career." Coleman played second base for the Yankees and had won the World Series over the Giants when, as he put it, "I traded my Yankee pinstripes for Marine greens in April 1952, with no hard feelings…I flew Corsair attack planes in Korea…sixty-three missions overall.[15]

Jerry Coleman was one of the few professional ball players to serve in World War II and Korea.

I wasn't the only major league player to go off to war, either in WWII or in Korea. Ted Williams, Bobby Brown, Bob Feller - there were many of them. But I think I was the only one who saw combat in both wars. By the time I returned from Korea in 1953, my record for both wars included two Distinguished Flying Crosses, thirteen Air Medals and three Navy citations." Coleman retired from the Marine Corps reserves as a lieutenant colonel in 1964.

Jerry Coleman's perspective was clear, "By any standard, I've had a great career. I played second base for the New York Yankees, was manager of the San Diego Padres and have been a sportscaster for almost five decades. But the most important part of my life was the five years I spent in uniform. I was a Marine Corps aviator in WWII and the Korean War…the Yankees are up there, but *not* as high."[16]

Between World War II and Korea, Jerry Coleman played second base for the New York Yankees and later became a sports announcer.

Major Albert C. Sebourn, USA

A Pioneer in the "MASH" Helicopter Concept During Korea

Albert C. Sebourn grew up in Mountainburg, Arkansas with a desire to travel and participate in adventure. Lying about his age, he joined the Army, serving first in WWII and then in Korea. Assigned to the Second Helicopter Detachment, 8th Army Headquarters, Captain Sebourn became the commanding officer of the four man unit. He was the first to fly an Army helicopter medical evacuation mission in Korea, picking up a wounded soldier from the battlefield and flying him to a Mobile Army Surgical Hospital (MASH). While Colonel Phillip Cochran made the first actual helicopter rescue during WWII in May 1943, regular use of the "egg-beater" for rescues became a reality in Korea with the 2nd Helicopter Detachment.

Flying the Bell H-13D, then Captain Albert C. Sebourn, (right) gained national attention after an article appeared in *Stars and Stripes*. The resourcefulness and heroism of the MASH units were the inspiration for the popular television series *MASH*.

Captain Sebourn received the Distinguished Flying Cross for a voluntary mission flown in the helicopter he called the *Mechanized Angel* on 13 January 1951, shortly after the unit became operational. The citation stated, "In response to an emergency request for air evacuation of casualties, Captain Sebourn volunteered, knowing that friendly troops were surrounded and under fire, to pilot his helicopter to the [battle] area. On arrival over the area, he was subjected to enemy automatic weapons fire from the hills surrounding the valley. Despite this hazard, Captain Sebourn landed and proceeded to load the seriously wounded, subjecting himself to direct enemy small-arms fire and a mortar barrage. Due to a mechanical failure, he was unable to take off…Captain Sebourn remained in the perimeter during the night." With help from the rest of his Detachment the next day, the wounded were evacuated safely.[17]

During January 1951, the first month of the operation, the unit of four evacuated more than 500 seriously wounded soldiers. In most cases, the injured were surrounded by the enemy and extracted them required skillful piloting to avoid being shot down. Over the next ten months, the unit rescued over 1,500 wounded troops.

Sebourn, who was promoted to major, wanted to protect wounded soldiers from enemy fire and adverse weather during the rescue missions so he designed an enclosed litter basket. His detachment also designed a tube to pipe hot air into the litter basket for warmth and created a means to deliver plasma in flight while en route to the MASH unit. With these innovations, the survival rate of the injured soared to more than ninety percent with eighty percent returning to combat.

After leaving the military, Albert Sebourn pursued a career repairing electronic equipment. His most profound achievement, though, was his contribution to helicopter rescue techniques, which changed the Korean battlefield and care of the wounded – quite a legacy for a man whose formal education extended only to the fifth-grade.

General Hsichun "Mike" Hua, ROCAF

U2 Miracle at Cortez

Nine months before Francis Gary Powers was shot down by the Soviets in the famous U-2 spy plane incident, Major Hsichun "Mike" Hua was one of six members of the Republic of China Air Force (Taiwan) selected to pilot the top secret U-2. Based out of Del Rio, Texas, he learned to fly the jet which had the appearance of a glider with its fifty foot fuselage and eighty foot wingspan. Developed in just eighty-eight days as a prototype, many performance factors were sacrificed in order to accomplish its high altitude and long range mission requirements. No doubt, this contributed to the destruction of seventeen U-2s, and ended the lives of eleven pilots during the first three years of flights involving fifty aircraft.

The pilots were unimpressed with the plane at first glance until they saw it take off with a seventy-five degree climb angle! While fast, it was a difficult aircraft to control. Major Hua stated, "The speed between stall and Mach buffet boundaries at high altitude was less than ten knots...which is why this region of the 'flight envelope' is called 'The Coffin Corner'."[18]

U-2 pilot, Major Hua, ROCAF

On his seventh training flight, at 8:30 p.m. on 3 August 1959, Hua left Laughlin Air Force Base in Texas to practice celestial navigation on a course to Ogden, Utah and back. On his return to the base, the aircraft engine flamed out. At 70,000 feet he also lost his generator and autopilot, entered the clouds at 40,000 feet and was unable to airstart the engine. To compound the emergency, he could not get a response from a nearby Air Force base. At 17,000 feet in near total darkness and still in the clouds, Hua remembered thinking, "many of the peaks of the Rocky Mountains rose above 14,000 feet – I was really in trouble...The only thing I could do was pray."

The U-2 spy plane rested safely on the ground.

Suddenly breaking out of the clouds at 7,000 feet, he saw lights on the ground and made an emergency landing at the Cortez Municipal Airport. To the surprise of the local inhabitants of Colorado, they saw a very strange craft land, without sound, and an "alien-like" figure emerge in an outfit that resembled a space suit. In 1989, *Air Force Magazine* depicted the incident in a cartoon. Major Hua was awarded a United States Distinguished Flying Cross for his heroic actions and it was determined that a broken fuel line had caused the emergency.[19] At lectures, Hsichun "Mike" Hua has continued to state that he doesn't believe this event involved just mere luck. He knew his prayer had been answered.

Colonel Jacqueline Cochran, USAF

WASP Commander who set Aviation Records_____

Jacqueline Cochran grew up in west Florida. Living in poverty, she didn't own a pair of shoes until she was nine-years old. With great determination however, Cochran became a pilot in 1932 and started air racing by 1934 alongside her friend, Amelia Earhart.

For decades, entrepreneur and pilot, Colonel Jackie Cochran inspired female aviators.

Before the US involvement in WWII, Cochran tried to get women involved in transporting military aircraft, but General Hap Arnold initially rejected the concept even though Eleanor Roosevelt supported the idea. Arnold reconsidered her plan in 1942 because of the severe shortage of male pilots. The Women's Auxiliary Ferrying Squadron (WAFS) was created and the Women's Flying Training Detachment (WFTD), headed by Cochran, was established to train pilots for the WAFS. In 1943, the two groups became one and Cochran was appointed director of the newly formed Women Airforce Service Pilots (WASP) which operated out of 120 air bases all over America. The program was unceremoniously disbanded on 20 December 1944 as the need for female pilots declined.[20]

After the war, Jacqueline Cochran resumed her participation in air races and established new transcontinental and international records. In an unusual manner, while serving in the USAF, Colonel Cochran received a Distinguished Flying Cross for a period of time between 1947 and 1951; during which she accomplished six world speed records while flying her F-51. Among those achievements were a new speed record of 469.5 mph and several speed records for flying specified courses.

Cochran received a second DFC in April 1962 when she set sixty-nine intercity, inter-capital and straight-line distance and speed records on a flight from New Orleans, Louisiana to Bonn, Germany flying a Lockheed JetStar C-140. She was also the first female pilot to fly a jet aircraft across the Atlantic Ocean. Her third and final DFC was conferred for flights made in May and June 1964, when she set a world speed record in an F-104C Starfighter for flying on a circular course, at 1429.297 mph – more than twice the speed of sound. She also set speed records for the 100 and 500 kilometer courses.[21]

In 1953, Cochran became the first woman to exceed the sound barrier and she still holds more international speed, distance and altitude records than any other pilot, male or female. In 1971 she was enshrined at the Aviation Hall of Fame in Dayton, Ohio.

Cochran received three DFCs for aerial achievement.

Colonel John Glenn, Jr., USMC

Combat Pilot, Test Pilot and First Man to Orbit the Earth_____

During WWII, John Glenn, Jr. served in the South Pacific as a Marine pilot and flew fifty-nine combat missions in F4U Corsairs. During that time, Glenn received two Distinguished Flying Crosses in 1944 for bombing and strafing attacks on enemy shipping and installations. Before the war ended in 1945, he was assigned to the Naval Air Station at Patuxent River in Maryland where he was promoted to captain.

After that assignment, Captain Glenn served as a flight instructor before flying another sixty-three combat missions in Korea. During his service in Asia, he flew the new F9F Panther jet and earned the nickname "magnet butt" for his misfortune of attracting enemy flak. On two occasions, he returned from combat with more than 250 holes in his aircraft.

Colonel John Glenn as he entered *Friendship 7* in 1962.

In 1953, Glenn completed a second Korean combat tour on an inter-service exchange program with the United States Air Force. He flew twenty-seven missions in the faster F-86F Saber near the Yalu River in the final days before the cease fire. Major Glenn received his third and fourth DFCs on 12 July and 19 July 1953 for shooting down MiG-15s and saving his wingman on the latter mission.

Once the Korean War was over, Glenn was stationed back at "Pax River" and became a test pilot. On 16 July 1957, Major Glenn flew "Operation Bullet" in a F-8U Crusader. His fifth DFC was awarded for being the first person to span the nation faster then the speed of sound.

In 1959, Colonel John Glenn, Jr. was selected to be one of the seven original NASA astronauts and on 20 February 1962, he completed a space flight on *Friendship 7*. He received his sixth DFC for being the first American to make a complete orbit around Earth.[22]

After he left the space program, Glenn was elected to the Senate from Ohio in 1974, where he served until 1998. As a surprise to many, he returned to space in 1998 as part of the *Discovery* space shuttle crew. On that flight, he became the oldest person to participate in space travel. In many respects, the mission became a nostalgic salute to one of the original astronauts and pioneers in space.

John Glenn returned to space thirty-six years after he first orbited the earth.

Captain James A. Lovell, Jr., USN

Carrier Pilot, Test Pilot and Astronaut

Before he was selected to be an astronaut by NASA in September 1962, James A. Lovell logged more than 7,000 hours of flying time in the Navy. His experiences as an aviator ranged from carrier pilot to test pilot. Among his many responsibilities at the Naval Air Test Center at Patuxent River, Maryland, Lovell served as program manager for the F-4H Phantom Fighter.

Once an astronaut, Lovell made his first trip into space on 4 December 1965 with Frank Borman on the historic *Gemini 7* spacecraft. The flight involved the first rendezvous of two, manned, maneuverable spacecraft. For this trip into space, which orbited the earth 206 times, Lovell was awarded a Distinguished Flying Cross. His next mission was *Gemini 12* which took place 11-15 November 1966. Captain Lovell was in command and was accompanied by Pilot Edwin "Buzz" Aldrin. A second DFC was awarded to Captain Lovell for this mission that accomplished sixty-three orbits of the earth and proved that man had conquered many of the challenges posed by space travel.[23] Following the *Gemini* flights, Captain Lovell served as command module pilot and navigator on *Apollo 8*, man's maiden voyage to the moon, during 21-27 December 1968. Lovell and fellow crewmen, Frank Borman and William A. Anders, became the first people to leave Earth's gravitational pull.

Captain James Lovell (left) received two Distinguished Flying Crosses for his Gemini flights but is best remembered for the safe return of Apollo 13.

Lovell's fourth and final space flight was his most memorable, *Apollo 13,* which has been referred to as the most successful failure. As spacecraft commander of the *Apollo 13* flight from 11-17 April 1970, Lovell became the first human to journey twice to the moon and he was responsible for managing an explosion and getting the severely damaged craft back to earth. Although Captain Lovell did not receive a DFC for this marvelous accomplishment, he did receive the Congressional Space Medal of Honor and the Presidential Medal of Freedom.

Combining his four space flights, Captain Lovell held the record for the greatest amount of time in space with a total of 715 hours and 5 minutes. This record stood until the *Skylab* flights. Captain Lovell reflected on his most challenging experiences while flying and noted that night carrier operations were among his most difficult, as they required as much or more skill than flying in space.[24] Of course, the most successful failure will always be at the top of his remarkable list of achievements.

Brigadier General James McDivitt, USAF

Korean Combat Pilot and Astronaut

James A. McDivitt joined the Air Force in 1951 and became a jet fighter pilot. During Korea, he flew 145 combat missions in F-80s and F-86s. While assigned to the 35th Fighter Bomber Squadron of the 8th Fighter Bomber Wing, he was awarded three Distinguished Flying Crosses.

His first DFC was conferred for flying a close air support (CAS) mission in defense of friendly troops who were in great peril. His accurately placed ordnance on the enemy forces, stopped the attack and protected American troops. The second DFC involved a successful attack on locomotives which, at the time were the number one target in Korea. However, his third DFC was the most harrowing. Flying with the entire wing on a mission to destroy the primary

McDivitt surveyed the damage to his aircraft during Korea.

North Korean radio station in the center of the capital, Pyongyang, McDivitt's horizontal stabilizer was hit and severely damaged. Using flaps, speed brakes, trim and throttle, he was able to bring the aircraft under some semblance of control and head back towards the base with his wingman. On the way to the base, they decided to bomb a bridge rather than return with their bombs. In spite of McDivitt's control difficulties, the bridge was destroyed and both planes landed safely.

James A. McDivitt received three DFCs for combat in Korea and a DFC for his 1965 space flight.

After his combat experience in Korea, McDivitt graduated from the USAF Experimental Test Pilot School and the USAF Aerospace Research Pilot course. He then served as an experimental test pilot at Edwards Air Force Base, California. McDivitt was selected as an astronaut by NASA in September 1962. He was command pilot for *Gemini 4*, a sixty-six orbit mission during 3-7 June 1965, which included a controlled extra-vehicular activity period and initial rendezvous experiments. For that space flight, he received his fourth DFC.[25] In March 1969, he served as commander of *Apollo 9* which included the first flight of the Lunar Module.

In addition to his space flights, McDivitt was the manager of Lunar Landing Operations in May 1969, leading a team that planned the lunar exploration program and redesigned the spacecraft that accomplished the task. In August 1969, he served as manager of the Apollo Spacecraft Program and managed *Apollo 12, 13, 14, 15* and *16*. General McDivitt retired in 1972.

Vice Admiral James Stockdale, USN

Naval Aviator, Test Pilot and POW

Throughout James Bond Stockdale's naval career, the courageous American had a pragmatic philosophy: "Follow Me!" This was not just a saying but a way of life for the amazing military leader.

In 1946, Stockdale graduated from the US Naval Academy and then completed flight training. His skills as a pilot quickly earned him a spot in the Naval Test Pilot School at Patuxent River, Maryland. During training, he came in contact with many individuals who later made their mark on aviation history; among them was John Glenn who Stockdale tutored in physics and calculus.

By 1958, Stockdale became the

Admiral James Stockdale, USN was awarded two DFCs, multiple Silver Stars and a Medal of Honor. He was a quintessential military leader.

flight leader of the first supersonic jets during the Taiwan Straits Crisis. He then went on to combat in Vietnam. Commander Stockdale received a Distinguished Flying Cross for repelling North Vietnamese torpedo boat attacks against a US ship while in international waters on 2-4 August 1964, and for a retaliatory air strike against North Vietnamese torpedo boats and supporting facilities on 5 August 1964.[26] This was the first air strike against North Vietnam following the Gulf of Tonkin incident. He was awarded a second DFC and multiple Silver Stars for his heroism in combat.

On 9 September 1965, Stockdale was shot down over North Vietnam, on what proved to be his last mission. He spent the next seven years of his life in the Hoa Lo Prison, known as the Hanoi Hilton. He was promoted to rear admiral while in captivity.

As the senior naval prisoner of war, he demonstrated exceptional courage by enduring agonizing torture, organizing the American POW resistance and establishing a code of conduct for the men in the infamous prison. He even passed information to Navy Intelligence through coded letters written to his wife, Sybil. Through his personal sacrifices, he convinced his captors that he would rather die than acquiesce to their demands. His resistance succeeded in bringing about the end of the American's severe torture and ultimately the replacement of the prison commander. While her husband was in captivity, Sybil, other POW wives and family members organized the National League of Families of American Prisoners in Southeast Asia which focused attention on the prisoners' plight and pressured Hanoi for more humane prisoner treatment. On 12 February 1973, the North Vietnamese released Stockdale.

For his acts of heroism, Admiral Stockdale was awarded the Medal of Honor in 1976. For his reputation and abilities he was selected as the vice-presidential candidate on Ross Perot's Reform ticket during the presidential election of 1992.

Colonel Leo Thorsness, USAF

A Wild Weasel with Six DFCs and a Medal of Honor

Leo K. Thorsness, an Eagle Scout from Minnesota, enlisted in the Air Force at the age of nineteen and became a jet pilot. In the fall of 1966, Thorsness completed his "Wild Weasel" training and was assigned to the 355th Tactical Fighter Wing based at Takhli RTAFB, Thailand. He was an aircraft commander of F-105s, charged with locating and destroying North Vietnamese surface-to-air missile (SAM) sites.

Demonstrating that the F-105 pilots were consistently engaged in significant action, from 2 December 1966 to 18 April 1967, Major Thorsness was awarded five Distinguished Flying Crosses.[27] Actions during that four-and-a-half month period resulted in the destruction of SAM missile sites; attacks and destruction of enemy fortifications; neutralization of hostile forces; conducting MiG "sweeps,"

Colonel Thorsness (second from the left) flew ninety-three missions as a Wild Weasel.

which resulted in the downing of several enemy jets and the destruction of convoys and barges laden with enemy supplies.

As head Weasel of the 357th Tactical Fighter Squadron, Major Thorsness and his backseater, Captain Harold Johnson, fought one of the epic solo battles of the war in a fifty-minute duel with SAMs, AAA and MiGs on 19 April 1967. The target for the mission was a compound near Hanoi; a most heavily defended area. Thorsness, leading a flight of four Weasels, split the planes into two groups for added diversion. He then proceeded to silence two SAM sites but Thorsness' wingman was hit with flak forcing the pilot and backseater to eject. The other two F-105s, sent north, were attacked by MiGs. A problem with an afterburner on one of the F-105s caused them to return to base. Therefore, Major Thorsness was left alone to battle the enemy on the ground and in the air, which he did with tenacity and great heroism while trying to rescue the downed pilots.

Eleven days later, while on his 93rd mission, Thorsness and his backseater, Captain Johnson were shot down, ejected and captured. Thorsness was interrogated for nineteen days and eighteen nights without sleep. Beatings with a fan belt were not uncommon. The Wild Weasel explained that the North Vietnamese were not sophisticated in their methods of torture but were brutal and unrelenting. After the lengthy interrogation, Major Thorsness was put into a cell with another prisoner and then endured solitary confinement. After six years of captivity, he was released on 4 March 1973 and was presented with the Medal of Honor by President Nixon. Thorsness retired from the USAF as a colonel.

Lieutenant Colonel Dick Rutan, USAF

Achieved One of the Last Aviation "Firsts"

Leaving from Edwards Air Force Base in Southern California on the morning of 14 December 1986, Dick Rutan and his copilot, Jeana Yeager, set out on a journey aboard *Voyager* to achieve something no other aviators had done before - to return to Edwards Air Force Base as the first pilots to fly around the world non-stop without refueling. In effect, they accomplished one of the last aviation "firsts" and joined the ranks of such aviators as Charles Lindbergh, Amelia Earhart and Wiley Post.

While Rutan obtained fame for his record breaking flights, his earlier aviation experiences are less well known. He joined the Air Force and became a navigator but later qualified as an F-100 jet fighter pilot in 1966.

In addition to flying F-100Fs with the Mistys, Lieutenant Colonel Rutan flew F-4s. (Rutan - right)

In Vietnam, he flew 325 missions serving on 105 of them as a member of the high-risk Fast Forward Air Controllers, commonly known as the Mistys.

Dick Rutan received five Distinguished Flying Crosses for combat between November 1967 and July 1968. His DFCs were awarded for close air support, working as a forward air controller and assisting the rescue of a downed pilot.[28] Captain Rutan also received the Silver Star in May 1968 for planning and coordinating a successful attack on a major anti-aircraft artillery site. While on his last strike reconnaissance mission over North Vietnam in September 1968, he was hit by enemy fire and forced to eject from his burning F-100. Rutan eluded capture and was later rescued by the Air Force's "Jolly Green Giant" helicopter team.

In 1978, Lieutenant Colonel Rutan retired from the United States Air Force and joined his brother, Burt, who had started the Rutan Aircraft Factory and then Scaled Composites, where the concept of *Voyager* was conceived. After six years of development, Rutan and Yeager flew *Voyager* to establish the coveted record of non-stop, around the world flight, with a time of nine days, three minutes and forty-four seconds.[29] The *Voyager* now hangs in the Smithsonian Air and Space Museum's "Milestones of Flight" gallery in Washington DC, alongside the Wright Brothers' first plane and Charles Lindbergh's *Spirit of St. Louis*. Dick Rutan, Jeana Yeager and Burt Rutan were awarded the Presidential Citizen's Medal of Honor by President Reagan.

After his combat experience, Rutan flew the *Voyager* non-stop around the world

General Richard A. Cody, USA

Leader of Apache Battalion who Fired First Shots During Operation Desert Storm

Often referred to as a "soldier's soldier" and an "aviator's aviator," Richard A. Cody received his commission as a second lieutenant in 1972 from the US Military Academy. From that time, Cody spent the next twenty-seven of his thirty-six year career in troop assignments, commanding at all levels, including his service as Deputy Commanding General of Task Force Hawk and Commanding General of the famed "Screaming Eagles" of the 101st Airborne Division (Air Assault).

When he was a lieutenant colonel, Cody served as battalion commander of the 101st Airborne Division's 1st Battalion, 101st Aviation Regiment (AH-64) and was the first unit deployed to the Persian Gulf. He

Lieutenant Colonel Cody in his Apache (AH-64) helicopter.

led the top secret Apache helicopter raid against two critical radar sites in Iraq and fired the first shots of Operation Desert Storm to create a forty nautical mile wide radar free corridor to Baghdad. He was awarded the Distinguished Flying Cross for that mission which occurred during the period 14 through 17 January 1991. The citation included the following rationale for the prestigious medal: "As Task Force Commander and AH-64 pilot, Lieutenant Colonel Cody's heroic actions, flawless combat pilotage, and tactical expertise resulted in the simultaneous and complete destruction of Iraqi Early Warning and Ground Control Intercept Radar Sites."[30] The extraordinary combat mission opened the air assault on Iraq, saved untold American and Coalition Forces' lives and immeasurably hastened victory.

To ensure mission success, Lieutenant Colonel Cody (bottom, center) handpicked his young pilots.

With over 5,000 flight hours, General Cody was an Army master aviator. His most significant leadership, however, was displayed during the period following 11 September 2001, when as the G-3/5/7 and then the 31st Vice Chief of Staff, Army, Cody led the most sweeping transformation in the Army and the aviation branch since the dawn of mechanized warfare. His actions provided the Army with the best prepared, trained and equipped force in the world. Cody introduced the most technically capable, modernized fleet of aircraft and unmanned aircraft systems. General Cody served with distinction until he retired from active duty on 4 August 2008.

Brigadier General Paul W. Tibbets, Jr., USAF and Colonel Paul W. Tibbets, IV, USAF

Grandfather and Grandson flew Historic Missions

It can be a daunting experience to grow up in the shadow of a prominent parent or grandparent. The situation can either make a person retreat into obscurity or encourage the younger generation to seize the opportunity, making his or her unique place in history. Paul Warfield Tibbets, IV chose the latter.

The name Tibbets has forever been linked to the dropping of the atomic bomb on 6 August 1945. Paul W. Tibbets, Jr. was the USAAF pilot of the *Enola Gay*, a B-29 named after his mother. Leading up to the historic mission, which impacted the end of WWII and brought about V-J Day, the senior Tibbets had established himself as an outstanding aviator. Paul W. Tibbets, Jr. ultimately became a USAF brigadier general and received two DFCs along with many other decorations.[31]

Lieutenant Colonel Paul W. Tibbets, IV was a B-2 mission commander.

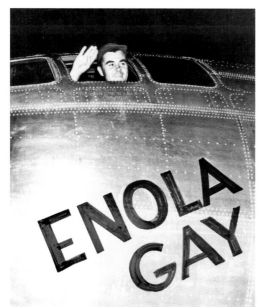

Colonel Paul W. Tibbits, Jr. waved from the B-29 that dropped the first atomic bomb.

More than half-a-century after the dropping of the atomic bomb, USAF Captain Paul W. Tibbets, IV was put into a position to make his own historic flight as a B-2 mission commander at or near Yugoslavia on 8 April 1999. On that date, Captain Tibbets made aviation history by leading the world's first B-2 combat sortie without support during Operation Allied Force. He targeted sixteen separate impact points and destroyed critical military production facilities near Belgrade, a radio relay facility and an arms production plant in Kragujevac. For that mission Tibbets received a DFC and later attained the rank of colonel.[32]

In the Tibbets family, the legacy has been passed on from grandfather to grandson; a tradition that is not uncommon in military families. Both are recorded in history as pilots, military leaders and Air Force officers who flew critical missions on behalf of the United States and received Distinguished Flying Crosses. They exemplify the proud tradition of service to their country.

Grandfather and grandson flew *FIFI,* the only remaining operational B-29.

Captain Eugene A. Cernan, USN

Astronaut and Visionary for Future Space Exploration

Before he left the gravitational pull of the earth, Gene Cernan received a Bachelor of Science Degree in Electrical Engineering from Purdue University in 1956 and was commissioned an ensign though the NROTC Program. As an aviator, he accrued forty-eight hundred hours in jet aircraft and accomplished over 200 jet aircraft carrier landings, prior to 1963, when he was selected by the National Aeronautics and Space Administration (NASA) to become an astronaut.

During two decades as a Naval aviator, including thirteen years with the National Aeronautics and Space Administration (NASA), Captain Eugene A. Cernan participated in three historic space missions. On his first flight, Cernan was the pilot of *Gemini IX-A* during 3 to 6 June 1966. For this heroism and extraordinary achievement while participating in aerial flight as an astronaut, he was awarded a Distinguished Flying Cross. The DFC citation stated that, "Cernan completed a space flight of seventy-two hours and twenty-one minutes for a total of forty-seven orbits. The primary objectives of this mission were rendezvous, and docking with the ATDA, and the extravehicular activity of Commander Cernan. The professional competence, aerial skill and devotion to duty displayed by Commander Cernan reflect great credit upon himself and the United States Naval Service."

Captain Eugene A. Cernan recently authored the book, *The Last Man on the Moon* and was featured in the Ron Howard film, *In the Shadow of the Moon.*

After this mission, Cernan was the Lunar Module pilot of *Apollo X* and the commander of *Apollo XVII.* While traveling in space, he flew to the moon twice, was the second American to walk in space and was the last man to leave his footprints on the moon.[33]

For his historic exploits, Captain Cernan has been honored in myriad ways. In addition to the Distinguished Flying Cross and several top naval and NASA awards, he was inducted into the US Space Hall of Fame. He was also awarded the FAA's Wright Brothers Master Pilot Award and the 2007 Lindbergh Spirit Award.

Since he last walked on the surface of the moon, Cernan has devoted nearly four decades of his life to the promotion, planning and development of future space travel. In the spirit of exploration, he has become well known for his challenge to the next generations of astronauts. Gene Cernan has stated, "Too many years have passed for me to still be the last man to have left his footprints on the moon. I believe with all my heart that somewhere out there is a young boy or girl with indomitable will and courage who will lift that dubious distinction from my shoulders and take us back where we belong. Let us give that dream a chance." [34]

Photographs courtesy of:

Page 268: President George Herbert Walker Bush
Page 270: National Museum of the United States Air Force
Page 271: Aleda E. Lutz VA Medical Center, Saginaw, Michigan
Page 272: The Family of Hamilton "Mac" McWhorter
Page 273: National Museum of the United States Air Force
Page 274: Donald Kilburg, Jr.
Page 275: National Museum of the United States Air Force
Page 276: Flying Leatherneck Museum
Page 277: Flying Leatherneck Museum
Page 278: The Major Albert C. Seabourn Korean War Collection
Page 279: Hsichun "Mike" Hua
Page 280: San Diego Air & Space Museum
Page 281: NASA
Page 282: NASA
Page 283: James McDivitt
Page 284: Tailhook Association
Page 285: National Museum of the United States Air Force
Page 286: Dick Rutan
Page 287: Richard A. Cody
Page 288: Paul W. Tibbets, IV.
Page 289: NASA

Notes

[1] President George Herbert Walker Bush, Distinguished Flying Cross citation, action date: 2 September 1944, Archives, the Distinguished Flying Cross Society, San Diego, CA.

[2] Timothy J. Chistmann, "Vice President Bush Called World War II Experience 'Sobering'." *Naval Aviation News*, March-April 1985, Naval Historical Center, Department of the Navy, Washington DC.

[3] Ibid..

[4] *Benjamin O. Davis: Brigadier General United States Army*, 20 May 1999, Arlington National Cemetery website, [www.arlingtoncemetery.net/bodavisjr.htm]. Accessed on 13 March 2011.

[5] General Benjamin O. Davis, Distinguished Flying Cross citation, action date: 9 June 1944, Archives, the Distinguished Flying Cross Society, San Diego, CA.

[6] *Aleda E. Lutz, World War II Female Army Nurse Corps, Remembered This Veteran's Day 2010*, United States Department of Veterans Affairs, 2010 [http://www.saginaw.va.gov/SAGINAW/features/Aleda_E_LutzWorld War II_Female_Army_Nurse_Corps_Remembered_This_Veterans_Day_2010.asp] Accessed on 13 March 2011.

[7] Lt. Aleda E. Lutz, Distinguished Flying Cross citation, action date: 1 November 1944, Archives, the Distinguished Flying Cross Society, San Diego, CA.

[8] Commander Hamilton McWhorter, Distinguished Flying Cross citations, action dates: 11 November 1943, 29 January 1944, 16-17 February 1944, 16 February 1945, 10 May 1945, Archives, the Distinguished Flying Cross Society, San Diego, CA.

[9] C.E. Daniel, *A Reel Real Hero: James "Jimmy" Maitland Stewart*, [http://www.danielsww2.com/JimmyStewart. html] Accessed on 13 March 2011.

[10] General James M. Stewart, Distinguished Flying Cross citations, action dates: 20 February 1944 and 27 May 1944, Archives, the Distinguished Flying Cross Society, San Diego, CA.

[11] First Lieutenant John Edwards and First Lieutenant Donald Kilburg, Distinguished Flying Cross citations, action date: 24 December 1944, Archives, the Distinguished Flying Cross Society, San Diego, CA.

[12] Colonel Francis Gabreski, Distinguished Flying Cross citations: Eleven citations, 1943-1944 and two citations, 1951-1952, Archives, the Distinguished Flying Cross Society, San Diego, CA.

[13] General Joseph Foss, Distinguished Flying Cross citation, action dates: 13-20 October 1942, Medal of Honor citation, action dates: 9 October to 19 November 1942, 15 January and 25 January 1943, Archives, the Distinguished Flying Cross Society, San Diego, CA.

[14] Lieutenant Jerry Coleman, Distinguished Flying Cross citations, action dates: 13 March 1945 and 16 May 1945, Archives, the Distinguished Flying Cross Society, San Diego, CA.

[15] Jerry Coleman, *The Yankees Are Up There, but Not as High*, unpublished paper by Jerry Coleman, undated, Archives, the Distinguished Flying Cross Society.

[16] Ibid..

[17] Major Albert C. Sebourn, General Orders #160, 8th United States Army, Korea, 22 March 1951, Archives, the Distinguished Flying Cross Society, San Diego, CA.

[18] Gerald L. Vincent, ed., *U-2 Landing at Cortez (3 August 1959)*, EAA Chapter 1451 [http://www.cortezeaa 1451.org] Accessed on 13 March 2011.

[19] Major Hsichun "Mike" Hua, Chinese Air Force of Taiwan, Distinguished Flying Cross citation, action date: 3 August 1959, Archives, the Distinguished Flying Cross Society, San Diego, CA.

[20] *Jacqueline Cochran*, US Air Force [http://www.af.mil/information/heritage/person.asp?dec=&pid=123006481] Accessed on 16 March 2011.

[21] Colonel Jacqueline Cochran, Distinguished Flying Cross citations, action dates: 1947-1951 April 1962, May-June, 1964, Archives, the Distinguished Flying Cross Society, San Diego, CA.

[22] Colonel John Glenn, Distinguished Flying Cross citations, action dates: 21-29 August 1944, 2-14 November 1944, 12 July 1953, 19 July 1953, 16 July 1957 and 20 February 1962, Archives, the Distinguished Flying Cross Society, San Diego, CA.

[23] Captain James A. Lovell, Jr., Distinguished Flying Cross citations, action dates: 4 December 1965 and 11-15 November 1966, Archives, the Distinguished Flying Cross Society, San Diego, CA.

[24] Captain James A. Lovell, Jr. Oral history interview, 2 March 2010, interviewed by Dr. Barry A. Lanman, Historian, Distinguished Flying Cross Society, The Distinguished Flying Cross Society Oral History Collection, the Distinguished Flying Cross Society, San Diego, CA.

[25] General James McDivitt, Distinguished Flying Cross citations, action dates: circa 1952-1953 and 3-7 June 1965, Archives, the Distinguished Flying Cross Society, San Diego, CA.

[26] Vice Admiral James Bond Stockdale, Distinguished Flying Cross citations, action dates: 2-5 August 1964 and 11 October 1966, Archives, the Distinguished Flying Cross Society, San Diego, CA.

[27] Colonel Leo Thorsness, Distinguished Flying Cross citations, action dates: 2 December 1966 to 18 April 1967, Archives, the Distinguished Flying Cross Society, San Diego, CA.

[28] Lieutenant Colonel Dick Rutan, Distinguished Flying Cross citations, action dates: 20 November 1967, 14 February 1968, 6 March 1968, 17 May 1968 and 2 July 1968, Archives, the Distinguished Flying Cross Society, San Diego, CA.

[29] Dick Rutan, *Voyager*, 2010 [http://www.dickrutan.com/voyager.html] Accessed on 13 March 2011.

[30] General Richard A. Cody, Distinguished Flying Cross citation, action date: 14-17 January 1991, Archives, the Distinguished Flying Cross Society, San Diego, CA.

[31] *Brigadier General Paul W. Tibbets*, Jr., US Air Force [http://www.af.mil/information/bios/bio.asp?bioID=7387] Accessed on 13 March 2011.

[32] Colonel Paul W. Tibbets, IV, Distinguished Flying Cross citation, action date: 8 April 1999, Archives, the Distinguished Flying Cross Society, San Diego, CA.

[33] Captain Eugene A. Cernan, USN, Distinguished Flying Cross citation, action date: 3-6 June 1966, Archives, the Distinguished Flying Cross Society, San Diego, CA.

[34] Captain Eugene A. Cernan, USN, *GeneCernan.com, The Official Website of the Last Man on the Moon*, http://www.marklarson. Com/genecernan/*bio.html*., Accessed on 2 September 2011.

Chapter 7

The Distinguished Flying Cross Society

The Distinguished Flying Cross Society
Preserving the Memory – Sharing the Heritage

From his experience in World War I, Senator Hiram Bingham developed a vision which led to the creation of the Distinguished Flying Cross in 1926. With similar foresight, another man recognized the need for an organization dedicated to recipients of the Distinguished Flying Cross and the family members of those who have received this prestigious honor.

Alexander D. Ciurczak, a retired Air Force Captain who was twice awarded the Distinguished Flying Cross in World War II, could not locate an organization that was dedicated to the DFC. Ciurczak, known to everyone as Al, best explained how he carried forth with incredible determination, in order to turn an idea into a national organization.

"It all started with an advertisement in the *Retired Officers Magazine* of September 1993. The ad read as follows:

> **USAF Distinguished Flying Cross**
> Is there an organization or society whose members have been awarded the USAF DFC? If not, why not? I would be willing to start one.
> Write: A.D. Ciurczak,
> 34552 Camino Capistrano
> Capistrano Beach, CA 92624-1232

With many individual responses, a letter from an editor of a military-oriented magazine and the Defense Department indicating there was no record of an organization made up of members who were awarded the DFC, a handwritten letter-writing campaign began. Letters went to HQ Air Force, HQ AFMPC/DPMASSA, Randolph AFB, Texas, the Legion of Valor Association, Airmen Memorial Museum, the Chief of Staff, US Air Force and any other address that sounded promising. Several negative responses almost led to abandonment and it wasn't until a reply was received from General Merrill A. McPeak, Chief of Staff, USAF, that he felt the Society could become a reality.[1]

The Chief of Staff's letter got the program going again. Letters went to every organization relating to aviation that could be found. In the meantime, the local library came in handy and solved the problem of how to get a non-profit organization started. Then we had to deal with the development of the articles of incorporation and the bylaws. About this time, wishes to win the lottery or have a family lawyer/friend to help were in order. Talk about paperwork! There were letters and forms to the Secretary of State, the IRS, phone calls, applications more complicated than income tax forms, etc.

Finally, in April of 1994, a letter from the Secretary of State indicated that the approval process was officially started, which meant the paperwork was forwarded to the IRS for review. Then more forms… then a letter from the IRS saying the review could take up to 100 days.

The letter-writing campaign continued with lists from '*Who's Who*' and a list of Vietnam organizations supplied by the Chief of Public Affairs in the Pentagon. The most disappointing aspect of this campaign was to find that none of the services maintained a listing of DFC recipients.

Meanwhile, individuals responded to notices placed in newsletters such as *Kings Cliffe*, published by the 20th Fighter Group Association; *Military*, published in California and covering all branches; *Journal*, published by the Second Air Division Association; *WWII Air Commando*, published by that association and *Flak News*, published by the 398th Bomb Group (H) Memorial Association.

It wasn't until 31 May 1994 that the Distinguished Flying Cross Society received recognition from the California Secretary of State. Then on 6 June 1994, the Internal Revenue Service gave its approval for a non-profit, tax-free organization under Section 501 (C) (19) of the Internal Revenue Code."[2]

The DFCS was Inaugurated on the Fiftieth Anniversary of D-Day

On the auspicious fiftieth anniversary of D-Day, the Distinguished Flying Cross Society became an official non-profit organization. In actuality, the real work of creating a fraternal society had just gotten under way. The first Board of Directors consisted of the following members and provided the direction for the DFC Society: Al Ciurczak, Bill Coats, Jack Mates and Wayne Turner.

Ciurczak's basement served as the initial headquarters for the fledgling organization. The formative meetings were held at Ciurczak's house in Capistrano Beach, California or in the homes of the other board members in San Diego. However, as the group swelled to twenty members, a suitable hotel was found for the gathering of DFC recipients.

While the base of the organization was in Southern California, written communication and telephone correspondence was conducted throughout all fifty states and Canada. As the months progressed, meetings were held and plans were developed for a convention. With the concentration of membership in San Diego, that location seemed the logical selection.

Al Ciurczak founded the Distinguished Flying Cross Society in 1994.

The first convention was held in San Diego, California in October 1996 at the Town and County Resort Hotel and concluded with a banquet on the final evening. It was attended by 275 people; a number which exceeded all expectations and got the DFC Society off to a successful start. Even more importantly, the organization accomplished its goal of bringing together the first significant group of individuals with a common background and purpose.[3]

The DFCS Matures Into a Respected National Organization

As the DFC Society's membership grew, so did its goals. In the first decade of its existence, the society had 4,100 members and created an Honor Roll listing its recipients on the organization's website (www.dfcsociety.org). As of the present time, the DFC Society has more than 5,700 members. To guide the Society and help focus its goals and objectives, a Mission Statement, Vision Statement and Statement of Heritage was developed (enclosed at the end of the chapter) along with the Society bylaws.[4]

The current bylaws state, "Regular members are individuals who have been awarded the Distinguished Flying Cross and have joined the Society. They are required to maintain membership in the National DFCS in order to be members of a regional chapter." Associate members are "spouses, relatives and descendants of individuals who were awarded the Distinguished Flying Cross and are members of the DFCS." Associate members are also required to maintain membership in the National DFCS in order to be members of a regional chapter.

To further the history and traditions of the men and women who were awarded the Distinguished Flying Cross, the Society

The DFCS Scholarship Fund was named after Ward Macauley.

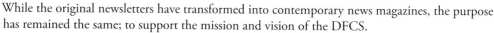

While the original newsletters have transformed into contemporary news magazines, the purpose
has remained the same; to support the mission and vision of the DFCS.

established the Ward Macauley Scholarship Fund in 1998 which has made financial awards annually to
deserving descendants of DFCS members. The program was first endowed by Lydia Macauley and named
in honor of her husband, Ward Macauley.[5]

Based on the success of the initial DFCS gathering, the organization has held biennial conventions
in various locations throughout the United States to reunite recipients of the Distinguished Flying Cross.
Each convention has included various programs, lectures, tours and other activities which have provided a
forum for patriotic, historical and social endeavors.

A DFCS news magazine is published three times a year to keep members informed of Society activities
and to highlight personal accounts of its members' exploits. As compared to the first mimeographed
newsletters, the contemporary news magazines, featuring color graphics and photographs, are digitally
produced and shared throughout the international aviation community.

Regional Chapters are Established

Shortly after the inception of the Society, it was determined that regional chapters were necessary. As
a model, the Lindbergh Chapter in San Diego was established and chapters were added as time progressed.
The DFC Society currently has twenty-two regional chapters.

At the chapter level, there is active recruitment for new members supported by regularly scheduled
social functions and civic endeavors. Each chapter pursues the national organization's goals in their own
unique way. They interact with their local communities and museums, establish memorials, talk with
young people, start their own scholarship programs, sell memorabilia and work with other local veterans
organizations. All of these efforts increase the awareness and importance of the Distinguished Flying
Cross.[6]

Desert Fliers Command Chapter
Palm Springs, California
Fort Walton Beach Pitsenbarger Chapter
Fort Walton, Florida
Great Plains Chapter
Papillion, Nebraska
Inland Empire Chapter
Riverside, California
Ira Eaker Chapter
Jacksonville, Arkansas
Kentuckiana Chapter
Louisville, Kentucky
Las Vegas Wings Chapter
Las Vegas, Nevada
Lewis and Clark Chapter
Milwaukie, Oregon
Mid-America Chapter
Wichita, Kansas
North Texas Chapter
Plano, Texas
Northwest Chapter of DFCS
Puyallup, Washington
Orange County California Chapter
San Clemente, California
Pensacola Chapter of DFCS
Pensacola, Florida
San Antonio Alamo Chapter
San Antonio, Texas
San Diego Lindbergh Chapter
San Diego, California
Southeast Florida Chapter
Hollywood, Florida
Southwestern Ohio Chapter
Troy, Ohio
Tampa Bay Area Chapter
New Port Richey, Florida
The Villages DFCS Chapter
The Villages, Florida
Tucson Arizona Chapter
Mariana, Arizona
Wilbur Wright Nation's Capitol Region Chapter
Lanham, Maryland
Wiregrass Chapter
Ozark, Alabama

Members of the Wilbur Wright Nation's Capitol Region Chapter meet near the College Park Airport, College Park, Maryland. The airport was one of the first in the country.

The San Diego Lindbergh Chapter has been highly active in southern California for more than seventeen years.

The Ira Eaker Chapter, like most chapters, participates in parades. These events serve to educate the public about the importance of the Distinguished Flying Cross.

The Society's Role in Preserving the History and the Heritage of the Distinguished Flying Cross

The Capistrano Beach Memorial was dedicated in 2002 and overlooks the Pacific Ocean.

The development of memorials honoring the Distinguished Flying Cross and its recipients has been a major undertaking for the DFC Society. The first memorial to the Distinguished Flying Cross was unveiled on 21 September 2002. The bronze plaque, embedded with an actual DFC medal, is located in Pines Park, Capistrano Beach, Dana Point, California. It captures the essence of the award and its initial recipients.[7]

The Distinguished Flying Cross Society's second memorial was the result of the Society's participation in the National Aviation and Space Exploration Wall of Honor. The Wall is a permanent memorial at the National Air and Space Museum's Steven F. Udvar-Hazy Center that recognizes those with a passion for flight. The DFC Society donated four metallic foils (plaques). Three of the foils list 750 names of DFC Society members who made a substantial contribution to the Wall of Honor. The fourth panel includes an engraving of a Distinguished Flying Cross medal and a brief dedication statement.

The Distinguished Flying Cross Society foils stand in association with other groups and notables associated with flight. Therefore, thousands of visitors each year witness the significance of the Distinguished Flying Cross. The money raised from the donations for the Wall of Honor were dedicated to the preservation of the world's largest and most historic collection of aircraft, spacecraft and related artifacts.[8]

In 2004, the Distinguished Flying Cross Society's third memorial was dedicated on Veterans Day at the Palm Springs Air Museum, Palm Springs, California. The striking memorial was placed to the right of the museum's entrance and sponsored by the Desert Fliers Command Chapter. Bob Pond and Dick Parker, along with several other contributors, were responsible for this tribute to all DFC recipients.[9]

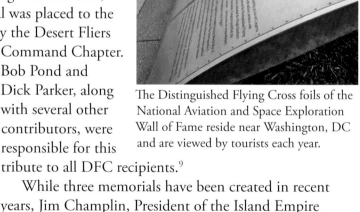

The Distinguished Flying Cross foils of the National Aviation and Space Exploration Wall of Fame reside near Washington, DC and are viewed by tourists each year.

The Distinguished Flying Cross Memorial greets patrons of the Palm Springs Air Museum.

While three memorials have been created in recent years, Jim Champlin, President of the Island Empire Chapter of the DFCS, realized the need for a national monument. With total dedication and focus, Champlin established the DFC National Memorial Committee to plan, fund and create an appropriate memorial. In addition to Jim Champlin, who served as National Chairman of the DFC National Memorial Fund, Eric Lindbergh, son of Charles A. Lindbergh, agreed to support the cause as honorary co-chairman. March Field Air

Museum in Riverside, California was selected as the site and it is in close proximity to the Medal of Honor and POW/MIA Memorials at the Riverside National Cemetery

After a major fundraising campaign, the designs were selected and artist/sculptor, Robert Henderson, was commissioned to create the bronze sculptures which included the Distinguished Flying Cross medal and ribbon, the *Spirit of St. Louis* and the Loening OA-1A aircraft. Tiles commemorating individual DFC recipients are an important part of the memorial, along with six large granite panels containing individual stories of heroism and a donor wall.[10]

While the planning and construction phases were taking place, Congressman Kenneth S. Calvert of the Riverside district introduced a bill into the House of Representatives to designate a Distinguished Flying Cross National Memorial at the March Field Air Museum (H.R. 2788). The bill in the House was passed unanimously in the spring of 2010 but was never passed in the Senate.

The Distinguished Flying Cross National Memorial was constructed at the March Field Air Museum in Riverside, California and dedicated on 27 October 2010.

It is currently being introduced again in both the House and the Senate. It is important to note that while many national memorials have been constructed with public funds, this endeavor was paid for by private and corporate donations without any cost to the American tax-payer.

The official dedication of the DFC National Memorial was conducted during the Society's National Convention in Riverside, California on 27 October 2010. The ultimate purpose of the monument is to honor, on a national scale, all Distinguished Flying Cross recipients for their, "extraordinary achievement and/or heroism while participating in aerial flight in service to their country."[11]

To preserve the individual biographies of the Distinguished Flying Cross, the DFCS Oral History Program was created in 2002. Since that time, more than 130 oral history interviews have been recorded in digital video. The collection is maintained at the organization's national headquarters and interview transcriptions have been produced, as time and funding permits. The collection is the largest source of individual accounts focused on the Distinguished Flying Cross.

In accordance with the development of memorials and the Oral History Program, the creation of museum displays have been another way in which the DFC Society has promoted its goals of educating the public about this military award. For example, the San Diego Air & Space Museum currently displays an original painting created for General E. Yul Yoon depicting a mission involving the destruction of the Seunghori Railroad Bridge in Pyongyang, the capital of North Korea. For those actions, as a

An artist's conception of General Yoon's DFC mission.

Ruth Mayer, painted the *Distinguished Flying Cross* to honor the military aviators who have protected the American way of life.

Republic of Korea (ROK) aviator, General Yoon received a DFC from the United States Government.

The Distinguished Flying Cross Society has also embraced the technology of the electronic media as a means of achieving its goals to educate the public. The DFCS website displays extensive information about the DFC medal, the Society and its members. An Honor Roll lists all members of the Society with many citations that depict the personal circumstances of being awarded this prestigious medal. A distinctive collection of DFCS gifts and emblems are also available on the website.

Video presentations are currently under production to provide interactive displays at a variety of museum venues relating to aviation history. The production of a television documentary is also in the planning stages and will, hopefully, become a reality.

One of the most creative and enduring ways in which the Distinguished Flying Cross and its recipients were immortalized was with the creation of a painting by American Master Artist, Ruth Mayer. Her husband, Randy Holden, described Mayer's reaction when Art Overman, a DFCS Board Member and long-time owner of a Mayer original, asked if she would accept the commission to honor the members of the Distinguished Flying Cross Society. "Ruth was not hesitant for a second - as she herself is a pilot, intimately aware of the unique contributions made by those who have love of flight."[12]

The painting, *Distinguished Flying Cross*, portrays a visual journey of America's history in military aviation and includes twenty-one DFC recipients and twenty-two aircraft. Holden continued to say that, "…renowned individuals in Distinguished Flying Cross history such as Charles A. Lindbergh and Amelia Earhart are included; however, many others with names not known to the American public are revered for their heroic contributions and epic bravery."

The painting was unveiled on Veteran's Day, 11 November 2007, in the Pavilion of Flight at the San Diego Air & Space Museum. Participants at the unveiling appropriately passed the only flying replica of Lindbergh's *Spirit of St. Louis* on their way to the special event. Attendees included many members of the DFC Society, some of whom appeared in the painting. They were unaware of their inclusion until the magnificent painting was unveiled with a stirring

American Master Artist, Ruth Mayer.

military ceremony.

Ruth Mayer donated the original painting to the Distinguished Flying Cross Society and it is on perpetual public display in the San Diego Air & Space Museum. She also allowed giclee prints and lithographs to be made from the original, in order to provide financial support for the Society. As a result of her passion and commitment to the DFCS, Ruth was made an Honorary Member of the Society.[13]

The critical acclaim of the painting has been astounding and the response from the public overwhelming. However, the appreciation expressed by DFC recipients has been the real story that touched Mayer's heart. For example, so taken by Ruth Mayer's painting, Ben Games, Ph.D., purchased several special edition prints and a DFCS Flag for each print. He then donated them to various military museums on behalf of the Society.[14]

Focusing on the Past, Present and Future: The Importance of the Distinguished Flying Cross Society_____

Dr. Robert "Bob" Frantz, former president and former chairman of the board of the Distinguished Flying Cross Society, expresses to members and the general public interested in DFC history, "We were pilots, bombardiers, navigators, radiomen, gunners, photographers and many other support personnel (including nurses) who were recognized for heroism and extraordinary achievement in aerial flight."[15]

The current DFCS Chairman of the Board, Bill Bradfield, added that, "the Society was established to give its members, who shared a piece of aviation history, the opportunity to meet in fellowship through its chapters, conventions and activities. In addition, one of the Society's visions is to educate the public about the Distinguished Flying Cross and the way in which its recipients impacted the course of American history. To accomplish this, the society works with museums, schools, community groups and other associations in order to ensure that this rich history endures along with the legacy of the DFC. I am proud and honored to represent nearly 6,000 DFC recipients in the Distinguished Flying Cross Society as the chairman of the board."[16]

The current President of the DFCS, Chuck Sweeney, shared his own perspectives which echoed the sentiments of the DFCS membership. "As recipients of the DFC, we are proud and honored but also humbled by the award because we believe we were only doing what we were trained to do. We represent many others who also deserved the medal but weren't awarded it for various reasons including making the ultimate sacrifice. While we wear the DFC with pride, we will never forget the maintenance and support personnel who enabled us to perform the missions successfully. The Distinguished Flying Cross Society is not about ego building but about capturing the personal stories of these fantastic events so that future generations will know what tremendous sacrifices military aviation personnel have made."[17]

Bill Bradfield, the current DFCS Chairman of the Board.

Jack Mates, a founding member of the DFC Society and Chairman Emeritus of the Board, summarized the importance of establishing the Distinguished Flying Cross Society. "You have to give an endless amount of credit to our founder, Al Ciurczak. The fact that the government did not keep a cumulative listing of DFC recipients meant that all of us who received the award would have otherwise gone on our merry way through life unaware of the many wonderful stories, deeds, happenings and lessons learned that helped us do our part in making this the greatest country on the planet.[18]

It is only by looking back on these lessons that the younger generations, their children and their children's children, can learn to make this world a better and safer place for all of mankind. So to all who have received the Distinguished Flying Cross, wear it proudly and know that you are a member of an elite group of persons who have contributed mightily to this great country."[19]

While the DFCS founder, Al Ciurczak, is no longer with us, his memory, his dream and his vision still provides guidance and inspiration to this vital organization. Like the Distinguished Flying Cross, the legacy he established continues to honor our heroes *On Heroic Wings*.

Mission Statement

The Distinguished Flying Cross Society is dedicated to the preservation, promotion and dissemination of the history and the heritage pertaining to the Distinguished Flying Cross and its recipients.

Vision Statement

Through the development of a strong national organization and active regional chapters, The Distinguished Flying Cross Society will:

1. Educate the general public about the Distinguished Flying Cross and the ways in which recipients impacted the course of American history by documenting, publishing, disseminating and preserving its history and heritage
2. Promote fraternity and fellowship among Distinguished Flying Cross recipients of all services, ranks, genders and races
3. Promote philanthropic endeavors supporting American values and ideals associated with The Distinguished Flying Cross Society
4. Acquire funding from internal and external sources in order to accomplish the mission, the vision and the goals of The Distinguished Flying Cross Society.

Statement of Heritage

Awarded to aviators and aircrew for heroism and/or extraordinary achievement during aerial flight, the Distinguished Flying Cross is the only medal conferred by all five military services, in all wars and campaigns from World War I to the present.

"May the Distinguished Flying Cross Society continue to build its membership of those who have earned the Distinguished Flying Cross and those who will be awarded the DFC in the future."

Alexander D. Ciurczak

Photographs courtesy of the Distinguished Flying Cross Society except for the following:

Page 297: Top, Wilbur Wright Nation's Capitol Region Chapter
Page 297: Middle, San Diego Lindbergh Chapter
Page 297: Bottom, Ira Eaker Chapter
Page 300: Ruth Mayer

Notes

[1] Al Ciurczak, Jack Mates and Michael O'Neil, editors, *The Distinguished Flying Cross Society*, (Paducah, CA: Turner Publishing Company, 2002), 16.

[2] Ibid., 16-17.

[3] Alexander D. Ciurczak, *The Flying Cross News and Review*, Newsletter, Convention Issue, No. 7, January 1997, (San Diego, CA: The Distinguished Flying Cross Society), 1-4.

[4] "Chapter Information," The Distinguished Flying Cross Society website, available from http://www.dfcsociety.org.

[5] Jack Mates, informal interview by Dr. Barry A. Lanman, 15 July 2010, San Diego, CA., notes, Archives, Distinguished Flying Cross Archives, San Diego, CA.

[6] "Regions," The Distinguished Flying Cross Society website, available from http://www.dfcsociety.org.

[7] Ciurczak, Mates and O'Neil, 10.

[8] "Memorials," The Distinguished Flying Cross Society website, available from http://www.dfcsociety.org.

[9] Chuck Sweeney, informal interview by Dr. Barry A. Lanman, 22 July 2010, San Diego, CA., notes, Archives, Distinguished Flying Cross Archives, San Diego, CA.

[10] Jim Champlin, informal interview by Dr. Barry A. Lanman, 26 July 2010, San Diego, CA., notes, Archives, Distinguished Flying Cross Archives, San Diego, CA.

[11] Ibid.

[12] Randy Holden, informal interview by Dr. Barry A. Lanman and Dr. Laura M. Wendling, 28 July 2010, Laguna Beach, CA., notes, Archives, Distinguished Flying Cross Archives, San Diego, CA.

[13] "Chapter Information," The Distinguished Flying Cross Society website, available from http://www.dfc society.org. Accessed 8 July 2011.

[14] Ibid.

[15] Ciurczak, Mates and O'Neil, 9.

[16] Bill Bradfield, unpublished notes, July 2010, Archives, Distinguished Flying Cross Archives, San Diego, CA.

[17] Chuck Sweeney, informal interview by Dr. Barry A. Lanman, 22 July 2010, San Diego, CA., notes, Archives, Distinguished Flying Cross Archives, San Diego, CA.

[18] Al Ciurczak, Jack Mates and Michael O'Neil, *The Distinguished Flying Cross Society*, (Paducah, CA: Turner Publishing Company, 2002), 8.

[19] Ibid., 8.

Epilogue

On a quest to circumnavigate Central and South America just five months following the enactment of the Distinguished Flying Cross, the Pan American Good Will Flight headed aloft with five aircraft. At the conclusion of a 21,000 mile journey, four planes returned to American soil with eight Army Air Corps pilots. Two of the men gave their lives in order to accomplish the mission and establish international relationships through aviation. For their courageous efforts while advancing the science of flight, the entire assemblage was honored with the first award of Distinguished Flying Cross citations. However, medals with the symbolic four-bladed propeller and cross were not part of the official ceremony as they had yet to be struck.

It was in San Diego, California, during the same relative era as the Pan American Good Will Flight, that the vision and dreams of a young airmail pilot and Army Air Corps reserve lieutenant, Charles Lindbergh, were shaped and crafted into the lovely silver lines of the Ryan Aeronautical Company's *Spirit of St. Louis*. The Lone Eagle and his plane – a partnership he referred to as "We" – vaulted across the Atlantic in 1927. In doing so, Lindbergh not only won the coveted Orteig Prize, he became the recipient of the very first Distinguished Flying Cross medal. From these historic events, the Distinguished Flying Cross was imbued with the integrity, courage, and spirit of great aviators. They established a standard by which all who have received the DFC have been measured and found deserving.

As a Naval Academy alumnus and the father of two Air Force Academy graduates and pilots, I try to find some common ground between my experiences in the Navy and my sons' experiences in the Air Force. It is not always easy. The cultures of the services, including the Army and Marine Corps and Coast Guard, sometimes seem more disconnected than connected. Certainly the missions are the same: Protect America and defend her against all enemies, foreign and domestic. It was an oath I took many years ago, an oath my sons took not that long ago, and an oath every soldier, sailor, airman, Marine and Coast Guardsman takes when they agree to set aside their civilian clothes for the uniform of the United States Armed Forces.

But beyond that noble oath, what binds us as a fighting force? What experience links warriors to one another in those moments when the pulsating glow of anti-aircraft and missile fire defines the fine line between life and death? What medallions proclaim commitment to a cause...faith in a principle...and fidelity to brothers-in-arms? Medals of Honor...Yes. Silver and Bronze Stars...unquestionably. Purple Hearts...of course. However, when it comes to valor in the skies, when it comes to recognizing the men and women who hurl themselves into the cauldron of aerial combat, the Distinguished Flying Cross is an honor unlike any other. Its recipients are American legends.

The American novelist, Herman Melville, once wrote, "We cannot live only for ourselves. A thousand fibers connect us with our fellow men; and among those fibers, as sympathetic threads, our actions run as causes, and they come back to us as effects." The actions of the men and woman who wear the Distinguished Flying Cross were caused by their selflessness in the face of personal peril; the effects of their actions were no less than the saving of lives and the protection of freedom.

During my service in Vietnam, I witnessed the heroic acts of aviators, rotary and fixed-wing pilots alike. They risked their lives to save lives in order to bring supplies to embattled outposts, to rescue downed pilots, to fly mercy missions to villages deep in enemy-held countryside. I watched vulnerable forward air controllers in single engine O-1s and O-2s work down to the treetops to mark targets for the "fast-movers" who themselves often took such pains to be on target that they left themselves exposed to ground-fire and SAMs. They would put themselves in harm's way to protect a River Rat like me, or a downed Air Force pilot a long way from home, or any comrade in uniform.

I was on the receiving end of support from slicks and Sandys and gunships, and I saw first-hand the compassion and "gutsiness" of aircrews flying into the fires of hell itself to snatch victory from defeat at great personal risk. Their actions remind me of a quote by John F. Kennedy from his book, *Profiles in Courage*, "For without belittling the courage with which men have died, we should not forget those acts of courage with which men have lived…A man does what he must, in spite of personal consequences, in spite of obstacles and dangers and pressures, and that is the basis of all human morality."

Today, American aircrews in every service continue the noble tradition of aerial bravery, performing with courage, heroism, and sacrifice: Navy and Marine Carrier pilots are patrolling the oceans – protecting our fleet – and flying countless sorties in Operation Iraqi Freedom and Operation Enduring Freedom.

Our Air Force Pilots are on the tip of Democracy's strategic spear, ready at a moment's notice to project our Nation's airpower to the far reaches of the globe. They are also guardian angels flying wounded troops home from the battlefield to Germany and then the States for care in the operating rooms at Walter Reed, Bethesda, and other fine military and VA hospitals across the country.

Our Army pilots take the fight to the enemy at 100-feet or fewer – often at night, under fire, in every terrain imaginable; but they also fly missions of mercy, carrying their wounded colleagues to field hospitals in life-saving time. Coast Guard aircrews brave incredible forces of nature to rescue hapless sailors, and they are tireless in their around-the-clock vigil over the security of our shores.

The Distinguished Flying Cross is bestowed on the best of the best – aviators whose aerial skills and indomitable courage propel them to the windswept heights of glory. Their citations are touchstones of courage, honor and pride representing generations of pilots…grandfathers, fathers, mothers, sons, daughters, and spouses who were born with wings on their hearts.

Antoine St. Exupery, an early 20th century aviator who was as elegant with his pen as he was graceful with an airplane wrote, "Although human life is priceless, we always act as if something had an even greater price than life. But what is that something?" I believe the answer is in every house where there lives a man or woman who has been awarded the Distinguished Flying Cross. The answer resides in every final resting place of a hero who gave his or her life in one final moment of flight. The Distinguished Flying Cross is not just about saving a life; it is about saving the way of life that we know as Democracy. A way of life blessed with the rights and freedoms that make our nation great.

By the selfless acts of aerial bravery, the Distinguished Flying Cross recipients secured freedom for all of us. They are our heroes and I thank them. All Americans should thank them.

Anthony Principi

The Honorable Anthony J. Principi
Secretary of Veterans Affairs, 1992-1993 & 2001-2005
Vietnam Combat Veteran, United States Navy
Honorary Member of the Distinguished Flying Cross Society

Photographic and Research Acknowledgements

Groups and Organizations

Coronado Library
Distinguished Flying Cross Society
Flying Leatherneck Museum
Library of Congress
Mighty 8th Air Force Museum, Savannah, Georgia
National Aviation and Space Administration
National Archives
National Historical Foundation
National Museum of the United States Air Force
National Naval Aviation Museum
National Personnel Records Center, Military Personnel Records
National World War I Museum
San Diego Air & Space Museum
Smithsonian Air and Space Museum
Tailhook Association
United States Air Force
United States Army
United States Army Aviation Museum
United States Coast Guard
United States Coast Guard Aviation Association
United States Coast Guard Historian Office
United States Marine Corps
United States Navy
Yale University Manuscripts & Archives Digital Images Database

Photographic and Research Acknowledgements

Individuals

Jeffrey Bowdoin, Collections Manager, United States Coast Guard Historian's Office, Forestville, Maryland

Jim Champlin, Chair, The Distinguished Flying Cross National Memorial Committee

Captain Charles F. Hahn, USCG, Retired, Researcher for United States Coast Guard Aviation Association

Bob Krone, Board Member, Distinguished Flying Cross Society

Dr. Barry A. Lanman, Historian and oral history interviewer, Distinguished Flying Cross Society

Jack Matz, Past-President, Distinguished Flying Cross Society

Dr. Charles P. McDowell, Past-President, The Orders and Medals Society of America

Michael O'Neil, Past-President, Distinguished Flying Cross Society

Reed Phillips, Chair, Oral History Committee, Distinguished Flying Cross Society

Catherine A. Sivils, Member, History Committee and Oral Historian, United States Coast Guard Aviation Association

Chuck Sweeney, President, the Distinguished Flying Cross Society and oral history interviewer

Dr. Laura M. Wendling, professor, College of Education, California State University San Marcos

Lucille Wendling

John D. Willard V, oral history interviewer and Associate Director, The Martha Ross Center for Oral History, University of Maryland, Baltimore County

Brennan Willard, Researcher, oral history interviewer, The Martha Ross Center for Oral History, University of Maryland, Baltimore County

Note: Unless otherwise stated in the text, photographic documentation and authority to use visual images is attributed to the Distinguished Flying Cross recipient and/or the recipient's family.

Glossary

AAA – Anti-Aircraft Artillery

Ace – A military aviator who has shot down more than five enemy aircraft.

Air Group – A unit of the United States Air Force larger than a squadron and smaller than a wing.

AIT – Advanced infantry training

Battalion – A ground force unit composed of a headquarters and two or more companies or similar units.

APAM – Antipersonnel/Antimaterial

BN – A bombardier/navigator

Bogie – An unidentified or possible enemy aircraft.

Bomb Group – The Air Force equivalent of an infantry regiment. The basic tactical control and administrative organization in all theaters of operation usually commanded by a colonel or lieutenant colonel.

Carrier Air Group – Two or more aircraft squadrons formed under one commander for administrative and tactical control of operations from a carrier.

Carrier Air Wing – an operational naval aviation organization composed of several aircraft squadrons and detachments of various types of fixed wing and rotary wing aircraft.

CASEVAC – Casualty Evacuation; The unregulated movement of casualties that can include both to and between medical treatment facilities.

CO – Commanding Officer

Coms – Short for communications (coms-out – no communication)

Company – A unit of about 100 troops, usually comprising two or more platoons.

DCNO – Deputy Chief of Naval Operations

Dihedral – A dihedral angle is the upward angle horizontal from the wings of a fixed-wing aircraft, or of any paired nominally-horizontal surfaces on any aircraft. A "buckle" that develops in a wing is called a dihedral.

Empennage – The section of the airplane that consists of the vertical stabilizer, the horizontal stabilizer, and the associated control surfaces.

FAC – Forward Air Controller

FCLP – Field Carrier Landing Practice

Feathering – Rotating the blades on variable-pitch propellers parallel to the airflow to reduce drag in case of an engine failure.

Feet dry – In air operations, a code meaning "operations over land."

Feet wet – In air operations, a code meaning "operations over water."

Flak – Anti-aircraft fire, especially as experienced by the crews of combat airplanes at which the fire is directed.

Flechette Rockets – A rocket that contains a large number of pointed steel projectiles. When the rocket is launched and explodes, the flechettes (French for little arrow or dart) can cover an area the size of a football field.

Fleet – An organization of ships, aircraft, Marine forces, and shore-based activities all under the command of a commander or commander-in-chief who may exercise operational as well as administrative control.

FLIR – Forward Looking Infrared Radar

GP Bombs – General Purpose Bombs

HARMs – High Speed Anti-radiation Missiles

HUREVAC – Hurricane Evacuation

Interdiction – Actions to divert, disrupt, delay, or destroy the enemy's military surface capability before it can be used effectively against friendly forces, or to otherwise achieve objectives. (interdiction bombing)

Jinking – Sharp maneuvering at random to avoid an enemy or enemy fire.

JOC – Joint Operation Command

Kamikaze – a fighter plane used for suicide missions by Japanese pilots in World War II. The term means "Divine Wind" in Japanese.

Lead Crew – The first/command aircraft in a formation.

LLLTV – Low Light Level Television

LOH – Light Observation Helicopter – "the hunter" of the "hunter - killer team"

LZ – Landing Zone

Mach 1 – "Mach Number" was named after the Austrian physicist Ernst Mach. Mach 1 is approximately 760 miles per hour at sea level. An airplane flying less than Mach 1 is traveling at subsonic speed, when flying faster than Mach 1 it is at supersonic speed and at Mach 2 it is traveling at twice the speed of sound.

Manual reversion – A changeover from powered controls to manual control. It may be done automatically in the event of a hydraulic failure.

MARK-77 – a type of fire bomb; a thin skinned container of fuel gel designed for use against troops that have "dug-in," supply installations, wooden structures, and land convoys. These bombs rupture on impact and spread burning fuel gel on surrounding objects.

MASH – Mobile Army Surgical Hospital

MEDEVAC – Medical Evacuation

Merchant Marine – The Merchant Marine is the fleet of ships which carries imports and exports during peacetime and becomes a naval auxiliary during wartime to deliver troops and war material.

MIA – Missing In Action

MiG – Russian-built jets

MiG Mauler – A term for an American pilot who shot down MiGs – first used in the Korean War

Napalm – Powdered aluminum soap or similar compound used to gelatinize oil or gasoline for use in napalm bombs or flame throwers.

NFR – Non-flying Officer

NOS – Night observation sight

OCS – Officer Candidate School

OPS – Abbreviation for "operations"

Port – Nautical left; directional left when facing the bow of a ship

POW – Prisoner of War - one who, while engaged in combat under orders of his or her government, is captured by the armed forces of the enemy.

R&R – Rest and Recuperation – the withdrawal from combat or duty for short periods of time.

Reserve Officer – A military officer who combines a military role or career with a civilian career and is available to serve or fight when a nation mobilizes for emergencies or military action.

ROE – Rules of Engagement

ROK – Republic of Korea

ROTC – Reserve Officer Training Corps

SAM – Surface-to-air missile

SCUD – A NATO reporting name (not an acronym) for a Soviet army short-range liquid propellant surface-to-surface ballistic missile system.

SEAL – A member of a Naval Special Warfare unit who is trained for unconventional warfare; SEAL is an acronym for Sea Air and Land.

SERE – Survival, Evasion, Resistance and Escape

Slicks – A term for helicopters that carry troops to and from battle.

Snake-eye bombs – Standard Mk 82 (unguided, low-drag general-purpose bomb) with folded, retarding petals.

SOP – Standard Operating Procedure

SPINS – Operating procedures, orders and/or special instructions

Squadron – The basic administrative aviation unit of the Army, Navy, Marine Corps, and Air Force. A squadron is also an organization consisting of two or more divisions of ships, or two or more divisions (Navy) or flights of aircraft. It is normally but not necessarily composed of ships or aircraft of the same type.

Starboard – Nautical right; directional right when facing the bow of a ship

Stealth fighter – F-117A

Tarmac – A common but inaccurate term referring to the paved areas of airports where aircraft park.

Task force – A temporary or semi-permanent grouping of units, under one commander, formed for the purpose of carrying out a specific operation or mission. A task force can also be a component of a fleet organized by the commander of a task fleet or higher authority for the accomplishment of a specific task or tasks.

TIC – Troops in Contact

Thach Weave – An aviation combat technique/tactic developed by naval aviator John S. Thach. Two fighter aircraft (side-by-side or two pairs of fighters) flying together turn in towards each other, cross paths, repeat the exercise, and bring the enemy plane into the hook's sights. Correctly executed, the Thach weave leaves little chance of escape to even the most maneuverable opponent.

Thud pilot – A term for a pilot of an F-105

Undercast – In-flight weather condition where a cloud layer of ten-tenths (1.0) coverage is viewed from an observation point above the layer.

Unit – Any military element whose structure is prescribed by competent authority, such as a table of organization and equipment; specifically, part of an organization. A unit is also an organization title of a subdivision of a group in a task force.

USA – United States Army

USAAC – United States Army Air Corps

USAAF – United States Army Air Forces

USAF – United States Air Force

USCG – United States Coast Guard

USMC – United States Marine Corps

USN – United States Navy

USS – United States Ship

Wild Weasels – Pilots dedicated to attack SAM sites during Vietnam

Willie Pete – Slang term for white phosphorus (WP), a material made from a common allotrope of the chemical element phosphorus that is used as an incendiary weapon that burns fiercely and can set combustibles on fire.

Windmilling – The action of a propeller when revolving freely under the forward airspeed of an aircraft but without engine power. The action usually causes drag and makes the aircraft difficult to control.

Wing Commander – United States Air Force duty title held by a colonel in charge of an air wing.

WST – Weapons System Test

WTO – Weapons Training Officer

X-1 Project – Project beginning in 1946 where two XS-1 experimental research aircrafts conducted pioneering tests at Muroc Army Air Field in California to obtain flight data on conditions in the transonic speed range.

USA & USAF Military Ranks

US Army

Pay Grade and Title

E-1 Private
E-2 Private 2
E-3 Private First Class
E-4 Specialist
E-4 Corporal
E-5 Sergeant
E-6 Staff Sergeant
E-7 Sergeant First Class
E-8 Master Sergeant
E-8 First Sergeant
E-9 Sergeant Major
E-9 Command Sergeant Major
E-9 Sergeant Major of the Army

W-1 Warrant Officer 1
W-2 Chief Warrant Officer 2
W-3 Chief Warrant Officer 3
W-4 Chief Warrant Officer 4
W-5 Chief Warrant Officer 5

O-1 Second Lieutenant
O-2 First Lieutenant
O-3 Captain
O-4 Major
O-5 Lieutenant Colonel
O-6 Colonel
O-7 Brigadier General
O-8 Major General
O-9 Lieutenant General
O-10 General

General of the Army (5-Star)
    Reserved for wartime only

US Air Force

Pay Grade and Title

E-1 Airman Basic
E-2 Airman
E-3 Airman First Class
E-4 Senior Airman
E-5 Staff Sergeant
E-6 Technical Sergeant
E-7 Master Sergeant / First Sergeant*
E-8 Senior Master Sergeant
E-8 First Sergeant*
E-9 Chief Master Sergeant
E-9 Command Chief Master Sergeant
E-9 Chief Master Sergeant of the
      Air Force

(No Warrant Officers)

O-1 Second Lieutenant
O-2 First Lieutenant
O-3 Captain
O-4 Major
O-5 Lieutenant Colonel
O-6 Colonel
O-7 Brigadier General
O-8 Major General
O-9 Lieutenant General
O-10 General

General of the Air Force (5-star)
Reserved for wartime only

Key: E – Enlisted   W – Warrant Officer   O – Officer   *Depends on job
Note: Some pay grades have more than one title

Source: United States Defense Department

For more data on United States Military Ranks including insignias and abbreviations, consult:
      http://www.defense.gov/specials/insignias/enlisted.html
      http://www.defense.gov/specials/insignias/officers.htm

USN, USCG & USMC Military Ranks

US Navy & Coast Guard

Pay Grade and Title

E-1 Seaman Recruit
E-2 Seaman Apprentice
E-3 Seaman
E-4 Petty Officer Third Class
E-5 Petty Officer Second Class
E-6 Petty Officer First Class
E-7 Chief Petty Officer
E-8 Senior Chief Petty Officer
E-9 Master Chief Petty Officer
E-9 Fleet / Command Master Chief Petty Officer*
E-9 Master Chief Petty Officer of the Navy
E-9 Master Chief Petty Officer of the Coast Guard

W-1 Warrant Officer
W-2 Chief Warrant Officer
W-3 Chief Warrant Officer
W-4 Chief Warrant Officer
W-5 Chief Warrant Officer

O-1 Ensign
O-2 Lieutenant, Junior Grade
O-3 Lieutenant
O-4 Lieutenant Commander
O-5 Commander
O-6 Captain
O-7 Rear Admiral – Lower half
O-8 Rear Admiral – Upper half
O-9 Vice Admiral
O-10 Admiral

Fleet Admiral   (5-Star)
     Reserved for wartime only

US Marines

Pay Grade and Title

E-1 Private
E-2 Private First Class
E-3 Lance Corporal
E-4 Corporal
E-5 Sergeant
E-6 Staff Sergeant
E-7 Gunnery Sergeant
E-8 Master Sergeant / First Sergeant*
E-9 Master Gunnery Sergeant
E-9 Sergeant major
E-9 Sergeant Major of the Marines

W-1 Warrant Officer
W-2 Chief Warrant Officer
W-3 Chief Warrant Officer
W-4 Chief Warrant Officer
W-5 Chief Warrant Officer

O-1 Second Lieutenant
O-2 First Lieutenant
O-3 Captain
O-4 Major
O-5 Lieutenant Colonel
O-6 Colonel
O-7 Brigadier General
O-8 Major General
O-9 Lieutenant General
O-10 General

Key: E – Enlisted   W – Warrant Officer   O – Officer   *Depends on job
Notes: Some pay grades have more than one title

Source: United States Defense Department

For more data on United State Military Ranks including insignias and abbreviations, consult:
        http://www.defense.gov/specials/insignias/enlisted.html
        http://www.defense.gov/specials/insignias/officers.html

Bibliography

Albion, Robert G. *Makers of Naval Policy, 1798-1947*. Annapolis, MD: Naval Institute Press, 1980.

Alexander, Joseph H., Don Horan and Norman C. Stahl. *The Battle History of the U.S. Marines*. New York, NY: Harper Collins Publishers, 1997.

Barrow, Clayton R., ed. *America Spreads Her Sails: U.S. Seapower in the 19th Century*. Annapolis, MD: Naval Institute Press, 1973.

Bartlett, Merrill L. and Jack Sweetman. *The U.S. Marine Corps: An Illustrated History*. Annapolis, MD: US Naval Institute Press, 2001.

Beach, Edward L. *The United States Navy: 200 Years*. New York, NY: Henry Holt and Company, 1986.

Beard, Tom. *The Coast Guard*. Westport, CT: Hugh Lauter Levin Associates 2006.

Bell, Ken. *100 Missions North: A Fighter Pilot's Story of the Vietnam War*. Dulles, VA: Potomac Books, Inc., 1993.

Benjamin, Walter. *War and Reflection, the Navy Air Corps: 1944-1946, Reflection on War Fifty Years Later*. Kennett Square, PA: Red Oak Press, 1996.

Berg, A. Scott. *Lindbergh*. New York, NY: Berkley Publishing Group, 1998.

Blair, Clay Jr. *The Forgotten War: America in Korea 1950-1953*. Annapolis, MD: Naval Institute Press, 2003.

Blakeney, Jane. *Heroes: US Marine Corps 1861-1955*. Washington, DC: Guthrie Lithographic Co., Inc., 1957.

Borch, Fred L. and Charles P. McDowell. *Sea Service Medals: Awards and Decorations of the Navy, Marine Corps and Coast Guard*. Annapolis, MD: Naval Institute Press, 2009.

Bowden, Mark. *Black Hawk Down: A Story of Modern War*. New York, NY: Atlantic Monthly Press, 1999.

Boyne, Walter J. *A History of the U.S. Air Force, 1947-1997*. New York, NY: St. Martin's Griffin Press, 1998.

Brady, James. *The Coldest War: A Memoir of Korea*. New York, NY: St. Martin's Press, 1990.

Bradley, James. *Flyboys: A True Story of Courage*. New York, NY: Back Bay Books, 2004.

Chaikin, Andrew. *Voices from the Moon: Apollo Astronauts Describe Their Lunar Experiences*. New York, NY: Penguin Group, 2009.

Chenoweth, H. Avery and Brooke Nihart. *Semper Fi: The Definitive Illustrated History of the US Marines*. New York, NY: Sterling Publishing Co. Inc., 2005.

Ciurczak, Al, Jack Mates and Michael O'Neil, eds. *The Distinguished Flying Cross Society*. Second Edition, Paducah, KY: Turner Publishing Company, 2004.

Clark, Wesley K. *Waging Modern War: Bosnia, Kosovo, and the Future of Combat*. Cambridge, MA: Perseus Books Group, 2002.

Collier, Peter. *Medal of Honor: Portraits of Valor Beyond the Call of Duty*. New York, NY: Artisan Publishing, 2003.

Crumley, B. L. *The Marine Corps*. San Diego, CA: Thunder Bay Press, 2002.

Daso, Dik Alan. *Doolittle: Aerospace Visionary*. Dulles, VA: Potomac Books, Inc., 2005.

_____. *US Air Force: A Complete History*. Westport, CT: Hugh Lauter Levin Associates, Inc., 2006.

Dryden, Charles W. *A-Train: Memoirs of a Tuskegee Airman*. Tuscaloosa, AL: University of Alabama Press, 1997.

Ford, Daniel. *Flying Tigers: Claire Chennault and the American Volunteer Group*. Summit, PA: Tab Books, 1991.

Fortin, Noonie. *Women at Risk: We Also Served*. Lincoln, NE: Writers Club Press, 2002.

Gaddis, John Lewis. *The Cold War: A New History*. New York, NY: Penguin Group, 2006.

Gilbert, Sir Martin. *The Second World War: A Complete History*. New York, NY: Henry Holt and Company, 1989.

Goldstein, Donald M. *Amelia: A Life of the Aviation Legend*. Dulles, VA: Potomac Books, Inc., 1997

Handleman, Phillip and Walter J. Boyne. *Brassey's Air Combat Reader: Historic Feats and Aviation Legends*.

Dulles, VA: Potomac Books, Inc., 2005.

Hawkins, Ian. *B-17s Over Berlin: Personal Stories from the 95th Bomb Group.* Dulles, VA: Potomac Books, Inc., 1990.

Hoover, Gerald R. *Brotherhood of the Fin: A Coast Guard Rescue Swimmer's Story.* Tucson, AZ: Wheatmark, Inc., 2007.

Jarrett, Phillip. *Modern War Machine: Military Aviation since 1945.* London, England: Putnam Aeronautical, 2000.

Karnow, Stanley. *Vietnam: A History.* New York, NY: Penguin Books, 1997.

Lazzarini, Tony. *Highest Traditions.* Larkspur, CA: Voyager Publishing, 2003.

Mahajan, Rahul. *The New Crusade: America's War on Terrorism.* New York, NY: Monthly Review Press, 2002.

Millett, Alan R., and Peter F. Maslowski. *For the Common Defense: A Military History of the United States.* New York, NY: Macmillan Company, 1984.

Morris, Rob. *Untold Valor: Forgotten Stories of American Bomber Crews over Europe in World War II.* Dulles, VA: Potomac Books, Inc., 2006.

Nalty, Bernard C. *Winged Shield, Winged Sword 1907-1950: A History of the United States Air Force.* Honolulu, HI: University Press of the Pacific, 2003.

Office of the Adjutant General. *American Decorations.* Supplement I (1 January 1927 – 30 June 1937), Supplement II. (1 July 1937 – 30 June 1938), Supplement III. (1 July 1938 – 30 June 1939), Supplement IV. (1 July 1939 – 30 June 1940), Supplement V. (1 July 1940 – 30 June 1941), Washington, DC: Government Printing Office, 1937. Reprint, Ft. Mayer, VA: Planchet Press Publication Co., 1992.

Olsen, John Andreas. *A History of Air Warfare.* Dulles, VA: Potomac Books, Inc., 2010.

Oppenheimer, T.A. *Flight: A History of Aviation in Photographs.* Buffalo, NY: Firefly Books Ltd., 2004.

Ostrom, Thomas P. *The United States Coast Guard: 1790 to the Present.* Oakland, OR: Red Anvil Press, 2006.

_____. *The USCG on the Great Lakes: A History.* Oakland, OR: Red Anvil Press, 2007.

Patrick, James W. *Wood & Canvas Heroes Awards of the Distinguished Flying Cross and other Airmen Stories 1927-December 1941,* Fullerton, CA: James W. Patrick Publishing, 2002.

Pisanos, USAF Colonel Steve (Ret.). *The Flying Greek: An Immigrant Fighter Ace's WWII Odyssey with the RAF, USAAF and French Resistance.* Dulles, VA: Potomac Books, 2008.

Polmar, Norman. *Historic Naval Aircraft.* Dulles, VA: Potomac Books, Inc., 2006.

_____. *The Enola Gay: The B-29 that Dropped the Atomic bomb on Hiroshima,* Dulles, VA: Potomac Books, Inc., 2004.

Skelton, William. *An American Profession of Arms: The Army Officer Corps, 1784-186.* Lawrence, KS: University Press of Kansas, 1992.

Smallwood, William L. *Warthog: Flying the A-10 in the Gulf War.* Dulles, VA: Potomac Books, Inc., 2005.

Smith, Starr. *Jimmy Stewart: Bomber Pilot.* Osceola, WI: Zenith Press, 2006.

Stanaway, John and Bob Rocker. *The Eight Ballers: Eyes of the Fifth Air Force: The 8th Photo Reconnaissance Squadron in World War II.* Chatsworth, CA: Challenge Publications Inc., 1999.

Wise Jr., James E. and Baron Scott. *The Silver Star: Navy and Marine Corps Gallantry in Iraq, Afghanistan and Other Conflicts.* Annapolis, MD: Naval Institute Press, 2008.

Weigley, Russell F. *The American Way of War: A History of United States Military Strategy and Policy.* Bloomington, IN: Indiana University Press, 1973.

_____. *History of the United States Army.* New York, NY: Macmillan Company, 1967.

Wolk, Herman. *Toward Independence: The Emergence of the United States Air Force, 1945-1947,* Washington, DC: Air Force History and Museums Program, 1996.

Wordell, M.T. and E.N. Seiler. *"Wildcats" Over Casablanca.* Dulles, VA: Potomac Books, Inc., 2007.

Index

Binh Dinh Province, Republic of Vietnam, 188, 198

Black Hawks, 244

Bloom, Charles H., 75

Bobcat, The, 37

Bocher, Gordon L., 196

Borman, Frank, 282

Bottriell, Ralph W., 9, 10

Bouley, Joe 219-221

Boyden, Hayne D., 17

Bradfield, William R., 193-194, 301

Brace, Richard N., 134

Bratt, Drew E., 207, 209

Bridges, Lonnie, 20

Bristol Bay, Alaska 208

British 7th Armored Brigade, Al Basra, Iraq, 257

Brodnan, Stephen J., 20

Bronze Star, 93

Brown, Bobby, 277

Bush, George Herbert Walker, ix, 268, 269

Butler, Paul, 90, 91-93

Byrd, Richard E., 12

C-4, 182

C-46, 72

C-47, 72, 77, 91, 105, 107, 143, 271

C-47 Airborne Ambulance, 271

C-47 "Gooney Bird," 194 C-109, 77

C-130, 209

C-133A, 161

C-140, 280

Caldwell, William W., 17

Calvert, Congressman, Kenneth S., 299

Cambodia, 181, 192

Camp Pendleton, California, 239

Campbell, Kim, 235-237

Campbell, Scott Christopher, 229-232

Cam Ranh Bay, Vietnam, 48, 177

Camp Radcliff, Vietnam, 197-198

Canton, China, 43

Capistrano Beach Memorial, 298

Cardenas, Robert L., 143-147

Caribou, (aircraft), 48

Carrier Task Force 77, 117

Carteret Islands, Papua New Guinea, 73

Cavite, The Philippines, 42

Cernan, Eugene, 267, 289

Cessna L-19/0-1, 182

CG-4a invasion glider, 143

CGAS Clearwater, 254

CGAS Kodiak, 254

CH-46, 240

CH-46E helicopter, 239, 258

CH-47, 194

CH-47 Chinook, 193

Challenge Coins, 184

Champlin, James L., 188, 298

Cheney, Richard, 260

Chichi Jima, Japan, 269

Chinese Air Force, 70

CIA, 146

Ciurczak, Alexander, 70, 294, 295, 301

Clement, Dave E., 191

Close Air Support (CAS), 283

Coast Guard Foundation Award, 210

Coats, Bill, 295

Coats, Wilbur L., 94, 95-97

Cobra, 169

Cochran, Jacqueline, 280

Cody, Richard A., 287

"The Coffin Corner," 279

Cole, Brent S., 261

Cole, Vanessa, 261

Coleman, Jerry, 277

Combat Air Patrol (CAP),

117

Combat Air Support, 189

Coolidge, Calvin, 2, 5

Cooper, Bill, 158

Cope, Alfred L., 73-74

Coral Sea, 213, 214, 216

Corpus Christi, Texas, 216

Corregidot, Philippines, 42

Cortez Municipal Airport, Colorado, 279

Croiz de Guerre, 273

Crenshaw, Lewis W., 252

Cronkite, Walter, 45, 49

Curtiss, Glenn, 8

Da Nang, Republic of Vietnam, 189

Davis, Benjamin O., Jr., 270

Davis-Monthan Air Force Base, Arizona, 236

D-Day, 57, 61

Deihl, Richard H., 99

Del Rio, Texas, 279

Delta Company 227, 170

Deputy Chief of Naval Operations (DCNO), 120

Desert Fliers Command Chapter, DFCS, 297

DeShazer, Jake, 31, 32

Detroit, 5

Direct Commission Aviator (DCA), 254

Discovery Channel, 254

Discovery Space Ship Crew, 281

Distinguished Flying Cross Metal, 4

Distinguished Flying Cross Society, 78, 97, 172, 295

Distinguished Flying Cross Scholarship Fund, 295

DFC Memorial Fund, 298

Direct Commission Aviator (DCA), 254

DFCS Scholarship, 78

Doolittle, James H., 29

Doolittle, Jimmy, 10

Numerical Index